URBAN LIFE AND URBAN LANDSCAPE
Zane L. Miller, Series Editor

READING LONDON

Urban Speculation and Imaginative
Government in Eighteenth-Century Literature

Erik Bond

The Ohio State University Press
Columbus

Copyright © 2007 by The Ohio State University.
All rights reserved.

Library of Congress Cataloging-in-Publication Data
  Bond, Erik.
  Reading London : urban speculation and imaginative government in eighteenth-century literature / Erik Bond.
    p. cm. — (Urban life and urban landscape)
  Includes bibliographical references and index.
  ISBN 978–0–8142–1049–9 (cloth : alk. paper) — ISBN 978–0–8142–9129–0 (cd-rom) 1. English literature—18th century—History and criticism. 2. London (England)—In literature. 3. Cities and towns in literature. 4. City and town life in literature. 5. London (England)—Politics and government—18th century. 6. Literature and society—England—London—History—18th century. I. Title.
  PR448.L65B66 2007
  820.9'32421—dc22
              2006035702

Paper (ISBN: 978-0-8142-5710-4)

Cover design by Fulcrum Design Corps, LLC.
Type set in Times New Roman.

For Sara, Darian, and "the story"

Contents

List of Illustrations ix
Preface xi
Acknowledgments xxv

Introduction   Two Cities, One London 1

Part I   Governing Others

Chapter 1   Archives of Conduct: John Gay on London's Street Level   31

Chapter 2   Novel Conduct: Imagined Authority in Henry Fielding's *Tom Jones* and Bow Street   68

Chapter 3   Pope, Westminster Bridge, and Other Imaginative "Things of Use"   97

Part II   Governing the Self

Chapter 4   Interchapter: The Print-Saturated City   129

Chapter 5   Agitation and Dramatic Criticism in Boswell's *London Journal*   138

Chapter 6   Frances Burney's "Inward Monitor" and the Self-Governing Woman   183

Conclusion   213

Glossary   217
Notes   221
Works Cited   257
Index   267

Illustrations

Figure 1. Marcus Willemsz Doornick. *Platte Grondt der Verbrande Stadt London.* Amsterdam. 1666. (Courtesy of the Map Library, Harlan Hatcher Graduate Library, University of Michigan)   32

Figure 2. William Faden. *A New Pocket Plan of the Cities of London & Westminster With the Borough of Southwark, Comprehending the New Buildings and Other Alternations to the Year 1790.* 1790 edition. (Courtesy of the Map Library, Harlan Hatcher Graduate Library, University of Michigan)   33

Preface

At the start of the twenty-first century, London's eighteenth-century foundations seem structurally familiar yet historically distant at the same time. Through pedestrian eyes, London's Georgian squares, plastered symmetry, Palladian architecture, and Portland stone may conveniently be read as the innocent, opening chapters of the same narrative that leads us to present-day London. For example, Ian McEwan's 2005 novel, *Saturday*, opens with his protagonist, Henry Perowne, rehearsing London's fictional history at his bedroom window in Fitzroy Square:

> Standing here, as immune to the cold as a marble statue, gazing towards Charlotte Street, towards a foreshortened jumble of facades, scaffolding and pitched roofs, Henry thinks the city is a success, a brilliant invention, a biological masterpiece—millions teeming around the accumulated and layered achievements of the centuries, as though around a coral reef, sleeping, working, entertaining themselves, harmonious for the most part, nearly everyone wanting it to work. And the Perownes' own corner, a triumph of congruent proportion; the perfect square laid out by Robert Adam enclosing a perfect circle of garden—an eighteenth-century dream bathed and embraced by modernity, by street light from above, and from below by fibre-optic cables, and cool fresh water coursing down pipes, and sewage borne away in an instant of forgetting.[1]

Using organic metaphors to comprehend London's diversity, McEwan's character interprets his urban environment as "an eighteenth-century dream bathed and embraced by modernity." McEwan's excerpt is notable since it describes a twenty-first-century Londoner "embracing" a dreamt (i.e., fictional) connection to eighteenth-century London. Acknowledging the historical distance between eighteenth- and twenty-first-century London, we may, however, question what is at stake in our waking from this dream. For example, did eighteenth-century Londoners really dream of being "bathed" and "embraced" by our modernity? When eighteenth-century Londoners dreamed of urban "success," did they dream of twenty-first-century London? Most importantly, to what extent are we interested in reading eighteenth-century London simply to anticipate ourselves? As McEwan suggests, the answers to these eighteenth-century questions are frequently, like the city's rubbish, "borne away in an instant of forgetting." *Reading London* revisits these questions and outlines the variety of answers made possible by writing in eighteenth-century London. Between the letters of eighteenth-century London and the telecom towers of its twenty-first-century version resides an entirely different story of urbanization and an entirely different set of alternatives to the modernity that Londoners now face.

Reading London traces an alternate urban history that begins with, and is made possible by, the destabilization of sovereignty during the 1688 Glorious Revolution and concludes with the self-governing strategies that James Boswell and Frances Burney developed to respond to the destabilizing effects of a print-saturated London. The evidence for why this alternative history should be told is predominantly literary since London's historical and geographical conditions provided fertile ground for eighteenth-century literature to offer alternatives for urban governance after the fall of absolutism. In the particular literary strategies, stylistic maneuvers, and rhetorical tools that writers used to reimagine London we may see evidence for this argument. These alternatives ultimately suggest that our twenty-first-century problems and conceptions of "the city" did not have to be this way—that our ideas about how to create, manage, and police centralized populations in urban settings do *not* have to be viewed as the culmination of an inevitable process. In other words, *Reading London* exposes the fictional status of what some may see as a natural, or determined, historical sequence.[2]

Two problems that encouraged writers to imagine new forms of government after 1688 are geographically and historically bound to eighteenth-century London. First, the rapidly expanding geography of eighteenth-century London presented writers with the opportunity to develop new strategies for organizing the city. Consider, for example, the popular fact touted by urban theorists: in 1700 there were roughly 500,000 people living in Westminster and the City of London; by 1800, one million people lived in London. While the one-hundred percent increase in the city's population is staggering, this statistic also suggests that between 1700 and 1800 two separate cities (the City of Westminster and the City of London) became one city (London). Two cities that had been traditionally defined by their separate administrative boundaries merged during "the long eighteenth century" into a city that was unified at least in name. No formal proclamation dictated this unity; no parliamentary law dictated this merger. By reading eighteenth-century texts as participants in shaping urban history, however, we can begin to understand the factors that made Westminster and the City of London appear as though they composed a single entity. Although eighteenth-century London lacked environmental architects and other accoutrements of urban planning as we now know them, London was nonetheless built. In particular, I argue that literary writing by and about London authors between 1716 and 1782 contributed to building post-Fire London. By "building," I mean an imaginative act in which urban writers developed strategies for conceptualizing themselves as legitimate authorities who could compete with London's traditional authoritative bodies, such as Parliament and the Corporation of the City of London, for control over an urban populace. To legitimize this imagined authority, these writers represented themselves as indispensable figures who could help readers comprehend and relate to a newly complex London. In one way similar to that used by twenty-first-century mapmakers, these eighteenth-century poets and novelists advertised their printed product as the proper technology for knowing the city. These writers catered to a market whose product was urban knowledge; thus, *Reading London* outlines how certain types of literary writing constituted essential blueprints for reimagining London's infrastructure. In the contest to render London a knowable object, writers presented themselves as victors armed with alternatives for organizing London. To eighteenth-century writers and readers, London was newly complex because its administrative geography posed new problems for the way individual Londoners defined their relationships to a diluted monarchy.

A second problem that enabled writers to imagine new forms of government involves the Glorious Revolution of 1688 and the fall of absolutism in England.[3] James II's abdication to the rule of William and Mary is not simply a matter of stabilizing Protestant succession; rather, it signifies a moment when monolithic, absolute rule was—or was *perceived* to be—shattered and its fractured remnants distributed among a variety of governmental and extra-governmental institutions.[4] For example, Carol Kay argues that when seventeenth-century institutions of English sovereignty confronted newly conceived "non-governmental forms of power" such as "commerce, the family, religion, the arts and sciences," there surfaced the Hobbesian theory of sovereignty that "required consent to shared law and agreement about which institutions have final authority to make law."⁵ What is therefore new to England after 1688 is that the task of garnering this "consent"—of consolidating a shared, communal opinion—is no longer in the hands of the monarchy. Instead, participants in formerly non-governmental practices, such as writers, merchants, and priests, now found themselves trying to shape the qualities, characteristics, and tastes that determined this shared consent. During the late twentieth century, these non-governmental practices became visible as a new type of cultural study emerged in the fields of literary and urban studies. Reading Restoration politics through the lenses of new historicism, critics have detailed the types of extragovernmental institutions that refashioned what Kay terms "consent to authority" after 1688, and as a result, the study of how non-governmental institutions fashioned public consent has matured into a valuable field of cultural study.⁶ For example, John Brewer and Roy Porter's *Consumption and the World of Goods* offers several essays that define trade and consumerism as extragovernmental institutions which assisted in shaping notions of community and shared consent.⁷ Alternatively, the work of Lawrence Klein and Carol Kay focuses on the community-building effects of political partisanship and philosophy.⁸ Linda Colley privileges Protestantism and the military as crucial elements for "forging" the common identities of London and Britain after the 1707 Act of Union.⁹ And Michael McKeon's comprehensive study on the origins of the novel reads the literature surrounding the Glorious Revolution through a historical perspective as he details how new forms of printed text tried to address as well as regulate social change.¹⁰ Building upon McKeon's connections between literature and socio-political change after 1688, Erin Mackie has analyzed how eighteenth-century periodicals such as *The Tatler* and *The Spectator* attempt to "fashion" categories of choice and discrimination for London's readers.¹¹ *Reading London* contributes not only to these emerging discussions about the nature of sovereignty after 1688, but also to McKeon's and Mackie's ongoing dialogue about the ways writers tried to shape new communal notions of authority. In particular, I focus on the specific problems and opportunities presented by London's geography and the way writers reimagined London's topography to generate consensus.

Although England still functioned as a monarchy after 1688, Londoners no longer defined themselves primarily in terms of being subjects to the King. This political realignment changed the terms of the seventeenth-century social contract and initiated a period of reassessing one's importance in a city no longer reliant upon unquestioned absolutism. This historical episode has even spawned a school of postmodern political theory that questions how notions of "liberal governmentality" negotiated absolutism.[12] In the introduction that follows this preface, I will clarify why speaking in terms of liberal governmentality is valuable; for the immediate moment, however, let me specify how eighteenth-century writers in London characterized these political changes. The Glorious Revolution affected the Cities of Westminster and London in very particular ways; for example, the medieval notion of a self-evident Londoner, separate from the King and Court, was not as inviolable as it was in the past due to the fact that the Great Fire of 1666 had forced Londoners to listen carefully to city-based regulations for rebuilding and to royal proclamations.[13] Readers from the City of London joined readers from previously disenfranchised areas located between the expanding cities (areas such as Soho and other fringes of the Town) in a communal attempt to comprehend their relationship to a non-sovereign city. With the shattering of absolutism and the rise of publication, a string of questions now accompanied the act of reading: to what extent should I trust an author's knowledge about London? Will I ever meet the writer who is supplying this information on how to structure my interior? How do I know that I'm part of a community of fellow readers and not just some alienated, misanthropic dunce? These questions highlight the speculative activity that reading about Restoration and eighteenth-century London encouraged. As Londoners questioned the governing ideas that united them as Londoners, many writers, politicians, architects, and priests vigorously competed to offer a wide range of answers and to provide viable alternatives to the sovereign foundation upon which London's government had previously operated. This realignment cannot be underestimated; it changed the way humans experienced the city since they no longer determined their identities solely by their distance from the King. It changed also the way humans viewed their individual significance and status in the city, before they even stepped onto the streets. Although the disorienting effects of a loss of absolute monarchy are historically foreign to twenty-first-century readers, they may be approximated by a modern counterpart.

Take, for instance, the experience of walking along Fifth Avenue in New York City and the communal assumptions about authority that we usually do not question while taking that walk. To whom do we owe unquestioned deference while walking down Fifth Avenue—to the police? To the mayor? To the hot-dog vendors? To citizens with guns? To your conscience? Now imagine all of the answers to these questions to be equally valid. Given the variety of literary strategies that writers developed to attend to these questions of authority after 1688, we may begin to access the sense of possibility that saturated London and infiltrated eighteenth-century imaginative thought. More importantly, these questions highlight the extent to which Kay's "agreement about which institutions have final authority to make law"[14] shapes the way we experience and perceive how we "fit" in a city—how we imagine our individual identities to relate to a larger metropolis. Determining one's place in an urban community is not, however, simply a matter of reading an urban guidebook. For example, John Bender describes this process of acquiring self-knowledge in cities as a type of internalized self-discipline that relies upon a continual, voyeuristic monitoring of oneself.[15] Bender's notion of speculative control contributes to my study since he outlines the philosophical, literary, and visual strategies developed by eighteenth-century artists to elicit readers' imaginations as tools for self-discipline and self-surveillance. But I want to extend Bender's work by exploring how writers reimagined the activities of reading and writing, specifically, to shape what it meant to be a Londoner after 1688.[16] As all of these questions suggest, the Glorious Revolution did not force writers simply to redefine the city, but also to adjust what it meant to be a reader. Just as readers speculated about their new relationships to authority in London, readers speculated about their relationships to writerly authority as well. At the same time that urban writers questioned their social responsibility, they seized a historical episode that enabled them to imagine that they could govern London's populace. In this historical context, writers participated in a new art of government by offering blueprints for new modes of urban authority. *Reading London* traces these writers' quest for supporting roles in London's government following the Glorious Revolution.

Each of the following chapters (whose arguments I summarize in the final section of the introduction) addresses a topographical problem that writers imagined they could resolve by using specific literary strategies (metaphors, abstract personifications, and strategies of interiority to name three) to change how readers interpreted London. I argue that by closely reading the strategies that eighteenth-century writers developed in London—and contextualizing these strategies in terms of London's government after the Glorious Revolution—we may draw several conclusions about the ways printed text projected or speculated upon futures for eighteenth-century London that are distinctly different from the one that twenty-first-century Londoners are living. In the remainder of this preface, I gesture towards these conclusions as well as explain the theoretical apparatus that helps me reach these points. Several theoretical lenses assist me in making the following claims, and I will explain how these lenses bring specific elements of London's printed text into focus.

The first conclusion involves the fluctuating status of eighteenth-century genre. In particular, a study that considers geography and genres as models for organizing London allows us to understand literary genre as an imaginative, experimental tool for organizing readers. Eighteenth-century writers recognize that both geography and textual traditions have the potential to become convenient tools for categorization and organization.[17] Each of the writers addressed in this book develops a distinct model for knowing London that is grounded in the terms provided by geography and textual traditions. Consider, for example, Henry Fielding's attempt not only to be a novelist but also to reimagine himself as a textual magistrate for the Bow-Street area while publishing the final volumes of *Tom Jones* in 1749. Consider also Alexander Pope's attention to London's civil projects such as Westminster Bridge in his *Epistle to Burlington* as well as his attempt to cast poets as moral engineers of urban improvement. Rather than advertising the novelist and poet as occupying socially acknowledged positions, Frances Burney's novels and John Gay's *Trivia, or the Art of Walking the Streets of London* present the writer as an urban guide who was essential for disseminating new knowledge about London by yoking imaginative tasks to specific geographic locales. All of these roles catered to and constituted a specific episode during London's urbanization as each writer uses printed text to envision a reader's relationship to London's administrative complexity. These roles and the textual forms writers used to create them served a unique social function: to render London a knowable object.[18] For these writers, geography and textual traditions constituted familiar patterns or structures that writers could fill with meaning to organize knowledge about London; more importantly, their goal was to train readers to interpret these models and metaphors as completely natural, inherent structures of the human mind. The didacticism of these texts is, therefore, their most imaginative trait.

Throughout this book, I examine genres within their constantly fluctuating eighteenth-century contexts. The work of Paul Hunter and McKeon is crucial to understanding this generic flux since it suggests that rather than approaching eighteenth-century genre as a system of concrete taxonomies, we should instead consider how cultural innovation relates to a continual cross-pollination of textual traditions.[19] Writers enlisted urban geography and genre as strategies for defining their functions as authors because they recognized that both entities were in flux and in need of definition. Boundaries were dissolving not only between the cities of London and Westminster, but also between the early modern textual traditions that writers had used to represent those cities. The "mock"-genres of the early eighteenth-century provide evidence of this generic instability. For example, John Gay's "mock"-genres (the mock-pastoral *Beggar's Opera* and mock-epic *Trivia*) blend classical textual traditions to result in an unfamiliar product that mirrored the unfamiliar, new urban landscape in which Gay wrote. My point is that writers enlisted geography and genre as their tools for organizing, categorizing, and establishing imaginative realms in which they could represent—and experiment with—the full range of possibilities for governing London's new future. In the metaphoric playground created by printed text, they imagined that they could reconcile readers with the unfamiliar and lead readers to participate in an art of government that was defined primarily by writers.

In the way writers conceived them, geography and genre constituted the raw materials that allowed writers in London to claim that they were socially indispensable figures. At this intersection of geography and genre, the functions of "writer" and "reader" in London surface, and we may begin to unpack the complex tasks that authors associated with or assigned to the practice of writing in eighteenth-century London. For example, lacking any concept of criticism as a professionalized practice as we have come to know the term, eighteenth-century writers had to approach writing not only as a rhetorical performance for generating social authority, but also as a tool for distinguishing their social contributions from those of franchised professions such as the law. Urban writers had to prove or legitimize their social value while creating the terms that would constitute this proof or legitimacy. *Reading London* explores this complexity by identifying some of the assumptions writers brought with them to the act of writing in London. The major difference between writing in eighteenth-century London and writing in twenty-first-century London involves the way eighteenth-century writers were in part creating their positions rather than adopting prefabricated, specialized titles such as "novelist" or "theorist" with which readers are now familiar. Eighteenth-century writers brought assumptions with them to the act of writing in or about London that are foreign to us, but there are specific reasons why writers could consider geography and genre to be valuable strategies for imagining urban authority during the eighteenth century.

One of these reasons involves the imagined effects of genres (or "species of writing") upon readers. Samuel Johnson categorized these species based upon a text's effect upon its reader.[20] G. Gabrielle Starr echoes Johnson's comments in the way "novels and poems are different objects of experience, objects we encounter in different ways because they 'ask' us to do so";[21] or, in Hunter's words, "preparing readers to read the text at hand is always the first task of any textual beginning."[22] The generic lens that I use to view London's literature is therefore not only a historically specific one but also a lens that considers eighteenth-century theories about genre as emergent rather than structurally static. Whether conscious of it or not, the generic frame through which a reader must pass before reading the first word of a text does shape *how* the text is read and experienced.[23] Thus, the creativity of eighteenth-century writers consists not only in a work's content but also in the way it guides readers to experience that content. Viewed through a historicized lens of genre theory, these instructions become essential to they way writers tried to guide readers to perform specific roles in London's changed environment. This careful positioning of the reader brings me to my next claim.

The second conclusion suggested by my study clarifies the governing role that eighteenth-century writers in London shaped for themselves. This role may be summarized as a conductor—a figure who, in the wake of 1688, led readers to recognize the boundaries of London's geography as well as the boundaries of literary genre. Similar to personal fitness trainers, writers trained readers to exercise skills of their own making. When readers applied these interpretive skills beyond the confines of the page, writers led them to believe that readers would be credentialized members of a healthy urban community. After 1688, writers stressed how geography and genre were in need of guidance, systematization, and organization.[24] In their attempt to provide this guidance and to participate in a growing market for conduct literature, writers first highlighted these problems and then offered specific solutions in the metaphors and abstractions that their printed texts produced. The writers that I examine in the first part of this book catered to these urban needs by yoking abstract notions of morality to a literal cityscape (Gay), recasting the relationships between textual traditions (Pope), and advertising writers as credentialized artisans of London's administration (Fielding). As the final chapters of this book show, Boswell and Burney recognized the potential of writing to reimagine London to such an extent that they imagine the possibility of a completely self-governed London—a London in which police are not necessary since Londoners police their own thoughts and actions. Although Boswell and Burney's self-governing techniques respond to a specific cultural problem that was new to late eighteenth-century London (i.e., the proliferation of printed text), they nonetheless inherit the idea that writing can reimagine the urban social environment. For twenty-first-century readers, the idea of a London where individuals govern themselves may seem difficult to imagine as an alternative to a thoroughly policed and surveyed metropolis; yet ultimately, the goals of these eighteenth-century urban writers are experimental and imaginative. I therefore suggest that one specific function of early eighteenth-century writers in London was to conduct projects—to guide readers to, and speculate upon, alternate futures.

As I emphasize throughout this preface, *Reading London* seeks to outline these alternate futures and contribute to the fields of literary and urban studies by avoiding the New-Critical tendency to overlook eighteenth-century London's differences for the sake of "seeing ourselves" in literature that perhaps does not refer to our age, our city, or our London at all. A reader's familiarity with the phrase "early modern London" attests to the popularity of reading eighteenth-century London in the manner that I am resisting here. For example, Elizabeth McKellar's *The Birth of Modern London* (1999) scans the literature and speculative building practices of late seventeenth- and early eighteenth-century London for the seeds of modernization, proclaiming, "the creation of modern London was an evolutionary not a revolutionary process."[25] While McKellar and other early modernist critics detail the connective tissue of this evolution, I closely read eighteenth-century literature not to draw similarities but to recover *alternatives* to our modern concept of "the urban." The theoretical lenses that allow us to see the "otherness" of eighteenth-century London are best described as those belonging to a tempered version of historicism, "tempered" in the sense of carefully avoiding the impulse to draw lightning-fast connections to the past while writing a history of the present. In other words, the concept of "a city" is present in both eighteenth-century London as well as modern London, but each version of this city is surrounded by different cultural contexts. *Reading London* therefore traces a genealogy of writers' alternate methods for organizing and conducting large populations of readers. This being said, I do not claim that the following chapters employ a magical theoretical apparatus for reading this literature in "the one way" that authors originally intended them to be read. But I do claim that by closely reading these texts for the metaphors they use, we may approximate one of the many assumptions that eighteenth-century writers brought with them to the acts of writing and reading in London. The evidence that justifies this interpretation surfaces by closely reading these writers' language and textual traditions, and this brings me to an additional lens that frames each of the following chapters—a lens that historicizes these close readings. Much of this book considers conduct as a metaphor for activities that we no longer associate with the word. By closely reading the contexts in which writers imagined they were conducting readers' behaviors, imaginations, and assumptions about literature's social function, we may understand why conduct literature was so vital to post-1688 London and begin to question why we are no longer familiar with its metaphoric connotations.

A final conclusion provided by this study is that the tradition of imaginative writing about eighteenth-century London is much larger than previously assumed. Works traditionally celebrated as "literature" (or, in Arnoldian terms, writing that is apolitical as well as disconnected from literal geography) may be seen to imagine new possibilities for governing London. For instance, many readers lament the fact that most eighteenth-century novels do not reflect eighteenth-century London with a Victorian novel's intense attention to detail; Defoe does not explicitly detail London's physical characteristics in *Moll Flanders* with the same intensity as Dickens details the city's exterior in *Dombey and Son* or *Bleak House*. However, most eighteenth-century novels like *Tom Jones* and *Cecilia* are not interested in mirroring London *as it was* but as these writers imagined it *could* be. In other words, the dominant mode of eighteenth-century writing about London is neither reflective nor mimetic; the mode is instead experimental and suggestive.[26] As I will suggest in the third chapter, this explains why it may be productive to read certain printed texts about London with the same interpretive lenses we use to approach eighteenth-century projects. This perspective allows us to understand eighteenth-century literature about London in two new ways; first, writers we have typically cast as "literary authors" can contribute to London's industry of urban planning; and second, these writers may be seen to rub elbows with London's pamphleteers as they compete to imagine alternate strategies for governing London's changing population.

Although an eighteenth-century conception of the imagination is not my primary object of analysis, I do outline some possibilities as to what eighteenth-century writers might have assumed they were doing when they "imagined" in printed text. The theoretical lens that helps us to understand what the act of imagining looked like before the romantic age is a decidedly historicist one, and this book describes the types of printed text that are produced when an eighteenth-century writer "imagines" (as a verb); however, I do not assume that these writers are familiar with a Wordsworthian entity know as "the Imagination" (as a noun) since a unified conception was not formulated until the final decade of the eighteenth century.[27] When eighteenth-century writers imagine, they, unlike Victorians and other post-romantics, perform a mental activity that does not refer to an object possessing essential characteristics. As my study suggests, eighteenth-century "imagining" resembles neither unrealistic fictionalization nor didactic prescription; instead, it gestures towards a third definition we have yet to recover. By thinking about imagination beyond a mere binary of creativity and didacticism, we may sense that reading and writing printed text were not alienating activities in eighteenth-century London; literary interpretation was not divorced from social use. Even if the metaphors, modes, voices, and tones employed by these writers are not legal trials, parliamentary motions, or written law, this does not mean that writers in London were barred from participating in an art of government after the Glorious Revolution. Just because writers designed their governing metaphors in printed text does not mean that we may dismiss these writers as lacking social efficacy or cast them as wishful dreamers of urban utopias. The reason for this involves the status of "imagining" during the eighteenth-century as well as the century's connotations for the word "imaginative"—connotations that need to be recovered. In other words, these eighteenth-century printed texts were socially useful since they provided patterns for systematizing, professionalizing, and ranking knowledge about Britain's largest urban community.

All of the mental activities that writers assigned to reading this imaginative writing about London lead to the title of this book. If writers were devising new literary forms to both alter and describe this changed urban environment, then it is not surprising that they supplied instructions on how to read and interpret their novelty. For example, hidden in Gay's meditative diversions to *Trivia* and couched within Fielding's introductory chapters to the books of *Tom Jones* are essential instruction-manuals for reading newly devised textual forms. As Fielding and Gay become interpretive guides for readers who are experiencing their works, they establish (by means of metaphors) strategies for experiencing London. From this perspective, writers reimagine the act of "reading" to constitute a guided, interpretive activity in which they encourage readers to speculate upon not only the nature of the writer's authority but also the nature of urban authority. This is why the act of reading printed representations of London during the eighteenth-century, as the writers in this study construct it, may best be described as communal speculation. I mean "speculation" here in the sense of (according to the *OED*) the "conjectural anticipation of something"—a conjecturing that is similar to the work of eighteenth-century projectors and their attempt to access an alternative future through the genre of the project. In this way, writers cast themselves as gate-keepers to readerly imaginations; writers try to generate an explicit sense of community in readers' minds.

One final lens that helps me reach the conclusions I have just summarized involves the question of agency—a question that is pervasive in contemporary materialist thought. In particular, I consider the agency of writers, and their ability to affect urban environments, not in oversimplified terms of cause (printed text) and effect (the city), but in terms of reciprocal engagement (known in Bakhtinian discourse as "dialogic criticism").[28] In other words, the historical status of post-1688 London made certain forms of imaginative writing possible, and reciprocally, the imaginative activity of these writers made certain interpretations and experiences of this urban environment possible. The evidence for this reciprocity exists, again, in language and shared diction. This approach contrasts with T. F. Reddaway's purely economic reasoning for why London looks the way it does—a reasoning that Marxist critics such as Raymond Williams have adopted as well.[29] Cynthia Wall carefully qualifies Reddaway, arguing that while the economic impetus to recover London's trade-based normalcy is part of the reason why post-Fire London "was largely rebuilt on its own old lines," the other half of this reasoning involves "a cultural stubbornness" that did not allow rebuilding to take place without architectural and topographical acknowledgement of the ancient City's foundations.[30] In a similar manner, *Reading London* does not offer an economically determined narrative to explain London's topography; instead, I offer an analysis of how writers imagined ways that London could function in its newly changed context. And this is where I differ from and extend Wall's carefully qualified thesis about post-Fire London's ability to "reconstruct the known" and "recreate the [fictionally stable] past in the context of the [likely unstable] future."[31] The cultural contexts of post-Fire London are not the contexts of post-1688 London. By the start of the eighteenth century, London was resurrected upon its medieval template, but this does not mean that eighteenth-century Londoners were required to experience this replicated, architectural space in the same way that their Restoration counterparts had experienced it. The streets may be the same, but the experiences available to Londoners on these streets have changed due to sovereignty's destabilization. The writers in this book recognize this, and they seize their pens in a desperate attempt to shape and to codify these experiences for a reading audience.

Although Wall traces how writers mapped meaning onto empty spaces in the wake of the Great Fire, I adapt her critical model to address a different period when writers mapped meaning not onto empty spaces, but onto a pre-existing geography whose relationship to Londoners was rendered politically obsolete after 1688. In contrast to absences and empty spaces that characterize the surveys, maps, and royal declarations of London between 1666 and 1688, the houses, streets, and buildings of post-1688 London were physically present (in terms of being "geographically" present) yet politically "empty" (in terms of their being "topographically" readable and interpreted by individuals who experienced an altered relationship to this physical geography). Also, whereas Wall sees an increasing "publicization" of spatial ideas after the Fire, I stress that not all eighteenth-century writers were comfortable participating in a monolithic march towards a supposedly freeing public sphere.[32] For instance, as I will show, Boswell and Burney promote a very private form of self-discipline as the necessary prerequisite for not only navigating public spaces but also securing the healthy interior of a self-governed Londoner who can therefore avoid drowning in a print-saturated London. Thus, the majority of this study details the new literary forms, techniques, and strategies that writers developed to attend to, and engage in, a changed urban environment. To recognize these new literary strategies, however, we need to be familiar with the specific types of changes in London that necessitated new kinds of writing. For readers who are uninitiated in the complex lexicon of eighteenth-century London, labels such as the City, the Court, the Corporation of the City of London, the City of Westminster, and the Town may amount to a nightmarish mass of obsolete signification. To approach a more comprehensive understanding of the ways London's changed urban environment made certain types of writing possible, the following introduction reviews the unique problems and opportunities represented by these various names.

Acknowledgments

I am extremely grateful to the following mentors for their academic prowess and professional guidance. To Mary Poovey for her academic and professional rigor matched only by her ability to temper this rigor with humility and humanity. To Ernesto Gilman for his urban *sprezzatura* as well as his matchless ability to open London's doors to wide-eyed assistant professors. To Paul Magnuson and Dustin Griffin for their early advice on London and its separation into Court and City. To Margreta de Grazia not only for her supplying a solid Red-and-Blue foundation upon which to build a responsible academic career, but also for launching London, King's College UCL, and the Strand into my life's trajectory and creating a spot of time in the form of a stellar study-abroad experience. To the following colleagues, I am grateful for their consistent, reliable advice. To Jonathan Smith and Deborah Smith-Pollard for their precise and balanced guidance. Thanks to my editors, Zane L. Miller, Sandy Crooms, Maggie Diehl, and Heather Lee Miller, as well as to my anonymous readers for their advice, direction, and encouragement to refigure the critical narrative that I needed to relate in this book

The origins of this book have been generously supported by a Halsband Fellowship from New York University. Thank you also to the staff members from the numerous research facilities that assisted in the production of this book, including the staff at the British Library, the University of Michigan's Hatcher Graduate Library, the Royal Institute of British Architects' British Architectural Library, the Mardigian Library at the University of Michigan-Dearborn, NYU's Bobst Library, and the library staff at the University of Nevada-Las Vegas and the University of Central Missouri. Special gratitude is extended to Karl Longstreth, Tim Utter, and the staff at the Map Library at the University of Michigan-Ann Arbor for their generous permission to reproduce the maps of London contained in this book.

And finally, to my parents, Clairann and Curt, who helped make it possible to not only access a life of the mind, but also meet all of the aforementioned mentors in the first place.

Chapter five has appeared in an earlier version as "Bringing Up Boswell: Drama, Criticism, and the Journals," *The Age of Johnson: A Scholarly Annual* 15 (2004): 151–76. An earlier form of chapter six has appeared as "Farewell, Mr. Villars: *Cecilia* and Frances Burney's 'Inward Monitor'" reprinted from *The Eighteenth-Century Novel, Volume 3* (© 2003 by AMS Press, Inc., New York) with permission. Sections from chapter six also appeared in "Flights of Madness: Self-Knowledge and Topography in the Cities of Burney and Dickens," *The Literary London Journal* 1.1 (2003), 21 December 2006: http://www.literarylondon.org/london-journal/march2003/bond.html. My gratitude to the editors and publishers of these works for their permission to reprint.

Introduction

TWO CITIES, ONE LONDON

To understand how writers tried to manage London during the eighteenth century, I organize the following chapters according to the goals that distinguish early eighteenth-century writers from those who inhabit a print-saturated London of the late eighteenth century. *Reading London* examines not only how early eighteenth-century writers developed imaginative strategies for governing other Londoners, but also how late eighteenth-century writers reinterpreted these strategies to govern themselves. This distinction between controlling others and controlling the self appears by mid-century, and it registers an important change in the cultural problem that London presented to writers. While early eighteenth-century writers such as Gay, Fielding, and Pope addressed the problem of how a diluted sovereignty following the 1688 Glorious Revolution affected a Londoner's perception of urban governance, late eighteenth-century writers such as Boswell and Burney addressed a completely new problem: the proliferation of print in London. To solve the first cultural problem (a problem unique to early eighteenth-century London's history), writers developed textual techniques for governing readers; to address the second cultural problem (a problem unique to late eighteenth-century London's history), writers reimagined textual strategies for governing the self. To clarify this distinction, the first three chapters of this book examine the innovative techniques that writers devised to manage and to conduct readers; the final two chapters show how Boswell and Burney adapted these techniques to stabilize and to shape the individual self. An interchapter punctuates these two stages of London's history and clarifies how the proliferation of London's print culture motivated Boswell's and Burney's efforts at self-government. I argue that the two tasks of governing others and governing the self respond to specific cultural problems that writers experienced during the eighteenth century.

By focusing upon these historical distinctions and time-dependent goals, I trace a critical narrative about London that involves three projects. The first project involves authors' efforts to imagine textual techniques to manage or conduct readers and help them relate to a newly conceived, post-Fire London. The purpose of this introduction is to outline London's unique historical and material conditions that make this first project possible. In particular, eighteenth-century London's changing administrative geography provided writers with a cultural problem that required an imaginative solution, and this solution involved a new, textual art of government or "governmentality." This is why conduct becomes a central concern for these writers, and I review the eighteenth-century status of conduct books to contextualize this first project. The first part of this book therefore details the solutions that Gay, Fielding, and Pope develop to address their problems with sovereignty and consensus in early eighteenth-century London.

The second project that I investigate involves readers' efforts to master a newly complex London. By "readers' efforts" I mean the way readers were to assume that certain textual genres constituted specific ways of interpreting, and therefore knowing, London. The second part of this book (chapters 4, 5, and 6) examines this second project by describing Boswell's and Burney's efforts at reading, interpreting, and relating to a London imagined by writers from an earlier generation. The third and final project that I consider involves readers' efforts to discipline themselves. As I clarify in the second part of this introduction as well as in chapter 4, a print-saturated London caused Boswell and Burney to adapt their predecessors' textual techniques so that Boswell and Burney could govern themselves. As exhibited by Boswell's and Burney's writing, the sheer heterogeneity of texts that tried to manage an individual's experience of London threatened their development of a single identity in the city. Boswell and Burney develop self-governing strategies to combat this threat. This third project imagines the completely self-governed Londoner (a Londoner ruled by neither police nor any other external authority) as a historical possibility, and this possibility originates in textual strategies for controlling others. In my attempt to contextualize these three projects, I trace a critical narrative that identifies several historical alternatives to the types of urban authority that currently police cities. Since London's historically specific geography was a foundational factor that enabled writers to imagine these alternatives, it is the issue to which I now turn.

London's Changing Geography

As the events of 1688 loosened the notion of urban authority from the Court's sole domain, writers were some of the first Londoners to connect this loss to changes in London's geography and the administrative tensions between the Court, Town, and City. One of the earliest writers to draw attention to London's changing administrative geography is Abraham Cowley. Cowley's 1668 poem, "On the Queen's Repairing Somerset House," adapts the seventeenth-century country-house poem to an urban setting. Cowley's poem represents a city in transition by reinterpreting a textual tradition (the country-house poem) to suit an urban environment. Cowley personifies Somerset House, a royal property on the banks of the Thames between Court and City, by giving it a voice. This voice does not try to detail Somerset House but instead calls attention to its peculiar surroundings:

> Before my gate a street's broad channel goes,
> Which still with waves of crowding people flows;
> And every day there passes by my side,
> Up to its western reach, the London tide,
> The spring-tides of the term; my front looks down
> On all the pride and business of the town.
> . . .
> My other fair and more majestic face
> (Who can the fair to more advantage place?)
> For ever gazes on itself below
> In the best mirror that the world can show.[1]

Cowley focuses our attention not on the house but the house's front entrance on the Strand ("a street's broad channel") and back entrance on the Thames ("the best mirror"). But Somerset House's location is privileged in another way:

> And here, behold, in a long, bending row,
> How two joint cities make one glorious bow;
> The midst, the noblest place, possessed by me;
> Best to be seen by all, and all o'ersee.
> Which way soe'er I turn my joyful eye,
> Here the great Court, there the rich Town I spy;

> On either side dwells safety and delight;
> Wealth on the left and power upon the right.[2]

Cowley's poem screams, "Location, location, location"; it suggests that "the midst, the noblest place," exudes authority because it forms a type of panopticon ("Best to be seen by all, and all o'ersee") that is unique to its location between "two joint cities." Although Cowley seems to unify Westminster and the City in "one glorious bow," he maintains each city's independence later in the poem when he refers to "two vast cities, troublesomely great."[3] From Cowley's perspective in 1668, the adjectival phrase "troublesomely great" highlights the revolutionary associations that people attached to the City of London after the Civil War—associations which Valerie Pearl reviews and questions in *London and the Outbreak of the Puritan Revolution*.[4] Although Cowley's phrase evokes the City of London's history during the Puritan Revolution, it also gestures towards a growing perception that the geographic distance between Court and City belied an even greater political distance between the two entities. In this sense, Cowely's "trouble" alludes to a divisive urban history that eighteenth-century writers would eventually inherit.

Cowley's "trouble" also emphasizes the fact that what we now recognize as London began as two separate cities: the City of Westminster, which was the home of the Court and parliament, and the City of London, which was the home of the Corporation of the City of London and trade. Discussing London's separate origins is an unusually difficult task. The names that we presently use to refer to London's spaces retain a confusing and faded sense of their separate, eighteenth-century referents. Consider, for example, how "the City" commonly refers to the ancient walled "City of London," but "the city" refers to Westminster and the City of London in general. Although the name "London" now subsumes Westminster, the City of London, and a number of other boroughs such as Southwark and Camden, tourists visiting London's West-End during the twenty-first century can claim without reproach that they are in "the city"; however, they would be technically incorrect to claim that they are in "the City of London."

Place-names therefore present particular difficulties for my attempt to discuss eighteenth-century London. For the purposes of clarity, I use "Westminster" to refer to the Court, "the City" to refer to the ancient, walled City of London, and "London" to refer to Westminster and the City of London informally combined. But this difficulty in referring to eighteenth-century London is more than a semantic problem; the difficulty attests to the problems surrounding the history of Westminster's and the City's relationship to a new "London." If language is a receptacle for cultural episodes, then by interpreting the names we have inherited to refer to London's urban spaces, we can understand how eighteenth-century literature tried to attend to, resolve, or amplify the confusion between Westminster and the City of London. Linguistic problems can be symptoms of historical impasses.

Part of this confusion stems from modern critics' desire to see Westminster and the City of London as the only two components of eighteenth-century London. The details surrounding Westminster's and the City of London's exponential growth during Charles II's restoration, however, offer a more complicated picture. In particular, speculative builders began to bring attention to the spaces between and on the margins of Westminster and the City of London.[5] Following the Great Fire of 1666, these spaces were waiting to be filled with not only inhabitants, but also meaning. What we now call "suburban sprawl" characterized Restoration London's building boom. This was the age of speculative estate-projects, the planning of Bond Street, and the building of Red Lion Square. Builders were not the only Londoners who speculated about the value of the spaces between and on the margins of Court and City, however. Speculative growth affected writers as well.

The middle ground between Court and City (commonly called "the Town") was a geographic novelty for eighteenth-century Londoners, and writers such as Cowley advertised the ramifications of this novelty. In particular, writers questioned what this novelty could do for their reputations. For example, Alexander Pope adopted Cowley's hyper-sensitivity to the unique space between Court and City in *Windsor Forest*. In particular, Pope seizes Cowley's "one glorious bow" to locate a new type of poetic authority:

> Behold! *Augusta*'s glitt'ring Spires increase,
> And Temples rise, the beauteous Works of Peace.
> I see, I see where two fair Cities bend
> Their ample Bow, a new *White-Hall* ascend!
> There mighty Nations shall inquire their Doom . . . .[6]

Like Somerset House's privileged perspective for observing and therefore indirectly controlling Westminster and the City, Pope's poet also occupies a privileged perspective ("I see, I see") from which he may prophesy the British Empire. Number 454 of Richard Steele's *Spectator* (commonly known as *Twenty-Four Hours in London*) also hinges upon a famous distinction between "two joint cities":

> The Hours of the Day and Night are taken up in the Cities of *London* and *Westminster* by Peoples as different from each other as those who are Born in different Centuries. Men of Six-a-Clock give way to those of Nine, they of Nine to the Generation of Twelve, and they of Twelve disappear, and make Room for the fashionable World, who have made Two-a-Clock the Noon of the Day.[7]

Steele suggests that Westminster and the City are so different that the cities cannot even be measured by the same timepiece. We should note that Steele, as an early eighteenth-century critic, observes this distinction from a privileged perspective beyond Court and City, and he begins the paper by describing the advantages of this distanced perspective: "It is an inexpressible Pleasure to know a little of the World, and be of no Character or Significancy in it."[8] Letter five of Daniel Defoe's *Tour through the Whole Island of Great Britain* considers the margins of Westminster and the City to constitute a completely new realm:

> Supposing now, the whole body of this vast building to be considered as one city, London, and not concerning myself or the reader with the distinction of its several jurisdictions; we shall then observe it only as divided into three, viz. the city, the Court, and the out-parts.
>
> The city is the centre of its commerce and wealth. The Court of its gallantry and splendour. The out-parts of its numbers and mechanics; and in all these, no city in the world can equal it. Between the Court and city, there is a constant communication of business to that degree, that nothing in the world can come up to it.[9]

"A constant communication of business" marks the area "between the Court and city" for Defoe. Depending upon the degree of "communication," this area could separate or unify London's two authoritative poles. Cowley, Pope, and Steele rendered the space between Westminster and the City visible; Defoe went a step further, describing London in three "parts" rather than two cities.

The desire to see London as two symmetrical parts is further complicated by the fact that London never adopted French boulevards, a rectangular matrix of cross-streets, or an elaborate symmetry, and, for this reason, historians tend to view London as "a muddle that always worked."[10] In an attempt to understand this "muddle," we may over-emphasize the administrative interaction between the Court and the City; in turn, Court and City come to resemble the opposite ends of a binary that serves to decode any complexity London's muddle might present. In this binary, Westminster is the symbolic pole for Tories, tradition, and sovereign monarchy, while the City of London is the location of rebellion, Whigs, and trade. This model might look good on undergraduate classroom blackboards, but it discounts "the Town"—that marginal, third term that Restoration and early eighteenth-century writers emphasize. This literature—"Town literature," one might call it—exposes the Court-City binary for what it really is: an oversimplification that distorts urban complexity. By understanding what this third term meant to urban writers, we may begin to witness how writers imagined themselves to be legitimate urban authorities.

Writers residing and working between Whitehall and Ludgate Hill occupied a space in which they could either promote or disassemble the informal tensions between Court and City. Their mediated residence between the poles of Court and City provided a point of entry into an administrative dialogue designed to reimagine London's cityscape. One of the reasons writers could more easily imagine their role in this middle ground than in either the Court or City was that several of these marginal spaces were organized into an antiquated administrative unit: the liberty. According to John Strype's updated edition of John Stow's *A Survey of the Cities of London and Westminster: Containing the Original, Antiquity, Increase, Modern Estate, and Government of those CITIES*, the space surrounding the Strand—the road literally connecting Westminster to the City—was still, in 1720, referred to by its medieval title, the "Liberty of the Dutchy of Lancaster."[11] Liberties were "formerly monastic precincts"[12] marked by "freedom from the jurisdiction of the customary administrative unit."[13] Recognizing these defunct administrative spaces, writers like Boswell, Fielding, and Burney filled these spaces with new meaning. In Boswell's case, the Town dominated his urban experiences, particularly his experiences at London's theaters, the majority of which were concentrated beyond the walls of the City and just outside Whitehall during the eighteenth century. Boswell's *London Journal* is filled with dramatic metaphors that actors and actresses used to define themselves onstage. For Boswell's particular experience of the Town, theatricality characterized this space. This middle ground also relates to Fielding's Bow Street career, which aimed to police these defunct spaces. Finally, as a woman writer, Burney reconceived this middle ground as a space of possibility for women to escape the gendered voyeurism that characterized Westminster and the City.

What all of these excerpts from Restoration and early eighteenth-century literature show us is that writers were assigning a unique value to London's geography. In particular, the areas between, beyond, and on the margins of Court and City were valuable to writers because these disparate areas (Grub Street, the Town, Holborn) appeared to require special regulation and new administrative apparatuses. I argue that writers living in or writing about London recognized these areas' administrative particularities as opportunities for participating in and constituting Defoe's prized "communication of business." The kinds of topographical opportunities that writers in this book observed include: reconceiving the Town as a known space (chapters 1–2), redirecting urban projectors and funding to address this space (chapter 3), managing street-level performances between Court and City (chapter 5), and defining alternative modes of interiority to comprehend the Town's "middling" influence on London as a whole (chapter 6). Paying particular attention to how this middle ground and the possibilities it represented affected urban writers, we may begin to unravel the sense in which London was "a muddle that always worked."

Shaping Political Consensus in Tudor and Stuart London

If early eighteenth-century writers considered London's administrative geography to represent a problem that needed solving, then the status of sovereignty and political consensus in late seventeenth-century London added a political element to this problem. Compared to its earlier incarnations, London was newly complex in a very specific way: London's geography changed as seventeenth-century concepts of political sovereignty accommodated new techniques for acquiring consensus. While these changes distinguish eighteenth-century London from Tudor London, these changes did not suddenly appear in a fit of revolutionary fervor as much as the title "The Glorious Revolution" might like to suggest. Instead, these eighteenth-century changes were enabled by a history that reaches back to sixteenth-century London. This prehistory begins with Tudor London's transition from a late-medieval marketplace to the uncomfortable centerpiece of an absolutist state, and it ends with Stuart London's restoration in the wake of the Puritan Revolution.[14] I do not recount the intricacies of this prehistory here since Lawrence Manley's *Literature and Culture in Early Modern London* offers that comprehensive analysis; however, part of Manley's thesis is worth repeating since it describes the exact nature of a "restored" London in 1660 and prefigures the changes that define eighteenth-century London:

> [T]he restored order that was promised, and to some extent the one that was eventually and fitfully delivered, had more in common with the revolutionary movement toward expansion, diversity, progress, and increase than with the ancient regime that had preceded it. And not least of the enduring legacies were the ethical innovations—a cosmopolitan disinvestment in the local and "parochial," a reliance upon reason, autonomy, and self-discipline, a self-restraint in the face of diversity—that, by linking personal liberty dialectically to new patterns of social discipline, helped to consolidate the urbanizing process. Perhaps typical of the revolutionary force of these innovations is [William] Walwyn's view that nothing "maintains love, unity, and friendship in families; Societies, Citties, Countries, Authorities, Nations; so much as a condescension to the giving, and hearing, and debating of reason." The emergence, from the Puritan Revolution, of views like Walwyn's and others makes it possible to see how the historical development of sedentarism could give moral force to [Edmund] Burke's later clam that liberty is a function of ethical maturity . . .[15]

Manley's point is that even after the revolutionary arguments of liberty and nonconformism that characterized 1642 to 1660, London's most liberal and individualistic qualities relied upon a type of general consensus and restraint to make the city resemble a communal (i.e., "sedentary") capital. After the Puritan Revolution, this new "Reason," with its origins in absolutist consensus, appeared to balance, moderate, and check London's civil society.[16] Manley's study ends at the Restoration with this conclusion, and this notion of a tempered civil society, liberated yet reliant upon shared consensus, is the context in which the 1688 Glorious Revolution, the discourse of sovereignty, and London's literature of conduct functions.[17]

New to late seventeenth- and early eighteenth-century Londoners, however, were not only the literary techniques developed by writers to generate shared consensus but also the type of writer and genres that were able to create these works. Whereas sixteenth-century writers distributed their manuscripts in courtly circles as they strove to become patronized "Courtier-Poets," an expanding print culture during the early eighteenth century brought about an entirely new audience of readers. New print technologies (marked by the popularity of new literary genres such as periodicals and novels) appeared beside the dissolution of the absolutist state, and the result was a window of opportunity for writers to define not simply their social value. If Manley's thesis is accurate in claiming that the type of absolute monarchy inherited by Restoration London rested upon a type of civil liberty (previously associated with the City of London's nonconformists) that was tempered by consensual discipline (previously associated with one's being "subject" to the King's sovereignty), then the shattering of absolutism in 1688 complicated the qualities that now constituted reasoned and enlightened discipline.[18] At this moment, the goal was neither to discipline oneself to be "subjects" in the same way that Tudor Londoners were "subject" to the King, nor to discipline one's mind according to the reasoned standards of Court-appointed philosophers, poets, and artists. Since the City of Westminster housed the Court, and the City of London came to be associated with civil liberty after the Puritan Revolution, writers throughout London (such as Cowley, Pope, Addison, and Steele) were quick to sense how these abstract notions of "reason," "consensus," and "liberty" easily mapped onto London's physical geography. And they recognized this geographic connection to absolutism's demise for a very specific reason. London's geography gave a substance to these previously inaccessible and unquestionable abstractions that organized seventeenth-century London. Geography presented the possibility to *all* writers (not simply Courtier-Poets) that they could seize these previously transparent notions of consensual rule, render them legible to readers by means of geographic metaphor, and reimagine a different London. As eighteenth-century writers in London saw it (and they witnessed it quite literally in the way London's geography and administrative boundaries were changing), consensus was now disenfranchised from the absolutist state. Therefore, it was fair game for ownership; consensus was now in the hands of priests, aldermen, the guilds, lawyers, politicians, and writers—the very people who were previously "the ruled" rather than "the ruling."[19]

Other recent work on London's pre-Restoration social organization has reassessed the nature of London's environmental changes by questioning the binary extremes that historians and literary critics have traditionally used to describe London's changed environment. The most familiar binaries employed by historians of seventeenth-century London include aristocratic versus bourgeois, Protestant versus nonconformist, Whig versus Tory, apocalyptic Hell versus City of God, gentry versus citizen, landed economy versus *rentier* economy, and Court versus City.[20] Although these studies have tried to rebalance these generalized binaries to more accurately represent London's growth, Ian Archer discards binary thinking altogether, arguing that "culture is best understood as a process, that people are constantly drawing upon a variety of different cultural forms, adapting them in the process to meet the needs of specific situations."[21] I suggest that we read London's eighteenth-century literature to recover the imaginative terms developed by eighteenth-century humans to shape their experience amid several overlapping binaries. From this perspective, we may begin to question how these binaries have oversimplified—or even ignored—the sensitive cultural work that eighteenth-century writers imagined they were accomplishing. For instance, when I claim that London's eighteenth-century geography was newly complex, I do not mean to polarize competing authorities for the sake of simplifying London. It is too simplistic to label the City of Westminster to be a "Tory" space and the City of London to be a "Whig" space, in the same manner that speaking of "red" and "blue" states in American elections oversimplifies political nuance and dissent. Instead, *Reading London* seeks to reveal the way eighteenth-century literature offers a variety of third-, fourth-, and fifth-terms that explode our preconceived binaries and allow us to sense the eighteenth-century alternatives to the terms we now use to account for urban change.

Recent studies of London's governance have also challenged strictly deterministic (i.e., economic) views of why London looks the way it does; that is, many critics consider personal experience to be as valuable as economic and political determinants for explaining London's changed environment. For example, J. F. Merritt's *Imagining Early Modern London* stresses "the human, the particular, and the personal" motivations for social change and vows to "restate citizens as active participants in the changing city—not simply as passive observers of a developing cityscape, but as individuals making creative, pragmatic responses to a changing urban environment."[22] In *Londinopolis: Essays in the Cultural and Social History of Early Modern London,* Paul Griffiths and Mark S. R. Jenner introduce their anthology by highlighting how the essays pose "questions about how the city was *experienced* and about the social relations of its inhabitants."[23] *Reading London* contributes to this analysis of the ways personal experience both shaped—and was shaped by—London's changing geography. This "shaping" and "being shaped by" are not mutually exclusive activities. Writers represented London's geography in a way that allowed readers to experience it as the writers intended. In this sense, writers shaped London's topography by offering mental maps that they imagined could be reproduced in readers' minds. Writers also inevitably had to respond to London's unprecedented growth and its growing, trade-based economy. In this sense, London social conditions shaped writers' responses. I argue that literature about London evinces both of these activities, operating simultaneously and almost inseparably. In this way, personal experience, when recorded in printed text, can both reimagine London and be shaped by it. After the Glorious Revolution's disenfranchisement of absolute power, carefully regulated experiences (i.e., experiences stylistically represented by writers and other previously disenfranchised professionals) became the tools for shaping consensus and shared consent in the city.

Vehicles for Reading London: Genre and Conduct

The second project that I examine in this book (readers' efforts at mastering a newly complex London) invokes the eighteenth-century status of genre and metaphors since these textual conventions were accompanied by strategies for reading, interpreting and knowing previously unknown objects. For Boswell and Burney, London constituted one of these unknown objects that they could understand by carefully interpreting a writer's metaphors and generic maneuvers. For Gay, Fielding, and Pope, the task of acquiring a reader's consensus made it incredibly important to train readers to interpret these metaphors and generic experiments properly. Although London's changed environment presented different writers with different generic and metaphoric opportunities, there is a common thematic element to these writers' responses to London's geographical changes: conduct. If the argument that eighteenth-century urban writers imagined their own authority seems abstract, it is because words such as "conduct," "authority," and "governing" are abstractions that require eighteenth-century contextualization—a context to which the remainder of this introduction is devoted. Writers cast these words as metaphors and abstract personifications because they constituted valuable tools for producing knowledge about London that preceded commercially available maps, aerial photography, and other modern techniques for relating to a city.[24] Readers with interests in literature's relationship to cartography will be particularly interested in the review in chapter 1 of the history of map making and its status at the beginning of the eighteenth century when Gay writes *Trivia*—a poem that exemplifies how literature's metaphoric play offered alternatives to mapping London. Eighteenth-century literature competed not only with visual technologies to represent London but also, as Hunter argues, with notions of seventeenth-century guidance: "By the beginning of the eighteenth century, the metaphor of the book as guide—a verbal map to space and time—had become fully established, words in print having replaced human leadership as the model for appropriate walking with God."[25] From this perspective, readers may witness how the titles of "sovereign God" and "the Poet" merge in London.

The geographic details that I have described in the preceding section were the material conditions that enabled writers to develop rhetorical strategies and, in turn, to imagine themselves governors over London's populace. Urban authors wrote about London's middling and marginalized areas because they experienced these environments in their daily lives. First, writers had to travel through these areas. Boswell, for example, tried to trace the footsteps of Steele's Mr. Spectator through Court and City. Fielding's jurisdiction as Bow Street Magistrate addressed both the City of Westminster and the middling liberties. Burney's interest in writing for the theatre and her career as Second Keeper of the Robes for Queen Charlotte suggest that Burney was familiar with not only with the Court, but also the theatrical, literary, and musical worlds operating just beyond Whitehall. Second, many writers take pains to advertise the Town as *their* realm—a textual kingdom where the courtiers of Whitehall and the aldermen of the City are woefully beyond their jurisdiction. For instance, Gay uses the final lines of *Trivia* to pay homage not only to his Fleetstreet publisher, but also to the location where his poetry advertises itself to the world: "High-rais'd on *Fleetstreet* Posts, consign'd to Fame, / This Work shall shine, and Walkers bless my Name."[26] Gay's self-referential ending is an eighteenth-century public-relations device; his poem first describes urban spaces and then guides readers to the spaces where his poem was published and advertised. Geographic citations like this example were meaningful to eighteenth-century writers and readers because they pointed to the realm of imaginative production. In Gay's case, these areas of production became unabashed subjects of his poem. Thus, we need to consider geographic locations in eighteenth-century urban writing not only as literal place names but also as important abstractions that writers used to moralize London and draw attention to the kinds of writing taking place there. If urban writers could utilize geography in this manner, then the tasks of "governing" and "conducting" readers through these geographic abstractions became valuable abstract tools for trying to help Londoners relate to a newly complex London. By yoking eighteenth-century London's geography to abstract notions of morality, these writers appeared to render London less complex. For instance, in order to yoke materiality to spirituality, writers used metaphors, abstract personifications, and other rhetorical textual devices whose purpose was to fill unfamiliar abstractions with familiar meaning. In this sense, a writer's governing takes place in the styles and rhetorical devices of printed text. Due to its figurative flexibility, conduct became one of these foundational metaphors for navigating the physical and moral treachery of London.[27] Since my phrase "the metaphor of conduct" may appear strange since it no longer functions as a primary strategy for knowing modern cities, a careful understanding of how conduct could operate beyond its literal meaning is in order.

Conduct literature is a familiar topic for readers of eighteenth-century literature—perhaps too familiar. I say "too familiar" because misinterpreting conduct literature as a purely didactic form, barren of stylistic qualities, may detract readers from seeing the social ramifications of such an omnipresent genre. Dieter A. Berger attributes this absence to a modern literary perspective that refuses to consider any type of book offering "rules to realize an acknowledged cultural ideal" as worthy of literary (or stylistic) analysis.[28] Nancy Armstrong's *Desire and Domestic Fiction* and her introduction to *The Ideology of Conduct* written with Leonard Tennenhouse are some of the first examples to seriously study conduct literature. In an attempt to comprehend the variety of conduct books in terms of their political and economic agendas, Armstrong argues that "conduct books imply the presence of a unified middle class at a time when other representations of the social world suggest that no such class yet existed."[29] For Armstrong, conduct books established a "domestic ideal" that promoted "a concept of the household on which socially hostile groups felt they could all agree."[30] Conduct books accomplished these social functions because, as Armstrong and Tennenhouse claim, these books "strive to reproduce, if not always to revise, the culturally approved forms of desire."³¹ Following Armstrong, critics like Berger and Lawrence Klein consider how standards of conversational conduct, in particular, fashioned a "culture of politeness" to promote a new type of public gentleman (with explicitly defined political and philosophical motivations) as the proper English citizen.³² In this sense, politeness does not refer to a timeless sense of inherent virtue; rather, politeness is a time-dependent concept shaped in part by different writers at different historical moments for different purposes.³³ Recalling that conversation refers to any type of social engagement, from a mercantile interaction to a personal chat with a lover, this concentration upon the proper conduct of conversation suggests that writers recognized how post-1688 authority resided partly in the ability to shape linguistic interactions among Londoners. What all of these critics agree upon is that conduct literature is a socially engaged and ideologically imaginative literary form; *Reading London* contributes to this critical conversation by examining the conducts that were available to eighteenth-century Londoners.

For eighteenth-century readers, conduct literature was not a new literary tradition. Seventeenth-century conduct literature consisted primarily in three forms: courtesy-books (guides for accessing and perfecting courtly mannerisms that were supposedly inherently natural characteristics for aristocratic courtiers), chapbooks (dialogues or ballads that offered standards of courtship), and phrase-books (fabricated phrases with their attendant occasions for conversational usage).³⁴ During the eighteenth-century, however, the lines between these textual traditions blur, and critics such as Jacques Carré, Tim McLoughlin, and Georges Lamoine find "the dissemination of [conduct literature's] subject-matter into a broad range of literary genres."³⁵ As this current work on conduct literature suggests, the degree of this "dissemination" was so great that it is difficult to understand what types of eighteenth-century writing are *not* conduct literature. A common explanation for why conduct and issues of courtesy seem to pervade a multitude of textual traditions during the eighteenth century involves the perception that London transformed from a society of well-bred aristocratic courtiers to a marketplace for middle-class professionals whose lack of breeding defined them as such.³⁶ As a result, Carré locates a "crisis of courtesy" at the start of the eighteenth century in which the courtly connotations of "*court*esy" were now in danger of becoming prescriptive rules of etiquette, available to everyone.³⁷

Although eighteenth-century conduct books may resemble lists of rules (and more analysis of conduct books' stylistic strategies may dislodge this resemblance), the literature of the period adopts the task of normalizing certain standards of physical and mental activity in London. They do so because writers acknowledged that the imaginative qualities attached to reading seventeenth-century textual traditions were perfect vehicles for helping readers envision new relationships to a newly changed London. This provides a reason for why a variety of eighteenth-century texts may be discussed under the rubric of conduct literature. It also explains the heterogeneity of these forms. All of the "Town literature" examined in this book conveys a mode of writing that is neither purely creative in the post-romantic sense of castles and unicorns nor purely didactic in the sense of formulaic lectures and textbooks. Their mode is neither laughably fantastical nor sternly prescriptive; instead, they display a species of generic play that mocks our oversimplified binaries of creative imagination versus didactic prescription—a species that begs to be caught with a more contextualized critical apparatus. Partly because of its seventeenth-century and aristocratic associations, conduct has become synonymous with "proper behavior" or "mannerism." But conduct is also a value-producing abstraction. As an alternative to Armstrong's discussion of actual conduct books and their "ideology," I suggest that we examine the topographical conditions that allowed the metaphor of conduct (and not just actual conduct books) to acquire social value and produce notions of morality in London.

Conduct literature was valuable to eighteenth-century writers because it was a familiar textual tradition; it brought with it explicitly defined ways of reading that emphasized the metaphysical reasoning for proper behavior and mannerism. Relying on this familiarity, writers seized conduct as a stable "known" amid the new "unknowns" of post-1688 London. And this is where writers' metaphoric play acquires value. Metaphors were particularly valuable to these writers since metaphors familiarize the previously unknown—a function that is perfect for helping readers know their place in a newly changed urban environment. In particular, writers interpret conduct as a metaphor because a reader's familiarity with conduct's seventeenth-century associations could be transferred, through figurative similitudes, to refer to new, urban unknowns such as self-government (Burney and Boswell), urban space (Gay), and policing (Fielding). In other words, writers use conduct beyond its familiar, literal meaning; readers may see the word "conduct" on the page, recognize its literal meaning, but are now asked to extend its literal and familiar meaning into new, unfamiliar and imaginative contexts.[38] A metaphor that is common to twenty-first-century readers may help to clarify the familiarizing effects of metaphors. For instance, when we say "my love is a red, red rose," we do not literally mean that there exists one rose that possesses all of our love; it would be laughable to have a rose permanently take our place in bed beside our significant other. The proclamation makes sense only if we read beyond its literal meaning. But it is an extremely valuable metaphor because it attempts to connect an intangible unknown ("love") with a tangible known ("a rose") and therefore familiarize readers with something previously unknown. In addition, this metaphor is so communally accepted that the roses actually acquire economic value; that is, roses are extremely expensive. Like the metaphor of the rose, writers use the metaphor of conduct to exceed literal meaning. For the writers in this study, conduct sometimes refers to instructive public behavior, and at other times it refers to a type of imaginative guidance which only a writer could provide, especially in the way John Locke uses it to title his essay, *On the Conduct of the Understanding* (1706). Sometimes conduct referred to the practical execution of a theory, and at other times it referred to what we now call the conscience.[39] Most importantly, conduct could refer to the set of specific rules that a reader followed to make sense of, and engage with, printed text. In this sense, conduct refers to emerging theories of genre, and these examples suggest that conduct is an important metaphor to writers because it could accomplish imaginative tasks in excess of its literal meaning. That is, writers could assign new tasks to conduct's familiar associations with social status, and in this way, they imagined they could manage London and fill the void left by the abdication of James II. By figuratively referring to conduct beyond its literal meaning and in ways that seventeenth-century writers never intended, eighteenth-century writers made conduct resemble a desirable object (almost tangible, like the cityscape) that printed texts embodied and conveyed to readers. Furthermore, writers were able to transform this abstraction into an almost priceless necessity for interpreting London properly; they did so by anchoring this abstraction to London's literal, physical geography. In this way, the intangible (love or self-government) is rendered tangible (through the vehicle of a rose or writing in a journal).

The metaphor of conduct could also refer to a writer's guidance for helping readers interpret new, urban spaces. Consider, for instance, how John Gay's long poem *Trivia, or the Art of Walking the Streets of London* guides readers through a literal cityscape by cataloguing street names.

Readers become familiar with Gay's London not by identifying and visiting monuments, streets, and churches but by yoking the way people act—their particular conducts, their "art of walking"—to specific named streets. Beyond referring to a literal cityscape, Gay's poem urges readers to develop imaginative activity in order to know a new London. Gay used material conditions (urban geography) to accomplish figurative work (to know London by reading properly). Many of the writers I address in *Reading London* use the word "conduct" as a metaphor for textual form. Boswell's "schemes," Burney's "plans," and Fielding's "Method" or "Conduct in Writing" are all closely related to "kind," "species," and the archive of words that eighteenth-century critics used as placeholders for "genre." Invoking the metaphor of conduct, writers could shuttle value between textual authority, which was performed by the narrator's or poet's self-conscious entry into a work, and social authority, which was performed by the writer's helping readers to relate to London in a new way. Interpreting the metaphor of conduct to relate to genre, we may account for the proliferation of kinds of writing about London during the first two decades of the eighteenth century and for the omnipresence of "mock" genres that translated classical Roman textual traditions into vehicles for addressing London's local conditions. This suggests why several of the texts discussed in this book may seem generically foreign to us. For example, Burney's *Cecilia,* Boswell's *London Journal,* and Gay's *Trivia* resist our categories of novel, journal, and poem because each is a textual vehicle designed to clarify specific traits that characterized eighteenth-century London. The idea that eighteenth-century urban writers developed textual modes that we neither have nor recognize as our own may seem strange, but it is completely consistent with writers' attempts to reconceptualize their authority in terms of the administrative geography and notions of conduct of eighteenth-century London. Thus, writers reconceived textual modes to address specific urban problems that were unique to London.

Genre and the features that defined individual genres were not self-evident or well defined for all eighteenth-century writers; therefore, to address only one genre in this book (such as novels, poetry, or drama) would imply that eighteenth-century urban writers viewed genres as natural categories. This is simply not true. Gay's *Trivia,* which could be described as a poem, a guidebook, an urban georgic, or a mock-epic, shows that the metaphor of conduct was valuable because it could shuttle value between geography and a variety of textual traditions to render a previously unknowable object, the city, familiar. Each of the following chapters suggests ways to expand our notion of eighteenth-century conduct to understand it not only as a synonym for some abstract notion of public propriety or an ideological vehicle for refiguring subjectivity, but also, when in the hands of urban writers, as a metaphor for London's new spaces, governance, and patterns of writing and reading. In the following chapters, the metaphor of conduct produces meaning where there previously was none. Writers in London recognize that metaphor is a crucial tool for making writers *appear* to be governing while they write, and making readers *appear* to be governed as they learn to read and interpret properly. This does not simply mean that we should interpret our city as we would interpret a book. Instead, conduct is an eighteenth-century metaphor for a complex system of knowledge production for both readers *and* writers.

Governmentality

By the middle of the eighteenth century, London's problematic administrative geography had encouraged writers to generate imaginative solutions, and these solutions participated in a new, textual art of government known as governmentality. By "governmentality" I refer to an important theoretical lens that assists readers in seeing the strategies of imaginative government that writers devised after 1688. Discussions about authority in eighteenth-century London frequently invoke language derived from twentieth-century theories about eighteenth-century notions of power and authority. These theories are dominated by the words "public," "civil," and "governmentality," and are generally derived from the writings of Jürgen Habermas and Michel Foucault.[40] The theory of liberal governmentality initially posited by Foucault and more recently examined by Graham Burchell, Colin Gordon, Mary Poovey, and Judith Butler forms the modern understanding of the social context that enabled eighteenth-century urban writing to resemble governing.[41] Modern critics use liberal governmentality to refer to an "art of government"[42] that appeared after 1688 to compete with a fading monarchial absolutism. In contrast to divine right, liberal governmentality did not strictly operate "by coercion"; instead, it "elicited voluntary compliance through the mechanisms of fashion and taste."[43] In twenty-first-century terms, Judith Butler suggests that we are familiar with governmentality in terms of post-9/11 military tribunals and "indefinite detention"; to Butler, governmentality "denotes an operation of administration power that is extra-legal.... [it] designates a field of political power in which tactics and aims have become diffuse, and in which political power fails to take on a unitary and causal form."[44] Although Butler uses governmentality to interpret twenty-first-century events, she nonetheless acknowledges the relationship of governmentality to eighteenth-century notions of sovereignty:

> Governmentality thus operates through state and non-state institutions and discourses that are legitimated neither by direct elections nor through established authority. Marked by a diffuse set of strategies and tactics, governmentality gains its meaning and purpose from no single source, no unified sovereign subject. Rather, the tactics characteristic of governmentality operate diffusely, to dispose and order populations, and to produce and reproduce subjects, their practices and beliefs, in relation to specific policy aims.[45]

Printed text in eighteenth-century London constitutes one of these "extralegal" tactics for replacing a "unified sovereign subject." From this perspective, we may consider the metaphors, rhetoric, and literary styles employed by early eighteenth-century writers as extralegal tactics for organizing London in new ways.

J. A. Pocock's work is also important since it carefully qualifies these theorizations of liberal governmentality by injecting "manners" into these discussions of eighteenth-century civic government.[46] In particular, Pocock traces how ancient notions of English virtue were redefined in terms of "manners," a concept of civic regulation that negotiated England's past with the onset of commercialism by combining "the ethical" with "the juristic."[47] Pocock's point here is that a technology of manners reconciled any ethical problems that people had with London's new materialism. While this argument offers one way to understand why eighteenth-century literature is obsessed with manners, conduct, and direction, I argue that in the way eighteenth-century writers theorized it, "conduct" was a technology not only suited for reconciling trade with an ancient regime, but also for projecting alternate futures that frequently, at least in their surface content, have nothing to do with trade. In its forward-leaning, goal-oriented movement towards imaginative speculation and projection, "conduct" is therefore distinct from "manners." Both metaphors target discipline and consensus, but each one reaches these goals via different modes (i.e., political, aesthetic, religious) and different cultural vehicles (i.e., writing, reading, performance).[48]

Early eighteenth-century literary writing, most notably Addison and

Steele's *Tatler* and *Spectator* papers (published between 1710 and 1712), frequently attempts to outline an individual's relationship to an urban community. In the shadow of divine right, textual discipline constituted a new prerequisite for a properly organized society. Conduct figured prominently in this periodical project as a monitoring device that left communal standards of taste intact, yet permitted readers to envision themselves as independent authorities. While critics such as Habermas have viewed Addison and Steele's project as the birth of bourgeois subjectivity,[49] I am more interested in how writers after Addison and Steele not only participated in liberal governmentality (their writings are attempts at controlling others), but also advertised printed text as a site of urban authority (their writings could govern other people in the place of divine right). Writers advertised their new method for knowing London as society's best and only way to comprehend a city filled with isolated individuals. These writers therefore had to define their social function while performing it; for them, governmentality implied self-authorization.

Each of the following chapters frames a cultural problem in London that writers attempted to resolve by shaping consensus in a post-1688 environment. In turn, each chapter also details the textual technologies and modes that interact with, or arise from, London's cultural geography, and it is these technologies and forms that constitute the writer's experiment in the art of government. My goal is neither to synthesize every chapter under a grand generalization nor to discount the differences between the projects of Gay, Fielding, Pope, Boswell, and Burney. Instead, I offer five different ways in which eighteenth-century literary writing about London may be seen to be experimental and exploratory rather than prescriptive and regulatory. In addition, each writer participates in textual governmentality by means of several different genres.

The principle that has guided my selection of the writers I analyze is based on my desire to show how the stylistic and rhetorical strategies of canonically "literary" eighteenth-century texts may, with the help of different theoretical lenses, be shown to strive for cultural goals that extend beyond traditionally literary goals (i.e., to be aesthetically pleasing or reflect an authentic "reality"). For instance, although she is a writer who was irretrievably influenced by London's physicality, Aphra Behn does not figure in the following study since she writes on the verge of sovereignty's realignment in 1688, much of her work being swan songs for the Stuart cause before her death in 1689. Writers such as Eliza Haywood and Daniel Defoe also do not figure prominently, but their absence is not due to their inability to imagine alternative Londons; instead, spatial limitations have caused me to test the validity of my thesis with texts that, with the exception of the past two decades, have traditionally been critiqued for their aesthetic and "realistic," rather than cultural or political, merit. Thus, the following chapters interpret traditionally literary works in frequently nonliterary ways to offer several conclusions about the ways writers administered urban and textual spaces to readers.

Not all of the writers in the following chapters contributed to ideas of liberal governmentality in the same way. For example, Gay, Pope, and Fielding aimed to present themselves and their textual products as unquestionable social authorities. They carefully focus a reader's attention on the new formal techniques that they were developing to guide the reader through unknown territories and textual forms. If the theory of governmentality can help suggest why writers in early eighteenth-century London were in the position to imagine themselves as authoritative figures, then this theory can also suggest how Gay's "Art of Walking the Streets of London" participated in an "art of governing." Boswell and Burney, on the other hand, offer detailed sketches of what should be taking place *within* Londoners' minds. Their works narrate what happens when Londoners internalize the disciplinary techniques posited by Addison, Steele, Gay, Pope, and Fielding; therefore, Boswell and Burney represent a generation of writers raised on the models of an earlier generation. But Boswell and Burney's self-governing techniques are not divorced from a specific experience of London; in fact, they are enabled by a new cultural problem that distinguishes late eighteenth-century London from its predecessor: the proliferation of print. To be sensitive to this cultural problem that distinguishes the motivations of early eighteenth-century writers from those of the late eighteenth-century, I organize the chapters of this book under two headings that refer to the changing functions that writers assigned to printed text: "governing others" and "governing the self." The final section of this introduction reviews the problems and arguments for each chapter that I include beneath these headings. In this way, the order of the chapters sketches a developmental history of these writers' experiments in eighteenth-century governmentality.

Governing Others

There are three reasons why I begin a study of how writers attempted to control others with Gay. First, Gay unapologetically anchors his poem to the material conditions of eighteenth-century London. The hypersensitivity with which Gay details street names provides us with an idea about how meaningful eighteenth-century London's geography was to writers. Desperate to refer to quotidian urban conditions and render them less complex, Gay also engineers over the course of the poem a powerful abstraction: urban space. In particular, Gay conceptualizes space as an archive of conduct (styles of walking, dress, and transport) each of which denotes a specific street. Another reason why a discussion of *Trivia* is important is that it details London's streets and conceptualizes space in a way that Fielding, Boswell, and Burney would eventually take for granted and consider to be common knowledge. The "art of walking" that Gay's poem describes allows us to view *Tom Jones* and the *Epistle to Burlington* as urban artifacts, even though they are not always viewed as such. My interpretation does not dispute that a work like *Tom Jones,* for example, may also be read as a mock-heroic *Bildungsroman,* but I do suggest that viewing this novel as an urban artifact reveals important facets of a shared artistic project. Finally, Gay's poem frustrates attempts to forge twentieth-century relationships to a 1716 long poem. The work wears its alterity on its sleeve; its specificity demands that we see the poem as a document written to address local conditions and to guide readers through a moment in London's history. Thus, I do not interpret the spaces that Gay conceptualizes in *Trivia* as primitive centers of modernity that reflect a modern "self."[50] One can only claim that eighteenth-century views of London prefigure twentieth-century perspectives on this or any other urban model by downplaying the sense of geographic and administrative specificity that *Reading London* strives to highlight.

I argue in the second chapter that the textual strategies Fielding used in *Tom Jones* to guide his readers through a new textual form (the novel) are identical to the strategies that he used in his Bow Street prose to introduce himself to the populace he governed as Magistrate on Bow Street. If we recognize how Gay relies upon the metaphor of conduct to fabricate ideas about urban space (as well as his social value as a poet), we may contextualize how Fielding's *Tom Jones* helped Fielding merge the novelist with the Bow Street Magistrate. The connection between Fielding's novel and his civil prose is stylistic; Fielding developed a specific way of guiding readers' relationships to their proper authorities that not only helped him police the liminal districts surrounding Bow Street, but also lent writers (whether novelists or writers of social treatises) legitimacy in an urban environment.

The third chapter contextualizes Alexander Pope's 1731 *Epistle to Burlington* in terms of London's industry of urban projecting and improvement. I argue that by using the final eight lines to Pope's verse-epistle as its epigraph, Nicholas Hawksmoor's 1736 *Proposition for a New Stone-Bridge at Westminster* points to the importance of Pope's poem for imagining London's mid-century cityscape. In particular, Pope's *To Burlington,* which Pope wrote to his architect-patron Lord Burlington, assigns a proper "Use" to wealth. Pope defined this use by using the poem to reinterpret the words "Taste" and "Use"; however, the way in which readers approached Pope's Horatian epistle as well as the poem's erratic publishing history suggests that *To Burlington* began to be read as a Humean—and definably British—essay. Witnessing the way Pope translates Roman textual tradition into a definably British form, readers were able to imagine that *To Burlington* transferred authority from Rome to London. In turn, Pope resembled a classically educated interpreter whom, in the absence of a sovereign monarch, London needed to render its social problems legible to an eighteenth-century populace. One of these problems involved the eighteenth-century competition between sovereignty and liberal governmentality. This problem of urban authority was best symbolized during the 1730s by the fervor over the construction of a bridge at Westminster that would compete with London Bridge, the City of London's ancient viaduct for trade. As Hawksmoor's epigraph suggests, Pope's poem, in both its form and its content, attempted to reconcile these immediate problems that threatened Court and City.

A New Cultural Problem: The Proliferation of Print

In an interchapter (chapter 4) that I position between the sections entitled governing others and governing the self, I detail not only the historical conditions that gave rise to the proliferation of print in London but also several reactions to this textual proliferation that recognize it as a new problem for Londoners. Writers moved from governing others to governing the self because the proliferation of governing projects that writers like Gay, Fielding, and Pope had popularized during the first half of the century had become incredibly varied, chaotic, and seemingly unrelated. From the perspective of late eighteenth-century writers such as Boswell and Burney, these early eighteenth-century experiments in textual government had failed to cause substantive political change due to the fact that Gay, Fielding, and Pope relied upon imaginative techniques to control Londoners. The "print-saturated London" which I outline in the interchapter therefore presents a cultural problem to late-century writers since they not only encountered early-century writers' failure to effectively guide readers' imaginations, but they also inherited a cacophonous number of proliferating textual voices that made urban unity seem impossible. The saturation of printed text in mid-century London therefore denies a reader's ability to fashion a single, individual self since there were an infinite number of different texts and forms that claimed to relate readers to London in the proper way. By the late eighteenth-century, a single "London" became more difficult to imagine since there was no single textual tradition in which to imagine London. The sheer heterogeneity of textual forms that constituted a print-saturated London threatened the notion of a single self. In short, the new cultural problem that London now presented to readers and writers was that a print-saturated London blurred London's readability.

The chapters that I devote to Boswell (chapter 5) and Burney (chapter 6) register two experiences of this cultural problem and result in Boswell's and Burney's developing textual modes of self-government. As a heterogeneous, print-saturated London threatens the conception of an individual self, Boswell and Burney respond by reappropriating the textual strategies that Gay, Fielding, and Pope had originally conceived to manage others. Boswell and Burney adapt these strategies to manage themselves, and as a result, they contribute to a late-century version of governmentality that involves self-government. In their self-governing responses to a print-saturated London, Boswell and Burney show how notions of private individuality both inherit and alter the terms of communal identity conceived by an earlier generation of writers.

Governing the Self

In chapter 5 I argue that Boswell responds to London's incongruous textual representations and images by internalizing the modes of government that Gay and Fielding had developed to address readers. If London's heterogeneity threatened Boswell's sense of an individual self, then he needed a way to reimagine unity in late eighteenth-century London. In his *London Journal,* Boswell recognized that the critical unity associated with dramatic metaphor represented a way to reimagine a unified self. For example, Boswell frequently adopts other personas in "scenes," and he introduces dialogues that contain parenthetical stage directions. To understand how Boswell's dramatic metaphor worked as a vehicle for recording his experiences within and between Court and City (the areas, not coincidentally, in which the majority of London's theaters were located), I historicize the connotations that the word "dramatic" would have carried in London between 1762 and 1763. Doing so, we can see that Boswell's use of dramatic metaphor originated in and was yoked not only to the Town's undisciplined geography but also to post-Restoration literary and social criticism. The *London Journal* represents Boswell's attempt to critique his every move in an effort to become, with the help of no one but himself, a proper Briton. To accomplish this feat, Boswell viewed the act of writing as synonymous with performing—and governing—the self; Boswell became both the authoritative actor-writer and the reflective critic-reader. Boswell's *London Journal* represents in many ways a logical conclusion to Addison and Steele's attempt to govern readers by means of printed texts.

Unlike Boswell's experience with the endless possibilities that a print-saturated city offered him, Burney recognized that these possibilities actually limited a woman's urban experience. Burney found that London's heterogeneity did not offer women a variety of choices; instead, London's endless possibilities for self-definition presented an endless number of ways to limit a woman's agency in London and render her a passive object. In the fifth chapter, I interpret Burney's second novel, *Cecilia,* as a sequel or attempt to recast these problems of London's gendered spaces by reimagining the gendered literary traditions that surface in her first novel, *Evelina.* Recognizing the formal limitations that a novel of letters had imposed upon her writing about a young woman's maturation in London, Burney wrote *Cecilia* not only to reappropriate the formal limitations that *Evelina* had allowed her to recognize, but also to write beyond the epistolary tradition so as to identify alternate sites of feminine authority in London. The forms in which male writers were producing knowledge about London frequently did not relate to women; for example, women lacking male conductors on eighteenth-century streets were considered prostitutes. Gay's "Art of Walking the Streets" therefore addresses male readers; it does not address women who were brought to and conducted throughout London by male escorts. In response to these masculine strategies for producing urban knowledge, Burney uses *Evelina* and *Cecilia* to suggest ways in which women could reimagine themselves as both the conducted individual and the conductor. One way to accomplish this imaginative task, Burney suggests, is to reject the idea that epistolary confession is the only means for knowing one's self. Women could instead interpret their own experiences rather than waiting for a reader to interpret and critique their urban experiences. Burney takes this suggestion to heart when she, as a woman novelist, rejects epistolary confession and reinterprets the role of letter writing in *Cecilia.*

Burney occupies the final chapter because she questions what a woman's authentic self might resemble in London. But she was also able to exploit the metaphor of conduct in a way that male writers such as Boswell and Gay could not. In particular, her first two novels question how notions of conduct and textual form made gender meaningful. She in turn exposed the metaphor of conduct for what it really was: a rhetorical device that writers used to imagine authority. Burney, however, did not discard the metaphor of conduct as a defunct or tainted strategy of authorization. She instead reinterpreted it in order to propose an alternative (and gendered) mode of soul-searching that did not rely upon confessional tactics. Burney's writing therefore outlined strategies of self-authorization that catered to women writers, but she continued to seize the opportunities that London's geography and its modes of governmentality made available to writers in general.

With these concrete examples in mind, I return to my central argument: eighteenth-century urban writers advertised an authority that they never really possessed, but imagined they held. None of the texts discussed here—not even Gay's *Trivia*—attempts to reflect London as it actually existed; instead, authors used their works to reimagine London and their roles in London's immediate present. To the extent that the guidebooks, novels, poems, journals, brochures, plays, periodical papers, and treatises I analyze tried to imagine a credentialized role for the urban writer that did not exist, these works should be seen as eighteenth-century projects. For example, Fielding's *Tom Jones* is just one example of what eighteenth-century novel writing looked like; Fielding had no way of knowing that his (or rather Cervantes's) self-conscious narrative voice and style would be adopted by later novelists as a defining characteristic of a British genre. Burney never fully resolved her problems with confessional literary vehicles in *Evelina* and *Cecilia;* she used each novel to make problems visible, not to solve them. We should also remember that Boswell's *London Journal* is not a self-contained work; it is just one volume in his recorded life. Boswell takes great pains to advertise that his *London Journal* does not end with a reformed, chaste hero. Instead, the *London Journal* tries to identify a British style of writing that Boswell could take with him on his Grand Tour. Fielding, Burney, and Boswell wrote without knowing what the end to their projects would be; thus, their works exemplify the eighteenth-century sense of the word "project" as Daniel Defoe had defined it: "a vast Undertaking, too big to be manag'd."[51] While none of these urban writers tries to "manage" the ends of these projects, each writer imagines exerting some control over London's present. It is not my intention to prove that Pope's poetry actually built a bridge or to prove that Londoners actually considered space in the way Gay imagined it; instead, I stress the important roles that writers' imaginations played in fabricating both London and the Londoner. I focus not only on textual projects that tried to clarify conduct's role in understanding London, but also on the textual strategies and formal traditions that defined and valorized the process of "conducting" or writing in eighteenth-century London.

By focusing on conduct as an abstract yet influential "governing idea," I offer one way to answer questions about why eighteenth-century urban writing differs from the urban writing from other centuries. I have chosen to focus on conduct because, although an abstraction, it had ramifications for London's daily life that demand further, sensitive clarification. Describing conduct as a governing idea allows me not only to visualize its relevance to theories of liberal governmentality ("governing") and imaginative thought (Hume's "ideas"), but also to question the self-evident status it enjoys as a governing idea in twenty-first century criticism about eighteenth-century literature. I have not attempted to make this study of conduct the last word on the subject of eighteenth-century urban writers' alterity; instead, I hope to provoke more questions that will render the peculiar complexities and lost subtleties of eighteenth-century writing visible to a twenty-first century audience.

The crucial characteristic about eighteenth-century urban literature that my study reveals is the experimental, exploratory tone of some of the most "canonical" works of the period. The experimental tone of these literary-urban-projects questions the post-romantic notion that eighteenth-century writing is prescriptive and unimaginative (according to a Wordsworthian definition of imagination). By closely reading the textual strategies that writers developed to contribute to London's government, I sketch an urban history that suggests that our ideas about how to create, manage, and police centralized populations in urban settings do *not* have to be viewed as the culmination of an inevitable process. In other words, *Reading London* shows how eighteenth-century literature offers alternatives for urban governance and ultimately suggests that our twenty-first-century problems and conceptions of "the city" did not have to be this way.

PART I

GOVERNING OTHERS

1

Archives of Conduct

JOHN GAY ON LONDON'S STREET LEVEL

When John Gay published *Trivia: or, the Art of Walking the Streets of London* in 1716, the long poem performed a function similar to the one that maps inherited by the mid-century. In particular, Gay's poem offers a variety of ways for readers to identify their position in London, which in Gay's terms means a position among a moral hierarchy of professions as well as among buildings and streets. Similar to twenty-first-century guidebooks, Gay's poem includes an index of London's street-names for a reader's convenient, quick reference; however, unlike our guidebooks, Gay's work offers no maps or visual representations from which to "take in" London. Instead, Gay provides mock-epic verse. *Trivia* offers an alternative to knowing one's place in London that has nothing to do with color-coded maps or aerial perspectives; in fact, Gay develops a relationship between readers and their urban environment that exists at the street level. The idea that visitors in London may have carried Gay's poem in their pockets to experience the city may seem humorous and counterintuitive, but it only appears foreign to us because other technologies (such as maps, global-positioning systems, and handbooks) now fulfill the duty that Gay assigns to his eighteenth-century "urban-pastoral" poem. The history of London's cartography, however, is linked to *Trivia* in some very specific ways.

Cynthia Wall's summary of London's cartographic history describes the changes in cartographic practice after the 1660 Great Fire as changes in perspective:

> Before the Fire there were relatively few maps of London. Most maps of London between 1550 and 1660 were printed on the continent or engraved

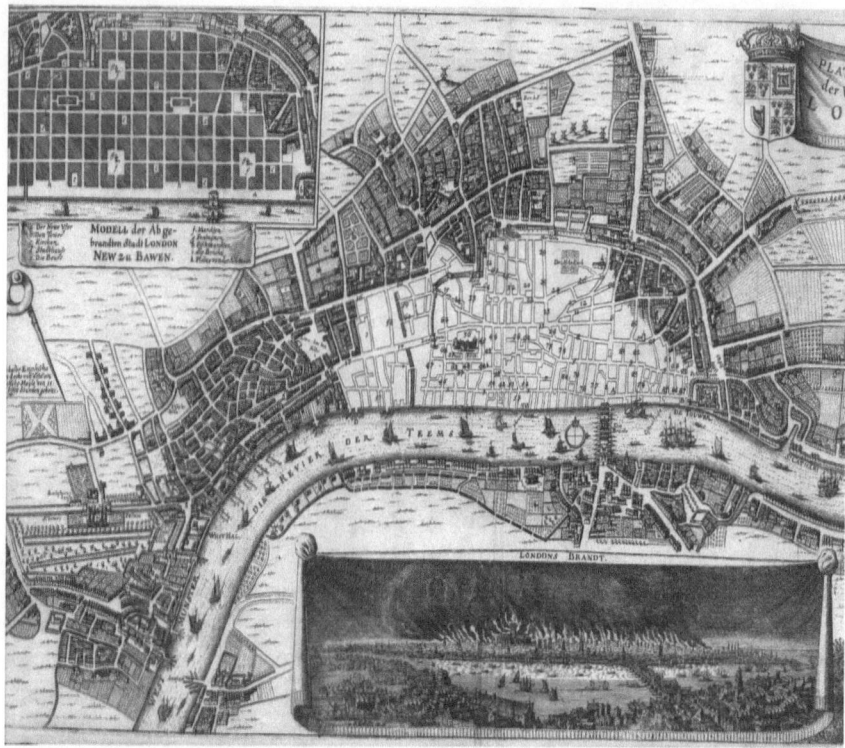

Figure 1. Marcus Willemsz Doornick. *Platte Grondt der Verbrande Stadt London.* Amsterdam. 1666. This post-Fire map of London exemplifies the two techniques for mapping London that Wall describes: 1) the three-dimensional representations of buildings beyond the outskirts of the ancient city that characterized early seventeenth-century maps and 2) the two-dimensional, vacant outlines of "empty" space that characterized maps following the Great Fire (see Wall, *Literary and Cultural Spaces,* 80 and 84, respectively). In the upper-left corner of the map, Doornick represents one possible plan for rebuilding the City—a symmetrical plan for squares, markets, and fountains. It is interesting that this transitional plan also evinces the transition between both techniques for mapping London. (For details concerning Doornick's map, see Ida Darlington and James Howgego, *Printed Maps of London Circa 1553–1850.* [London: George Philip & Son Ltd., 1964], 60) (Courtesy of the Map Library, Harlan Hatcher Graduate Library, University of Michigan).

by foreigners, and were sponsored by royal or military events. Over the next hundred years or so a few of the maps of London were published, but they were almost entirely derivative of the Tudor maps.... The Fire also, in a manner of speaking, literally and theatrically interrupted the whole

Figure 2. William Faden. *A New Pocket Plan of the Cities of London & Westminster With the Borough of Southwark, Comprehending the New Buildings and Other Alternations to the Year 1790.* 1790 edition. In this late eighteenth-century map of London, we can see how blank, disenfranchised blocks of topographical detail take the place of personalized buildings (see Wall, *Literary and Cultural Spaces,* 83 and 90–111). Yet this topographical detail still preserves the administrative tradition of carefully separating the City of London (with a painted red line) from the surrounding liberties of Westminster. The map's title also emphasizes this distinction as it constitutes a "plan" of "the *Cities* of London & Westminster" (emphasis mine). (For details concerning Faden's map, see Darlington and Howgego, *Printed Maps of London,* 137) (Courtesy of the Map Library, Harlan Hatcher Graduate Library, University of Michigan)

> tradition of three-dimensional cartography in London, and generated a very
> different perception of cartographic discipline.[1]

This "different perception" centered upon the change from early seventeenth-century "pictorial bird's-eye-views . . . in which buildings and landmarks are privileged over topographical accuracy" (figure 1) to the two-dimensional foundation lines of post-Fire maps that "literally as well as figuratively represents blank space, emptiness, the inexpressible" (figure 2).² The result of this perceptual change was a new spatial awareness that is evident not only on maps, but also in London's "textual topographies."³ In her comparative study of Restoration maps and literary texts, Wall argues that "in fact the *literary* remapping of London is part of the *literal* remapping, grounded both imaginatively and technologically in the innovations of cartographic reappropriation, borrowing explicitly and implicitly from its vocabulary and conceptual apparatus."⁴ For Wall, this borrowing consists in the way maps and texts before 1666 stressed "owner and history over space and structure" whereas maps and texts after the Great Fire outlined immolated, empty spaces in need of an owner and a history.⁵

The history of London's literary mapping (as opposed to its visual mapping) usually begins with John Stow's 1598 *Survey of London*.⁶ In his portrait of sixteenth-century London, Stow infamously exhibits a "nostalgic antiquarianism" for pre-Reformation London.⁷ Stow's *Survey* is important to eighteenth-century London because, as J. F. Merritt notes, John Strype updated Stow's work in a 1720 edition; therefore, between Stow's original and Strype's "Protestant" 1720 edition, Merritt traces how writers adapted the *Survey* to satisfy "a public thirst for the reassuring spatial and temporal continuity implied by the inclusion of the Elizabethan Stow's reminiscences among accounts of early eighteenth-century building."⁸ Wall offers additional evidence of Stow's nostalgia by noting how Stow's pre-Fire "grammar of space . . . is primarily fixed by verbs of stasis and by passive constructions of 'to be'—streets and structures are grammatically inert."⁹ After the Fire, this grammar of space turns to a grammar of motion, as suggested by the title of Defoe's *Tour* and John Macky's *A Journey*.¹⁰ Published in 1716, Gay's *Trivia* stands at the end of this cartographic-textual history, and it evinces a grammar of motion; however, whereas Wall claims that "Gay's poem is closer to the agendas and tones of the textual topographies," I argue that the meaning Gay attached to "conduct" throughout *Trivia* occupies a third term between the extremes of seventeenth-century static space and a post-Fire grammar of motion.¹¹ In particular, Gay's metaphor of conduct presents readers with the impression of a regulated, directed, and therefore safe, brand of guidance—peripatetic and moving, yet stable and secure. The idea of meditating upon the communal experience of the street level, rather than considering it to be an unremarkable, faceless vehicle for harried transport to a destination, may indeed represent an alternative to the way we conceive the twenty-first-century street level. In addition to theorizing conduct as a textual alternative to visual maps, *Trivia* offers its readers a quality that is frequently not associated with maps: morality. By yoking morality to geography, Gay's poem produces a "mental map" for readers on the go. But to understand Gay's eighteenth-century alternative to mapping London, we, as twenty-first-century readers, must acknowledge at least three early eighteenth-century problems that Gay's poem sought to address.

First, the status of the areas between Court and City after 1688 presented Gay with problems for representing a single "London." Because a unified concept of "London" before 1716 did not exist, *Trivia* offered to resolve this problem by engineering space as a concept that could transform previously under-emphasized parishes and liberties into meaningful components of an international—and newly British—capital. A second problem involved the competing technologies that Londoners used to gain knowledge about early eighteenth-century London. Although maps proved to be one of the most valued technologies for knowing cities during the twentieth century, we should understand *Trivia* as Gay's attempt to position poetry in a place where maps would eventually come to exist. *Trivia* is therefore not a "poem" in the way modernists might use that term but a textual technology in the sense that Gay's long poem fashioned new ways for describing, reading, and knowing a specific object. Not only was this object—the city—in need of description but Gay's audience also needed to be named, described, and addressed. Taking advantage of the rise of a definable print culture and the variety of audiences it created, Gay fashions his own audience in *Trivia*. Thirdly, the way Gay's poem fashions its readers shows that Gay was making a statement about the nature of poetry—a highly contested topic in early eighteenth-century London. Eighteenth-century poets repeatedly questioned their century's relationship to classical poetic traditions, and British writers cast themselves as the people who would determine the fate of a poetic lineage that originated in Rome. Gay's poem questions poetry's relevance to a newly formed nation, and the answers that he provides are complex and related to the history of print.

As a textual artifact, *Trivia* occupies a crucial moment in the history of print in London. The proliferation of printed text in London during the late seventeenth and early eighteenth centuries brought with it an infinite number of ramifications for the way Londoners understood their relationships to urban authority. For example, Paula McDowell focuses on the period from 1678–1730 to contextualize the "democratic possibilities inherent in the new literary marketplace" that specifically related to women and their political empowerment.[12] McDowell details how the different opportunities for affecting urban communication open to hawkers, informants, ballad-singers, and mercury-women can go unnoticed if we ignore the nuanced material conditions of early eighteenth-century printing practices.[13] McDowell's concentration on the "oral activism" of ballad singers and its effects upon sedition laws shows that writing, reading, and printing were more complicated during the early eighteenth-century than previously assumed.[14] As McDowell reappropriates textual agency during this episode in the rise of urban print culture, she generates a theory that we may relate to *Trivia* since the poem both participates in and censors the "democratic possibilities" that this marketplace presented to Gay. To stress his participation in and relationship to this marketplace, Gay's poem draws our attention to "Ballad-Singers," the "Bookseller," the "Hawker," Gay's publisher "Lintott," and the "Author" himself. In particular, Gay sees in *Trivia* the opportunity to answer one question that had acquired particular importance after 1688: how can writers govern people they will neither meet nor see?

With the proliferation of print during the early eighteenth century came doubts about print's ability to be a vehicle for truth. Adrian Johns has detailed this "epistemic indeterminacy" of early modern print: "Fixity was in the eye of the beholder, and its recognition could not be maintained without continuing effort. At no point could it be counted on to reside irremissibly in the object itself, and it was always liable to contradiction."[15] Throughout *Trivia,* Gay assigns meaning to geography, or, in Johns's terms, attempts to make "fixity" and truth "reside irremissibly in the object itself." Gay yokes London's materiality—its bookshops, its churches, its paving stones—to abstract notions of truth and morality. Truth, Gay seems to suggest, was inherent in London's material objects. To access this truth, one needed to read these objects correctly. For Gay, walking through London therefore came to resemble both a moral activity—an "art"—and a newly specialized mode of reading. If the "Art of Walking" was a moral activity, then Gay's ability to conduct readers through his poem acquired a similar moral responsibility. Walking, conducting, and reading embodied similar critical activity for Gay because they were his tools for connecting materiality to ethics. Consequently, these tools allowed Gay to imbue printed text with moral value. To assign this intangible value to a printed poem and a physical city, Gay also created his own readership by teaching them how to read *Trivia.* If the early eighteenth-century literary marketplace opened up possibilities for certain readers to view themselves from outside a framework of sovereignty, then new forms of reading were not only possible but also necessary for readers to comprehend this new framework. Thus, part of this chapter is devoted to magnifying the ways Gay's poem instructs his audience on how to read the city as well as the poem. "How to read" is as much a part of Gay's moral project as "what to read."

Finally, before explicating Gay's work as "a poem" or attempting to phrase arguments about *Trivia,* it is crucial to note the way *Trivia*—and Gay's entire career—defies what we might see as "genre."[16] To interpret this "defiance," we might describe Gay's work as rebellious or in terms of "mock"-genres as a way to salvage generic categorizations. This chapter does not try to catalogue the satiric twists and heroic turns of Gay's text since that job has been done elsewhere.[17] Instead, I interpret Gay's use of textual tradition to see how formal devices perform a type of work that constituted an eighteenth-century version of urban planning. For example, using "mock" to describe the tone of *Trivia* presents significant difficulties. Consider how Tom Woodman uses the term "mock-georgic" to bridge a critical binary: "Gay cannot find a convincing form of work as the georgic art of living in his period, and it is for this reason that he needs the saving grace of the mock-georgic. Through the mock mode he expresses his ambivalent yet affectionate attitude toward city life as a whole."[18] Woodman views the "mock mode" as a way to nurture a contradictory "attitude"; however, I want to push the way Woodman reads Gay's contradictions a bit farther. The labels "mock" or "anti" (i.e., mock-heroic, mock-georgic, anti-pastoral) are frequently placeholders for an emergent interpretation of Gay's complexity. The adjectival "mock," when yoked to "georgic," suggests that the mode is precisely *not* georgic. Instead, "mock" signifies that we are reading an episode that is something other than purely georgic. From this perspective, "mock" descriptions are symptoms of *Trivia's* eighteenth-century "otherness"; they demand a second look because they overgeneralize and obscure Gay's very sensitive textual work.

Current critiques of *Trivia* also center upon the slipperiness of Gay's tone, and a controversy has developed over whether *Trivia's* tone is ultimately serious or satiric.[19] Pat Rogers attributes this ambivalence to "a complex feat of rhetorical engineering" as the poem "is no more a straightforward mock-heroic than it is straight reportage"; however, the work ultimately succeeds in Rogers's view since it "employs social observation to make permanent moral comment; it employs moral emblems, such as the Fleet, to state sociological truth."[20] It is not always easy to distinguish between places where Gay is ironic and passages where he is completely serious; however, an argument that only interprets "tone" is not my target. While drawing attention to *Trivia*'s generic complexity, I am also interested in how combinations of modes, tones, and voices create different ways of reading—or more to the point, interpreting—*Trivia*. These different ways of reading accomplish *Trivia*'s hidden work. Episodes marked by changes in mode, tone, and voice signal that the poem is accomplishing new tasks.

Acknowledging these three problems that Gay faced while writing *Trivia* as well as the issues involved with the terms we use to interpret Gay's poem, the first part of this chapter poses two arguments: first, *Trivia* contributed to building London because it forced readers to relate to their urban surroundings in completely new ways. Second, *Trivia* engineered a specific metaphor to make a new vision of London possible: urban space. In her study of "empty" urban space after the Great Fire, Wall privileges the metaphor of space to such an extent that she structures her chapters around different spatial manifestations (parks, streets, houses, and even "novels"), and I also consider alternatives to organizing post-1688 London that reside in imaginative metaphors (such as conduct) that coexist with spatial thought. Indeed, space is a complex abstraction conceived by architects, map makers, surveyors, and writers to which they assign arbitrary value. For example, as frequent-flyers know all too well, the precious "space" purchased by first-class airline customers (leg room, etc.) is a major factor in differentiating their ticket-price from their fellow travelers squeezed into coach. Space can be empty or full, yet either version can carry a weighty price tag; thus, this seeming inconsistency (some would call it a dialectic of space) suggests that a discussion of historicized space, or space and its different manifestations as it has been reconceived over centuries, is required. Wall attempts to tell this history, as she describes her study as "largely phenomenological";[21] however, rather than assuming that eighteenth-century writers agreed upon a universal meaning of "space" and to avoid my placing an anachronistic importance upon this modern phenomenon, I am more interested in exploring the literary alternatives to a theorized, spatial vocabulary that writers developed to reorganize London after 1688. Space, in its twentieth-first-century manifestation, therefore implies a three-, four-, or five- dimensional interpretation of a "place" (the "dimensions" being cultural issues of politics, economics, identity, nationalism, etc.), and Wall carefully explores Restoration notions of space in this manner. But writers such as Gay devise other methods for reading eighteenth-century London—methods that do not always resemble our versions and conceptions of place and how we register it.

The textual techniques Gay used to engineer space allowed readers to envision their relationships to a changing cityscape. Gay's particular concept of space addressed and was irretrievably linked to a crucial problem of London's urbanization that I have outlined in the introduction in more detail: the tension between the encroaching administrative boundaries of Westminster and the City of London. From a twentieth-century perspective, "space" in London is usually seen as either a historical product of traditional English party structures (i.e., a Tory Court and a Whig City) or as the faded boundaries of an antiquated parochial system.[22] I suggest that *Trivia* fashioned space in a completely different way, in a way that adjudicated the three problems faced by early eighteenth-century London.

Once again, these are questions about the boundaries of London, the nature of contemporary textual technologies, and the function of poetry itself at the time. Gay's concept of space offers to render the system of legislative and textual practices that operated in a realm between Court and City less imposing.

Trivia is an intersection of textual traditions and social concerns precisely because it attempts to catalogue the experience of an entire city at street level. This concentration on street-level experience has caused many critics to label *Trivia* a distinctly "urban" text.[23] I do not argue that "inclusiveness" is Gay's contribution to "urban" literature, however. I am not trying to discover a primordial definition of "the urban" that is applicable to the literature of other cities or other times.[24] This is because *Trivia* does not participate in a universal urban tradition; it nurtured complexity to manage one city during a transformative period of its history. It is essential to understand that the complexity that *Trivia* continually refuses to resolve for the reader—in both its form and tone—did specific work to a "London" of 1716. *Trivia* navigated a complex web of administrative concerns and became just one early eighteenth-century version of urban planning.[25]

Gay's version of urban planning designs two objects: London and the Londoner. Gay juggles, at one time, several different practices, professions, genres, modes, classical texts, and contemporary allusions to make London and the Londoner recognizable entities. As a result, *Trivia* appears multi-voiced, complex, and confused; however, this textual complexity may have accomplished work. That is, Gay considered complexity to be an integral textual component to his design of London. To make this work visible, the latter half of the chapter interprets *Trivia* with a critical lens that accounts for eighteenth-century ideas of civil conduct.

The final section of this chapter interprets the ramifications of these issues on Gay's role as an eighteenth-century poet in London. In particular, an interesting parallel arises when we compare Gay to an urban architect, especially in light of how a textual "art of walking" managed and governed civil society. This is where I differ from studies which send *Trivia*—and Gay's career—to a critical graveyard of generic ambiguity.[26] *Trivia* is not simply a satiric playground of detached signifiers; *Trivia* participates in its own type of textual tradition—a tradition which accomplished some very necessary work during the first three decades of the eighteenth century.

"To Tread in Paths to Ancient Bards Unknown"

The most tempting way to approach *Trivia, or the Art of Walking the Streets of London* is by seeing it as some sort of Michelin guide. A famous example of this approach is William Henry Irving's curiously titled study, *John Gay's London, Illustrated from the Poetry of the Time*. Irving reads Gay line by line and uses Gay's references to hidden haunts like Seven Dials and Watling Street as touchstones from which to cut and paste other references to these places from roughly a decade of eighteenth-century verse. Irving reads *Trivia* to "recover" London, and this method raises an interesting question: does Gay's text ask us to read it as a historically accurate portrait of early eighteenth-century London or simply a theme-park reconstruction of what it could have been? This question is unnecessary if we first consider the formal and structural devices of *Trivia* that inform these readings.

There must be something in *Trivia* that produces the impression of an actual experience of—and thus an incitement to recover—a "real London." This "something" involves more than the text's incessant reference to London's locales. Gay's formal decisions structure any reading of the poem. I discuss Gay's complex use of satiric, heroic, epic, and pastoral traditions later beneath the topic of "mode" and "tone" because these modes and tones alter the content of a seemingly traditional textual form. But Gay's formal vehicle is not traditional because Gay uses a reader's recognition of these formal traditions to point *Trivia* in a new direction.

There are at least two reasons for interpreting *Trivia* as a "guidebook," and both are reactions to the text's structure.

First, *Trivia* consists of three self-contained books, and Gay advertises the criteria which justify this triptych-like organization in the subtitle to each book. For example, Gay subtitles book one, "Of the Implements for walking the Streets, and Signs of Weather"; book two, "Of Walking the Streets by Day"; and book three, "Of Walking the Streets by Night." It is worth noting how these subtitles parallel essay titles of the time or even the separate "papers" of *The Tatler* and *The Spectator*. By titling each book in this manner, Gay implies two things: first, that the function of each book is to instruct us, and second, that each book organizes this instruction by catering to a specific stage of a London-walk. If we are trying to lunch at Will's, we would turn to book two; if we accidentally wander into a dark alley, we turn to book three; if we encounter a tempestuous downpour, we turn to book one. Gay's formal vehicle seems to be a guidebook because its function is to guide or to instruct us, and it creates the impression that he will show us the "real" London. He is able to create this impression by relying upon a way of reading supplied by the formal conventions of guidebooks. For this reason, it is tempting to read *Trivia* as a "real" description of 1716 London.

The second way *Trivia* encourages "realist" readings involves the formal conventions suggested by its marginalia. Gay's glosses, which punctuate the literal margins, are similar to each book's subtitle. For instance, the glosses "Of narrow Streets," "Of whom to enquire the Way," and "Of avoiding Paint" present the main text as instructive reading. Gay's glosses refer to the knowledge being developed in the main text; they substantiate a way of reading the main text as factual information. The glosses are for reference more than they are for commentary and therefore echo Jeremy Collier's description of marginal notation—that is, they "stand like rocks in the margin."[27] As quick-reference tabs that allow readers to access information with a bookmark rather than by memory, Gay's glosses are a technology for conveying knowledge in a reading environment that is distinctly not a parlor-room armchair. On the streets and during a moment of crisis, they direct readers to knowledge that might save their lives. As a result, the glosses present—or even validate—the main text as legitimate, "real" knowledge. However, this impression of reality is a direct result of the way Gay expected readers to approach a guidebook. He therefore relies upon a recognition of formal textual tradition to create the impression of a literal environment.

As mentioned earlier, Gay provides an index to his poem. Indexes are familiar elements of guidebooks, but this is an unusual editorial device in the context of eighteenth-century poetic practice, especially when the poet (rather than the publisher) writes this index.[28] Gay's alphabetized index contains over 250 entries, which become the "fourth book" of the poem because the index does as much work to present the first three books as legitimate urban knowledge as does the poem. There are at least three types of entries in Gay's index, each of which advertises or reinterprets the function of the poem. One type of entry advertises *Trivia* as an employment catalogue: "Fishmonger, *the description of his Stall*" and "Broker, *where he usually walks.*" It is important to note that Gay links each occupation to a workplace: "*his Stall*" and "*where he usually walks.*" Another type of entry advertises *Trivia* as a journalistic fact-book that allows us to "know" street-level details. These details provide knowledge about both time and people: "Wednesday, *how to know it*"; "*Whore, how to know one.*"[29] Gay's diction—"know it" and "know one"—suggests that we only need to turn back to the line numbers to "know" London. A final type of entry advertises the poem's variety of textual traditions. Examples of this type of entry include "*Evening Described,*" "Vulcan *metamorphos'd to a Country Farrier,*" "Œdipus," and "*Reader, the Author addresses him.*" This type of entry draws our attention to Gay's formal maneuvers and classical allusions. Gay, in turn, advertises himself as a poetic genius who is able to evoke all of these poetic tropes in one poem while sharpening a reader's recognition of these tropes. The index first structures a way of reading and then suggests that readers reinterpret the poem's content.[30] From this perspective, the index represents *Trivia*'s content as legitimate knowledge.

We might be especially wary of an eighteenth-century long poem that uses georgic, heroic, satiric, and pastoral modes *and* only resembles a guidebook in its form. Seventeenth- and eighteenth-century guidebooks, as Hunter argues, occupy a unique historical moment when "lost personal contact and radically changed institutions" dictated that the metaphoric direction offered by printed texts replaced first-hand experience.[31] Hunter reads eighteenth-century guidebooks as revised sermons and interprets their popularity as a symptom of increased "cultural redefinition."[32] The metaphor of direction, culled from seventeenth-century sermons and lifelong guides to spiritual journeys, that Hunter finds in these guidebooks is redefined by Gay to organize a rapidly changing Town. For example, Gay mobilizes all of these textual traditions to enact his version of the proper

London poet, and the specific task of that poet is to conduct readers to proper interpretations of their city. I use the word "conduct" purposefully since Gay's formal vehicles—the triptych structure and marginalia—suggest one manner by which a reader may interpret poems to acquire knowledge about London. Yet *Trivia* is not merely a guidebook. If the poem seems realistic, it is only because the function of formal conventions, for Gay, is to supply a way of reading his poem *like* a guidebook. *Trivia*'s content, in turn, appears to be factual knowledge. But this content, which I will now address, does more than just guide readers to landmarks; it shapes them.

While this tendency to read *Trivia* as a guidebook might also stem from a way of reading that searches for a proto-modern version of "ourselves" or "our London" in Gay's verse, the more glaring assumption implicit in this tradition is that Gay "illustrates" an object that is already there—a city that merely wants proper description by a proper poet. At this point we might recall Irving's title: *John Gay's London, Illustrated from the Poetry of the Time*. It is not "John Gay's London" simply because Gay happens to describe its minute particulars. It is "John Gay's London"—shaped and possessed by Gay—because all of these formal, minute particulars design his concept of what should constitute London's "urban" traits.

Consider, for instance, how Gay advertises his function as poet early in *Trivia:* "To tread in Paths to ancient Bards unknown / And bind my Temples with a *Civic* Crown."[33] It is worth noting that Gay's "paths" are "unknown" to "ancient" poets; that is, *Trivia* moves beyond classical formal conventions because it describes a stage of urbanization unknown to the ancients.[34] Furthermore, the *Civica Corona*—the office awarded to the less-respected "City Poet" of the City of London—for which Gay ambivalently aims (he puns upon the word "bind") is an eighteenth-century path not available to "ancient" counterparts.[35] This introductory couplet stresses, above all, the novelty of Gay's textual "path." In the type of urban planning *Trivia* offers, Gay's poem presents an urban prototype.

Gay's *Trivia* does not simply illustrate a pre-existing London; rather, it creates what counts as urban experience and, at the same time, tries to make a unified vision of London possible. The poem accomplishes these tasks by engineering a tool suited to early eighteenth-century London's needs; that tool is urban space. I will outline Gay's particular concept of space in a moment, but for now allow me to stress the administrative conditions that I see Gay's spatial technology addressing.

"WALKING ADVANTAGEOUS TO LEARNING":
FASHIONING THE STREET LEVEL

Gay's poem is not self-sufficient; it does not generate a reproducible, international model of a city that could be shipped beyond the Thames to Paris, Venice, or Vienna. It is London-specific. Gay clearly states that he will not "wander from my native Home, / And (tempting Perils) foreign Cities roam" (1.83–84). He also specifies his target by rejecting foreign "streets"; he will neither enter Paris, "where Slav'ry treads the Street" (1.86), nor navigate the "sloping Pavements" (1.91) of the Netherlands. Through a process of elimination that interprets streets as metaphor for national character, the poet represents London's streets as the only thoroughfares worthy of his labor. That is, *Trivia* occupies—and contributes to—an important moment during London's integration when the separate, partisan cities of Westminster (the aristocratic Court) and the City of London (the mercantile City) began to be known by the single, more general title of "London." Between these two extremes of Court and City was a mediating area inhabited by poets, architects, and preprofessionals: the Town. For Gay, the Strand—a literal street linking Whitehall to the City—represented a means for comprehending this area of London since streets enabled one to *experience* the Town's differences. More specifically, the three books of *Trivia* make the Town visible because they show how differently one is to experience and behave in the Town than in either the Court or the City.[36]

This differentiation of experience and behavior is the foundation for Gay's urban spatialization. From the street-level perspective of the Town, Gay reads space as what I wish to call "archives of conduct." This is shown in Gay's invocation to his Muse, Trivia:

> Through Winter Streets to steer your Course aright,
> How to walk clean by Day, and safe by Night,
> How jostling Crouds, with Prudence, to decline,
> When to assert the Wall, and when resign,
> I sing: Thou *Trivia*, Goddess, aid my Song
> Thro' spacious Streets conduct thy Bard along. (1.1–6)

Here Gay yokes space to streets; the streets are where ideas of "the spacious" originate. However, we are not to loiter about, or simply occupy, these streets; we are to travel "thro[ugh]" them and, with the help of our

Bard by the end of the same line, "along" them as though to suggest a more disciplined, pointed action than the simple "thro'" which begins line six. In short, the entire line balances metrically and turns upon the word "conduct"—the central iamb of the pentameter.[37] Conduct playfully begins to acquire meaning in this line.

Archives of conduct lend meaning to space by making it visible in two very specific ways. These ways hinge upon the double meaning of the word conduct. First, this is a poem about walking—"the art of walking," as the subtitle tells us. Gay is obsessively concerned with walking as the proper vehicle for urban travel and as a means of conducting (or transporting) oneself between Court and City. Second, the differences between Court and City can only be felt if one consciously designs or adapts one's behavior while traveling. In other words, Gay's readers come to recognize an abstract entity known as "space" only by recognizing changes in both their physical and mental conduct through the poem's genres and, by metaphor, through London's geography. Henri Lefebvre's *The Production of Space* is the source for tracing why and how notions of physical, mental, social, and finally, abstract space were produced and reified; however, I am interested in how Gay privileges the metaphor of eighteenth-century conduct *over* abstract space as a proper way of knowing London.[38] In both of these senses, conduct (an abstraction that Gay shapes in *Trivia*'s poetry) shapes, imagines, and legitimizes space (an abstraction to which Gay only gestures—an abstraction beyond the text). From our twenty-first-century perspective, *Trivia* is invested in producing abstractions that differ from the ones which presently shape our lives.

Trivia's metaphor of conduct engineers space, and this is the work that the poem accomplishes. Whereas Miles Ogborn has interpreted walking in *Trivia* as a way for an eighteenth-century reader to negotiate a private self amid public crowds,[39] I am more interested in how an "art" of walking, specifically walking in the Town, imbues space with meaning. Walking is a quotidian vehicle for producing knowledge about an everyday setting. It allows us to know our object in the same way that travel was frequently Daniel Defoe's vehicle for establishing knowledge through a narrative. For Gay, any knowledge of the interactions between Court and City was intimately tied to the behavior, morals, and thoughts that accompanied an individual passing through these areas.

The title of the poem supports his conception of space. For example, just as Trivia—or Gay's Muse—is the vehicle which inspires Gay to master and to know his art, the poem offers itself as a vehicle for making

London known to us. "Trivia" does not mean the modern sense of "small importance" but refers to "the goddess of Streets and High-Ways"; she is literally an embodiment of "three roads" and grounded in the Latin root "*via.*"[40] More importantly, she is a goddess of three distinct thoroughfares: "Where winding Alleys lead the doubtful Way, / The silent Court, and op'ning Square explore, / And long perplexing Lanes untrod before" (1.8–10). The "spacious Streets" of line six above are neither "winding Alleys" nor "perplexing Lanes"; there is a careful distinction of kinds of thoroughfare here. And while *Trivia* may have nurtured the British practice of using a street name to refer to a more generalized urban area (e.g., "Pall Mall," "Whitehall," "Fleet Street," and "The King's Road"), *Trivia*'s street names do more than just refer to pre-existing neighborhoods. Rather than assuming that names refer, Gay considers street names to be hollow vehicles that can be filled with new meaning. This is why Trivia so desperately calls our attention to the streets and pedestrian thoroughfares; she makes us know what lies before us, beside us, between us—and perhaps, if Gay works hard enough—even within us. Gay uses at least two means of developing our street-level attention.

First, the street generates sensory experience. Our walker-poet[41] is hypersensitive; therefore, anything associated with walking—including preparation—is as much a self-contained experience as it is a vehicle to register other types of experiences. In an introductory book which strongly parallels the arming scene of medieval epics, Gay catalogues "the Implements" or tools "for walking the Streets." Gay clearly treats walking as a type of poetic labor, which involves specific tools. Armed with "True *Witney* Broadcloth" (1.46), a "*Kersey*" (1.59) coat, the walker adopts a work uniform that is distinctly British. But this is not merely nationalistic propaganda. If the walker sports shoes made with "*Spanish* or *Morooco* Hide," the body will register the punishment: "Each Stone will wrench th' unwary Step aside: / The sudden Turn may stretch the swelling Vein, / The cracking Joint unhinge, or Ankle sprain" (1.36–38). Foreign shoes are not part of the standard-issue uniform because they fail to conduct the walker correctly—that is, safely—through British streets. Gay rejects foreign tools and therefore makes *Trivia* more than just a nationalistic eighteenth-century long poem; it suggests that proper walkers do not adopt Courtly fashions. For instance, the choice of a proper cane involves a similar principle of selection:

> Let Beaus their Canes with Amber tipt produce,
> Be theirs for empty Show, but thine for Use,

> In gilded Chariots while they loll at Ease,
> And lazily insure a Life's Disease;
> While softer Chairs the tawdry Load convey
> To Court, to *White's,* Assemblies, or the Play. (1.67–72)

Our cane should *not* be like those seen in chairs bound for Parliament or West End coffeehouses—all Court-specific activities.[42]

A proper walker also laments the Court's fashionable means of transport and ponders a golden age when cities catered to walkers:

> O happy Streets to rumbling Wheels unknown,
> No Carts, no Coaches shake the floating Town!
> Thus was of old *Britannia's* City bless'd,
> E'er Pride and Luxury her Sons possess'd:
> Coaches and Chariots yet unfashion'd lay
> Nor late invented Chairs perplex'd the Way. (1.99–104)

Gay's use of "unfashion'd" during this elegiac episode has two meanings: "not of current value" or "not yet invented." The second sense is extremely suggestive. "Fashioning"—in the sense of engineering behavior to accomplish specific tasks—is *Trivia's* function. As Gay fashions the uniform of the walker in book one, he begins to reassign meaning to walking. Of course, walking assumes a primordial, even classical, origin, and he relies upon this assumption to make *Trivia* work. That is, an "Art of walking" seems frivolous unless we pay attention to *what* we are walking through. Walking, for Gay, requires constant street-level attention as opposed to the leisured ignorance that chairs, coaches, and chariots promote. As a result, walking reinvests streets with potential; it opens up possibilities for Gay to direct this street-level attention to acknowledge or sense space. In turn, a walker's "sense" of space fashions Gay's London.

The poem also arms its readers with intangible tools of knowledge anchored to the Town's local conditions. That is, Gay fashions a way of reading "Signs" in book one that constitutes a skill.[43] This skill is more than just a defensive warning to "Watch your Step"; it details the proper way to "watch"—to read and to observe—every step. In this part of the poem, Gay explicitly responds to another problem of London's literal geography: an exponentially increasing amount of signage. Text-based wooden signs (for both streets and shops) crowded London's skies, and navigating the city now required additional skills, as Wall observes:

"In the earlier, transitional period, the city that had been to some extent navigable by illiterate sight now required knowledge of different kinds of codes. As the streets were physically cleared and opened, making it easier to *see*, they increasingly required to be *read*."[44] *Trivia* establishes its own protocol of reading and, by means of repeated practice in books two and three, eventually credentializes the reader in the skill of recognizing archives of conduct. *Trivia*, from this perspective, constitutes a self-help workbook with lessons and practice tests.

Directly following the uniform-catalogue, Gay explains how to predict the weather by interpreting the street level. For a walker, the skies do not present credible "Signs"; instead, the street level possesses its own reliable signs, and the poem develops a sensitivity to them:

> The changing Weather certain Signs reveal,
> E'er Winter sheds her Snow, or Frosts congeal,
> You'll see the Coals in brighter Flames aspire,
> And Sulphur tinge with blue the rising Fire . . . . (1.133–36)
> . . .
> Nor do less certain Signs the Town advise,
> Or milder Weather, and serener Skies.
> The Ladies gayly dress'd, the *Mall* adorn
> With various Dyes, and paint the sunny Morn . . . . (1.143–46)
> . . .
> But when the swinging Signs your Ears offend
> With creaking Noise, then rainy Floods impend;
> Soon shall the Kennels well with rapid Streams,
> And rush in muddy Torrents to the *Thames*.
> The Bookseller, whose Shop's an open Square,
> Forsees the Tempest, and with early Care
> Of Learning strips the Rails . . . . (1.157–63)[45]

The "swinging Signs" encourage readers to develop a sensory reading of the street level; that is, the signs are more valuable for their "swinging" during an approaching storm than for the text written on them. As a person skilled in text, the Bookseller (the first of many in this poem), applies an "early Care of Learning" to read the "open Square." Gay grounds this reading lesson to an episode where books are sold at the Town's street level, and he makes a very specific point about the skill he is developing at the start of book two:

> Thus far the Muse has trac'd in useful Lays,
> The proper Implements for Wintry Ways;
> Has taught the Walker, with judicious Eyes,
> To read the various Warnings of the Skies. (2.1–4)

Those who possess "judicious eyes" have internalized the protocol of reading Gay developed in book one and are ready to test this skill.

Book two supplies several practice examinations, each of which offers readers a hypothetical situation for testing their street-level, interpretive skills:

> If drawn by Bus'ness to a Street unknown,
> Let the sworn Porter point thee through the Town;
> Be sure observe the Signs, for Signs remain,
> Like faithful Land-marks to the walking Train.
> Seek not from Prentices to learn the Way,
> Those fabling Boys will turn thy Steps astray;
> Ask the grave Tradesman to direct thee right,
> He ne'er deceives, but when he profits by't. (2.65–72)

This passage is central to *Trivia*'s function for two reasons. First, it strengthens a protocol of reading developed in the Town. It sternly rejects City protocols; the knowledge of "Prentices" and "Tradesmen" is suspicious and unreliable. Second, the couplet, "Be sure observe the Signs, for Signs remain, / Like faithful Land-marks to the walking Train," punctuates this crisis on a "Street unknown" and conducts the reader back to a more valid protocol of reading "Signs" established in book one. Even more notable is the simile that links "Signs" to "Land-marks." This important couplet establishes a dialogue between a protocol of reading signs and a protocol of walking past landmarks. This simile works because the similarity between signs and landmarks turns on methods of interpretation: between a way of interpreting our reactions to text and a way of interpreting our sensory reactions to walking. It is also crucial that Gay conflates "reading" with "observing." For example, the walker's "judicious Eyes" should "read" (2.4, 5) the streets and later "observe the Signs" (2.67). Reading text is "like" observing the street level. The link forged by this simile also credentializes Gay as an urban planner—a figure who seems to control the value of urban landmarks by carefully designing and crafting textual signs. Gay yokes the poet to a physical sphere by assuming that readers react to texts and cityscapes in the same way. Signs and landmarks, in turn, become explosive sites of knowledge production for Gay. Previously common "Land-marks" now acquire intense meaning.

I have suggested that Gay arms the reader with a uniform protocol of interpretation unique to the Town. Books two and three of *Trivia* then use this protocol to develop a sensitivity to different—almost foreign—styles of walking. Gay does not elaborately describe the Town's architectural landmarks; rather, Gay details the way one should pass these landmarks. He assigns to each "fam'd" tourist trap a style of walking through it:

> Where fam'd Saint *Giles*'s ancient Limits spread,
> An inrail'd Column rears its lofty Head,
> Here to sev'n Streets, sev'n Dials count the Day,
> And from each other catch the circling Ray.
> Here oft the Peasant, with enquiring Face,
> Bewilder'd, trudges on from Place to Place;
> He dwells on ev'ry Sign, with stupid Gaze,
> Enters the narrow Alley's doubtful Maze,
> Trys ev'ry winding Court and Street in vain,
> And doubles o'er his weary Steps again. (2.73–82)

The walker-poet marks St. Giles and its seven emanating streets with "bewildered" peasants who "trudge" and "dwell" rather than maintain a directed pace. Their "stupid Gaze" clashes with the proper walker's "judicious Eye," for this "stupid Gaze" does not specify its reading material but "dwells on ev'ry Sign." The result of this conduct is a hopeless, labyrinthine nightmare of "winding Court and Streets" and "weary Steps." We might note how this type of description consumes the one line of architectural detail: "An inrail'd Column rears its lofty Head." Gay suggests that the juncture of seven streets is not a problem if we know how to conduct ourselves through them.

Covent Garden presents a striking contrast to this meditative, dolorous pace. Here, walking turns into an impromptu jog when, in a fit of terror, our walker-poet encounters a Football match:

> Where *Covent Garden*'s famous Temple stands,
> That boasts the Work of *Jones'* immortal Hands;
> Columns, with plain Magnificence, appear,
> And graceful Porches lead along the Square:

CHAPTER 1: ARCHIVES OF CONDUCT 51

> Here oft' my Course I bend, when lo! from far,
> I spy the Furies of the Foot-ball War:
> The 'Prentice quits his Shop to join the Crew,
> Encreasing Crouds the flying Game pursue.
> Thus, as you roll the Ball o'er snowy Ground,
> The gath'ring Globe augments with ev'ry Round;
> But whither shall I run? the Throng draws nigh,
> The Ball now Skims the Street, now soars on high;
> The dext'rous Glazier strong returns the Bound,
> And gingling Sashes on the Penthouse sound. (2.343–56)

Following two couplets that briefly mention architect (Inigo Jones) and landmark ("Columns, with plain Magnificence"), the walker-poet presents a situation of increasing anxiety. In a panic, the walker-poet asks, "But whither shall I run?" and brings the rhythm to a frightened standstill with the caesura which immediately follows this question. The source of this rhythmic void and the anxiety that it echoes is the "augment[ing]" Football's trespass on the "Street." For Gay, Covent Garden's open square—its lack of a defined street—encourages anarchy. Gay directs our attention to an over-magnified football precisely because it usurps the street's function as a vehicle for walking. He also suggests that the City (the "'Prentice" and the "Glazier") is to blame for this anarchic interruption in the Town.[46]

A final example of Gay's approach to architectural landmarks involves St. Clement's—a structure located directly in the middle of the Strand:

> Where the fair Columns of Saint *Clement* stand,
> Whose straiten'd Bounds encroach upon the *Strand;*
> Where the low Penthouse bows the Walker's Head,
> And the rough Pavement wounds the yielding Tread;
> Where not a Post protects the narrow Space,
> And strung in Twines, Combs dangle in thy Face;
> Summon at once thy Courage, rouze thy Care,
> Stand firm, look back, be resolute, beware. (3.17–24)

This landmark dictates that the walker adapt to its impeding position directly on the street—a dictum that the penthouse and surrounding pavement echo. More specifically, walkers must "bow" their heads to traverse this particular part of the Strand; the connotations of "bow," especially in the shadow of a religious structure, imbue street-level attention with a sort of virtue.[47] The episode at St. Clement's is especially notable because it takes place in the final book of *Trivia;* therefore, Gay feels comfortable enough at this point in the poem to refer directly to the technology he has been developing. Because the sanctuary of the street—the "narrow Space" of conduct itself—is threatened here, Gay names his precious "Space." Gay follows this revelation by increasing the walker's hypersensitivity: "Stand firm, look back, be resolute, beware." As Gay reveals the technology *Trivia* actively develops, he deliberately heightens our skills of reading, observing, and interpreting.

What all of these excerpts show is that architectural landmarks become meaningful spaces only when Gay provides a style of navigating around the landmark. Different streets produce different effects on the walker's body based upon overhanging "Penthouses," "rough Pavement," or sports matches made possible by a street's absence. In general, different ways of walking signify that we have entered a different space. We should note that Gay attaches an introductory tag of "Where" to each of these architectural landmarks, for Gay tailors his diction during these moments to engineer space. By claiming that these examples "engineer" space, I return to how Gay imbues walking with new meaning and reproduces it as a new technology for knowing London. Walking produces the impression of space as different streets inscribe different conducts on the walker's body. For instance, readers recognize Seven Dials and Covent Garden by a change in pace: by a helpless wandering or a frantic run. Gay highlights styles of walking—not the mimetic descriptions of architectural facades, and these stylistic archives, in turn, allow walkers to maneuver between these different styles by recognizing the different way in which they should manage their pace. By yoking these different conducts directly to the streets, Gay naturalizes the conduct he designs. That is, he may claim that the streets—not the poet—control walkers. As the poem progresses, our primary goal is to become "careful Observers, studious of the Town" (2.285) rather than careful critics, studious of the poet.

What is remarkable about all of the above excerpts is how much work walking now involves, as opposed to what was once such a quotidian or arguably natural act in the country. Gay's version of walking is inseparable from reading, observing, and interpreting, and it is in this sense that walking is an art—specifically, a necessary skill. If we interpret conduct as the act of registering details, then the "art" of walking is a discipline requiring mastery for those who do not "naturally" possess it. We are meant to register and to study these thoroughfares because they are both the sites and the vehicles for conveying knowledge about London. In Gay's London, the streets are the planes upon which knowledge is organized and, as I will now suggest, where conduct is registered.

Engineering Conduct

Gay's "Art" of walking is different from the art of mapping. Walking is the vehicle for temporal experience; it provides an unfolding, continuous experience of each space rather than merely describing or diagramming the boundaries delimiting those spaces. This is the crucial difference between Gay and map makers: Gay draws archives of conduct while map makers draw parochial and administrative lines. His particular brand of spatiality (recognizing different conducts) relies upon temporality (reflecting upon experience). This distinction brings me to the second way Gay develops street-level attention. Gay fills archives with behavioral nuances. One way Gay yokes specific behaviors to specific streets is by focusing street-level attention on the way other people, who are native to the street Gay describes, walk. As I have shown above, Gay alters the rates of walking and reading to fashion correct modes of traveling at the Covent Garden football match. But now I shift my interpretation of "conduct" to modes of behavior. For example, pace affects temporal experience, and any alteration in the rate of walking or reading directly affects how a walker or reader experiences a setting. Variations in pace, however, also appear in *Trivia* when a walker must interpret or react to the way other people walk. These reactions, introduced as "due Civilities" (2.45), contribute to what has been Gay's task all along: to design a vision of London by fashioning the conduct of its inhabitants through a printed text. The way walkers react to foreign behaviors differentiates how walkers act—that is, behave themselves—on the Strand, near the Court, and in the City. Space, fashioned by different conducts of the walker, builds Gay's London.

For example, Gay intentionally makes us recognize that we are near the Town during an episode in which walking turns to "stray[ing]":

> But sometimes let me leave the noisie Roads,
> And silent wander in the close Abodes
> Where Wheels ne'er shake the Ground; there pensive stray,
> In studious Thought, the long uncrouded Way.
> Here I remark each Walker's diff'rent Face

> And in their Look their various Bus'ness trace.
> The Broker here his spacious Beaver wears,
> Upon his Brow sit Jealousies and Cares;
> Bent on some Mortgage, to avoid Reproach,
> He seeks bye Streets, and saves th' expensive Coach.
> Soft, at low Doors, old Letchers tap their Cane,
> For fair Recluse, who travels *Drury-lane*.
> Here roams uncomb'd, the lavish Rake, to shun
> His *Fleet-street* Draper's everlasting Dun. (2.271–84)

The references to Drury Lane and Fleet Street clearly situate this episode in the Town, and we should note the behavior that the walker-poet assigns to the Town. Gay's lines slow in pace: "Where Wheels ne'er shake the Ground; there pensive stray, / In studious Thought, the long uncrouded Way." The caesura in line 274 provides the time to rub our feet, a rare break amid this poem of incessant walking. In an environment that seems to encourage reflection, Gay magnifies our attention to "remark each Walker's diff'rent Face / And in their Look their various Bus'ness trace."[48] We are to "remark"—that is, interpret—the "differen[ces]" of each Face, and the end rhyme of the couplet links "various Bus'ness trace" to "each Walker's diff'rent Face." This couplet establishes a protocol of reading faces in the Town that hinges upon the adjectives "diff'rent" and "various." The walker's "judicious Eye" is trained to notice these distinctions, which defend the eighteenth-century idea that exteriority reveals identity. In the same manner, the "close Abodes" of the Town provide the walker-poet with the opportunity to be "pensive" and to reflect upon the differences generated by these walks. Mental activity and meditative thought constitute the behavior that "marks" the Town's archive of conduct.

An encounter in the City contrasts nicely with the Town's "pensive" tenor. We know that we are in the City in the following excerpt because this section immediately follows both the entrance of "a draggled Damsel" from East End *"Billingsgate"* (2.9–10) as well as a catalogue of City trades and "Industry" (2.21):

> Let due Civilities be strictly paid.
> The Wall surrender to the hooded Maid;
> Nor let thy sturdy Elbow's hasty Rage
> Jostle the feeble Steps of trembling Age:
> And when the Porter bends beneath his Load,

> And pants for Breath; clear thou the crouded Road.
> But above all, the groaping Blind direct,
> And from the pressing Throng the Lame protect.
> You'll sometimes meet a Fop, of nicest Tread,
> Whose mantling Peruke veils his empty Head,
> At ev'ry Step he dreads the Wall to lose,
> And risques, to save a Coach, his red heel'd Shoes;
> Him, like the *Miller,* pass with Caution by,
> Lest from his Shoulder Clouds of Powder fly.
> But when the Bully, with assuming Pace,
> Cocks his broad Hat, edg'd round with tarnish'd Lace,
> Yield not the Way; defie his strutting Pride,
> And thrust him to the muddy Kennel's side;
> He never turns again, nor dares oppose,
> But mutters coward Curses as he goes. (2.45–64)

This episode in the City is notable for at least three reasons. First, Gay focuses on the behavior of different walkers—not on the quality of different streets; our attention is just slightly above the literal street level. This shift in focus is a subtle difference, but it changes the sense of conduct from verb to noun. Walkers must proactively manage themselves to maintain a standard of "due Civilit[y]."[49] Second, the walkers here differ greatly from walkers in the Town; it is impossible to "remark each Walker's Different Face" when these walkers are "the hooded Maid" and the Fop, whose "mantling Peruke veils his empty Head." The encounter with "the assuming Pace" of "the Bully" of the City also requires a different reaction from us than our reaction to "the Rake" of the Town required. This City "Bully" will not yield the safety of "the Wall" to those on (what we now refer to as) the sidewalk. Gay's near-didactic tone makes us read this City episode differently, as well. Here, we are to "defie his strutting Pride, / And thrust him to the muddy Kennel's side"; we are to proactively correct the impudent behavior of a mercantile citizen. We are conscious of where we are because we are behaving quite differently here than we would on the Town or near the Court.

A third reason why this City episode is pivotal is because it yokes "Civilit[y]" to walking. This pairing is important not because it establishes standards of "civil" courtesy, propriety, and charity; rather, it allows Gay to participate in the larger eighteenth-century project of civil rule and the model of liberal governmentality following the fall of absolutism in 1688.

This context of liberal governmentality imbues *Trivia* with the power to imagine what counts as urban conduct and civil behavior. This context also explains why Gay spends so much time promoting walking as both a "Vertue" (2.590) and an "Art." To walk properly—that is, to interpret and to react properly to other walkers—we should temper our own "hasty Rage" as we encounter the elderly's "feeble Steps." We should also protect or guide "the groaping Blind" and "the Lame" who require our assistance. All of these suggestions nurture a self-control and self-regulation grounded in social responsibility. Only walking provides us with the opportunity to exercise this necessary, street-level civic responsibility, and our walker-poet shores up this responsibility in the final section of book two:

> See, yon' bright Chariot on its Braces swing,
> With *Flanders* Mares, and on an arched Spring,
> That Wheels, to gain an Equipage and Place,
> Betray'd his Sister to a lewd Embrace.
> This Coach, that with the blazon'd 'Scutcheon glows,
> Vain of his unknown Race, the Coxcomb shows.
> Here the brib'd Lawyer, sunk in Velvet, sleeps,
> The starving Orphan, as he passes, weeps;
> There flames a Fool, begirt with tinselled Slaves,
> Who wastes the Wealth of a whole Race of Knaves.
> That other, with a clustring Train behind,
> Owes his Honours to a sordid Mind.
> This next in Court Fidelity excells,
> The Publick rifles, and his Country sells.
> May the proud Chariot never be my Fate,
> If purchas'd at so mean, so dear a Rate;
> O rather give me sweet Content on Foot,
> Wrapt in my Vertue, and a good *Surtout!* (2.573–90)

"*Flanders* Mares," as Vinton Dearing stresses, drew aristocratic coaches. This fact, in combination with the phrase "Court Fidelity," positions the episode in Westminster. The walker-poet seems extremely close to us here for a reason. With the phrases "that other" and "this next," the walker-poet points over our shoulder to be certain that we witness irresponsible, courtly waste, especially the individual who "the Publick rifles, and his Country sells." This behavior is doubly sinful because this type of courtly conduct—wedded to detailed descriptions of chariots—involves corrupt agents of the Parliament and the law ("the brib'd Lawyer"). If we consider that Gay is also trying to fashion conduct or even civil laws of conduct, then these courtly figures are Gay's foils; they are his patronized, West End enemies. This is why Gay moves to the first person in the final four lines; he justifies a "correct" conduct that hinges upon social responsibility to "the Publick." If he cannot purchase a chariot through the virtuous labor of writing poetry, then he will remain "Content on Foot, / Wrapt in my Vertue." The suggestion here is that walking inherently provides a shield of virtue against the lavish temptations of courtly Westminster. It also suggests that the ability to distinguish the Court's archive of conduct from other conducts is a guarantee of both moral and physical security.

I mean "moral" here in two senses. First, I mean the way in which walking gestures toward an inner "Vertue." Gay casts walking as an external sign of inner strength.[50] Second, I mean a "moral" that implies inherent and undeniable value. One of Gay's tasks throughout this poem has been to assign value to a previously unnoticed or quotidian street level. The moral element that underwrites Gay's concept of walking represents walking as a conduct—a systematized practice that is neither a trade nor an apprenticeship; rather, conduct is an "art" that can only be mastered or cultivated by those who are already naturally and inherently moral. People who are able to navigate the infinite number of behaviors in the Court, Town, and City—or more specifically, those who can adapt to and recognize these different spaces—show "certain Signs" (1.133) of inner worth. Their style of walking is "valuable" because it shows that they "know" London. Walking is visible evidence of an inner knowledge and mastery of London's behavioral cityscape. Because Gay's walker sounds like a version of the Puritan "elect," a review of the walker's *curriculum vitae* is important.

I have used "reader" and "walker" interchangeably throughout this chapter for two reasons. First, if "signs" are "like faithful Land-marks," then "reading" is like "walking." Second, Gay also uses both walker and reader; however, his use of them suggests that "a reader" can only aspire to become "a walker." A walker is a peer—a "friend"—of our walker-poet-professor: "O ye associate Walkers, O my Friends, / Upon your State what Happiness attends!" (2.501–2). At the close of *Trivia*—where we would expect to graduate as fully accredited walkers—Gay refers to the "Reader":

> Consider, Reader, what Fatigues I've known,
> The Toils, the Perils of the wintry Town;
> What Riots seen, what bustling Crouds I bor'd,
> How oft' I cross'd where Carts and Coaches roar'd;
> Yet shall I bless my Labours, if Mankind
> Their future Safety from my Dangers find. (3.393–98)

This excerpt distances us from a laboring walker-poet. At the conclusion, we are "Reader[s]" again, and to secure the credentials of a "walker" seems to require more of our *own* work. That is, *Trivia* does not credentialize readers into walkers; it instead identifies a uniform, a protocol of reading, and archives of conduct. The transformation from "reader" to "walker" therefore depends upon self-conduct and, in terms of "Vertue," self-improvement.

Gay's reliance on his readers, however, should not be taken at face value. A reader's transformation into a walker through self-regulation effects an even greater transformation: "the Town" becomes "London." There is a double-purpose here: readers are the agents of Gay's change—they are human tools for transforming London from Town to Cosmopolis. The walker, in turn, fashions London while Gay sits back and counts his "Praise":

> But more, my Country's Love demands the Lays,
> My Country's be the Profit, mine the Praise. (1.19–20)
> . . .
> For you, O honest Men, these useful Lays
> The Muse prepares; I seek no other Praise. (1.119–20)

By yoking morality to the walker, Gay also fortifies his blueprint of London as the proper, inherently correct version. *Trivia* ultimately succeeds in nurturing Gay's London because the readers inherit the skills needed to make London's future sink or swim. *Trivia,* Gay could claim, projects an alternative future.

If we interpret conduct as behavior, then Gay's "art" of walking involves the cultivation of the self. In this cultivation, only the body of the walker is the proper instrument to register, to feel, and to construct spatial difference. Archives of conduct work because they yoke the production of space to specific strategies of virtuous self-management. This link allows Gay to accomplish several complex tasks at once. First, it allows him to fashion the "Londoner" as a person who is skilled in highly sensitive techniques of observation and interpretation. Second, it allows him to fashion "London" as both a new metropolis and a "Town." While I believe that Gay clearly assigns specific conducts to Court, City, and Town and therefore distinguishes them (he even distinguishes smaller spaces within these three areas), his creation of a unified image of London is less obvious; thus, I end this section by clarifying how space contributes to "building" Gay's London.

Walking appears to be a component of self-mastery, but it also shapes a city by making different spaces clearly visible. The differences among these spaces, however, are only visible because Gay's text immediately compares streets separated by incredible distances—a method that is impossible for a walker to recreate. That is, the walker-poet's path is impossible to recreate because there is no continuous "path." Gay's attention jumps randomly from a street in the Court to a street in the City without ever narrating a passage through the Town. We frequently enter a street in the Town from a point not even close to the Town. And we usually do not know where we are until a street-name appears in the final lines of a stanza. This creates the surface effect of a unified "London" and effaces Court, Town, and City; conversely, Gay's archives of conduct preserve and maintain some very strict distinctions beneath this unified surface. My point is that walking is the perfect vehicle to provide an impression of continual experience *and* differentiation. Gay's archives of conduct work because they rely upon walkers to reinforce difference and, at the same time, to unify London by walking through and registering these differences in contemplation. In this context, *Trivia* participates in a larger project of legitimizing spatial knowledge as the only way of knowing or relating to the almost unimaginable state of a unified London beneath which City, Court, and Town are distinct spaces.

Gay's final couplet returns our attention to the walker-poet: "High-rais'd on *Fleetstreet* Posts, consign'd to Fame, / This Work shall shine, and Walkers bless my Name" (3.415–16). If we recall that the Strand turns into Fleet Street as it approaches the City's walls, then the poem concludes by returning us to where his muse first visited Gay. Furthermore, this end of the Strand houses Gay's publisher, "Bernard Lintott between the Temple Gates in Fleetstreet." If we further recall that these "posts" are not only the areas where a bookseller would hang advertisements for newly published texts, but also the physical land-markers that define that part of the street reserved for walkers, we might also conclude that Gay's name may be celebrated because his text defines a concept of space that was entirely necessary for London to become an urban center. If there is an art to knowing John Gay's London, it exists at the street level.

"Read Me": Fleet Street Signage and the Poet

I return to Gay's crucial distinction between "guiding" and "instructing"—a distinction which I need to clarify because of the way it highlights Gay's duty as a poet. *Trivia* does not literally guide readers through London; it establishes no reproducible "tour." This is why we should not consider *Trivia* strictly as a guidebook. The purpose of *Trivia* is not to help a tourist enjoy a leisured holiday in London. Reading *Trivia* for a mimetic tour of London would result in terrible confusion and aggravation because the order of its tour is not reproducible. Only printed text can make the leaps which Gay makes. Its purpose, again, is to create what counts as "London" and "the Londoner." Yet *Trivia*'s tone frequently positions Gay somewhere between guiding and instructing—a position where he can govern London and Londoners using textual means. I use the word "govern" to describe Gay's function as a poet because I interpret *Trivia*'s mixture of modes, voices, and tones as an attempt to manage or to fashion a reader's experience of this text. The idea of liberal governmentality is one way to support my use of "govern"; however, I am more interested in specifying the textual maneuvers Gay uses to participate in liberal governmentality. Archives of conduct do not simply appear because of a reader's increased sensitivity to exterior behavior; they exist because the poem's modes, voices, and tones—part of what I have been calling the "textual traditions"—offer one very specific and seemingly classical manner in which to read the poem. If Gay could govern the way a reader interprets *Trivia,* then he imagined that he could govern the way a walker interprets the street level. The way he managed his own text—the way he crafted it by combining various textual conducts such as the pastoral, georgic, elegiac, and heroic—determines how clearly a reader could interpret space as archives of conduct.

Similar to the guidebook, the mélange of modes, tones, and voices of *Trivia* constitutes a new technology for knowing London. Gay does not accomplish this reinscription by linking a specific mode to a specific archive of conduct; it is not as though "the heroic" corresponds to Watling Street and "the pastoral" relates to Seven Dials. Instead, these modes, voices, and tones are tools or behaviors with classical origins that Gay fashions, like walking, to accomplish new work. I use the phrase "like walking" to reemphasize the earlier simile Gay establishes between "Signs" and "Land-marks" (2.67–68). Similes are vehicles of knowledge production: by comparing an unknown object to a familiar one, similes make the reader "know" previously foreign entities. In this way, Gay couches traditional modes, voices, and tones in similes that will make the conduct of "a Street unknown" (2.65) more familiar. In this poem, similes accompany a mixture of textual modes, tones, and voices and, in turn, are vehicles that help Gay specify his role as poet.

The walker-poet does not conceal the fact that writing is work. Indeed, the poet's labor is a blatant part of the poem's content. Using first-person voice, Gay advertises "my gen'rous Labours" (3.407) and the "Fatigues I've known" (3.393). The georgic mode underwrites this constant spotlight on the poet's own labor, which explains why a careful analysis of *Trivia*'s combination of modes, tones, and voices—that is, an analysis of the poet's "work"—can clarify the London poet's task. Gay's georgic mode, however, is irretrievably connected to other poetic voices, and, in combination with other modes, tones, and voices, Gay's georgic mode establishes similes. This is why the question "What work does Gay accomplish?" is misleading; a more pertinent question is "What is Gay's work like?" There are at least four different answers, each of which involves a combination of textual modes, tones, and voices rather than a solitary mode, tone, or voice.

One simile that generates knowledge about London's street level uses epic and heroic modes to describe manual labor. For example, a "Dustman's" accident with a "Beau's" chariot ends with "So when dread *Jove,* the Son of *Phœbus* hurl'd" (2.535); an evening traffic-jam of livestock and commuters concludes "So when two Boars, in wild *Ytene* bred, / Or on *Westphailia*'s fatt'ning Chest-nuts fed" (2.45–46); and an episode which traps a pedestrian in the middle of a busy street concludes, "So Sailors, while *Charybdis*'s Gulph they shun, / Amaz'd, on *Scylla*'s craggy Dangers run" (2.183–84). Traditions of interpreting epic catastrophe allow the reader to "know"—or, if the reader does not recognize the exact references to "*Charybdis*" or "*Scylla*," at least to know how to approach—this part of Gay's London.

A second pattern involves the georgic mode (specifically, the tradition established by Virgil's *Georgics*), national origin myth, *and* the tone of satire. Book two, for example, develops a mythic ancestry for the shoe-shine boy of Fleet-Ditch.[51] Cloacina, the goddess-mother of the shoe-shine boy, makes her son "useful to the walking Croud, / To cleanse the miry Feet, and o'er the Shoe / With nimble Skill the glossy Black renew" (2.154–56). This myth makes the boy's work—the assistance he offers to walkers—heroic. And although Gay's presentation of a shoe-shine boy whose mother is a goddess named "Cloacina" is satiric in the tradition of Swift's scatological satire, we should not consider this episode to be a throwaway joke that plays on a high-low binary; instead, this episode juggles several modes *at the same time*.[52] Dearing's annotations clearly trace how this origin myth mirrors "Virgil's account of how the art of engendering bees from the putrid blood of cattle was discovered, which closes the *Georgics*."[53] Gay combines the modes of national origin myth and Virgil's *Georgics* while using a satiric tone to refashion traditional ways of reading. We cannot locate a "tone" because there are *many* tones. During the transition from this Town-based origin myth to "the busy City," we also encounter a simile:

> Like the sweet Ballad, this amusing Lay
> Too long detains the Walker on his Way;
> While he attends, new Dangers round him throng;
> The busy City asks instructive Song. (2.217–20)

The phrase "Like the sweet Ballad" offers a way of comprehending Cloacina's origin myth in terms of the larger context of *Trivia*. This simile advertises that the poem will now shift modes from this "amusing Lay" or "sweet Ballad" of the Town to an "instructive Song" for the City. That is, the medieval "Lay," the English "Ballad," and the "Song" offer different ways of reading the Town. Just fifty lines later, the "amusing Lay" becomes the "Elegiac Lay" (2.375) when Gay recalls the decapitation of "*Doll*" on the icy-banks of the Thames. That is, the form of the "Lay" can adopt multiple tones, and this interchangeability allows Gay's similes to make anything on the street level appear "like" something more familiar.

When the walker approaches bookstalls on the Strand, Gay refers even more directly to Virgil's "art of engendering bees": "Here, like the Bee, that on industrious Wing, / Collects the various Odours of the Spring, / Walkers, at leisure, Learning's Flow'rs may spoil" (2.555–57). This simile links the browser of Strand bookstalls to a type of "leisure[d]" labor. Printed text acquires value here regardless of the type of reading—georgic, nationalistic, or satiric—we use to interpret these lines.

A third type of simile combines epic with the eighteenth-century prospect poem. I use "prospect poem" here in one specific sense: the tradition of distanced observation that allows the poet to project and to prophesy a nation's future by using personified abstractions. By alluding to the destruction of Troy and Rome during a London fire, Gay envisions London's future via *The Aeneid*. In particular, the fire of book three is like a historical conflagration:

> 'Twas such a Light involv'd thy Tow'rs, O *Rome*,
> The dire Presage of mighty *Caesar*'s Doom,
> When the Sun veil'd in Rust his mourning Head,
> And frightful Prodigies the Skies o'erspread.
> Hark! the Drum thunders! far, ye Crouds, retire:
> Behold! the ready Match is tipt with Fire,
> The nitrous Store is laid, the smutty Train
> With running Blaze awakes the barrell'd Grain;
> Flames sudden wrap the Walls; with sullen Sound,
> The shatter'd Pile sinks on the smoaky Ground.
> So when the Years shall have revolv'd the Date,
> Th' inevitable Hour of *Naples*' Fate,
> Her sap'd Foundations shall with Thunders shake,
> And heave and toss upon the sulph'rous Lake;
> Earth's Womb at once the fiery Flood shall rend,
> And in th' Abyss her plunging Tow'rs descend. (3.377–92)

This specific combination of epic and prospect traditions relates this apocalyptic destruction to London and yokes London's success to Britain's success. Another fire in London will destroy the nation; if London dies, so will the promised empire.

A final pattern of simile pairs georgic and journalistic modes. Following his plea to the reader to "Consider . . . what Fatigues I've known" (3.393), Gay compares the figure of the walker-poet to a "Bold Traveller." The simile begins with "Thus"—here a placeholder for "Like":

> Thus the bold Traveller, (inur'd to Toil,
> Whose Steps have printed *Asia*'s desert Soil,
> The barb'rous *Arabs* Haunt; or shiv'ring crost
> Dark *Greenland*'s Mountains of Eternal Frost;
> Whom Providence, in length of Years, restores
> To the wish'd Harbour of his native Shores;)
> Sets forth his Journals to the publick View,

> To caution, by his Woes, the wandring Crew. (3.399–406)

The textual conduct of travel "Journals" is similar to the walker-poet's work. In these lines, the georgic mode melds with a "Citizen of the World" tone. Gay completes this simile by applying an elegiac tone, and this tone allows Gay to envision his own death:

> And now compleat my gen'rous Labours lye,
> Finish'd, and ripe for Immortality.
> Death shall entomb in Dust this mould'ring Frame
> But never reach th' eternal Part, my Fame. (3.407–10)

I have argued that the "gen'rous Labours" are "complete" because Gay's use of the georgic mode—in combination with an infinite number of other modes, tones, and voices—offers a way of comprehending *Trivia*'s textual work. *Trivia* not only imagines that it performs work in "the publick View," but also creates the impression that the knowledge which these similes produce fills a gaping void in the temper of its own time. *Trivia* is "ripe for Immortality" because it provides overdue knowledge.

These combinations of modes, tones, and voices constantly force readers to use several protocols of reading at the same time to finish *Trivia*'s three books. The experience of surviving *Trivia*, in Gay's view, requires a constant interpretation of—and therefore, sensitivity to—*the poet's* conduct as well as street-level conduct. Again, it is not as though Gay connects "the heroic" to specific spaces; it is simply that different modes, tones, and voices force readers to change their interpretive approaches. *Trivia*'s interpretive exercise therefore produces an impression of differentiation.

The *Civica Corona*, the Attorney, and the Architect

I end this chapter by reading an episode in which one of the most famous architects of the eighteenth century appears: Lord Burlington, the close friend of both Pope and Gay.[54] This episode reveals the larger purpose of *Trivia*, which is to govern London and Londoners. The episode begins by introducing another friend of Gay's, attorney William Fortescue:[55]

> Come, F * * * sincere, experienc'd Friend,

> Thy Briefs, thy Deeds, and ev'n the Fees suspend;
> Come, let us leave the *Temple*'s silent Walls,
> Me Bus'ness to my distant Lodging calls:
> Through the long *Strand* together let us stray,
> With thee conversing, I forget the Way.
> Behold that narrow Street, which steep descends,
> Whose Building to the slimy Shore extends;
> Here *Arundell*'s fam'd Structure rear'd its Frame,
> The Street alone retains an empty Name. . . . (2.475–84)

On "the long *Strand*," the walker-poet laments Arundell Street's "empty Name" because the estate home for which it was originally named no longer exists. Only "Arundell Street" remains, and Gay stresses the futility of the street's "empty Name"—its empty purpose. The lament continues with Gay telling us how to read or navigate this "empty Name":

> Where *Titian*'s glowing Paint the Canvas warm'd,
> And *Raphaels*'s fair Design, with Judgment, charm'd
> Now hangs the Bell-man's Song, and pasted here,
> The colour'd Prints of *Overton* appear.
> Where Statues breath'd, the Work of *Phidias'* Hands,
> A wooden Pump, or lonely Watch-house stands.
> There Essex' stately Pile adorn'd the Shore,
> There *Cecil*'s, *Bedford*'s, *Villiers*', now no more. (2.485–92)

In alternating couplets, Gay compares the past to the present, and for a split second, we imagine the interiors of famous seventeenth-century inner-city estate homes on the Thames, on the literal strand (or beach of the river). The moment is elegiac, but the tone offers more than just a nostalgic lament; it heightens the intensity of Lord Burlington's entrance:

> Yet *Burlington*'s fair Palace still remains;
> Beauty within, without Proportion reigns.
> Beneath his Eye declining Art revives,
> The Wall with animated Picture Lives;
> There *Hendel* strikes the Strings, the melting Strain
> Transports the Soul, and thrills through ev'ry Vein;
> There oft' I enter (but with cleaner Shoes)
> For *Burlington*'s belov'd by ev'ry Muse. (2.493–500)

Burlington's appearance offers at least two suggestions about what Gay views as "architecture." First, the phrase "but with cleaner Shoes" seems to be a throwaway, parenthetical expression; however, it distinguishes the poet's work from Burlington's work. Gay's shoes, muddied from cataloging London's infinite number of archives of conduct, do not enter Burlington's estate. The vehicles of Gay's "art of walking"—his shoes—insist upon disciplinary distinction. Gay stresses this distinction to suggest that the poet's task is not to revive "declining Art" but rather to fashion what counts as art. Second, Burlington is "belov'd by ev'ry Muse," and in the context of *Trivia*'s muse, a very important question arises: is Burlington "belov'd" by all nine classical Muses—*and* Trivia? Gay separates himself from Burlington because the two men employ different formal vehicles to convey their "art," yet Gay identifies with Burlington's patronage of multi-disciplinarity (art, music, literature). We may further specify the foundational similarity between Burlington and Gay if we remember that a third person is experiencing this part of the poem: Gay's attorney, William Fortescue. This communal "stray" is taken by three law makers: poet, attorney, and architect. Significantly, their stray is a conduct specific to "the long *Strand*." Author, administrator, and architect ultimately converge on "the long *Strand*" because the way in which they conduct their discourse about London's art is similar. Their goal is to manage conduct. The attorney interprets texts to reinforce standards of behavior, the architect designs buildings to govern spatial behavior, and Gay does both of these. Gay's concept of the proper poet assigns him, like the walker he designs, a "moral" position—a position that replaces the obsolete "Watchmen" of the antiquated Restoration "Town":

> Yet there are Watchmen, who with friendly Light,
> Will teach thy reeling Steps to tread aright;
> For *Sixpence* will support thy helpless Arm,
> And Home conduct thee, safe from nightly Harm . . . . (3.307–10)

As the walker-poet in *Trivia* inherits the "friendly" task of the "Watchmen," Gay injects conduct as a new technology, and Gay's final conception of the poet as a moral architect appears. We may describe this poet as a "spatial architect" since space—when seen as manifesting archives of conduct—is a moral technology that governs conduct. Gay shores up his claim that moral work is an integral component of the poet's task when he addresses his own publisher, Bernard Lintott:

Chapter 1: Archives of Conduct

> O *Lintott,* let my Labours obvious lie,
> Rang'd on thy Stall, for ev'ry curious Eye;
> So shall the Poor these Precepts *gratis* know,
> And to my Verse their future Safeties owe. (2.565–68)

The spatial architect is always charitable—but complex. The clause "let my Labours obvious lie" is a pun that readers will recognize only if they have inherited *Trivia*'s protocols of interpretation. Gay suggests that anything "obvious" in *Trivia* deserves a second glance with a more sensitive, "judicious Eye." Gay's definition of architecture needs to be approached in this manner.

In the end, Gay's "*Civic* Crown" refers to neither the position of City Poet held by Elkanah Settle nor the Roman *Civica Corona* given "to those who saved the life of a fellow-citizen in battle."[56] The function of *Trivia*'s poet may be summarized in this word: *Civic.* That is, archives of conduct serve a civic duty in their complex creation and simultaneous management of space, behavior, and city. The poet who creates these archives of conduct considers printed texts to be a medium of moral engineering, and it is in this context that writers could contribute to building London. *Trivia* shows us a position previously inaccessible to writers who did not narrate at the street level. Gay's poem grounds itself in the conducts available on the Strand, and in this way, *Trivia* designs the Town. It makes the Town visible and consequently available for other authors to manage the possibilities of this new space. Each of the following chapters participates in the textual possibilities fashioned by John Gay's London.

2

Novel Conduct

IMAGINED AUTHORITY IN HENRY FIELDING'S *TOM JONES* AND BOW STREET

Henry Fielding's dual career as novelist and Bow Street Magistrate—careers that may seem incompatible from a twenty-first-century perspective—was not strange to eighteenth-century readers. For example, given Fielding's preoccupation with the notorious Jonathan Wild, recent work on Fielding has explored the connection between novel writing and eighteenth-century crimes such as thief-taking—that infamously profitable practice of employing thieves, taking their stolen goods, reselling these goods to the victims, and informing against the thieves when their capture turns profitable. In reviewing the Restoration origins of thief-taking, Tim Wales claims that "thief-takers filled a void, providing services that a public watch patrolling the streets did not," especially during the 1690s when "a campaign for moral reformation, triggered by providential interpretations of the events of 1688, merged with concerns about rising London crime."[1] In this anxious climate, Fielding offered to fill another administrative void, and in turn, render London's borderline-criminal practices, such as thief-taking, obsolete. In particular, Fielding recognized that the Town required a new type of regulation that could attend to the questionable behaviors taking place there. His conception of the literary Magistrate developed amid these conditions.

I argue that Fielding's literary and juridical roles were completely consistent with the functions that writers were assigning to printed text after the Glorious Revolution. To recover a sense of this consistency, I begin by tracing Henry Fielding's metaphor of conduct through *Tom Jones* (1749) and his Bow Street prose (1749–1751) to identify how Fielding reimagined the urban writer's social function in mid-eighteenth-century London. The metaphor of conduct created the impression that Fielding policed the proper behaviors of two specific audiences: the readers of his novels and the Londoners he governed as Bow Street Magistrate. Fielding was able to serve these two high-profile roles in London because this metaphor not only grounded claims of authority in the local geographic and administrative tensions of London but also supplied a vocabulary for Fielding to articulate authority in *Tom Jones* and his civil prose. In particular, Fielding's metaphor of conduct tried to resolve literal tensions by figurative and imaginative means.

The factor that allowed Fielding to believe that he was competing with London's politicians, lawyers, and priests involved the way his metaphor of conduct referred to Bow Street, a street located within a unique district caught inside the traditional Court–City binary.[2] Similar to John Gay, Fielding recognized that the district between these two cities did not conveniently fit into either pole of the Court–City binary. As I introduced earlier in this book, between the cities of Westminster and London stood the "liberties" of Westminster, which were "formerly monastic precincts"[3] marked by "freedom from the jurisdiction of the customary administrative unit."[4] John Entick's *A New and Accurate History and Survey of London, Westminster, Southwark, and Places Adjacent* (1766) records that "the management of the civil power [in the cities and liberties of Westminster] has been, ever since the reformation, in lay hands, elected from time to time, and confirmed by the dean and chapter."[5] John Strype's 1720 updated edition of John Stow's *A Survey of the Cities of London and Westminster* refers to this liminal district by its medieval title, "the Liberty of the Dutchy of Lancaster."[6] Taken together, these texts suggest that Fielding's jurisdiction resembled a patchwork of liberties and parishes, which was, not incidentally, also the district where the nation's textual production and distribution were concentrated.

In this chapter I argue that the dual nature of Fielding's career was made possible by the way his metaphor of conduct referred to, and was irretrievably influenced by, the geographic and administrative conditions of the Town. His control over the readers of *Tom Jones* and the civil prose hinges upon the way the metaphor could imagine types of authority beyond those already in place.[7] In particular, the two texts refer readers to a literal cityscape but gesture towards a completely new way of organizing, or interpreting, London. The metaphor of conduct, in combination with the gap left by the fall of James II and the literal gap between Court and City, helped Fielding represent himself as a surrogate governor, competing with both the politicians of Westminster and the aldermen of the City of London. Thus, Fielding valued the metaphor of conduct because it could accomplish tasks beyond simply referring to existing governmental apparatuses; more specifically, it helped him believe that the techniques he developed to guide his readers through *Tom Jones* could also direct interpretations of a newly complex London. In turn, Fielding developed a specific way of presenting these techniques that became its own style, its own discourse.[8] In this context, the didacticism of *Tom Jones* and the civil prose is, therefore, these texts' most imaginative trait.

I support these claims by reading Fielding's *A Charge Delivered to the Grand Jury* (1749), *A True State of the Case of Bosavern Penlez* (1749), and *An Enquiry into the Late Increase of Robbers* (1751) as manuals of conduct that regulated both the reader's and the writer's relationships to London. Fielding uses words like "conduct" and "manner" when debating, organizing, and regulating the task of the urban author; thus, we must interpret his language in terms of these administrative projects.[9] I conclude by outlining how Fielding's administrative discourse, with its attempt to control public behavior, aligned the novelist and the magistrate in a surprisingly consistent eighteenth-century project of urban administration.

TOM JONES AS ADMINISTRATIVE VEHICLE

The claim that Fielding used *Tom Jones* to develop ways of managing the Town is supported by his official appointment as the Magistrate of Westminster in January of 1749. For example, *Tom Jones* was published in February of that year, and we have evidence suggesting that Fielding had campaigned for this appointment while finishing the final three volumes of the six-volume novel.[10] This overlapping period of textual production suggests that Fielding was at least thinking about how the metaphor of conduct could affect public representations of his social function. If the English novel tested the limits of its own novelty at mid-century, then Fielding was working with a new textual technology. What makes *Tom Jones* a "new" technology is the way Fielding created the impression that the novel as a genre possesses essential characteristics, such as its abilities to incorporate many textual traditions simultaneously and to debate closure. When it appears in *Tom Jones,* the metaphor of conduct helps Fielding regulate the possibilities that this interrogation presents. The ending of *Tom Jones* is not, of course, open; like all texts, the novel ends. If Fielding could, however, make the novel look like it would never end, however, and then conclude it, he could create the impression of regulating or administering order to the possibility of open-endedness. We may witness the way Fielding uses *Tom Jones* to regulate and manage the novel's formal characteristics, such as unending or alternative narratives. The techniques that Fielding developed to regulate these possibilities are chiefly stylistic changes in voice, mood, tone, and mode. This description of "style" is purposefully vague; the terminology now used to describe novelistic devices (characterization, point of view, enplotment) is an anachronistic imposition on Fielding's texts because these terms were codified primarily during the late nineteenth century. Therefore, speaking in stylistic terms other than our own, we may begin to see the textual traditions or modes that Fielding valued for accomplishing several specific tasks.

The model around which Fielding organizes *Tom Jones* depends upon a habitual order. In other words, the novel assigns certain functions to certain episodes and then places these episodes in a narrative order with which the reader eventually becomes familiar. For example, an introductory chapter for each of the eighteen books presents didactic knowledge while the remaining chapters house the plot. Changes in voice also organize this narrative: the narrator of the introductory chapters directly addresses the reader, while the narrator of the remaining chapters only intervenes during moments of crisis. As Hunter has argued, even when the narrator's voice "claims to be apprehensive about readers it is always part of some elaborate ironic scheme to outwit them, and even when he comments accurately he leaves readers with a sense that they themselves have earned the conclusion by listening carefully to tone, evaluating, and finally judging for themselves."[11] This "apprehensive" yet seemingly omniscient voice nurtures a reader's sensitivity to changes in voice. In particular, Fielding assigns a specific voice to specific sites, and the repetition of this combination advances the novel. One of the best illustrations of this stylistic specificity occurs at the start of Book VI, immediately following the fistfight between Jones and Blifil: "In our last Book we have been obliged to deal pretty much with the Passion of Love; and, in our succeeding Book, shall be forced to handle this Subject still more largely. It may not, therefore, in this Place, be improper to apply ourselves to the Examination of that modern Doctrine . . . ."[12] On the level of content, this chapter critiques essays "On Love," and it delivers this content in a voice that includes the reader: "our Last Book." Because these introductory chapters are the sites where practical or didactic knowledge is expected, Fielding frequently adopts a textual mode or tradition that the reader would recognize as a vehicle for producing knowledge. For instance, this chapter presents an ordered list of "Concessions" with paragraphs beginning "First," "Secondly," etc. (*T,* 6.1.270), and the opening reference to "Dr. *Swift*" and the sustained metaphor of Love as a "Hunger" ("Appetite," "Glutton," "Flesh," "Sir-loin of Roast-beef") transform this chapter into a proposal that resembles Jonathan Swift's famous exemplar (*T,* 6.1.268–72). Fielding adopts the proposal's mode, which implies a certain way of reading; therefore, the conduct associated with the way a proposal produces knowledge helps Fielding substantiate the position of the novelist. Put another way, Fielding reinterprets conducts linked to specific textual modes to accomplish other tasks. Here, the proposal is the generic template whose conduct or way of reading Fielding uses to develop the proper conduct of the novelist. This ability to empty out the content of an established textual tradition and then to import the conduct associated with interpreting that tradition is a technique that became important to the way Fielding was able to write his way into Bow Street. By importing conduct from the proposal to the novel, Fielding identifies how to transfer administrative language from the novel into his social treatises. For Fielding, this transferal of distinct readerly conducts into new modes of writing defined the task of the skilled novelist.

Another instance of site-specific conduct involves Fielding's use of dialogue and the epistolary mode during the London scenes. As the scene shifts to London, Fielding adapts his style to reflect the way London's administrative geography organizes its inhabitants. Elaborate passages of topographical detail do not make us recognize that we are in London; instead, we recognize that we are in London because Fielding's style changes. In the Somerset section, for example, Fielding assigns a separate paragraph to each character's dialogue. Such self-contained speeches and oral conducts are not possible in London; from book XIII onward, paragraphs lengthen as Fielding no longer signifies a change in speaker with a new paragraph. As many as four characters compete with each other for the right to speak in one paragraph, with each speaker frequently finishing the sentences of the preceding characters. Speakers wage this competition especially during episodes that characterize London, such as the masquerade (*T,* 13.7.712–17). This change in Fielding's representation of dialogue also increases the pace of conversation, and Fielding therefore creates the impression that this style reflects a conduct that is specific to, and capable of interpreting, London.

The Somerset section of *Tom Jones* does not include a single letter, but the London section is a virtual epistolary novel. Characters who live less than a two-minute coach ride from each other write as though they are total strangers, and Lady Bellaston communicates with Jones in letters more than she does in person. In a style particular to the urban letter, Lady Bellaston's letters have three postscripts, as though she needs to write beyond the confines of this scripted textual conduct (*T,* 14.2.744–45). Even Thwackum and Square adapt to the textual conduct of London; chapter IV of book XVIII, simply titled "Containing two Letters in very different Stiles" (*T,* 18.4.924), translates the pair's countrified opinions through the urban sieve of the epistolary. Fielding shores up the epistle as London's popular means of communication when he reprints a letter from Sophia's servant, Mrs. Honor, in which he conceals a pivotal moment:

> ["]I beg ure Onur not too menshon ani thing of what I haf sad, for I wish ure Onur all thee gud Luk in thee Wurld
> . . . . I begg ure Onur to say nothing of what past, and belive me to be,
> Sir,
>
> Ure Onur's umble Sarvant
> To Cumand till Deth,
> *Honour Blackmore.*"
>
> Various were the Conjectures which *Jones* entertained on this Step of Lady *Bellaston* . . . . (*T,* 15.10.825)

The narrative voice that follows Honour's letter does not clarify what "this Step of Lady Bellaston" is; it simply refers to the revelation of "this Step" in Honour's letter. If we were to skip this letter because of an impatience with Honour's writing style, we would miss the revelation of her promotion, which is a clue to Bellaston's motivations. This episode is important because it shows how Fielding can import a mode of writing as well as the way of reading that mode without importing its content. Honour's letter is entirely consistent with an established trend of urban, textual conduct, and readers must participate in this conduct—that is, endure her letter—to continue to participate in *Tom Jones*. Fielding's epistolary mode serves the same function as his use of the proposal; he empties out the content and then uses the customary expectations about reading that mode or textual tradition to dictate a new interpretation.

Fielding also reassigns functions to traditional textual modes by using what we might call retrofitted narratives, episodes marked by the narrator's instruction to turn back to earlier episodes. This stylistic device not only creates the impression of a conscious, providential order that miraculously transforms the plotted events of *Tom Jones* into "accidents" and "surprises," but also provides time for readers to comprehend earlier episodes. Leo Damrosch argues that the type of providence that Fielding imitates throughout *Tom Jones*'s narrative (a type of providence that is "aware that paradise is lost but willing to perceive an ideal harmony in the universe that survives it") positions the novel as "a terminal moraine, the comprehensive ending of an old tradition rather than the herald of a new one."[13] While Fielding definitely wishes readers to sense how writing conveys "an ideal harmony" in the eighteenth-century universe, I argue that Fielding's constant glances over his shoulder serve to associate the novelist with not only a metaphysical or aesthetic-religious authority, but also a type of regulatory, social guidance that extends beyond the plot's fictional content. Consider, for example, how Sophia remembers what happened at the Inn at Upton:

> This Incident, however, being afterwards revived in her Mind, and placed in the most odious Colours by *Honour,* served to heighten and give Credit to those unlucky Occurrences at *Upton,* and assisted the Waiting-woman in her Endeavours to make her Mistress depart from that Inn without seeing *Jones.* (*T,* 10.9.564)

The moment evinces a type of *nachträglichkeit,* a reconstructed comprehension of a past (or "revived") episode. But the narrative seems to unfold before us because most of Fielding's revived episodes address the reader, not the characters:

> Before we proceed any farther in our History, it may be proper to look a little back, in order to account for the extraordinary Appearance of *Sophia* and her Father at the Inn at *Upton.*
> The Reader may be pleased to remember, that in the Ninth Chapter of the Seventh Book of our History, we left *Sophia,* after a long Debate between Love and Duty, deciding the Cause, as it usually, I believe, happens, in Favour of the Former. (*T,* 10.8.554)

The style of this excerpt, due to its first-person voice, is conversational and creates a familiar mood in which to ponder past events. But Fielding supplies such intense specificity ("in the Ninth Chapter of the Seventh Book") that the revived narrative serves only one purpose: to advertise the way Fielding makes his plot appear accidental and providentially designed at the same time. Fielding eventually labels what I am calling "the revived episode" as "our Method":

> The Reader may now perhaps be pleased to return with us to Mr. *Jones,* who at the appointed Hour attended on Mrs. *Fitzpatrick;* but before we relate the Conversation which now past, it may be proper, according to our Method, to return a little back, and to account for so great an Alteration of Behaviour in this Lady. . . . (*T,* 16.9.866–67)

"Our Method" seems to be created by the narrator as we read, yet it also assigns a premeditated, proper function to the novelist: to regulate the "Methods" or styles of writing. Every mode of writing in *Tom Jones* has its proper place, and this placement becomes a conduct that readers eventually expect from the novelist, even if Fielding uses these textual modes to reach nontraditional ends.

Tom Jones also experiments with alternative endings to professional, legal practices. For example, *Tom Jones* repeatedly takes the legal trial and offers alternatives to the rigid acts of sentencing that usually conclude a trial. Each of these episodes constitutes a mock-trial because the style or tone loosely follows a legal tradition without reaching a conclusion. These episodes appear when Fielding applies technical legal diction to quotidian situations, such as when legal conduct suddenly operates in domestic spaces. Because Fielding dramatizes these episodes in a space outside a formal courtroom, he is able to suggest an alternative ending that could not occur in a trial. For example, Magistrate Allworthy's mock-trial in chapter VII of book I, (which is prefaced by Fielding as a "kind of instructive Writing" [*T,* 1.6.50]), "tries" Jenny Jones for the "crime" of Tom's birth. Moving closer to the point of sentencing, Allworthy's diction changes. Technical phrases, such as "Part of your Offence," "Defiance of the Laws of our Religion," "Breach of the Divine Commands," give way to lists of abstract qualities: "Sophistry," "Delusion," "Terror," "Passion," and "Reason" (*T,* 1.7.51–52). The change in Allworthy's diction from the technically specific to the philosophically abstract allows Fielding to introduce an alternative to Jenny's conviction. Jenny also exonerates herself by appealing to a realm of judgment beyond a mortal law court. She appeals to her "future Conduct":

> As to my Concern for what is past, I know you will spare my Blushes the Repetition. My future Conduct will much better declare my Sentiments .... But now, Sir, I must on my Knees intreat you, not to persist in asking me to declare the Father of my Infant. I promise you faithfully, you shall one Day know; but I am under the most solemn Ties and Engagements of Honour, as well as the most religious Vows and Protestations, to conceal his Name at this Time. And I know you too well to think you would desire I should sacrifice either my Honour, or my Religion. (*T,* 1.7.54)

Jenny's "future Conduct" values "Honour," and Allworthy's own honor forces him to dissolve the trial before a final sentencing. Because this mock-trial takes place in Allworthy's study and not in a formal, legal space that prescribes social behavior, Fielding creates and manages a conduct that is specific to domestic conflict. Fielding removes professionalized legal conduct from the trial's performance to address a new type of domestic episode that is in need of attention. Typically, the mock-trial appears whenever Fielding needs to catalogue proper domestic conducts: to dissolve the debate of Thwackum and Square (3.3); to dismiss the blame for the boxing match between Tom and Blifil (3.4); to dissolve the controversy surrounding what Tom does with the money he receives for selling his Horse (3.8); and to excuse Jones's selling his Bible (3.9).[14]

This device shows how a novel can assign new conducts to unregulated spaces; Fielding applies it to episodes that lack systemized or conventional conducts. One of the most important examples of these episodes takes place in the barn where Jones and Partridge encounter a band of gypsies (12.12). In the absence of Magistrate Allworthy, Fielding begins this mock-trail by relating the "King of the Gypsies" to a "great Magistrate":

> It is impossible to conceive a happier Set of People than appeared here to be met together. The utmost Mirth indeed shewed itself in every Countenance; nor was their Ball totally void of all Order and Decorum. Perhaps it had more than a Country Assembly is sometimes conducted with: For these People are subject to a formal Government and Laws of their own, and all pay Obedience to one great Magistrate, whom they call their King. (*T,* 12.12.667)

Joining this gypsy wedding ceremony, Jones and Partridge experience an alternative society in which Partridge's over-eagerness with one of the married gypsies positions him as a defendant in another mock-trial. However, when it is discovered that the gypsy's husband had encouraged his peers to watch his wife tempt Partridge (and that the husband had designed the entire scene), this mock-trial dissolves with an atypical sentence for the erring husband. The Gypsy-King's sentence corrects conduct:

> [M]e do order derefore, dat you be de infamous *Gypsy*, and do wear Pair of Horns upon your Forehead for one Month, and dat your Wife be called de Whore, and pointed at all dat Time: For you be de infamous *Gypsy*, but she be no less de infamous Whore. (*T*, 12.12.671)

Jones lauds this punishment of shame: "*Jones* afterwards proceeded very gravely to sing forth the Happiness of those Subjects who live under such a Magistrate" (*T*, 12.12.671). After a lengthy debate over absolute monarchy, however, the narrator suggests that the gypsies' conduct is possible only because they occupy a unique part of British society:

> Nor can the Example of the *Gypsies,* tho' possibly they may have long been happy under this Form of Government, be here urged; since we must remember the very material Respect in which they differ from all other People, and to which perhaps this their Happiness is entirely owing, namely, that they have no false Honours among them; and that they look on Shame as the most grievous Punishment in the World. (*T*, 12.12.673)

The narrator's concluding disclaimer makes it clear that shame, as an alternative ending to the mock-trial, applies only to a very specific community in a very specific space. Thus, a specific, alternative conduct accompanies each mock-trial in *Tom Jones*.

While all of these mock-trials appear to destabilize legal practice, they actually assign specific conducts to episodes that take place in unregulated realms of British society. This is why the word "conduct" appears throughout the mock-trials. During the final meeting, or final mock-trial, between Sophia and Jones, Sophia uses "conduct" in a legal context: "'I think, Mr. *Jones*,' said she, 'I may almost depend on your own Justice, and leave it to yourself to pass Sentence on your own Conduct'" (*T*, 18.12.971). As the author of *Tom Jones*, Fielding develops ways to "pass Sentence" on new conducts, especially in the first chapters to every book. In chapter I of book XII, the narrator describes plagiarism as an improper "Conduct in Writing" (*T*, 12.1.619); therefore, I am interested in what *Tom Jones* presents as the *proper* "Conduct in Writing." This brings me to my final point about the ways Fielding uses *Tom Jones* to administer the novelist's practice to readers.

The entire novel constitutes a mock-trial for Fielding's right to claim the title of novelist. Fielding's mock-trial uses a system in which regulating the stylistic opportunities presented by this genre leads to a more definable role for the writer. In the exact middle of the novel (9.1), in a chapter entitled "Of those who lawfully may, and of those who may not write such Histories as this" (*T*, 9.1.487), Fielding catalogues the qualifications for "Historians of our Order" (*T*, 9.1.492):

> For Nature can only furnish us with Capacity, or, as I have chose to illustrate it, with the Tools of our Profession; Learning must fit them for Use, must direct them in it; and lastly, must contribute, Part at least, of the Materials. A competent Knowledge of History and of the *Belles Lettres*, is here absolute necessary; and without this Share of Knowledge at least, to affect the Character of an Historian, is as vain as to endeavour at building a House without Timber or Mortar, or Brick or Stone. (*T*, 9.1.491–92)

An ease of "conversation" is also required in this act of "building": "Now this Conversation in our Historian must be universal, that is, with all Ranks and Degrees of Men: For the Knowledge of what is called High-Life, will not instruct him in low, nor *e converso*, will his being acquainted with the inferior Part of Mankind, teach him the Manners of the superior" (*T*, 9.1.494). The task of learning "the Manners" of "all Ranks and Degrees of Men" is tied to Fielding's larger project as a Bow Street Magistrate. Between the mock-trials of the Somerset section, Fielding presents "a very useful Lesson" to those who "administer to an honest Pride in their own Minds" (*T*, 3.7.141). The proper administration of one's "self" is promoted here and alludes to the function shared by *Tom Jones* and Fielding's writings as Magistrate. In *Tom Jones,* Fielding introduces this administrative function with one of the most blatant instances of the first-person voice in the novel:

> I ask Pardon for this short Appearance, by Way of Chorus on the Stage. It is in Reality for my own Sake, that while I am discovering the Rocks on which Innocence and Goodness often split, I may not be misunderstood to recommend the very Means to my worthy Readers, by which I intend to shew them they will be undone. And this, as I could not prevail on any of my Actors to speak, I myself was obliged to declare. (*T*, 3.7.141–42)

In eighteen introductory chapters, this intrusive voice encourages the reader to rely on the narrator's presence. The novel produces this reliance and, at the same time, defines the specific sites where this presence should be administered to the reader. Whether or not Fielding professionalizes the activities of the novelist in the modern sense of the term is not at stake here because the phrases "the poetical Trade" (*T,* 12.1.621) and "Tools of our Profession" (*T,* 9.1.492) position writing somewhere between "Trade" and "Profession." As a result, *Tom Jones* is an experiment, or essay, in the means of systematization rather than a handbook on how to professionalize the practice of writing. Fielding writes the novel partly "to pass Sentence" on what the conduct—not the profession—of the novelist might be.

All of the techniques described here—site-specific modes, the revived episodes, and mock-trials—constitute a style, a conduct, and finally, a discourse that develops through *Tom Jones*. This discourse is administrative because Fielding mobilizes all of these stylistic techniques to explore, to instruct, and to validate proper behaviors of both the reader of *Tom Jones* and its novelist. By writing *Tom Jones,* Fielding was able to ask himself how well he was able to administer a new literary form to an audience. The task now was to apply these new textual conducts to a new job: Bow Street Magistrate.

The Civil Prose

Before interrogating the ways in which Fielding's Bow-Street project inherited an administrative discourse that he had developed in *Tom Jones,* we might note the complex forms that these writings adopt. I call the texts Fielding published as a magistrate his "civil prose" to allude to Fielding's own definition of their task: to "rouse the CIVIL power."[15] Each of the works discussed below may be seen as a textual vehicle that accomplishes a different task, and these distinctions are evident in Fielding's titles: *A Charge, An Enquiry, A True State of the Case.* To avoid discounting the specific work accomplished by each of these textual traditions, I organize the following discussion around the specific textual conduct that each vehicle imposes upon its audience. Thus, we may witness not only the type of knowledge being generated by Fielding's revision of the traditional ends and expectations of these specific titles, but also the different roles each text played in organizing and advertising Fielding's duties as Magistrate.

Fielding's fiction and his Bow Street writings are linked only by the works' shared use of the administrative discourse. For example, Magistrate Allworthy might be "like" Magistrate Fielding, but Magistrate Allworthy does not write *Tom Jones*. The following works are rarely similar in content to either each other or to *Tom Jones*, and this dissimilarity has led critics to be surprised, or even betrayed, by the supposedly "conservative" writer they find in the civil prose. To establish this discursive connection between *Tom Jones* and the civil prose, the following discussion addresses not only the content of Fielding's texts, but also the style that deliver that content. I am interested in Fielding's texts as administrative vehicles because his positions as novelist and Bow Street magistrate forced him to shape them as such. The remainder of this chapter analyzes these three pieces of civil prose to see how each text imposes a traditional way of reading, or a specific conduct, on its audience. Thus, their variety of titles and forms can be understood in terms of the administrative discourse Fielding used in *Tom Jones*.

Fielding Delivers His *Charge*

Fielding's first task as Bow Street Magistrate was to define the importance of his position. As the final volumes of *Tom Jones* appeared in 1749, Fielding prepared for his first appearance as magistrate at the quarterly meeting of the Westminster Commission. Fielding chose the genre of the charge to accomplish this credentialization because, as a familiar textual tradition, the charge would have been expected to accomplish at least two specific tasks.[16] First, readers expected eighteenth-century charges to be self-reflexive commentaries about—or updates on—the effectiveness of public administration in London.[17] The charge was read, or "delivered," during a ceremony when qualified individuals were sworn in to their profession; therefore, the charge seems to have been an integral part of credentialization.[18] Second, the *Charge* publicized Fielding's duty as a new type of magistrate. Nowhere in the *Charge* is there a detailed proposal for handling specific crimes. Instead, the *Charge* uses metaphors of conduct to systematize the proper behavior of the Town-based administrator.

Malvin Zirker has claimed that the form and style of Fielding's *Charge* are consistent with those of other charges of the time.[19] Indeed, Fielding begins by advertising a historical pageant of the English legal privilege of trial by jury, and he "trace[s] the Original of this great and singular

Privilege"[20] back to Alfred and the Normans. However, Fielding draws attention to the way his *Charge* swerves away from textual tradition:

> The usual Method of Charge hath been to run over the several Articles, or Heads of Crimes, which might possibly become subject to the Enquiry of the Grand Jury. . . .
>
> But, Gentlemen, I think I many be excused at present from taking up so much of your Time; for tho' we are assembled to exercise the Jurisdiction of a very antient and honourable Liberty, yet, as there is another Sessions of Justices within that County of which this Liberty is a Part, before whom indictments for all Crimes of the deeper Dye are usually preferred, it seems rather to savour of Ostentation than Utility, to run over those Articles which in great Probability will not come before you. (*Charge,* 12)

Fielding advertises his *Charge*'s novelty; he even narrows the type of knowledge his version of the charge will convey. Jettisoning procedural concerns tied to "Crimes of the deeper Dye" that are addressed only in the Middlesex sessions, Fielding's administrative voice addresses crimes taking place in a very specific area of the Town: the "Liberty" of the Strand. The *Charge*'s production of specialized, site-specific knowledge is, in Fielding's terms, a swerve away from "the usual Method of Charge." I argue that what Fielding does to the "usual Method of Charge" is to add his own "Method," which we have already seen in *Tom Jones:* an administrative discourse that employs the metaphor of conduct. "Method" is again used here as an eighteenth-century placeholder for the model of imaginative, textual government that I am outlining in this book.

If Fielding tailored his charge to cater to the administrative possibilities of the Town, then he also explored what additional functions the charge could serve. Fielding recognized with the *Charge,* as he did in *Tom Jones,* a way to systematize his position while performing it. In particular, a charge is "a task or duty laid upon one; commission, trust, responsibility; an office entrusted to one."[21] In this sense, a duty or task is "Delivered to the Grand Jury"; that is, Fielding has the power to administer positions and offices to the jury. As a magistrate, Fielding administers work—that is, he authorizes professional positions—for others. In another sense of the word, the "charge" refers to the actual body of people "entrusted to the management of"[22] the jury. In this sense, Fielding delivers the audience of the Town to their proper administrators. In both cases, to deliver a "charge" is to possess the right to confer an office on an audience. When Fielding delivered the *Charge* to the grand jury, he was both defining and performing, quite publicly, the protocol of his own office and the protocol of his audience. *A Charge* is in many ways Fielding's inter-office memo notifying others of his own promotion, and what, exactly, that promotion entails.

Because the *Charge* administers offices to others, there is a tendency to read the work as the text where Fielding professionalizes himself. Zirker, for example, deems the Bow Street position a "profession": "Certainly . . . he intended to display a distinguished expertise in his profession. . . . The *Charge* is both a public display of his credentials and an anticipatory response, inevitably unheeded, to those who would ridicule his sober posture at the bench."[23] I would push this further. The *Charge* is where Fielding performs his credentials; it is his dramatization of his own résumé to validate his new role as a magistrate—a figure who derives his basis for administrative power from printed text.[24] From this perspective, Fielding's position as magistrate was not as professionalized as Zirker would assume. Entick's job description for Fielding's Bow Street Magistrate was still, in 1766, a position for "lay hands." This is anything but "professional," in the modern sense of that term, and the "lay" status of Fielding's magistrate reflects the same absence of systematization that characterized Fielding's other role, that of eighteenth-century writer.

Fielding repeatedly foregrounds the disclaimer that all of his topics are time and place specific; that is, they are "Characteristic of the present Age" (*Charge,* 25). He again uses history to validate claims and to generate knowledge in the same way that the title of *Tom Jones* (*The History of Tom Jones, a Foundling*) relies upon history as a means of acquiring textual credibility. But the *Charge* also stresses the timeliness of the crimes into which the jury must "enquire." Consider, for example, the way Fielding contrasts how past laws have dealt with libel as compared with present laws. He suggests that libel may develop its own means of professionalization if not curbed: "I have mentioned these Laws to you, Gentlemen, to shew you the Sense of our Ancestors of a Crime which, I believe, they never saw carried to so flagitious a Height as it is at present; when, to the Shame of the Age be it spoken, there are Men who make a Livelihood of Scandal" (*Charge,* 29). "The Shame of the Age" is that crime could be made "a Livelihood." While discussing those who commit libel—a crime, we should note, involving a printed text—Fielding charges his audience with a duty: "Of these [libelers], Gentlemen, it is your Business to enquire; of the Devisers, of the Writers, of the Printers, and of the Publishers of all such Libels; and I do heartily recommend this Enquiry to your Care" (*Charge,* 29). Fielding confers "Business" onto the jury; he literally delivers his charge.

At the end of the *Charge,* Fielding shores up his own administrative position by combining all of these issues—the conferral of offices, the specificity of the Town, and the duty of his own office:

> To conclude, Gentlemen, you will consider yourselves as now summoned to the Execution of an Office, of the utmost Importance to the well-being of this Community: Nor will you, I am confident, suffer that Establishment, so wisely and carefully regulated, and so stoutly and zealously maintained by your wise and brave Ancestors, to degenerate into mere Form and Shadow. Grand Juries, Gentlemen, are in Reality the only Censors of this Nation. As such, the Manners of the People are in your Hands, and in yours only. You, therefore, are the only Correctors of them. If you neglect your Duty, the certain Consequences to the Public are too apparent. . . .
>
> To this Censorial Office, Gentlemen, you are called by our excellent Constitution. To execute this Duty with Vigilance, you are obliged by the Duty you owe both to God and to your Country. You are invested with full Power for the Purpose. This you have promised to do, under the sacred Sanction of an Oath; and you are all met, I doubt not, with a Disposition and Resolution to perform it, with that Zeal which I have endeavoured to recommend, and which the peculiar Licentiousness of the Age so strongly requires. (*Charge,* 29–30)

Fielding heads "this Censorial Office" to which members are "invested with full Power for the Purpose." His task as "Censor," the office he holds by delivering this charge, is to maintain specific conducts ("the Manners of the People are in your Hands"). The textual vehicle of the *Charge* therefore allowed Fielding's "lay hands" to appear to do business themselves.

It is important to see Fielding's position as the writer of the *Charge* as separate from the position of his audience. Fielding alters his style to acquire this authority just as he does in *Tom Jones.* In the above excerpt, Fielding uses the passive voice to deliver the deity-like proclamation, "You are invested with full Power for the Purpose." Fielding appears only when he needs to stabilize his own position; he only appears to recommend "Zeal" or to "recommend this Enquiry" (*Charge,* 29). By using this construction, he leaves the content of his job description open, yet he plainly separates his task from that of the jury: "the Duties of [the Office] it is incumbent on me concisely to open to you; and this I shall endeavour in the best Manner I am able" (*Charge,* 11). His only duty is to regulate the infinite number of possible administrative duties his jury will perform and to do so with the proper conduct, "the best Manner," that the charge will permit. Because this is only a charge, Fielding assigns duties to others: "it may be therefore proper to awaken *your* Enquiry" (*Charge,* 20, emphasis mine); "you are the only Correctors of [the People]" (*Charge,* 29). But this is where the work of the charge ends. Because the *Charge*'s function was only to "recommend Enquiry," Fielding would turn to the textual traditions of the enquiry to investigate questions of causation. *A Charge* presents Fielding as the public relations manager of Bow Street, and it represents Bow Street as a newly credible component of London's governmental cityscape.

Privileging Civil Conduct: *The Case*

Before Fielding even had a chance to think about his next act as magistrate, the Town presented him with a complicated example of its unregulated status. On 1 July 1749, a sailor named Bosavern Penlez accused the owner of a brothel next to St. Mary's-le-Strand of theft while Penlez was patronizing that same "Bawdy-House."[25] When bounced from the house, Penlez amassed several fellow sailors and attacked the house. Within hours, Penlez's group was joined by citizens of the Town who burned the structure to the ground. For two days, the group continued to target and destroy houses in the Town until Penlez was finally captured and jailed on 3 July. The execution of Penlez, which took place in October, was highly contested because some citizens viewed his destroying a house of prostitution to be a civil service. Fielding's reaction to this—one of his first acts as magistrate—is crucial to our understanding the relationship of administrative discourse to his civil prose. In fact, after Fielding encountered this behavior in the Town, he could begin to imagine what his Bow Street writing should do. Should it make new claims or should it nurture traditional possibilities? Should it proactively, offensively police or should it passively, defensively react to the unrest? The Penlez case therefore offered Fielding a choice to manage conducts that were already common in the Town or to dictate what new conducts should exist there.

If Fielding had defended Penlez's attack against the "Bawdy-Houses," then he would have fully authorized riot as a credible response to robbery. If he had condemned Penlez, then he might have appeared to legitimate the practice of prostitution. Fielding chose the latter, but he supported the acquittal of Penlez's accomplice, John Wilson.[26] My point in briefly jumping from a discussion of form to content is to note that Fielding made a decision based on conducts specific to this case. For instance, the case was not strictly measured against the permanent rule of the Riot Act established by George I. In many ways, the act of rioting was part of the Town's archive of conduct. Fielding's task was not to stipulate laws (the Riot Act did that) but to quell the act of riot via textual means. *A True State of the Case of Bosavern Penlez* presents a narrative that tried to interpret and to regulate the variety of possible ways to respond to episodes of civil unrest in the Town. Fielding recognized that rioting was a conduct that needed regulation and management—*not* outright suppression.

It is extremely important to clarify what was at stake in Fielding's response "in this Case."[27] His commentary on the conduct of the "Mob" is specific only to the Town in July of 1749. The *Case* is not a proposal that outlines future contingency plans or details laws; it is a revived and almost journalistic narrative that produces knowledge about the past to stabilize the "True State" of what just occurred. Fielding's *Case* uses two textual modes to engineer authority over the "True State of the Case." The first mode involves the use of sworn accounts to recreate the night of 1 July from several different points of view. After reviewing the existing Riot Act and clarifying the distinction between a public and a private riot, Fielding introduces six different accounts of the Penlez Riot.[28] These accounts were not testimonies since they had no binding legal power, but they take on the appearance of civil testimony in print. They do not retry a man already in his grave; instead, these accounts create the effect of objective knowledge (of "A True State of the Case") from a variety of perspectives. Thus, the points of view supplied by these accounts serve a narrative function: they establish an unfolding history. The *Case*'s catalogue of sworn accounts reproduces a journalistic means of generating knowledge and validating past events.

Fielding's use of eyewitness accounts was obviously not an innovation; however, what was new was how the accounts attempted to create and to manage the author's position. In the *Case,* the accounts create the impression that the Town's daily life revolves around the magistrate's text. For example, all six accounts are notarized by Fielding's name; that is, Fielding authorizes all six of the accounts as possible versions of the same riot. His authorization of each account not only validates the number of possible points of view, but also constitutes another stylistic technique that creates and manages his new position as magistrate. For example, the "Information" in each account is related by people who hold positions in an administrative model which Bow Street was updating: beadles, constables, high-constables, and tradesmen. This continual retelling of the same story by members of London's traditional administrative apparatus makes Fielding's *Case* subsume that rigid, traditional system. All of the street-level administrators report to Fielding, and they even advertise their subservience to him. For example, Saunders Welch, the "Gentlemen, High-Constable of Holbourn Division" (*Case,* 50), offers a hypersensitive narrative that carefully details Fielding's role in the Penlez Riots:

> And this Informant [Welch] further saith, that on the *Monday* Morning, about Twelve of the Clock, he attended *H. Fielding,* Esq; one of his Majesty's Justices of the Peace for the County of *Middlesex,* who had been out of Town during all the preceding Riot, and acquainted him with it. That immediately the said Justice sent an Order for a Party of the Guards to conduct the aforesaid Prisoners to his House, the Streets being at that Time full of Mob, assembled in a riotous and tumultuous Manner, and Danger of a Rescue being apprehended. And saith, that the above mentioned Prisoners, together with *Bosavern Penlez,* who was apprehended by the Watch in *Carey-street,* were brought before the said Justice, who, after hearing the Evidence against them, and taking the Depositions thereof, committed them to *Newgate.* And this Informant saith, that whilst he attended before the said Justice, and while the Prisoners were under Examination there was a vast Mob assembled, not only in *Bow-street,* but many of the adjacent Streets, so that is was difficult either to pass or repass. (*Case,* 52)

This excerpt is notable for the way Fielding narrates his own participation through an observer's account, and Fielding considers this method to be more objective. As a result, Fielding's magistrate position is born from the words of his employees.

A second function of these accounts is to spotlight the conduct of the mob. The way Fielding characterizes the mob for the purpose of interpreting its social function parallels Fielding's method of characterization in *Tom Jones*. For example, in the six accounts, the mob is constantly represented as a single person, complete with a "Disposition" and character: "And so riotous did the Disposition of the Mob appear that whole Day . . ." (*Case*, 53). This personification is important because it allows Fielding to address the unrest in terms of a conduct that applies to all people in the Town. Fielding regulates the mob by appealing to its definable "Manner." The accounts are particularly attentive to the mob when it displays a specific mannerism: "The Mob . . . continued in a very riotous and tumultuous Manner" (*Case*, 49); "at that Time . . . assembled in a riotous and tumultuous Manner" (*Case*, 52). The reason for this repetition of "riotous and tumultuous" is clear when we compare these accounts to Fielding's interpretation of the third definition of a "Riot" from George I's Riot Act: "Persons unlawfully, riotously, and tumultuously assembled together" (*Case*, 43). When "Persons" adopt this "Manner," they officially become "the Mob"; however, Fielding does not use the phrase "riotous and tumultuous" each time the mob appears in the six accounts. This suggests that a "proper" riot (that is, one that is conducted properly and with proper morals in mind) is still possible in the Town. The Penlez Mob, after reaching the number of persons necessary to qualify its actions as "illegal," conducted itself incorrectly due to its intolerance. In this way, Fielding regulates possibility in the Town. Fielding exploits the subjective accounts to manage the infinite range of conducts available to people living in the Town.

The second textual mode that further defines Fielding's administration of the Town involves expectations of reading. In fact, reading distinguishes a proper riot from an improper riot. When the number of rioters exceeds the limit allowed by the Riot Act, the Act requires that the magistrate read the proclamation as a warning. If the rioters do not "[disperse] themselves within an Hour after the Proclamation is read to them by a proper Magistrate" (*Case*, 42), then the magistrate may consider the riot to be improper. The reading of the proclamation was so important that a person's hindering its oral performance was considered villainous by George I's Riot Act:

> 4thly. If any Persons obstruct the Magistrate in reading the Proclamation so that it cannot be read, such Obstruction is made Felony without Clergy; and the continuing together, to the Number of Twelve, after such Let or Hindrance of reading the Proclamation, incurs the same Guilt as if the Proclamation had really been read. (*Case*, 43)

The important point here is that the magistrate is empowered by reading text on Bow Street. In the *Case,* Fielding considers it to be one of the most important laws ever written:

> . . . I shall here repeat the Sentiments of our present excellent Lord Chief Justice, as I myself hear them delivered in the *King's Bench, viz.* That the Branch of the Statute which empowers Magistrates to read the Proclamation for the dispersing Rioters was made, as the Preamble declares, on very important Reasons, and intended to be applied on only very dangerous Occasions; and that he should always regard it as a very high Crime in any Magistrate wantonly or officiously to attempt to read it on any other. (*Case,* 46–47)

This is also the reason why Welch's account carefully remembers the moment Fielding read this proclamation in the Penlez case:

> And this Informant [Welch] farther saith, that he was present when the said Justice [Fielding], from his Window, spoke to the Mob, informed them of their Danger, and exhorted them to depart to their own Habitations: For which Purpose, this Informant likewise went among them, and entreated them to disperse, but all such Exhortation were ineffectual. (*Case,* 53)

In Penlez's case, Fielding evoked textual authority when his "Duty" demanded him to do so. The act of reading contributed to Fielding's administrative discourse because part of Fielding's power as a magistrate stemmed from reading text. Fielding imagined that by performing his writing, he was administering authority. The metaphor of conduct helped Fielding perform authority in the Town, and, in the *Case,* helped to clarify the line between proper and improper conduct.

While concluding the *Case,* Fielding mentions "Zeal," a term also present during the conclusion of the *Charge:*

> But I am willing to see these Clamours in a less culpable Light, and to derive them from a much better Motive: I mean from a Zeal gainst lewd and disorderly Houses. But Zeal in this Case, as well as in all other, may hurry Men too far, and plunge them headlong into the greater Evils, in order to redress the lesser. . . .
>
> When I mention this Zeal as some kind of Excuse or Mitigation, I

would be understood to apply it only to those Persons who have been so weak (at least) to espouse the Cause of these Malefactors: as to the Rioters themselves, I am satisfy'd they had no such Excuse. The Clamour against Bawdy-Houses was in them a bare Pretence only. Wantonness and Cruelty were the Motives of most, and some, as it plainly appeared, converted the inhuman Disposition of the Mob to the very worst of Purposes, and became Thieves under the Pretence of Reformation. (*Case*, 58)

I concentrate on Fielding's "Zeal" since it appears whenever the Town's range of possible conducts becomes endangered. Zeal "may hurry men too far"; it is the condition upon which the Town's possibilities collapse into law. Yet Fielding argues against dictating new laws related to the Penlez Riot; in fact, he tells us that he never wanted to write the *Case* in the first place.

Fielding opens and closes the *Case* by clearly stating that proposing laws is not his job. He begins by calling attention to "that Reluctance with which I am drawn forth to do an Act of Justice" (*Case*, 33), and he concludes by referring to this "Act" as "this ungrateful Task" (*Case*, 60). Fielding supplies two reasons for this reluctance: first, his "Character hath been so barbarously . . . aspersed" by other writers; and second, he wishes Penlez to "be permitted to rest quietly in his Grave" (*Case*, 33–34). This advertised reluctance is not simply an expected, textual mannerism; rather, it constitutes a thin, tonal smokescreen that he maintains throughout the *Case* to generate social credibility for his new position as magistrate. Fielding crafts his revelation of this reluctance. He states that he is "drawn forth" rather than actively choosing to write this piece. His use of the passive voice makes it appear as though the magistrate is forced to step outside his proper position. Fielding comes closest in the *Case* to dictating laws for the Town, and, for this reason, he delivers his proclamations with a certain reluctance in order to salvage what he considered to be the real part of his job: reinterpreting traditional conducts to regulate the Town's public conducts. When his voice surfaces in the *Case*, Fielding adopts a defensive tone, the same tone that appears every time Fielding systematizes the critic-novelist position in *Tom Jones*. The *Case*, therefore, is "novelistic" only in its use of the administrative discourse.

The main function of the *Case* may have been to promote distinctions between modes of civil administration: "the Distinction between an Object of Mercy, and an Object of Justice at last prevailed, to my Satisfaction,

I own entirely, and I hope, now at last, to that of the Public" (*Case*, 60). In its attention to distinction and specialization, *A True State of the Case of Bosavern Penlez* made Town riots possible if they were conducted correctly. The *Case* also explains the Town's conduct to its people. As with the *Charge,* the title of this textual vehicle is important. This work attempts to stabilize the "State of the Case"—not Bosavern Penlez's character or reputation. The textual conduct of the case was Fielding's target; his administrative discourse was again on trial.

Defining Civic Novelty: *An Enquiry*

An Enquiry into the Causes of the Late Increase of Robbers (1751) is Fielding's most famous civil text not because it potentially affected the Town's crime rate but because of the way it is now read. Critics routinely cite *An Enquiry* when trying to reconcile Fielding's novels with his appointment as Bow Street Magistrate. For example, Zirker, in his general introduction, tries to generate a canonical importance for the text:

> The *Enquiry* may be seen as the major result of Fielding's activities as magistrate and as innovating creator of that police force which historians have come to see as the progenitor of Scotland Yard. The *Enquiry* is easily the most distinguished and ambitious of Fielding's social pamphlets . . . and it reflects, within the limits of its context, Fielding's impressive learning [and] his considerable but necessarily imperfect grasp of the implications of the social and cultural changes he perceived to be taking place . . . . [29]

To place this much value on just one of Fielding's civil texts is a bold move since the *Enquiry* is time and place specific, and for this reason, it neither presents any detailed outlines for the Bow Street Runners nor does it prefigure today's Scotland Yard. By stressing Fielding's "considerable but necessarily imperfect grasp" of some sort of undefined "cultural" knowledge, Zirker's introduction presents *An Enquiry* as a text that miraculously embodies abstract and generalized "social and cultural changes." It is difficult to categorize exactly what the *Enquiry* does if we only attend to the work's content rather than its formal strategies for generating knowledge. In this way, the *Enquiry* does not embody a proto-modern reflection of ourselves or our concept of policing; it is specific to the Town of 1751. In fact, *An Enquiry* reimagines and elucidates the Town in order to govern it.

As with the *Charge* and the *Case,* Fielding reinterpreted textual traditions in terms of an administrative discourse. In the *Charge,* Fielding specifically described the Grand Jury's task as "the Business to enquire" (*Charge,* 29). Fielding expands this business in *An Enquiry into the Late Increase of Robbers,* and he designs a way to comprehend "the Late Increase" of crime in the Town. The work is, again, time and place specific, and it stabilizes Fielding's own position as magistrate since the *Enquiry* can serve as an example—or a textual appendix in the employee handbook—of what he expects from his fellow justices of the peace. The enquiry also produces knowledge by providing a forum for "seeking"[30] it out. As I suggested in the previous chapter, John Gay searches for knowledge by using the trope of walking to conduct the reader through the streets of London. Movement, for Gay, represented the action of seeking and recording knowledge; it was an action that defined the eighteenth-century peripatetic poet. "Seeking" knowledge was tied to "visualizing" knowledge. On the microcosmic scale of Fielding's Bow Street, the primary function of the *Enquiry* was to inquire into the nature of civil power and to visualize what aspects constituted "the Public."

The *Enquiry* begins by reviving a history of the English Constitution to make the point "that the Constitution of this Country is altered from its antient State."[31] Against this revived historical narrative, Fielding makes it clear that definitions of power were at stake in the Town. Fielding concentrates on the word "political" in its most basic sense; his use of the word refers to the administration of power. Each "evil" (drunkenness, gaming, luxury, and the nonworking poor) gets its own section, and each section follows the same narrative: presentation of the vice, the history of English law in relation to the vice, and the imperative that the magistrate intervene to update the administration of these vices. What surfaces from this repeated pattern or narrative is not only an interrogation of the causes of each evil, but also a query into the ways administrative power should address them. That is, the form of the enquiry allowed Fielding to write on a discursive level; thus, he could critique the nature of English authority in the Town as well as specific crimes. The magistrate was necessary to critique London's administrative strategies.

Manners stand at the boundary between the political and the moral traditions with which Fielding was working. It is not surprising that Fielding's *Enquiry,* which examines previous ways of administering power, includes conduct as an integral component of "Power":

> Now in this Word, *The Constitution,* are included the original and fundamental Law of the Kingdom, from whence all Powers are derived, and by which they are circumscribed; all legislative and executive Authority; all those municipal Provisions which are commonly called *The Laws;* and, *lastly,* the Customs, Manners, and Habits of the People. These, joined together, do, I apprehend, for the Political, as the several Members of the Body, the animal Oeconomy, with the Humours and Habit, compose that which is called the Natural Constitution. (*Enquiry,* 65)
>
> . . .
>
> The Customs, Manners, and Habits of the People, do, as I have said, form one Part of the Political Constitution; if these are altered therefore, this [Constitution] must be changed likewise; and here, as in the Natural Body, the Disorder of any Part will, in its Consequence, affect the whole. (*Enquiry,* 67)

The above passages make it clear that power partly resides in conduct, in "the Customs, Manners, and Habits of the People." Like Fielding's characterization of the mob in the *Case,* the Constitution, the management of power itself, is humanized here and given "Customs, Manners, and Habits" that render it "Natural." In conflating the "Natural Constitution" with the "Political Constitution," Fielding represents his job as a natural duty because it uses conduct ("Customs, Manners, and Habits of the People") to administer power.

The *Enquiry* begins to make space visible as it targets a "Commonalty" (*Enquiry,* 73) and tries to specify "the Public." Fielding never outrightly defines what he means by "the Public," but he does clearly define "the Commonalty" by illustrating the archive of conduct that this group inhabits. The conducts he describes were common to the Town at mid-century:

> Now what greater Temptation can there be to Voluptuousness, than a Place where every Sense and Appetite of which it is compounded, are fed and delighted; where the Eyes are feasted with Show, and the Ears with Music, and where Gluttony and Drunkenness are allured by every Kind of Dainty; nay where the finest Women are exposed to View, and where the meanest Person who can dress himself clean, may in some Degree mix with his Betters, and thus perhaps satisfy his Vanity as well as his Love for Pleasure? (*Enquiry,* 79)

Fielding's question is rhetorical; these conducts define the Town. Fielding never directly mentions the Town, yet his catalogue of conducts make the "Place" visible. Following this maneuver, references to "the Commoner" subtly change to "the inferior Tradesman" (*Enquiry,* 80). Fielding's alteration of diction is a stylistic way to address the demographic makeup of the realm surrounding Bow Street, a place where conducts of Court and City intermingle to constitute a new "Commonalty." Indeed, one of the hidden tasks of the *Enquiry* is to stabilize the identity of the people who fall under the Bow Street Magistrate's jurisdiction.[32] For Fielding, "the Commonalty" refers to people; "the Public" refers to the matrix of power that Fielding uses the *Enquiry* to reimagine and reinforce. He addresses issues in which "the Public becomes interested, and consequently the Legislature is obliged to interpose" (*Enquiry,* 78) to maintain "the Public Safety" (*Enquiry,* 172). The mercantilism of the city, the vagabonds of the country, and the misled nouveau riche of the Court constitute a "common" threat to quotidian stability, which is alluded to in the phrase "the Public." To maintain this stability, the *Enquiry* seeks ways to administer "the Public" to the Town's "Commonality."

To outline strategies for exercising administrative power in the Town, Fielding organizes the *Enquiry* around a narrative that "trace[s]" the past, present, and future of a Town tainted by uncontrollable luxury "which *Rome* itself had run before it; from virtuous Industry to Wealth; from Wealth to Luxury; from Luxury to an Impatience of Discipline and Corruption of Morals, . . . [and to] its original Barbarism" (*Enquiry,* 74). Rome's historical narrative underwrites Fielding's Town, and he concludes the *Enquiry* by proposing to intercept this historical narrative:

> Thus, I have, as well as I am able, finished the Task which I proposed, have endeavoured to trace the Evil from the very Fountain-head, and to shew whence it originally springs, as well as all the Supplies it received, till it becomes a Torrent, which at present threatens to bear down all before it.
>
> And here I must again observe, that if the former Part of this Treatise [addressing robbery, gaming, and drunkenness] should raise any Attention in the Legislature, so as effectually to put a Stop to the Luxury of the lower People, to force the Poor to Industry, and to provide for them when industrious, the latter Part of my Labour [addressing manners of execution] would be of very little Use; and indeed all the Pains which can be taken in this latter Part, and all the Remedies which can be devised,

> without applying a Cure to the former, will be only of the palliative Kind, which may patch up the Disease, and lessen the bad Effects, but never can totally remove it. (*Enquiry*, 171–72)

The guiding assumption in this conclusion is that the Town's criminal narrative can be derailed. "If" customs of luxury are properly addressed, then Fielding suggests that executions will not be necessary. "If" customs of luxury are ignored, then Fielding can suggest ways to systematize the proper conducts of executions. The *Enquiry* offers a catalog of corrective solutions that readers can use to derail Rome's apocalyptic narrative in London. Interception is not Fielding's job as Bow Street Magistrate; he simply enables others to make this interception.

Finally, similar to Gay's self-conscious maneuvering at the close of *Trivia,* Fielding uses the *Enquiry* to clarify the function of his new position. Fielding never represents his position as a "professional" office. Bow Street is instead an administrative realm separate from those of established professions: "The mere Lawyer, however skilful in his Profession, who is not versed in the Genius, Manners, and Habits of the People, makes but a wretched Politician" (*Enquiry,* 66). To be Bow Street Magistrate, it is not enough to be "skilful in" a "Profession"; instead, one must manage the "Genius, Manners, and Habits of the People." Fielding delegates to himself an authority beyond that of professionalization:

> It is a common and popular Complaint, that the Justices of Peace have already too much Power. Indeed a very little is too much, if it be abused; but, in truth, this Complaint proceeds from a Mistake of Business for Power: The Business of the Justice is indeed multiplied by a great Number of Statues; but I know not of any (the Riot Act perhaps excepted) which hath all enlarged his Power. And what the Force of that Act is, and how able the Magistrate is, by means of the Civil Power alone, to execute it in any popular Commotion, I have myself experienced. But when a Mob of Chairmen or Servants, or a Gang of Thieves and Sharpers, are almost too big for the Civil Authority to suppress, what must be the Case in a seditious Tumult, or general Riot of the People? (*Enquiry,* 72–73)

The phrase "a mistake of Business for Power" exposes a crucial distinction that Fielding makes while creating and regulating the position of magistrate. The magistrate's "Business" is to perform duties; however, "Power" refers to something much more complicated. The Bow Street Magistrate has the power to regulate, or even support, the Town's possible conducts, and Fielding recognizes that no other established profession can address this issue. Fielding promotes a completely different practice using the discursive model we see in *Tom Jones;* he develops an "administrative" practice.

By "administrative practice" I mean Fielding's systematized "Method" for presenting alternative endings and alternative conducts. When Fielding writes the *Enquiry*, the moment is ripe for distinguishing and specifying this new type of administrative power:

> In plain Truth, the principal Design of this whole Work, is to rouse the CIVIL Power from its present lethargic State. A Design which alike opposes those wild Notions of Liberty that are inconsistent with all Government, and those pernicious Schemes of Government, which are destructive of true Liberty. (*Enquiry*, 73)

As in the *Charge*, the Magistrate's duty operates on a discursive level—that is, on the level of administering power to others through printed text. His decision to aggrandize the power of the magistrate is entirely consistent with his conceptualizing the areas of his jurisdictions in terms of conduct. Fielding dispenses with antiquated legal machinery that has failed to update itself to deal with the Town's contributions to an image of London. At the same time, Fielding's version of administrative power subdues at least one possibility: "Anarchy." This new, middle-of-the road practice creates and manages power while maintaining a constant discussion of alternative endings. Fielding explicitly phrases these administrative goals in terms of civil power in the preface to the *Enquiry:* "[T]he Power of the Commonalty hath received an immense Addition; and that the Civil Power having not increased, but decreased, in the same Proportion, is not able to govern them" (*Enquiry*, 73). "Rous[ing]" the "Power" does not mean reviving a previously defunct administrative model; instead, it signifies a need for the magistrate to launch a temporary mechanism—a project—that will make the power of the Bow Street Magistrate exceed the commonalty's power. In Fielding's specific case, this temporary mechanism consists of printed text and the metaphor of conduct. Printed text, and its proliferated use in Fielding's office, is the new technology for "rousing CIVIL Power"; it is the means by which he can force new modes of government to apply, or to catch up to, the Town's population. Textual technology eventually brings the Bow Street Runners into being; however, this model is only temporary. Scotland Yard is not yet necessary.

Fielding exploited the administrative possibilities of the eighteenth-century charge, case, and enquiry, as he did those of the eighteenth-century novel, to create and manage a way of publicizing his own behavior and social function. In combination with the self-defining potential Fielding saw in textual traditions of civil prose, the metaphor of conduct generated public credibility. Fielding's civil prose, in accruing social authority by rearranging readers' expectations, made the writer of the Town a newly visible and credible component of London. Thus, Fielding's Bow Street prose suggests a more complex London in which writers and publishers perform a specific social function: they provide readers with the moral instructions necessary to interpret urban surroundings and their occupants properly. Although Fielding was able to accomplish this instruction from a position outside traditional professionalized and authoritarian practices, the stylistic manner in which he acquired credibility as a textual magistrate suggests that urban planning was exercised in the Town during the mid-eighteenth century, even if this planning operated on the imaginative level of metaphor. Although these metaphors were conveyed in printed text, Fielding imagined that they were powerful enough to effect social change by operating in his readers' minds. Not surprisingly, Fielding's Bow Street project was designed concurrently with the 1751 appearance of Westminster Bridge. In the next chapter, I address how poets tried to reimagine poetic traditions so that they could participate in building London's projects for urban improvement.

3

Pope, Westminster Bridge, and Other Imaginative "Things of Use"

This chapter begins by questioning an epigraph's function—specifically, the epigraph to an architectural proposal written in London during the 1730s—and concludes by considering how epigraphs help us understand the literary strategies that eighteenth-century writers developed to reimagine London. Epigraphs, or excerpts of text read in entirely new contexts, are interpretative puzzles since several different critical schools offer several different ways to frame an epigraph's function. For example, the epigraph may be an essential device for influencing the way a reader experiences a text. As a political disclaimer, the epigraph is a suggestive tool, whispered to readers as they pass through the formal threshold of the text and impressing upon them a specific way of reading. In another case, a writer could use the epigraph less intrusively and not require the reader's recognition. Perhaps the epigraph merely alludes to another text with which the writer has an extremely personal or even subconscious association. But the epigraph could also signify a writer's attempt to efface the epigraph's original author and to strike out in a new direction via a Bloomian misreading of the original text. All of these possibilities seem valid when we first approach the epigraph that emblazons the title page to Nicholas Hawksmoor's 1736 *Proposition for a New-Stone Bridge at Westminster:*

> Bid Harbours open, Publick Roads extend,
> Bid Temples Worthier of the Gods ascend;
> Bid the Broad Arch the Dangerous Flood contain,
> The Mole projected break the Roaring Main;
> Back to his Bounds their Subject Sea command,
> And roll obedient Rivers through the Land;

> These Honours, Peace to happy BRITAIN brings;
> These are Imperial Works, and worthy Kings.¹

Although these lines present a litany of epic commands calling for a national project of British public works, they are even more noteworthy because Alexander Pope wrote them. By citing the final eight lines to Alexander Pope's *To Richard Boyle, Earl of Burlington,* Hawksmoor encourages readers to ask several questions from several disciplinary standpoints. From the architectural standpoint: why did Hawksmoor, a hard-core devotee to the baroque architectural school, quote Pope, a poet who seemed to promote Palladianism, the inveterate enemy to Hawksmoor's baroque school? From the biographical and interdisciplinary standpoint: how did Pope react to his being cited by a writer who was not a man of letters? From the literary standpoint: how should we read these eight lines in relation to Pope's entire literary career and his "stages" of poetry? Or, from a New Critical standpoint: what does Hawksmoor, an architect, have to do with Pope, a poet?

I argue in this chapter that the significance of Hawksmoor's Popean epigraph, and in turn, Pope's contribution to imaginative government, may be viewed from a critical perspective that takes into account all of these questions as well as the standpoints that ask them. By citing a Popean epistle, Hawksmoor was not shattering any disciplinary boundaries; he instead enlisted himself in a common interpretative project of the mid-eighteenth century that did not distinguish between poet and architect. Indeed, much of the standard critical work surrounding Pope's *Epistle to Burlington* notes the similarities between Pope's cultivating function in the poem and the architect's (in the city) or gardener's (in the country) cultivating functions for the British nation.² The conjoined title of Maynard Mack's *The Garden and the City* reminds us that Pope's concept of cultivation, due to its metaphoric flexibility, nurtured not only individual identity but also participation in an imaginative community as well.³ Indeed, Pope began imagining himself as a poetic conductor through London's geography as early as *An Essay on Criticism* (1711): "For diff'rent Styles with diff'rent Subjects sort, / As several Garbs with Country, Town, and Court."⁴ In the *Essay,* Pope casts writers as poet-critics—figures whose creativity *is* their didacticism.⁵ By yoking the poet to the critic, Pope does not distinguish between creative writing and literary criticism; as a result, the poet-critic guides, reigns, and rules in readers' imaginations. As in *The Rape of the Lock,* the poet-critic creates this imaginative kingdom since the poet-critic evinces "faith in the power of poetry to restructure a world" as well as encourages "interpretive battle."[6] From these socially situated and imaginative perspectives, an important question arises: in what ways may we interpret Hawksmoor's adoption of Pope's poetry as evidence of Pope's attempt to "restructure a world" and solicit "interpretive battle"? Just how did Pope's poem shape London's cityscape?

The answers to these questions involve how the *Epistle to Burlington* tries to reimagine London by reimagining the formal and moral traits of verse. In particular, Pope reassesses the verse epistle and the status of wealth in London during the 1730s. Consider, for instance, the functional parallels that Pope might identify between the classical verse epistle, the essay, and the economically motivated project. Similar to conduct-books in they way they fulfilled functions that eighteenth-century readers expected from urban writers, the urban project and "Projector" were infamously familiar to eighteenth-century readers in London.[7] But eighteenth-century projectors need not be stereotyped as polemicists or writers of propaganda whose social value is suspect due to their supposedly hidden, political agendas. As Joyce Kennedy, Michael Seidel, and Maximillian Novak clarify, Defoe's *An Essay upon Projects* (1697) strove to bathe "projectors in a potentially positive light":

> Defoe's more productive projector, his merchant entrepreneur who through wit and ingenuity sustains himself and increases the wealth and well-being of his nation in the process, vies for supremacy throughout *An Essay upon Projects* with the greedy throw-back projector of a more insidious nature—unscrupulous, greedy, and maddened. . . . What he does for the term "projector," he will do for the systems he projects upon: he will "essay" to make them worthy.[8]

By focusing upon the positive economic ramifications of a newly redefined projector, Defoe's *Essay* relates to Hawksmoor's Westminster Bridge as well as Pope's *To Burlington* in two specific areas: the use of wealth and the art of essaying. First, the proposition for a bridge at Westminster was a highly contested topic for Londoners for a variety of reasons, not the least of which involved the future of British trade. Since 1176, London Bridge had been the only bridge of the urban environment, and both cities, Westminster and London, used it to traverse the Thames and to access the traditional heartland of England's southern landscape. London Bridge was anchored on its north side to the City of London and crossed to the southbank at Southwark; thus, the bridge was, literally, a City-based monument and praised as a lifeline for British trade.[9] Westminster had no direct access to its southbank, Lambeth, save by the leaking, incommodious ferries that dotted the shores of the Thames. Therefore, as seventeenth-century politicians contemplated the idea for a bridge at Westminster, residents of the City became defensive. To combat Westminster's plans, the City based its reasoning (or hatred) in economic terms and stressed the ruin that a bridge at Westminster would bring to the ancient marketplace of England and the stronghold of the new Great Britain. The *Daily Journal,* however, advertised the other side of what by then became interpreted as purely an economic project:

> It is computed that when the new Bridge is built from Lambeth to Westminster, provisions will be sold at least 20 per Cent cheaper than they now are in all the Markets from Temple Bar to Hide Park Corner, as well as in Westminster.... [V]ast quantities of Fish, Fowl, Beef, Mutton, &c. which comes from Kent, Surry, and Sussex, are (for want of another Bridge) obliged to come over London Bridge so that the out Markets are served at second hand.[10]

According to this excerpt, Westminster Bridge should be seen almost entirely in terms of money rather than as a romanticized public-works project conducted for the good, and use, of all people. Pope would work to change this debate. In this way, the issue of Westminster Bridge is a "project" in the commercialized terms that Defoe uses in his *Essay.*

The second connection between Defoe's projector, Hawksmoor, and Pope, involves the status of the essay form during the early eighteenth century. Defoe's conception of the "entrepreneur-projector" is made possible by the literary form in which he reconceives this projector: the essay. If we recall that one of the meanings available to eighteenth-century readers of the verb "to essay" is "to attempt," then we may begin to understand not only the reasons for why Pope's poem is a verse essay, but also its connections to Hawksmoor's architectural attempt to span the Thames. As I argue in this chapter, Pope's *To Burlington* is an epistle essay in the Horatian tradition with all of its accompanying ironies and contradictions, as well as a definably English essay on "the Use of Riches"—an essay in which Pope "essays," interprets, and experiments with London's trade-based wealth. It is at this generic intersection of the essay and the project that Pope's poem attempts to shape London's geography. And I claim that

Hawksmoor's *Proposition* suggests that other readers understood Pope's poem in this manner as well. Therefore, rather than discounting the projector as a "bad" writer, I suggest that it may be more productive to trace how literary writing (or "Literature," as it was broadly conceived) borrowed the socio-political aims of eighteenth-century projectors to become gatekeepers of imaginative writing.

By evoking the phrase "imaginative writing," I want to recover the crucial differences that eighteenth-century readers and writers made between projects and utopias. Eighteenth-century projects are not utopias, and the reason for this distinction is that projects explicitly referred to London's local conditions. Projectors anchored their plans to London's administrative geography; their imaginative writing detailed and extended an existing place rather than "no place" (the literal definition of "utopia"). In this way, certain writers previously associated only with literary writing may be seen to resemble projectors since both figures produce texts that are to be interpreted in a type of realm that is neither purely real nor purely imagined.[11] Even if writers used fiction to convey these alternate modes of government to readers, this does not mean that their metaphors, literary styles, and governing rhetoric lacked social efficacy. In fact, straddling this boundary between the real and the artificial, eighteenth-century writing about London constitutes one piece of evidence that enables twentieth-century conceptions about civic community, liberalism, and governmentality to be theorized.

Moral-Ethical Essay-Epistles to Several Persons?

The first task of this chapter is to show how Pope's *To Burlington* outlined for Londoners something that was, during the 1730s, initially more valuable than architectural theory. In particular, *To Burlington* began a project that tried to design a new and definably British imagination that could resolve the tension between Court and City. Pope's attitude towards imagination has always been contested partly because the view of the imagination as a positive and creative faculty is supposed to be a romantic discovery.[12] Within the last two decades, however, a body of critical work has tried to sketch an eighteenth-century version of imagination by opening up discussions of what constituted an imaginative act before Coleridge and Wordsworth.[13] Eighteenth-century imagination has therefore come to resemble a socially complex and multifaceted issue that is distinct from the romantic reincarnation we have come to know so well. This chapter builds upon these ideas by stressing the otherness of the eighteenth-century imagination, but departs from it as I focus on the way Pope disciplined this complexity to accomplish a very specific task during a crucial moment of London's urbanization.[14] This task was to render wealth useful to an area of London that had grown allergic to a trade-based economy. In particular, the City of Westminster's proposition for a new bridge must have been unimaginable to those living in the City of London. This task was also imaginative because it required Pope to reconceptualize not only the value that Westminster had been attaching to trade but also the textual forms that would allow him to enact this reconceptualization.

The second task of this chapter is to analyze how these strategies enabled Pope to reimagine himself as a governor or an interpreter of British society. That is, *To Burlington* does not simply conduct us to a proper, moral imagination; it also calls our attention to the figure performing this imagination. Pope seemed to acquire administrative authority because he presented himself as an interpreter who clarified for Britons the problems and textual traditions that they had inherited from Rome. Pope, however, cast these problems and traditions in newly British as well as urban terms. As a result of this interpretative performance, Pope shored up the poet as a figure who was essential to understanding and making decisions about London's social, economic, and physical infrastructure. From our perspective, we can see how an eighteenth-century version of imagination not only allowed Pope to adjust British values, but also enabled him to envision himself as a new species of social authority.

This poem is ostensibly about neither urban architecture nor "the urban architect," and that is Pope's point. Richard Boyle, the third Earl of Burlington, rallied to promote Palladianism as London's architectural standard, and as a result, he tried to establish a "national Taste" for a burgeoning architectural industry in Britain.[15] Palladianism was, in every sense of the word, a project for Burlington; he, with the help of those architects enjoying his patronage, promoted Palladianism as Britain's only possible future. Pope also enjoyed Burlington's patronage; however, *To Burlington* is a dubious paean to Palladianism. In fact, the poem's "ambivalences and contrarieties," which Julian Ferraro outlines, cast Burlington as "the victim of changes in the tone and emphasis of the poem which leaves his status as an example within the emerging structure increasingly open to question."[16] The context in which Pope published *To Burlington* is partly to blame for these Palladian interpretations. This context is complex and involves at least three interrelated issues: the connection of *To Burlington* to a Roman precedent; the almost infinite number of revisions Pope made to at least four published versions of the poem; and Pope's inability to stick to a consistent title for not only *To Burlington* but also the other epistles he wrote between 1730 and 1734.

For Pope, a discussion about architecture was inseparable from debates over social conduct and moral philosophy. Pope casts these debates in those seemingly familiar capitalized, universal abstractions: Taste, Sense, and Nature. In the argument of *To Burlington,* Pope clarifies that this poem about "the Use of Riches" will be "Instanced in Architecture and Gardening." Architecture is merely an instance or an example of Pope's larger concern: "the Use of Riches." I claim that rather than waging a war over architecture, *To Burlington* initiates a debate over "Use." Proper "Use," another abstraction capitalized by Pope, is at stake in this poem along with, secondarily, its different manifestations: literary, architectural, and economic. Rather than looking for Pope's hidden references to Vitruvian or early modern theories of architecture, we may instead view Pope's poem through the lens of what eighteenth-century readers would have recognized as a classical generic template: the epistle. Consistencies of form, rather than content, made this poem legible to an eighteenth-century audience trained to read classical templates. Interpreting the poem in this manner, we can see Pope's agenda, which was to translate Horace's epistle into an English essay, in terms of Burlington's agenda, which was to translate Palladio into a British environment. In both cases, London was projecting itself upon, or reimagining, Rome.

Thanks to the work of Mack and Julian Ferraro, we have hypersensitive analyses of the changes Pope made to his manuscript before its publication.[17] Ferraro's study has taken this sensitivity to another level, stressing that we cannot ignore that at least four different versions of *To Burlington* were published during Pope's lifetime.[18] The idea that many literary critics have been discussing completely different poems while referring to a single, nonexistent *To Burlington* is noteworthy, and this has undoubtedly led to misreadings that do not take into account the number of times Pope felt it necessary to recast this poem to accomplish different yet equally important tasks.[19] Thus, another complicating factor in interpreting *To Burlington* is its complex publishing history.[20]

A final context that is crucial to interpreting *To Burlington* is Pope's anxiety over what he wanted to label the series of four epistles that *To Burlington* initiated. Pope first referred to them as *Epistles to Several*

Persons. He also originally conceived the *Essay on Man* and the four epistles to be two "books" of a larger poem-in-progress, which Pope described as an "ethic work in four books,"[21] entitled *Ethic Epistles*. But in an infamous deathbed anecdote, Pope agreed with Warburton, "to whom he left the task of preparing a complete posthumous edition [of Pope's poems]," that *Moral Essays* would be a more appropriate title.[22] Pope's constant revision suggests that he was particularly anxious about genre and the way these poems were read. The deathbed scene also suggests that the form and content of *To Burlington* needed to be classified, and therefore stabilized, under the heading of "essay" in order for readers to interpret it correctly. Stressing the sensitive connections between *To Burlington* and what it meant to write an essay with Horatian overtones in the 1730s allows us to outline the poem's ostensible goal.

To recognize this goal, I suggest viewing *To Burlington* not as a self-sufficient poem but as the beginning of an imaginative project as we have seen Defoe redefine the word. *To Burlington* is at once a grandly general "moral essay" and an intensely specific epistle written to a patron in the style of Horace. The first part of this interpretation—the poem as a general moral essay—has escaped critics. *To Burlington* is not an important poem because Pope wrote a letter to an architect but because Pope used it to merge Horace with the tradition of the English essay. *To Burlington* presented a new forum in which to debate London's future. It also presented the poet, or more generally the writer, as an agent for realizing this projected future.

Formal Schemes:
From Horatian Epistle to British Essay

To Burlington qualifies as a project because it begins a series of poems that reimagine the poet as a figure who translates classical problems into British terms. For this reason, *To Burlington* neither resolves problems nor presents a single moral. This claim seems counterintuitive at first. Eighteenth-century poetry is supposed to be didactic, prescriptive, and moralistic—not open-ended or exploratory. But Pope eventually labeled the project which *To Burlington* began *Moral Essays* because reading these poems represented, or attempted to stand in for, moral experience.[23] By reading *To Burlington* and becoming entangled in the number of times Pope backtracks, switches tonal gears, and contradicts himself, readers exercised the eighteenth-century equivalent of imagination. This type of imagination seems strange to twentieth-century readers who consider imagination to be merely a creative faculty.[24] Imagination was a tool Pope used to test a reader's decision-making skills. But *To Burlington* does not specify what a correct decision is; rather, the decision-making process constitutes imagination itself. This is why it is useful to label Pope's function in *To Burlington* that of an interpreter. The poem does not solve problems; it translates classical problems into British terms so that Britons can grasp these problems as immediate concerns rather than as antiquated historical phenomena. Thus, *To Burlington*'s goal is accessibility; it brings problems that seem to have no human agents back into the realm of human agency. While reading *To Burlington*, readers gain moral experience, and Pope exercises a moral function that seems essential to Britain's imperial inheritance. To convince his audience that he was the right poet for this job, Pope used two techniques of authorization: formal imitation and nonreferential language. The topic of imitation is its own field in eighteenth-century studies but relates to my argument in the way Pope used classical and English literary templates to accomplish new tasks. Pope, as his title revisions suggest, used form to signal to readers the correct way to approach, or to experience, the poem's content. In particular, Pope recognized how crucial the classical epistle was as a tool for legitimizing, or imagining, his role as national interpreter. He needed to strike a careful balance between reproducing a classical epistle to accrue credibility for his content and deviating just enough from this form to clarify new British values and philosophies. Maintaining this balance is what Pope means by imitation. Pope's self-conscious diction constitutes another technique by which he was able to appear to be performing a function necessary to London's future survival. Together, formal imitation and nonreferential language constitute Pope's tools for establishing an imaginative project that authorized him as London's necessary social interpreter.

To understand the poem's relationship to the eighteenth-century trend of imitation, we need to look at an excerpt from *The Master Key to Popery, or A True and Perfect Key to Pope's 'Epistle to the Earl of Burlington'* (1732), a text that was "never published during Pope's lifetime [and which] masquerades as an attack on Pope but in fact was probably written by him."[25] In *The Master Key*, our fictitious writer voices an opinion about Eastbury, an estate designed by John Vanbrugh for George Dodington. When Dodington died, his cousin, Bubb Dodington, was forced to complete the estate as part of the will regardless of the contemporary contempt for Vanbrugh's baroque style. *The Master Key*'s narrative persona writes:

"It would be like this Poets Injustice, to reflect on a Gentleman's Taste for a thing which he was oblig'd to build on another Man's scheme. . . ."[26] Bubb Dodington was "oblig'd to build" the frivolous Eastbury estate "on another Man's [Vanbrugh and his uncle's] scheme." In other words, Bubb Dodington built without aesthetic discretion, and this earned him a cameo appearance as "Bubo" in *To Burlington:*

> See! sportive fate, to punish aukward pride,
> Bids Bubo build, and sends him such a Guide:
> A standing sermon, at each year's expense,
> That never Coxcomb reach'd Magnificence![27]

Although Pope satirizes Dodington in the poem, the phrase "oblig'd to build on another Man's scheme" calls into question Pope's own role as an imitator of classical poetry. In particular, Pope inherits, or builds upon, Horace's epistle. Unlike Bubb Dodington, however, Pope does not blindly follow precedent. Pope is "oblig'd to build on" Horace's scheme to acquire credibility, but Pope also uses this scheme to reach new, British goals.

Much work has been devoted to tracing parallels between Horace and Pope, so I do not review all of it here. However, to understand how Pope extended Horace's epistle to initiate an imaginative project, a summary of some of these parallels is helpful. Although *To Burlington* does not explicitly state that it imitates Horace, Frank Stack reminds us that Pope had begun to write his imitation of Horace's *Satire II.i* "as a defence of the satire of the *Epistles to Burlington* and *Bathurst.*[28] Thus, *To Burlington* contributed to Pope's imitative career that ended with his conscious imitations of Horace's epistles.[29] Stack offers a descriptive summary of Horace's epistles:

> These epistles have been given the shape of casual conversation: they are purposeful, but they seem to have no purpose. Related to this is the notorious obliqueness of Horace's handling of the "theme," and the equally famous subtlety of his transitions. These characteristics, evident in all Horace's poetry, are used with particular effect in the epistle form of his maturity: it is as if one could not have a "subject" or a "purpose" in writing to a friend.[30]

A subtle elusiveness, which a conversational tone helps to nurture, characterizes Horace's epistle. Stack's summary coincides with R. A. Brower's more detailed comparison of Pope's *To Burlington* to Horace's poetry in general:

> The poem [*To Burlington*] moves along conversationally through exempla of bad taste to reflections and hints on good taste, to the grand narrative-portrait of Timon and the brief epilogue in which Burlington is hailed as the author of "Imperial Works, and worthy Kings." In its broad outline and type the poem is Horatian, as can be seen from the briefly sketched portraits in the first half of the poem, the casual introduction of pieces of doctrine, and the concentration in the second half on a single bad case and its nobler opposite. But the poetic life and the more subtly Horatian quality of the epistle come out in the masterly variation of tones, with all the attendant qualities.[31]

With Stack's and Brower's help, we may identify two parallels between Pope and Horace: conversation and narrative. Indeed, *To Burlington* generates knowledge by resembling a question-and-answer session between the poet and the reader. This question-and-answer scheme not only generates a conversational tone, but also produces knowledge. Pope uses questions to make his satire work. For example, we know what Pope means by "bad Taste" not because he tells us, but because the answers to his questions always involve "a more or less direct allusion to the Roman achievement" as an "ideal civilization."[32] Horace's Rome underwrites *To Burlington*'s value system because Pope employs Horace's own question-and-answer tactics to produce knowledge.

At least the first part of Pope's narrative is Horatian. Pope's narrative involves at least three stages: first, a shouting match between passages of pseudoaphoristic doctrine and negative examples; second, a case study; and third, a *deus ex machina* in which moral philosophy and a proposal ironically save the day.[33] This third part, however, is where Pope deviates the most from the Horatian "scheme." It is also where he is able to accomplish new work that is specific to London. I explicate the poem to detail these first two stages and will address the third stage in a separate section of this chapter.

The poem's first 98 lines constitute a tennis match between positive statements and negative examples. We learn more about Horace's Roman ideal by means of negative examples than through the positive pseudoaphorisms. Consider, for instance, one of the poem's defining couplets: "You show us, Rome was glorious, not profuse, / And pompous buildings once were things of Use" (23–24). The "You" refers to the recipient of this Horatian epistle, Burlington; thus, for architectural historians trained in rhetoric, this couplet appears to be "the poem's imaginative germ, the nucleus of its felt relationships" and its "ideal that ratifies the ironies and makes them meaningful."[34] Although this couplet seems to lay down didactic ground rules, critics rarely cite the lines that immediately follow this supposed moral anchor:

> Yet shall (my Lord) your just, your noble rules
> Fill half the land with imitating Fools;
> Who random drawings from your sheets shall take,
> And of one beauty many blunders make;
> Load some vain Church with old Theatric state,
> Turn Arcs of triumph to a Garden-gate;
> Reverse your Ornaments, and hang them all
> On some patch'd dog-hole ek'd with ends of wall,
> Then clap four slices of Pilaster on't,
> That, lac'd with bits of rustic, makes a Front.
> Or call the winds tho' long Arcades to roar,
> Proud to catch cold at a Venetian door;
> Conscious they act a true Palladian part,
> And if they starve, they starve by rules of art. (25–38)

Pope betrays the couplet's positive tone with a passage of negative examples beginning with the qualifier "Yet." Pope details a cutting irony here; although Burlington tried to improve Britain by composing his "noble" British-Palladian rules on a Roman palimpsest, Burlington's Palladian campaign generated a British industry of "imitating Fools" who, without discretion, copied Burlington's copies of Palladio's "random drawings." In other words, imitation had gone awry. "Another man's Scheme" enters a house of mirrors where substandard copies consume the "noble" original. The irony is that Pope firmly attaches the blame for this imitative chaos to Burlington, the parenthetical "(my Lord)."[35]

Pope also generates irony in this passage by mixing a particularly Latinate, technical diction ("Arcades," "Pilaster," "Arcs," "Ornaments") with mid-eighteenth-century street slang ("dog-hole," "ek'd," "clap," "bits"). As a result, Pope ties Burlington's "noble rules" to ignoble products. In a later passage, this technical diction is purely laughable:

> Behold Villario's ten-years toil compleat;
> His Qunicunx darkens, his Espaliers meet,
> The Wood supports the Plain, the parts unite,
> And strength of Shade contends with strength of Light;
> A waving Glow his bloomy beds display,
> Blushing in bright diversities of day,
> With silver-quiv'ring rills mæander'd o'er—
> Enjoy them, you! Villario can no more;
> Tir'd of the scene Parterres and Fountains yield
> He finds at last he better likes a Field. (79–88)

This highly technical—and foreign ("Qunicunx," "Espaliers")—diction almost supplies us with a baseline of bad taste, but a hyphen-break in line 85 violently throws any conclusions we may have deduced into question. For instance, does the "you" in line 86 refer to the reader, or does it refer to Burlington, the epistle's recipient? Does Pope actually yell at his patron here, gaining supremacy over him? Not only must we navigate Pope's tennis match between pseudoaphorism and negative example, but we must now also interpret, or moralize, sudden exclamations. The effect is disorienting.

The lightning flashes of irony generated by Pope's tonal maneuvering echo a defining trait of the Horatian epistle. In fact, *To Burlington*'s ultimate irony is that Pope never stabilizes architectural precepts; he only seems to do so. Consider how Pope ends the passage cited above with more pseudodoctrine:

> Oft you have hinted to your brother Peer,
> A certain truth, which many buy too dear:
> Something there is more needful than Expence,
> And something previous ev'n to Taste—'tis Sense:
> Good Sense, which only is the gift of Heav'n
> And tho' no science, fairly worth the sev'n:
> A Light, which in yourself you must perceive;
> Jones and Le Nôtre have it not to give. (39–46)

This passage states that "Sense" is a guiding precept. So far, so good. But this clarifies nothing; sense is "something" "which only is the gift of Heav'n" and "which in yourself you must perceive." There is no architectural handbook here, no aesthetic outline. Pope even ends this stanza with negative examples: "[Inigo] Jones and [André] Le Nôtre have it not to give." We only learn that an amorphous "Sense" cannot be given to us by other architects; thus, Pope defines "Sense" negatively. I label these seemingly positive statements "pseudoaphorisms" because Pope's Horatian irony never allows readers to locate a serious aphorism. Each time Pope gets close to being didactic, an ironic tone or negative example undermines its seriousness. Pope eludes us here. As he writes a Horatian epistle, he plays a game in which only the losers assign rules. Pope's goal hides in the final two lines of this stanza: "He gains all points, who pleasingly confounds, / Surprizes, varies, and conceals the Bounds." Poetry, for Pope, is one of these practices "where half the skill is decently to hide." In fact, most of Pope's disorienting ironies generate an impression of secret agency. Take, for example, an episode that again sounds entirely didactic:

> Still follow Sense, of ev'ry Art the Soul,
> Parts answ'ring parts shall slide into a whole,
> Spontaneous beauties all around advance,
> Start ev'n from Difficulty, strike from Chance,
> Nature shall join you . . . . (65–69)

Richard Steiger raises an interesting question: should we read the verbs "start" and "strike" in line 68 as imperatives or indicatives?[36] The question has no answer. Steiger's point is that Pope's poetry makes it "impossible to tell precisely who the creator is."[37] Like a poetic version of free indirect discourse, Pope's language transports us to a realm where art "confounds" its origin.

When I state, therefore, that *To Burlington* is not a debate about architecture but a debate about the nature of experience itself, I mean that Pope uses Horace's verse epistle to situate his readers in a moral impasse that was to appear "natural" to Londoners, the supposed inheritors of Rome's imperial lineage. As a social interpreter, he is "oblig'd to build upon another Man's scheme" in order to make London conscious of its inheritance and its present foibles. *To Burlington* "surprises, varies, and conceals the Bounds" because it must constitute, and be the site of, a new nation's moral experience. Readers must decide what to do with this disorientation; they must make decisions. Pope merely guides them to what he considers to be the natural and proper interpretation of their society's present value problems.

The second narrative stage, (the case study of Timon's villa), exemplifies this point. Stack, while analyzing Horace's epistles, notes that Horace is always conscious of his position as poet, and the Timon scene in *To Burlington* shows Pope's inheriting this self-consciousness.[38] By positioning his appearance precisely at the dinner scene and immediately following the tour of the pseudolibrary, Pope suggests that his target is British consumption. Our poet suddenly appears to "curse such lavish cost" (67). We should note, however, how careful Pope is to place the blame for his being "sick" on one cause: Timon's "civil Pride" (66). "Civil Pride" is a curious phrase; it yokes the politics of a civil society, which would include liberal governmentality, to one of Pope's great universal, capitalized abstractions. I focus on this "civil Pride" because it sickens Pope just three lines before he sanitizes *To Burlington* of its Horatian irony. In addition, when Pope begins another stanza with "Yet hence the Poor are cloath'd," he enters Bernard Mandeville's realm of economic self-interest. It is as though a new poem begins with the "Yet" in line 169, and this impression is a symptom of Pope's break with Horace. A new type of economic and definably British irony replaces Horace's classically playful, "pleasingly confounding" version.

What we finally learn from comparing Horace to Pope is that Pope used Horace's epistle to generate versatility, irony, and open-endedness. It is fitting that Pope chose lines from the tenth satire of book two of Horace's *Satires* as his epigraph to the *Moral Essays* to stress this versatility (here translated): "You also need a style now grave, often gay in keeping with the role, now of orator, or poet, at times of the wit, who holds his strength in check and husbands it with wisdom."[39] Pope uses Horace to preserve a type of *concordia discors* in eighteenth-century poetry. But eighteenth-century imitation did not mean plagiarism. How often we forget that eighteenth-century imitation was not strictly *mimesis,* but novelty. Horace gave Pope a template for producing irony, but Pope extended the boundaries of this template by alluding to the English tradition of the essay.

The eighteenth-century essay relates to the Horatian epistle because both forms nurture thematic versatility, irony, and experimentation. Like its three sister epistles, *To Burlington* projects readers onto an uncomfortable poetic and often satiric landscape where they, as Britons, face unanswered philosophical and social problems that had plagued classical civilizations and were now threatening London in new ways. Our inability to locate an episode where Pope is completely serious is unsettling, but it is completely consistent with the genre of an epistle essay. We also need to view

To Burlington in terms of an essay because, while interpreting the *Moral Essays,* twentieth-century critics have dropped Pope's original co-titles: the "Epistle to Cobham, or, Of the Knowledge and Characters of Men"; the "Epistle to a Lady, or, Of the Characters of Women"; the "Epistle to Bathurst, or, Of the Use of Riches"; and the "Epistle to Burlington, or, Of the Use of Riches." These titles (beginning with "Of") squarely situate these poems in the tradition of mid-eighteenth-century essays. These details suggest that Pope wanted his readers to approach *To Burlington* as an essay or philosophical conversation, an approach that Pope's Horatian epistle also fortifies. We may therefore view *To Burlington* not only as a Horatian epistle with all of its accompanying ironies and contradictions, but also as "Of the Use of Riches"—an essay in which Pope "essays," experiments, performs, and interprets a new social condition: trade-based wealth.

A Return to the City: From "Taste" to "Use"

Viewing *To Burlington* as an essay, we may begin to see Pope reinterpreting Horatian irony to suggest a completely British irony: just as wealth underwrote this poem dedicated to an architect (Pope's patron), unprecedented luxury underwrote London's physical infrastructure. London looked the way it did, Pope may have anxiously claimed, because of self-interest rather than because it was a chosen "City of God." *To Burlington* therefore constitutes an imaginative project first to clarify, or interpret, this irony and then to outline a way to resolve wealth's ironic influence by making it useful to the imagination. This essay is, after all, "Of the Use of Riches."[40] Of course, much has been written about Pope's ambiguous relationship to British trade, but I mean "wealth" here in the sense that Pope would have recognized. To Pope, wealth was a philosophical, political, and economic phenomenon intimately tied to London's imperial role. In this sense, wealth plays into the eighteenth-century trends of moral philosophy and liberal governmentality—two trends that the mid-eighteenth-century essay frequently addressed. David Hume, for example, began publishing his essays in 1740. This date is important because it punctuates the two different titles of Pope's epistle sequence. Pope referred to these poems as *Epistles* during the 1730s and then changed the title to *Moral Essays* just before his death in 1744.

Hume's examples of the genre suggest that the mid-century essay represented a textual technology with great potential.[41] As Mary Poovey explains, the essay was "a dialogic, self-refining style [that could] supplement, or even compensate for, the limitations of experimental moral philosophy":

> Like experimental moral philosophy, the essay was a genre in which eighteenth-century writers explored both human motivation and its relation to liberal governmentality. Unlike philosophers, however, essayists did not produce systematic knowledge so much as they engaged readers in the exercise of that discrimination by which (self-) government was assumed to proceed. . . . Indeed, because it both sought to generate knowledge—in the form of a conversation—and elicited identification with a more or less particularized speaker, the essay constituted the generic bridge between experimental moral philosophy and the novel, where yet another mode of knowledge production was being codified.[42]

The essay could easily incorporate Horace's conversational style into its agenda and was tied to the generic problems (the "generic bridge[s]") that Pope faced throughout his career. From Pope's perspective, the essay privileges moral discrimination and experience over "systematic knowledge"; thus, writing an essay at this time was irretrievably tied to the mechanisms of government. By calling *To Burlington* a "moral essay," Pope is able to reimagine himself as a discriminating, interpretative governor over London's populace. Pope was again "oblig'd to build on another man's Scheme"; however, this scheme was an English one.

As suggested by these examples, Pope's formal imitation was a strategy of authorization that allowed him to accomplish new goals. One of the immediate goals of this poem was to change the nation's vocabulary. In fact, the disorientation that we experience while reading this poem is actually a symptom of Pope's assigning new meanings to words. Pope's semantic adjustment centers upon two words: "Taste" and "Use."[43] Most of *To Burlington*'s pseudoaphorisms use one of these two words; "Taste" saturates the first two narrative stages of the poem, and "Use" dominates the final narrative stage involving the moral proposal. The poem's publishing history corroborates this linguistic shift. *To Burlington* appeared as "Of Taste" in 1731, but Pope revised the title in his 1735 *Works* to "Of the Use of Riches." The result is that "Use"—with all of the new meanings and values Pope assigns to it—subordinates "Taste." This shift was necessary because it allowed Pope to assign a new imaginative function, or use, to wealth's influence over London's infrastructure. In *To Burlington*, Pope's diction changes just as his Horatian scheme transforms itself at the end into an essayistic one. Pope's language and his form are irretrievably interrelated.

To Burlington juggles four moral abstractions at once: taste, sense, nature, and use. These words carry different and subtle nuances throughout Pope's career; however, in *To Burlington,* Pope privileges "Use" above the rest. In fact, Pope's entire point in writing *To Burlington* is to hunt down words to describe, as best he can, an almost indescribable and nameless moral function that he can attach to wealth. Pope needs to clarify the "Use of Riches," and he does so by questioning whether "Taste," "Sense," and "Nature" are the proper conceptual vehicles to convey wealth's moral function to his readers. *To Burlington* is a search for the right words; it is an essay in lexicography.[44] When the right words cannot be found, Pope assigns new meanings to old ones. Consider, for example, the poem's most famous pseudoaphorism: "You show us, Rome was glorious, not profuse, / And pompous buildings once were things of Use" (23–24). Although this couplet appears early in the poem, it interrupts the passage listing sensationalized figures of bad "Taste": Virro, Sir Visto, Ripley, Bubo. Seventeen lines later, "Sense" subordinates "Taste": "Something there is more needful than Expence, / And something previous ev'n to Taste—'tis Sense" (41–2). This couplet literally translates the values that the poem is generating; it translates those values formerly associated with "Taste" into "Sense." Our interpreter does not dictate precepts in these pseudoaphorisms but realigns old words in a new hierarchy.

Pope determines that "Sense" is an insufficient word to describe the poem's central concern, and he immediately qualifies his use of it: "Good Sense, which only is the gift of Heav'n, / And tho' no science, fairly worth the sev'n" (43–4). "Sense" is "no science," but reluctantly equivalent. Six lines later, "Nature" constitutes an alternate term: "In all, let Nature never be forgot" (50), and in the Timon episode, "The suff'ring eye inverted Nature sees" (119). William Gibson sees Pope's "Nature" as a unifying principle: "'Nature' was as much the 'aesthetic norm' in architectural theory as in literary criticism, and its meanings were very similar in both disciplines. Nor was 'Use' an entirely different basis for aesthetic and moral judgment from 'Nature'; they were, in fact, believed to be inseparable."[45] This is comprehensible in extremely general terms of eighteenth-century moral philosophy, but even Gibson overlooks what Pope has been trying to do all along: to render a change in what was "Natural" by changing his diction. In particular, the poem is busy recasting "Use" as a natural, universal quality that governs the meanings of every other abstract noun in the poem. Thus, even after Pope mentions "Nature," he continues to search, to essay, for just the right word.

We previously saw how Timon's case study in luxury abruptly and ironically ends with hateful "civil Pride" and a strange turn towards Mandevillian economics: "Yet hence the Poor are cloath'd, the Hungry fed" (169). Regardless of Pope's opinions about Mandeville, this passage interrupts the poem. This interruption, be it serious or satiric, shatters the self-satisfying case study and brings the reader out of a personal communion with the poet and into an impersonal, distant economic sphere. Adopting the stance of a prophet, Pope suddenly projects us into a different future. Pope continues to employ Horace's question-and-answer motif during this prophecy:

> Another age shall see the golden Ear
> Imbrown the Slope, and nod on the Parterre,
> Deep Harvest bury all his pride has plann'd,
> And laughing Ceres re-assume the land.
> Who then shall grace, or who improve the Soil?
> Who paints like BATHURST, or who builds like BOYLE. (173–78)

Pope's final translation takes the form of a thesis: "'Tis Use alone that sanctifies Expence, / And Splendor borrows all her rays from Sense" (179–80). The parallels that this heroic couplet draws subordinate "Splendor" and "Expence" to privilege "Use alone." Furthermore, the 1731 edition of the poem originally read: "In you, my *Lord,* Taste sanctifies Expence, / For Splendor borrows all her Rays from Sense."[46] Thus, Pope's revisions literally replace "Taste" with "Use." Quite simply, *To Burlington* foregrounds "Use" in every possible way.

If this poem needs any more historicizing, it relates to answering the question why *To Burlington* is an essay on the word "Use." Like the essay, the word "Use" relates to two issues that were crucial to forming London's identity during the 1730s: liberal governmentality and moral philosophy. "Use" relates to these issues because Pope relies upon the word to reconcile—or literally reinterpret—the archive of economic problems associated with "Taste." In terms of moral philosophy, "Taste" brought with it the problem of individual subjectivity. In terms of liberal governmentality, "Taste" was a tool for creating consensus in London after the fall of absolutism. Pope encapsulates these problems of subjectivity and self-interest in one phrase: "civil Pride." Pope, "treated, caress'd, and tir'd," grows "sick of his [Timon's] civil Pride." In this context, "civil Pride" not only refers to the way Timon self-consciously calls attention to his own civility, but also alludes to the new social model around which theories of liberal governmentality attached themselves: civil society. By yoking the word "civil" to "Pride," Pope introduces a new universal abstraction to us and reinterprets a specific type of civility as a universal sin. Thus, *To Burlington* taints a word philosophers used to project new models of government by pairing it with a universal sin (pride) and bringing its self-interested economic terms ("lavish cost") to the surface. The problems posed by subjectivity and economic self-interest seem, at Timon's villa, to pose an irreconcilable and uninterpretable irony that threatens to consume the poem. At this point in the poem, Pope seems to condemn civil society and register its demise in fractured, self-interested people who have nothing in common with their neighbors. It seems as though liberal governmentality has failed to replace sovereignty.

Enter "Use alone." The end of this poem attempts to eradicate the problems associated with subjectivity and self-interest by giving wealth an imaginative function, or in Pope's terms, a proper use. For Pope, "Taste" was too heavily ensconced in these problems; his own use of it was, in fact, tainting his own career and reputation.[47] Instead, the poem employs the word "Use" to yoke the right type of interest to the right type of imagination. Thus, trade-based wealth now becomes useful to society through the work of a moral interpreter, or in Pope's case, a poet. *To Burlington*'s final two stanzas map the value that the Whigs had been attributing to wealth onto the interpreter's imagination. In fact, an "interpreter" appears in these lines as a distantly prophetic and nameless figure:

> His Father's Acres who enjoys in peace,
> Or makes his Neighbour glad, if he encrease;
> Whose chearful Tenants bless their yearly toil,
> Yet to their Lord owe more than to the soil;
> Whose ample Lawns are not asham'd to feed
> The milky heifer and deserving steed;
> Whose rising Forests, not for pride or show,
> But future Buildings, future Navies grow. (181–88)

This is classic georgic revelry, or, in Mack's phraseology, a paean to "agrarian capitalism."[48] But the agent of this ostensible content is an unnamable figure doing a special type of work: interpretation. Pope injects this figure into the poem without warning, and this suggests that the interpreter figure is someone with whom we are already familiar. Not only does this figure translate labor into wealth, but the figure also interprets "rising Forests" as "future Buildings, future Navies." The interpreter's imagination is important here. In Pope's world of landscaping and gardening, readers do not look at England's forests and immediately see wooden townhouses and bulkheads. We cannot interpret our surroundings properly until a figure steps forward and reimagines these trees for us in terms of their wealth-potential. This figure is, of course, crucial to Pope's own position as our poet, for he is our own social interpreter. Pope interprets our surroundings for us, and he determines what we should value. "What we should value" is the basis of Pope's moral technology. Thus, Pope is useful because he imagines things properly.

Our poet ends his introduction of the interpreter figure with an entirely new voice: "Let his plantations stretch from down to down, / First shade a Country, and then raise a Town" (189–90). In this suggestive voice, Pope proposes an intriguing interpretation: country-based labor can build the City. The interpreter's plantations not only "shade a Country," which in this sense means to shelter or protect, but also "raise a Town," which implies physical construction as well as moral instruction. As we return to the City with out interpreter, we should note that Pope's punning increases. Pope fills his lines with double meanings as though to drive readers to seek interpretative help. This maneuver makes the interpreter's ability to see beyond single meanings more valuable. The ability to see multiple meanings where there previously was only one defines the value of Pope's interpreter figure.

The final stanza seems to propose separate didactic commands, but it is actually one long sentence in which Pope again offers proclamations in a suggestive voice:

> You too proceed! make falling Arts your care,
> Erect new wonders, and the old repair,
> Jones and Palladio to themselves restore,
> And be whate'er Vitruvius was before:
> Till Kings call forth th' Idea's of your mind,
> Proud to accomplish what such hands design'd,
> Bid Harbors open, public Ways extend,

> Bid Temples, worthier of the God, ascend;
> Bid the broad Arch the dang'rous Flood contain,
> The Mole projected break the roaring Main;
> Back to his bounds their subject Sea command,
> And roll obedient Rivers thro' the Land;
> These Honours, Peace to happy Britain brings,
> These are Imperial Works, and worthy Kings. (191–204)

This final stanza is a treasure trove for the literary critic because, due to Pope's diction, every line suggests multiple meanings. The "You" in line 191, for example, could refer to Burlington, the reader, or Timon. We cannot specify to whom Pope addresses this stanza because the end of this essay addresses an unknown future. "Jones," "Palladio," and "Vitruvius" seem to be important because they are names of architects, but Pope lists them only to lend credibility to his position as interpreter and to the definition of imagination he outlines in the subsequent lines. Pope does not detail Palladian precepts or Vitruvian rules; he uses these names as signposts to gain attention for what follows.

The most striking characteristic of these concluding lines is the trio of lines beginning with "Bid" (197–99). In the context of this entire stanza, or single sentence, Pope's repetition of the word creates a type of incantation that softens the commands of the first lines ("make falling Arts," "erect new wonders," "the old repair") and adopts a new tone for making suggestions or possibilities. We cannot afford to misread these lines in their full, sentence-long context because this trio changes the entire tone of the sentence. The trio is not instructing readers to open harbors, build temples, and establish bridges but to imagine them. Pope clarifies this distinction in the couplet immediately preceding this trio: "Till Kings call forth th' Idea's of your mind, / Proud to accomplish what such hands design'd" (195–94). That is, until the King asks to see our ideas and plans, we must continually cultivate, adjust, and refine these ideas and plans in our imagination. "Bidding" constitutes an act of proposing, projecting, and, most importantly, refining. Furthermore, pride, a sin Pope had previously associated with civil society, is now reinterpreted as a positive motivation for this bidding: "Proud to accomplish what such hands design'd." Thus, Pope is not dictating rules for architecture; he is sketching, proposing, and exemplifying something much more important: the imagination's moral function.

In this final stanza, Pope redesigns the imagination although he would like us to think that he is simply interpreting its self-evident function for us. For Pope, the imagination is a faculty where "Ideas's of your mind" are constantly refined, redesigned, and reinterpreted. As an example of this faculty, Pope uses the final stanza to resolve the problems of liberal governmentality by adopting the language in which these problems were debated. In highly charged, political language, Pope maps the image of a bridge's construction onto the debate between sovereignty and liberal governmentality. Consider, for example, the final "bid" Pope proposes: "Bid the broad Arch the dang'rous Flood contain" (199). The bridge's stone piers (or "Moles") "projected break the roaring Main" while "back to his bounds their subject Sea command / And roll obedient Rivers thro' the Land" (201–2). Pope's use of the word "subject" is loaded in 1731 with connotations of sovereignty, and it is embedded in the debate over the state's identity: do people derive their identities from being "subjects" to the King or as citizens of a community? What results from this densely metaphorical language is an interpretive house of mirrors: Pope interprets a political debate by mapping it onto a public-works project within the context of a poem about "the Use of Riches." Thus, Pope's metaphors suggest that political debates, public-works projects, and poetry are part of the same interpretative project.

Poised between Mandevillian self-interest and a disinterestedness previously associated with sovereignty, Pope assigns to the imagination a moral duty: to experiment, to essay, and to project. Pope writes *To Burlington* to posit a middle ground in which individual wealth can serve both the monarchy and a civil society. By positioning the King as the person who "calls forth th' Idea's of your mind" (195), Pope maintains a subtle respect for the monarchy's role in a new London. But Pope does not call for a complete return to sovereignty. While he does position the King as the sovereign figure who issues vocations (who "call[s] forth" ideas) to individuals, these ideas still originate in individuals' minds and even their individual subjectivities. Pope's definition of the imagination, as a faculty that allows us to design what we wish but which is ultimately judged by the King, therefore reconciles subjectivity with economic self-interest. In fact, the final couplet plays upon this balance between monarchy and self-rule: "These Honours, Peace to happy Britain brings, / These are Imperial Works, and worthy Kings" (203–4). The "worthy Kings" not only refer to royalty in the sense that these "Honours" are "worth" presentation to Kings, but the phrase also, in the structure of this final line, refers to the "Imperial Works"—London's public works—themselves. These ideas—the imagination itself—possess value; they are "worthy" objects. To Pope, wealth resembles less a tangible banknote than a capitalized, universal abstraction imbued with moral authority. We must remember, "'Tis Use alone that sanctifies Expence"; that is, use "sanctifies," or raises, wealth from a commodity to a value, and then maps this nameless value or "worth" onto the imagination.

It is at this point that we can finally grasp what Pope means by "Use." Horace was, not surprisingly, concerned with the word "use," or *usus,* and employed it to refer to "a kind of historical necessity."[49] The eighteenth century inherited this sense of "use" as an "opportunity, occasion"—a moment when specific things were possible that would become impossible later.[50] This time-sensitive definition of "use" relates to Pope's poem because it suggests that wealth could accomplish tasks specific to London during the 1730s. Pope does not suggest that wealth would eternally benefit London; however, for a very specific moment, and more precisely, for the purpose of imagining the "Town" during this moment, wealth was necessary because it could "call forth th' Idea's of your mind."[51] For Pope, exploitative wealth was not an eternal component of Britain; however, it was necessary in the early 1730s to design a permanent London. Thus, to be "useful" in *To Burlington* is to possess ideas worthy of expense and immediate royal investment. Pope's "Use" is, in this light, a very public concept.

We should remember that Pope wrote the *Moral Essays* during the final stage of his career. If we can map Pope onto the interpreter figure he illustrates in this poem (and we should, given that our poet actually appears in the poem), then Pope's task is to "First shade a Country, and then raise a Town." By this I mean that *To Burlington* began an imaginative project that attempted to "raise the Town." In particular, this project began with "Imperial Works" and ended with the "dread Empire" of *The Dunciad.* If *To Burlington,* as the first epistle to the *Moral Essays,* stands at the threshold of Pope's final stage in his career, then it is one of Pope's most important poems because it accomplished three tasks. First, it defined the poet's function as an interpreter. Second, the poem performed this interpretative duty by exemplifying what ought to constitute an individual's imagination. Finally, the poem tried to accomplish a goal that was very specific to the early 1730s: to make wealth serve this interpretative project via the word "Use." Pope was able to juggle these three tasks simultaneously because he chose a multi-voiced form (the Horatian epistle and the English essay) that allowed him to debate the subtle ironies and blatant problems that liberal governmentality presented to a growing city. Formal imitation not only provided a template for interpreting some very complex problems in London, but it also lent Pope a sense of credibility and authorization. The final stage of Pope's career begins, then, with a poet "oblig'd to build on another Man's scheme." Pope, however, translated "build on" to refer to novelty. During the 1730s, one of Pope's new goals was to render wealth a compatriot, rather than an enemy, in the campaign to help London reimagine its inheritance.

Imagination therefore constituted a project for Pope because it allowed him to believe that he was strengthening, or even linking, the value of text and the value of the British capital. First, Pope advertised imagination as one of the products of reading poetry; it stood in for moral experience as readers were forced to deal with the ironic twists and fine-tuned questions that Pope's text presented to them. Second, Pope exercised this definition of imagination to readjust the social value attached to his own position as poet. Pope was in this way able to reimagine himself as a socially relevant writer whose national *quo warranto* lay in his interpretative talent. This interpretative activity was equally as creative as what we now call the romantic imagination, but was markedly different. Pope's version was valuable because he anchored it to three eighteenth-century strategies of authorization: imitation (Horace, Palladio, Vitruvius); moral philosophy (the essay and theories or problems of individual subjectivity); and liberal governmentality (self-interest). Thus, the type of imagination Pope outlined in *To Burlington* tried to project, or invent, new roles for wealth, inherited textual forms, and the eighteenth-century poet.

Imagining Pope's London and Hawksmoor's Bridge

Throughout the previous section, I have labeled Pope as "London's necessary social interpreter" rather than "Britain's necessary social interpreter" because of the relationship that Hawksmoor's epigraph establishes between Westminster Bridge and *To Burlington*—a relationship that becomes clear when we consider what Pope's lines could possibly contribute to an architectural proposal. Lest we be tempted to read *To Burlington*'s final lines as nothing more than metaphors, Pope mobilizes the ultimate critical tool for guiding our interpretations back to historicizing: the footnote. In fact, Pope's final footnote addresses practically the entire stanza:

> [lns.] 195–204. The poet after having touched upon the proper objects of Magnificence and Expence, in the private works of great men, comes to those great and public works which become a Prince. This Poem was published in the year 1732, when some of the new-built Churches, by the act of Queen Anne, were ready to fall, being founded in boggy land (which is satirically alluded to in our author's imitation of Horace Lib. ii. Sat. 2 [1.119]: Shall half the new-built Churches round thee fall) others were vilely executed, thro' fraudulent cabals between undertakers, offices, &c. Dagenham-breach had done very great mischiefs; many of the Highways throughout England were hardly passable, and most of those which were repaired by Turnpikes were made jobs for private lucre, and infamously executed, even to the entrances of London itself: The proposal of building a Bridge at Westminster had been petition'd against and rejected; but in two years after the publication of this poem, an Act for building a Bridge past thro' both houses. After many debates in the committee, the execution was left to the carpenter above-mentioned (1. 18), who would have made it a wooden one; to which our author alludes in these lines:
>
> *Who builds a Bridge that never drove a pile?*
> *Should Riply venture, all the world would smile.*
> See the notes on that place. (*Imit. Hor., Ep.*, II i 186)⁵²

This footnote is important for three reasons. First, Pope continues to use Horace as a strategy of authorization—even in the critical commentary about his own poem. Pope calls attention to his own Horatian imitations to substantiate *To Burlington* as a factual interpretation of reality. Pope repeatedly draws our attention to his Horatian allusions ("which is satirically alluded to," "which our author alludes"). These allusions, and his advertising them, constitute a foundational strategy by which he authorizes himself as a social interpreter, a figure completely necessary to imagining Britain's future. Second, this footnote assigns agency to his poem: "but in two years after the publication of this poem, an Act of building a Bridge past thro' both houses." It is as though Pope wants us to see *To Burlington* as a proactive element that ultimately influenced the debate over, and building of, a bridge at Westminster. But even more important is how this entire footnote reinterprets *To Burlington* as a poem about London's public works.

Up to this point, I have interpreted the importance of Pope's *To*

Burlington in terms of its strategies of formal imitation. I now argue that this literary critique is necessary in order to contextualize why Hawksmoor used part of the poem's final stanza (the concluding eight lines) as his epigraph to *A Proposition for a New Stone-Bridge at Westminster* in 1736. The case of Pope and Hawksmoor interests me because we need to use an inverted historicism to understand the subtleties of their textual relationship. Instead of approaching Hawksmoor's *Proposition* by means of an elaborate historical context (its partisanship, its impact on London's traffic, Hawksmoor's biographical details), we need to interpret the *Proposition,* and the building of Westminster Bridge, by means of its literary context to comprehend fully what Pope's poetry might have meant to an architect. This type of analysis suggests how integral a role printed text, or even categorical "Literature," was beginning to play in mid-eighteenth-century London. It also suggests how important literary analysis is to understanding or contextualizing eighteenth-century historical events.

Hawksmoor's epigraph begins in the middle of Pope's seemingly endless sentence devoted to reconciling liberal governmentality and sovereignty:

> Bid Harbours open, Publick Roads extend,
> Bid Temples Worthier of the Gods ascend;
> Bid the Broad Arch the Dangerous Flood contain,
> The Mole projected break the Roaring Main;
> Back to his Bounds their Subject Sea command,
> And roll obedient Rivers through the Land;
> These Honours, Peace to happy BRITAIN brings;
> These are Imperial Works, and worthy Kings.[53]

This epigraph ignores, at the very least, the couplet that introduces what I have been calling Pope's trio of imaginative biddings. The effect of this is striking. In Pope's poem, the introductory couplet ("Till Kings call forth th' Idea's of your mind, / Proud to accomplish what such hands design'd" [195–96]) acts as an introductory clause, influencing our reading of the subsequent biddings as actions taking place in the mind rather than as proactive commands. In Pope's version, this couplet also maps the bidding onto a chronological vector; Pope in effect says that *until* the king acknowledges your vocation, you should bide your time refining and perfecting your own, individual imagination. But Hawksmoor's epigraph does not convey this sense and therefore translates Pope's imaginative bidding into didactic commands issued by a god-like, external authority. In terms of Pope's original sentence, the *Proposition* gives us the predicate without the nominative's influence over its tone. Hawksmoor's epigraph boils down to a lesson in contextual clues.

Hawksmoor's epigraph is therefore important for two reasons. First, the epigraph trashes the allusively complex lines that refer to a nameless "You" and that mention Palladian heroes. Noticing this fact, we may witness how Hawksmoor's text shares the value that Pope had previously generated by using formal strategies of authorization. Consciously or not, Hawksmoor also "builds on another Man's scheme" by alluding to Pope's imitative "scheme" as a strategy of authorization. Second, the epigraph spotlights the political diction ("subject," "obedient," "worthy Kings") we have seen governing the poem's conclusion. Hawksmoor's epigraph drops Pope's lines about the vocational power of "Kings," so we might be tempted to claim that Hawksmoor's editing conceals political motives. We might wish to argue that because Hawksmoor was an architect, he could neither vacillate nor "essay." We might say that Hawksmoor, because he was an architect, needed to actualize himself by providing a visible use to society that was not as ambiguous or impractical as the poet's social function. We might also like to claim that by using Pope's words, Hawksmoor was indirectly authorizing himself by means of literary schemes; therefore, the architect was doing a job with more value to society and subordinating the poet's function to his own. Hawksmoor, after all, was trying to build a bridge with plans, schemes, and mathematical equations. But these claims would be erroneous and spurious. Hawksmoor's bridge never was built.[54] Another plan, engineered by Charles Labelye, was instead "call'd forth" and realized.[55] Therefore, although Pope's *To Burlington* and Hawksmoor's *Proposition* may not have resulted in physical products, they did contribute to shaping the terms in which these urban projects were imagined, designed, and made possible.

I do not argue that Hawksmoor's epigraph reveals some larger political affiliation or hidden characteristic about Hawksmoor because this is a much larger and complex argument requiring sociological research. In fact, we cannot attribute to Hawksmoor the sole responsibility for placing Pope's poetry in this *Proposition;* the publisher or any other participant in the *Proposition*'s publication could have easily added these lines without explicit motivation from Hawksmoor himself. Instead, I argue that Hawksmoor's epigraph is an important cultural artifact because it suggests one way in which Pope was read and interpreted by his eighteenth-cen-

CHAPTER 3: IMAGINATIVE "THINGS OF USE" 125

tury readers—in particular, those readers linked to London's architectural practices. In the context of what Hawksmoor's *Proposition* attempts to do to London's cityscape, Hawksmoor's epigraph supports the reading I have just proposed about Pope's reconceiving wealth's imaginative function in the City of Westminster. Thus, while it is difficult (and part of a completely different theoretical study) to determine whether the *Proposition*'s epigraph signifies that Pope's poetry changed London's cityscape, it is possible to analyze the epigraph as a barometer of how wealth's imaginative function, projected by Pope in *To Burlington,* was received and interpreted by those associated with an additional, extralegal institution in London during the 1730s.

Pope's poem—in its ability to incorporate wealth into developing models of liberal governmentality—addressed a cultural tension that was increasingly occupying and interfering with London's daily operation: the tension between the City of London and Westminster. Hawksmoor's epigraph suggests that *To Burlington* shaped the debate over Westminster Bridge, and helped to cast this debate in terms of money and whether it could promote public-works projects that were conducted for the good of all people. As Hawksmoor's epigraph suggests, *To Burlington* offered a way to reconcile wealth and self-interest with an individual's imagination and vocation. The epigraph therefore promotes that Pope be read as a social interpreter whose ideas about the imagination could be of use to an architect who wanted to serve his country. As an imaginative project still on the drawing board in 1736 and not yet "call[ed] forth" by the King, Westminster Bridge was in need of a proper conductor.

In drawing literary as well as cultural conclusions between Hawksmoor's *Proposition* and Pope's *To Burlington,* it is interesting to note how Hawksmoor might have employed certain words in the same way Pope used them in *To Burlington.* For example, Hawksmoor appeals to trade to make his plan attractive to Westminster, and he does so in terms that helped Pope reimagine wealth in *To Burlington:*

> But it is hoped, that the City of London, of such mighty Commerce, and in all other respects, managed with such admirable Police (since it is now so much increased as to be eight Miles in length, the Suburbs included) will not only not oppose, but readily promote another Bridge, for a better Communication of trade, and Joint-advantage of both London and Westminster.
> . . .
> . . . as the Cities of *London* and *Westminster,* &c. and their Suburbs, have

been so enlarged, Necessity and Convenience calls for another Bridge, to expedite and forward the transacting of Business and make it easy for Passengers, whether Citizens, Gentleman, or others of the Country.[56]

Just as Pope advertised himself as a poet-interpreter who helped us to see "Buildings" and "Navies" in the trees of forests, Hawksmoor interprets Westminster Bridge as an urban lynchpin that will be essential to the "Joint-advantage of both *London* and *Westminster.*" "Business" unites "*London* and *Westminster, &c.* and their Suburbs" in Hawksmoor's plan; it makes their unity valuable. Therefore, using Pope's scheme in which wealth possesses an imaginative use, Hawksmoor could imagine or project London's future as a "fam'd Metropolis, and universal Emporium of *Europe.*"[57] We should also compare Pope's sensitivity surrounding the word "civil" to the opening to Hawksmoor's *Proposition* where Hawksmoor addresses governmental regulations, "particularly in those Branches which relate to Commerce, Navigation, Manufacture, and Agriculture, and the Advancement of such Arts, Sciences, and honourable Professions as tend to civilize and profit the Community. . . ."[58] Hawksmoor enjambs "Commerce" with the "Arts and Sciences" and then pairs "civilize" with "profit" when discussing "Community." The paradox of liberal governmentality—self-interest within a community—is at stake here just as it was in Pope's poem. This gestures toward the methods that Pope utilized to make it acceptable, or "moral," to yoke British wealth to imaginative acts, such as the planning of Westminster Bridge, during the 1730s. In the end, Hawksmoor's epigraph suggests a way in which Pope's *To Burlington* began what twentieth-century critics might call an interdisciplinary project that repositioned writers as urban interpreters. These writers, some of whom were poets and architects, interpreted not only the immediate complex social surroundings in terms that readers would be able to understand; they also interpreted textual traditions to lend credibility to their proposals and goals. Pope used Horace to authorize himself as a writer with a new interpretative social function; Hawksmoor also tapped into this literary lineage by mobilizing Pope's definition of the imagination to begin London's translation into an "Emporium of Europe."[59]

PART II

GOVERNING THE SELF

4

Interchapter

THE PRINT-SATURATED CITY

The purpose of this interchapter is to clarify a pivotal moment in London's cultural history when writers, due to a rapidly expanding print culture, moved from imagining that they could govern others to imagining that they could govern an interior self. In particular, late eighteenth-century London differed from its earlier incarnation in at least three ways. First, London's institutional organization had been reconceived. For example, Boswell and Burney's urban framework now included several well-advertised, centralized institutions of authority, such as the Fieldings' Universal Register Office and the Bow Street Runners. The generation that preceded Boswell produced new, extralegal apparatuses that communities of readers now imagined to be assisting as well as governing every late eighteenth-century Londoner's daily existence. Second, Boswell and Burney were raised on the literary techniques, imaginative strategies, and projects of Addison, Pope, Fielding, and Gay. My claim in the preceding chapter is that Pope's eighteenth-century version of imagination not only attaches a new social value to the urban writer, but it also questions the comfortable role that imagination presently plays in attempts to secure literary periodization and explicate poetry about London. In the next two chapters, I explore the psychological ramifications of this type of eighteenth-century imagination on the textual traditions of the journal and the urban-domestic novel. In this way, *Reading London* concludes with two analyses of the *internalized* strategies of self-government that writers developed to cater to a very specific cultural problem in London's changed environment. This problem constitutes a final difference between late eighteenth-century London and its earlier incarnation: the proliferation of urban print.

The most important reason why writers moved from controlling others to controlling the self involves the status of London's print culture after

1750—a culture defined by an explosive proliferation of the governing projects that writers like Gay, Fielding, and Pope had popularized during the first half of the century. Indeed, the phrase "the proliferation of print culture" is now a critical commonplace; however, the careful work by critics such as James Raven, William Warner, and Jon Klancher demands that we contextualize exactly what it means as well as define what its ramifications were for late eighteenth-century Londoners.[1] I devote the majority of this chapter to reviewing the evidence for and criticism about the ways late eighteenth-century print culture saturated Londoners with guidebooks and conduct-based literature that fractured the notion of a single London and blurred the imaginary ideal of London's unified readability. By this I mean that the governing projects of the early eighteenth century constituted a large part of the "popular literature" of the late eighteenth century, especially in the instructive tone and moral guidance that this popular literature offered readers.[2] Given London's traditional stereotype as a monstrous den of vice, it is not surprising that, as James Raven shows, London's readers, critics, and booksellers expected instructive moral guidance from London's novels, poems, and periodicals: "The testimony of dozens of autobiographies and private journals of these years [by William Temple, Frances Burney, Hester Thrale, etc.] suggests that the readers of both fiction and more serious literature were conscious that they should be reading for improvement."[3] Raven contextualizes this frenzied, late-century proliferation of textual instruction in terms of the new ways that booksellers (rather than authors) dictated the "Taste of the Town":

> By 1790 most reviewers insisted that the age was one of unprecedented corruption and that a contributory evil was the mushrooming of illicit literature and circulating libraries. . . .
>
> . . .
>
> In the face of such attacks, both writers and booksellers sought more explicit justification for the content of their publications. The result was to introduce greater melodrama and stereotyping in fiction in the cause of public usefulness. Identifiable social nuisances were to be set up and exposed. Direct and stern prefaces or addresses were to be included where necessary. Moral responsibility and general utility were made the selling points. . . .
>
> All this produced powerful and energetic booksellers, responding to and also creating the wants of a leisured reading class. Where most authors and contributors to best-selling literature remained poor, power-

less, and prolific, the successful London bookseller selected, promoted, and suppressed. The public may not always have been given what it wanted: it was given what it was said to want.[4]

If a bookseller's economic and cultural authority surpassed that of late-century writers, then these writers could not imagine the same degree of agency over their urban environments that Gay, Fielding, and Pope originally imagined in the wake of 1688. Mid-century London therefore presented writers such as Boswell and Burney with a new cultural problem that involved the saturation of London with a dizzying variety of texts, each vying to govern a Londoner's conduct with a different agenda. Amid this variety, the dream of a "single London" became desperate and complicated. We find evidence for this growing complexity in a variety of forms: in London's legal attempts to curtail this proliferating print, in guides to London, in Londoners' letters and journals, and in the current fields of literary study (such as materialist histories of the book) that attempt to recover the intricacies of London's print culture and textual marketplace.

According to John Entick's *A New and Accurate History and Survey of London, Westminster, Southwark, and Places Adjacent* (1766), London's street signs had, by 1766, become so omnipresent that an act was proposed to remove overhanging street-signs.[5] This law offers a juridical example of how the textual signs designed by an earlier generation (such as the street signs that Gay trained early-century readers to understand and interpret) had replicated themselves so rapidly that London's legal apparatus was called upon to control this growth. Although the 1766 act that Entick cites was particularly designed to "improve" London's streets via paving, the eighth recommendation focuses upon street signs:

> That the daily increasing rivalship in the size and projection of signs in a great measure defeats the purpose of them, obstructs the free circulation of the air, (so desirable in a large and populous city) in times of high wind often proves dangerous, and in rain always an annoyance to foot-passengers, and at night, more or less, intercepts the light of the lamps.[6]

The signs are not only physically dangerous ("in times of high wind") but also representationally dangerous (in the way their proliferation "defeat[s] the purpose" of a sign). I begin with this legal example since it exemplifies not only the literal proliferation of Gay's textual project, but also a historical episode when Londoners where threatened by a complete saturation of textual authority. In fact, they felt threatened to such an extent that "the Law" began to intervene to curtail this textual proliferation.

Another realm that registers the effects of a proliferating print culture in late eighteenth-century London involves the numerous guidebooks that warn readers about the dangerous effects of printed text, even though these warnings contribute to this proliferation as well. For instance, Raven focuses on a prime example of the kind of advisory text that generated preconceived ideas about London to readers who were unfamiliar with the city: John Trusler's *The London Adviser and Guide: Containing Every Instruction and Information Useful and Necessary to Persons Living in London and Coming to Reside There* (1786).[7] Beneath the heading "Conveniences in London," Trusler details "the principal Circulating Libraries in town," their location, and their loaning charges. He also lists "the French booksellers," where to buy "Law-books, in great variety," and under a separate heading, "A List of the News-papers published in London" in which he helps readers contribute to these self-aggrandizing newspapers: "Letters, or essays, set up in the larger letter of newspapers, are generally paid for according to their length, at the rate of one guinea a column."[8] My point is that the type of information contained in Trusler's *London Adviser* catalogues how a massive variety of printed texts encourages the Londoner to participate in London's "Conveniences"; this is evident as the *Adviser* explicitly reveals its function on its title page: "In order to enable them to enjoy Security and Tranquility, and conduct their Domestic Affairs with Prudence and Economy." In R. Campbell's 1757 *London Tradesman* (a guide to the professions of London and Westminster), Campbell emphasizes the saturation of writers and booksellers in London: "There are a Number of Men of Letters, and Men without Letters, possessed of the Itch of Writing. . . . A Man must be much reduced in his Circumstances before he is obliged to sell his Labours to the Bookseller. Of these there is a numerous Tribe in and about *London;* and, as in all over-stocked Trades, each underworks another for the Sake of Bread."[9] Recognizing this "over-stocked" trade in which "the press is loaded with so much trash of late years," Campbell humbly offers a solution:

> This naturally leads me to offer a Word of Advice to my Brother Authors: I mean such as are obliged to work for Bread, and offer their Labours to the Trade. Let them write less, and digest their Works with greater Accuracy, and though they must not raise their Price all of a sudden, yet in the End they will find their Advantage in it.[10]

Campbell tries to derail a narrative of proliferating print by stressing textual "accuracy" over immediate wealth. In this way, Campbell's *London Tradesman* registers the threat that hastily produced texts posed as they produced inaccurate knowledge about London. Campbell's and Trusler's texts each offer, of course, just one opinion of how to evince proper urban "conduct"; however, they represent the type of printed text that supposedly helped a person become a Londoner. By the late eighteenth century, the problem now resides in knowing *which* guidebook or newspaper possessed the single key to knowing London properly. An expanding print culture made this singular knowledge increasingly difficult.

In terms of the current field of print studies that analyzes mid-eighteenth-century London, Warner, Klancher, and Raven provide the most comprehensive support to illustrate this mid-century cultural problem in London—a problem to which, I argue, both Boswell and Burney respond by developing textual modes of self-government. For instance, Warner examines the proliferation of print in terms of an eighteenth-century "media culture" or a "feedback loop between a type of print media—novels in small-book format—and a practice—avid reading for pleasure."[11] By analyzing the multiplying forms of critical and promotional writing that packaged novels such as Richardson's *Pamela* and Fielding's *Joseph Andrews,* Warner suggests how "out of the amorphous matrix of media culture come new forms of 'formula fiction,' such as the gothic novel, which render their respectable double, *the* novel, an opaque and ambivalent cultural object."[12] Warner's work is important since it posits a cultural history to explain a proliferating textual form. By doing so, Warner accounts for the proliferation of novels not only in terms of their cultural agendas ("the debate about the effects of novel reading, the nationalization of the novel, and the development of the novel's realist claims"),[13] but also in terms of the previously marginal types of writing (readers' guides, critical reviews, and other promotional materials) that surround a novel's publication. Because London's marketplace, readership, and booksellers devised many of these promotional materials, Warner suggests that London's marketplace had saturated readers with culturally motivated printed materials by mid-century.[14] Most importantly, Warner suggests not only how this marketplace both responded to and shaped a reader's perception over whether novels should be read for entertainment or instruction, but also how any attempt to develop a consensus on this issue became increasingly complex.[15]

An additional factor that complicated the idea of a single London was that London's heterogeneity was not confined to a single textual tradition.

Klancher's work, for instance, highlights how periodicals and journals had, by the late eighteenth century, established a contradictory definition of community which relied upon diversifying smaller reading audiences:

> The sheer array of journals at a bookstall or coffeehouse afforded the Englishman a veritable map of national reading. Such audience-building expanded that middle-class public whose very scope and diversity would, finally, work against the more traditional intimacy of reader and writer. As the journals multiplied, they registered the increasingly heterogeneous play of sociolects—the discourses of emerging professions, conflicting social spheres, men and women, the cultivated middle-class audience, and less sophisticated readerships. This contradictory role—cementing the small audience while subdividing the larger public—made the periodical a singular but socially unstable institution for defining, individualizing, and expanding the audiences who inhabited the greater cultural landscape.[16]

Klancher shows how a textual tradition becomes "a singular but socially unstable institution" in its attempt to "map" community atop individual readers. According to Klancher, printed text's "contradictory role" threatens to erase the individual by the 1790s: "The social text of periodical writing thus joins two dissonant orders: inside the text, a communal, democratic exchange; outside the text, a hierarchically ranked world. . . . Effacing social differences, the pages of a journal became a phantom social world—an alternative society of the text."[17] Klancher's "increasingly heterogeneous play of sociolects" therefore denotes not only a proliferation of diverse discourses but also a proliferation of diverse textual traditions. Amid this exponentially increasing "diverse diversity," Boswell and Burney face a new cultural problem: to define a single Londoner amid a heterogeneous print culture.

The "print-saturated London" to which I refer in the following chapters therefore denotes a cultural problem in which late-century writers faced the failure of early-century writers to effectively manage reader's responses to London. Since Gay, Fielding, and Pope could not guarantee that readers would function in London as these writers had imagined, we might say that the projects of early eighteenth-century London were destined to fail, if by "failure" we mean the texts' inability to cause political change. The problem of these early-century writers' attempts to exert external control over Londoners surfaces when we see that a major selling-point of London's proliferating print culture was its instructive guidance. Mid-century readers therefore face a series of new questions: given the hundreds of different texts in a variety of different genres that claim to relate readers to London, whose imaginative guidance will allow us to become functioning individuals? Which author? Which bookseller? Which genre? In the context of a proliferating print culture, the textual strategies devised by Gay, Fielding, and Pope to imaginatively manage readers now lacked its previously imagined coherence. By the late eighteenth century, the possibility of a single "London" did not exist because an imagined "London" now existed in a seemingly endless variety of print forms. There was no "single" London because there was no single textual tradition to represent London. London's dizzying heterogeneity—its blurred readability in terms of its printed representations and actual experiences—therefore forced late-century writers to face a new problem for organizing and managing the city's population that earlier writers did not have to face in the same degree. In particular, the variety of forms that constituted a print-saturated London threatened the notion—and even the possibility—of a single, individualized self.

The sheer heterogeneity of the textual images, genres, and actual experiences that London presented to individuals such as Boswell and Burney causes them to reappropriate the textual strategies that Gay, Fielding, and Pope had developed to manage others. Rather than writing to manage others, Boswell and Burney adapt these earlier strategies to manage themselves. In the following chapters, I argue that Boswell and Burney position the individual self to be the object of their governing techniques since the heterogeneity of late eighteenth-century London's print culture threatened their conception of a single, individual identity. Reacting to the way a print-saturated London endangered the notion of an individual self, Boswell and Burney adapt the textual strategies that Gay, Fielding, and Pope had initially devised to govern London's population. Boswell and Burney instead use these strategies to develop modes of self-government.

Boswell's and Burney's texts represent two different experiences of a print-saturated London that result in self-government. For Boswell, London presented the male individual with an endless number of morally questionable experiences and unrelated diversions that threatened a single, disciplined (or self-governed) identity. As his *London Journal* shows, Boswell also viewed London through a seemingly endless number of fictionalized lenses, referring most famously to the writings and characters developed by Gay, Addison, and Steele as prototypes for interpreting and organizing his own London experiences. Facing these multiple personalities and experiences that London's texts offered to him, Boswell records his experience in London during the 1762–63 season as an attempt to govern and stabilize his authentic self amid these endless possibilities. Similar to the way Gay, Fielding, and Pope used writing to manage others and relate them to a single community of Londoners, Boswell relies upon his journal to manage himself and develop a single, fortified urban identity. Unlike early eighteenth-century writers, however, Boswell faces the added problem of imagining himself to be an object (or product) of these experimental forays into imaginative urban governance *as well as* a subject (or agent) in his own writing. Therefore, Boswell's task is to become a writer who produces printed text through the lenses of well-rehearsed, early eighteenth-century imaginations. He initiates a unique eighteenth-century project by imagining himself to be an Addisonian critic of his *own* recorded experience. If the goal of Addison and Steele's critical project was to produce a disciplined Londoner, as studies such as Mackie's argue, Boswell is a complex example of such a product.[18]

Unlike Boswell's tortuous indecision over the seemingly infinite and morally ambiguous ways that a man could relate to London, Burney's experience with a print-saturated London shows how London's ambiguous signs and boundaries actually limited a women's urban experience. They were especially limiting since they detailed an infinite number of ways to represent women as passive objects. For this reason, Burney writes *Evelina* and *Cecilia* to expose how a print-saturated London limited a woman's urban experience by excluding her from the strategies for acquiring urban agency. As a result, Burney tries to resolve the problems that London presented to women by imagining self-governing textual strategies that would deter women from being written into a state of passivity. Burney's first two novels try to sketch what an authentic sense of selfhood resembles among an infinite number of ambiguous textual signs and conventions in London that placed boundaries upon a woman's urban experience. In outlining this new selfhood, Burney develops modes of textual self-government in *Cecilia* that try to surmount the heterogeneity of London's textual representations and street-level experiences.

Part II of this book, in which I address Boswell's and Burney's projects, is entitled "Governing the Self" since it analyzes two writers and their reactions to a print-saturated London. With these chapters I move from analyzing how writers imagined that they were managing other readers (the first project of *Reading London*) to how readers try to master a newly complex London and how they exhibit this "mastery" by disciplining themselves (the second and third projects of the book). I argue that late eighteenth-century London presented Boswell and Burney with a new task: to develop modes of self-government and to define an authentic self amid a saturation of unrelated images and printed texts that tried to govern Londoners. Although these final two chapters register two different experiences of this cultural problem, both Boswell and Burney arrive at self-government as a solution to this new cultural problem. Inhabiting an urban framework that is saturated with projects of urban conduct originally conceived by Gay, Fielding, and Pope, these late-century writers try to understand their interior identities by adapting the techniques that Gay, Fielding, and Pope originally established to address London's changing environment. As a result, Boswell and Burney show how the notions of a private, interior self both inherit and contain the terms of communal identity from an earlier generation.

5

Agitation and Dramatic Criticism in Boswell's *London Journal*

A print-saturated London—a cultural problem whose conditions I outline in the preceding interchapter—shaped Boswell's writing in more ways than he imagined. In particular, Boswell's *London Journal: 1762–1763* differs significantly from the governing projects that came before him since he experiences an urban framework that varied greatly from the administrative geography of his predecessors. By 1762, Boswell's London not only housed new, centralized institutions of authority but also a familiarity with the literary strategies that writers from a previous generation had devised to imagine that writers could contribute to almost every late eighteenth-century Londoner's daily existence. This proliferation of "improving" institutions combined with a proliferation of printed texts in London generated a new cultural problem for writers such as Boswell. Unlike the dissolution of sovereignty that had motivated early eighteenth-century writers to devise textual strategies for governing London, late eighteenth-century London presented Boswell with an entirely new problem or reason for writing: the threat that these seemingly infinite, heterogeneous, and proliferating textual forms posed to an individual's conception of a stable, unified self. Unlike the way Pope, Gay, and Fielding designed textual strategies to imagine that they were governing *other* readers (strategies that addressed the problem of the 1688 dissolution of sovereignty), Boswell develops strategies for self-government (to address the problem of individual identity in a print-saturated London). As we watch Boswell wrestle with London's heterogeneity and uncomfortably adopt multiple textual personas in his *London Journal,* we also witness him adopt the textual strategies of his predecessors in a desperate attempt to represent himself as a stable and disciplined Londoner. Inheriting a variety of "Londons" that were not of his own making, Boswell faced the added problem of being a contested object in these earlier, experimental forays into imaginative urban governance *as well as* a subject in his own writing. In this way, Boswell initiates a unique eighteenth-century project by imagining himself to be an Addisonian critic of his *own* recorded experience.

As the following excerpts from his *London Journal* show, Boswell uses the word "agitation" to characterize London's influence upon him; London's agitation is both exciting (in its endless possibility and permissive accessibility to moral temptation) and threatening (in the way these possibilities may dissolve moral boundaries). For Boswell, the most important aspect of London's permissive heterogeneity involved the way early eighteenth-century literature about London had presented him with an archive of preconceived textual images and personas to experience London. Yet these same textual images were perpetually in conflict with one another. We find evidence of this conflict not only in what Boswell chooses to describe in his *London Journal* (i.e., the *Journal*'s thematic content), but also in *how* Boswell chooses to deliver this description to the page (i.e., the *Journal*'s generic maneuvers). In particular, a print-saturated London causes Boswell to translate the textual strategies that Gay, Fielding, and Pope had devised to govern others and realign these strategies to govern the individual self. Boswell's attempt to live—or to actualize—the competing and chaotic experiences of London's seemingly infinite textual representations therefore shapes his innovative adoption of textual strategies that were devised for one function (disciplining others) to serve a more pressing function for 1762 (disciplining the self). On the pages of Boswell's *London Journal,* we therefore witness what happens when a late eighteenth-century reader tries to resolve conflicting textual representations of the individual Londoner *by writing himself.* In this way, Boswell's *London Journal* presents us with an example of what I deemed in my introduction to be the second and third projects of this book: readers' efforts not only to master a newly complex London, but also to discipline themselves. Self-government therefore figures prominently in Boswell's late-century project.

This chapter differs from the eighteenth-century projects that I outline in the preceding chapters since a London inundated with print caused Boswell to address interiority, especially the textual strategies that he develops to shape, describe, and comprehend his identity. By "interiority" I refer to the eighteenth-century conceptions of selfhood that writers used to describe psychological complexity before Sigmund Freud assigned a vocabulary to this complexity. Although both early and late eighteenth-century authors write to manage cultural problems that were unique to London, Boswell employs his eighteenth-century imagination not to target the mental processes of Londoners beyond himself; instead, he critiques his own mind. Boswell's goal is to instruct himself and, in the process, reject exterior authority. In twenty-first-century terms, Boswell's *London Journal* offers an alternate method for gaining self-knowledge that does not require an interpreter, a therapist, or a priest. I argue that Boswell's *London Journal* is valuable not simply because he inherits Addison and Steele's critical project but because his *London Journal* presents alternatives to twenty-first-century versions of interiority by answering one question: what if Addison and Steele critiqued their own writing? The answer involves the way Boswell reimagines journal writing and dramatic metaphor to suggest that eighteenth-century Londoners may someday write to discipline, govern, and police themselves. Boswell's response to the fragmentary effects of a print-drenched London reasserts a Londoner's singular identity through dramatic metaphor because he found the unities of traditional drama to represent a valuable method for acquiring a unified character amid London's heterogeneity. After providing examples of how London's heterogeneity "agitated" Boswell, I address this sense of unity that Boswell yoked to dramatic metaphor as he searched for a stable identity in late eighteenth-century London.

"My mind is strangely agitated"

Immediately upon his arrival in London in 1762, Boswell optimistically tries to comprehend the city from a distant, totalizing perspective: "When we came upon Highgate hill and had a view of London, I was all life and joy. . . . I gave three huzzas, and we went briskly in."[1] As Boswell descends to London's street level, however, London's totality becomes an increasingly distant ideal. Responding to the signs that lined London's streets, Boswell initially describes the city's pluralistic, representational complexity as an "agreeable" type of confusion: "The noise, the crowd, the glare of shops and signs agreeably confused me" (44). Yet Boswell's positive reaction to London's confused "glare of shops and signs" is short-lived. Just six days later, Boswell condemns the city's influence upon him: "I lay abed very gloomy. I thought London did me no good. I rather disliked it; and I thought of going back to Edinburgh immediately. In short, I was most miserable"

(49). Boswell's sudden misery in London replaces his previous agreeableness with a frantic mood swing. Although these mood swings may be evidence of Boswell's melancholic temper, I argue that they respond to the endless variety of incongruous textual identities (such as Gay's Macheath and Addison's Mr. Spectator) and lived experiences (such as Boswell's engagements with London's executions, crime, social traditions, and prostitutes) that London presents to him as he desperately tries to formulate a unified identity. Although he is initially attracted to London's endless opportunities to be "in some degree whatever character we choose" (47), the proliferating textual images and representations of the proper Londoner threaten his ability to "choose" an authentic identity.

Facing a print-saturated London that presents him with an infinite number of fictional textual guides and conduct books, Boswell grows increasingly anxious over whether he has wasted his time by imagining himself to be these fictional characters. His anxiety is not ungrounded. Throughout the *London Journal*, Boswell repeatedly imagines himself to be a number of fictional personas including Gay's rakish Macheath (264) and Steele's restrained Mr. Spectator (68, 76, 130). He also imagines himself to be actual producers and performers of text such as Addison, Steele, and personal friends such as West Digges (62, 94, 137), Andrew Erskine, and Sir James Macdonald (79). So which textually influenced persona represents the authentic Boswell? Amid all of these textually produced possibilities for self-definition, Boswell considers London to offer too many choices. Consider, for instance, how the Fieldings' Bow Street legal enterprise launches Boswell into a fictional realm as he recalls reading London's crime narratives:

> By the advice of Mr. Coutts, I went to Sir John Fielding's, that great seat of Westminster justice. A more curious scene I never beheld: it brought fresh into my mind the ideas of London roguery and wickedness which I conceived in my younger days by reading *The Lives of the Convicts,* and other such books. There were whores and chairmen and greasy blackguards of all denominations assembled together. (290–91)

This excerpt is notable not only for the way Boswell's youthful reading lists color his experience of London's legal apparatus, but also because we cannot confidently identify whether the "whores and chairmen and greasy blackguards" are from Fielding's courtroom or *The Lives of the Convicts.* Thus, Boswell's authentic experience of London is filtered through an archive of fictional associations (or "ideas"). There are moments, however, when Boswell is conscious that these imaginary ideas are controlling his identity. For example, he is particularly worried that his imagination has misrepresented London and deterred him from securing a comfortable living as an officer of the Guards. Boswell's depression unfolds as he questions his imaginative activities:

> I was very dull this day. I considered the Guards as a most improper scene of life for me. I though it would yield me no pleasure, for my constitution would be gone, and I would not be able to enjoy life. I thought London a bad place for me. I imagined I had lost all relish of it. Nay, so very strange is wayward, diseased fancy that it will make us wish for the things most disagreeable to us merely to procure a change of objects, being sick and tired of those it presently has. (165)

In this passage Boswell questions whether his "diseased" imagination has misrepresented his relationship to London. Anxious episodes such as this one appear throughout the journal, and several link Boswell's experience of London's heterogeneity to his interior self. For example, after taking a three-day "jaunt to Oxford" to gain a change of perspective, Boswell returns to London unrefreshed: "When I got to London I could not view it in the usual light. My ideas were all changed and turned topsyturvy" (248). Boswell's experience of London is marked by "change" and "topsyturvy" values, and this incessant variety eventually affects Boswell's sense of self-worth: "I had lost all relish of London. I thought I saw the nothingness of all sublunary enjoyments. I was cold and spiritless" (213–14). Here, Boswell yokes London to his "spiritless" condition; he suggests that the city has somehow emptied his body of an individual "spirit." Unable to successfully define his spirit amid London's diversity, Boswell experiences "nothingness" in London. Considering these examples, it is not surprising to see that one of Boswell's goals in writing the *London Journal* is to fill this "nothingness"—to discipline and individualize himself amid London's dizzying diversions.

As the *London Journal* suggests, Boswell considered London's textual representations—as well as the experiences that they shaped—to threaten not only his future but also his ability to write a journal that properly represented a single, authentic self. For this reason, he writes the *London Journal* to discipline himself while living in an environment that many considered to be undisciplined and permissive—especially in terms of its proliferating textual representations and its variety of moral temptations. Boswell explicitly reveals this goal when he associates London to other areas of his life that need critique, regulation, and guidance:

> I told [Mr. Sheridan] that I could not study law, and being of a profession where you do no good is to a man of spirit very disagreeable. That I was determined to be in London. That I wanted to be something; and that the Guards was the only scene of real life that I ever liked. I feel a surprising change to the better on myself since I came to London. (82)

Here Boswell no longer reads London as a direct threat; instead, he reinterprets the city as an environment that may test, improve, and discipline him to become a "better" man. In addition to desiring a paid post in the Guards, Boswell's other motivation for traveling to London was to entertain a possible conversion to Catholicism.[2] These biographical motivations suggest that Boswell imaginatively linked London's heterogeneity not only to his maturation and self-government, but also to a sense of communal belonging and consensus that the Guards and the Catholic church advertised. Little did he know that his own writing style would eventually constitute the moral reform for which he was searching.

As Boswell represents it, London's physical environment also offered him a perfect environment in which to test his ability to refine himself into a stable, single individual. Consider, for example, his ascent to the top of the Monument:

> I then went up to the top of the Monument. This is a most amazing building. It is a pillar two hundred feet high. In the inside, a turnpike stair runs up all the way. When I was about half way up, I grew frightened. I would have come down again, but thought I would despise myself for my timidity. Thus does the spirit of pride get the better of fear. I mounted to the top and got upon the balcony. It was horrid to find myself so monstrous a way up in the air, so far above London and all its spires. I durst not look around me. There is no real danger, as there is a strong rail both on the stair and balcony. But I shuddered, and as every heavy wagon passed down Gracechurch Street, dreaded that the shaking of the earth would make the tremendous pile tumble to the foundation. I then got *The North Briton* and read it at Child's. I shall do so now every Saturday evening. I then came to Dempster's, where Erskine and I drank tea. This seems now to be an established rule on Saturdays. (232)

Tottering above the city in the Monument to the Great Fire of 1666, Boswell does not provide the kind of elaborate description that characterizes a prospect poem written from a privileged perspective. He instead narrates the degree to which the Monument provides him with the opportunity to refine his conduct and "luxuriant imagination." We should note that this refinement involves reading text as "an established rule" or habit every Saturday. The familiar coffeehouse ends this nightmarish excursion, and Boswell therefore suggests that he can cauterize needless anxiety by reclaiming textual habits.

Boswell gives himself another chance to govern this anxiety more effectively when he climbs to the top of St. Paul's:

> Here I had the immense prospect of London and its environs. London gave me no great idea. I just saw a prodigious group of tiled roofs and narrow lanes opening here and there, for the streets and beauty of the buildings cannot be observed on account of the distance. The Thames and the country around, the beautiful hills of Hampstead and of Highgate looked very fine. And yet I did not feel the same enthusiasm that I have felt some time ago at viewing these rich prospects. (310)

Boswell's indifference to these observations is a very eighteenth-century reaction. Getting above London today, be it via the Monument, St. Paul's observation deck, or the intensely popular Millennium Wheel, seems to be a requisite activity for twenty-first-century tourists who want to "know" London. Yet when Boswell does take in the tourist traps, he abhors them. Overhead maps of Boswell's London, however, were not yet the primary means of knowing London. As we have seen with Gay, to know eighteenth-century London meant to act and recognize conducts unique to eighteenth-century Londoners. In fact, Boswell's anxious experiences at the Monument and St. Paul's show how the idealistic, totalizing "view of London" that he experienced upon arriving in London is no longer valuable to him. It is no longer valuable because he recognizes how London's heterogeneous experiences and textual representations have become inevitable parts of urban identity.

One way to understand why these prospects of London disturbed Boswell so much is to realize that they detached Boswell from the very material that he considered to be "urban": individual conduct.[3] His ascents up the Monument and St. Paul's suggest that he eventually considered the value of London to reside not in the landscape or in its "prospects" but in the chaotic and random opportunities for exemplifying and correcting his conduct that its streets and drawing rooms presented to him. Boswell values London's agitations since they present opportunities to discipline and govern himself. In this way, the *London Journal* constitutes a workbook that tests Boswell's self-restraint and his ability to remain stable and centered in an environment that seems to deny this stability. We need to remember that Boswell, upon first experiencing London's agitation, restrains his "agreeable confusion" by evoking the central truths of philosophical discourse: "I had recourse to philosophy and so rendered myself calm" (44). In particular, Boswell uses his *London Journal* to imagine a philosophy of writing that could evoke a centered, authentic self.

Boswell repeatedly uses one word to represent how a print-saturated London and the heterogeneous experiences it shaped motivated his writing: "agitation." Using the word "agitation" instead of "diversion" or "confusion," Boswell sanitizes the threat that London's heterogeneity presented to his individual self. By "agitation," Boswell refers to an experience of London's incongruous textual representations and experiences that encourages him to control his imagination by textual means. For Boswell, agitation defines London; it is the raw material upon which Boswell may exercise discrimination, test his self-worth, and discern proper conduct. Boswell eventually uses "agitation" to replace the "agreeable confusion" that he experienced earlier in London:

> Mrs. Gould and Mrs. Douglas and I went in the Colonel's chariot to the Haymarket. As we drove along and spoke good English, I was full of rich imagination of London, ideas suggested by the Spectator and such as I could not explain to most people, but which I strongly feel and am ravished with. My blood glows and my mind is agitated with felicity. (129–30)

While speaking "good English," Boswell desperately searches for words to describe a reaction to London that he finds impossible "to explain to most people." "Agitation" is as close as he gets to naming this inspiration; London's agitation provokes not only thought but also "rich imagination." London's agitation motivates Boswell to "study" himself, especially as he pursues one "object"—a place in the Guards:

> Yet I do think it is a happiness to have an object in view one keenly follows. It gives a lively agitation to the mind which is very pleasurable. I

am determined to have a degree of Erskine's indifference, to make me easy when things go cross; and a degree of Macdonald's eagerness for real life, to make me relish things when they go well. It is in vain to sit down and say, "What good does it do to have a regiment? Is a general more happy than an ensign?" No. But a man who has had his desire gratified of rising by degrees to that rank in the Army, has enjoyed more happiness than one who has never risen at all. The great art I have to study is to balance these two very different ways of thinking properly. It is very difficult to be keen about a thing which in reality you do not regard, and consider as imaginary.... Although the Judgment may know that all is vanity, yet Passion may ardently pursue. Judgment and Passion are very different. (79)

In this passage, Boswell imagines his "great art" to be the way he disciplines London's agitation by carefully balancing "Judgment and Passion." Acknowledging that "it is very difficult to be keen about a thing which in reality you . . . consider as imaginary," Boswell considers disciplining his textually produced, imaginary ideas and fictional notions about the "real" Londoner by keeping "an object in view." With the word "agitation," Boswell transforms a previously threatening characteristic of London into a useful provocation for self-discipline—a transformation that we can trace in his diction:

> London is undoubtedly a place where men and manners may be seen to the greatest advantage. The liberty and the whim that reigns there occasions a variety of perfect and curious characters. Then the immense crowd and hurry and bustle of business and diversion, the great number of public places of entertainment, the noble churches and the superb buildings of different kinds, agitate, amuse, and elevate the mind. (68–69)

Experiencing London's dizzying pluralism (its "liberty," "whim," "immense crowd," "bustle of business and diversion," and "buildings of different kinds"), Boswell establishes a narrative progression in which he may reimagine this heterogeneity to "agitate, amuse, and elevate the mind." If Boswell can reinterpret London's pluralistic agitation to improve himself, then he will have denuded London's pluralism of the threat it posed to his individual identity. What once was threatening is now capable of being disciplined in writing.

As these examples from his *London Journal* indicate, Boswell experienced the city's heterogeneity in such a way that it produced a sense of chaos that initially threatened the possibility of his becoming a disciplined individual. In the next section, I examine the way Boswell responds to the fragmentary effects of London by reasserting a Londoner's singular identity through dramatic metaphor. Boswell valued dramatic metaphor because he found the unities of traditional drama to represent a viable model for acquiring a unified character amid London's heterogeneous environment. By "character" I mean both public reputation and constructed, personal identity, and in the following section, I address the ramifications that dramatic metaphor had on his search for a stable character in late eighteenth-century London.

Boswell's Dramatic Metaphor

For reasons related to the way critics discuss Boswell's use of metaphor, the *London Journal* and perhaps even Boswell the writer have had trouble becoming independent analytic objects. The days when Boswell's name was just a byline to Samuel Johnson's biography have almost passed; however, Boswell's journals, letters, and poems have inherited a peculiar critical dependency. Consider, for example, the critical reincarnations that the *London Journal* has experienced since its publication in 1950. To a generation of scholars trained to teach and analyze a definable "Age of Johnson," the *London Journal* is Boswell's immature, experimental test run in which he sketches primitive rhetorical strategies that he would eventually perfect in *The Life of Johnson.* This view of the *London Journal* as a prequel to the *Life* hardly pushes Boswell out of Johnson's shadow, and it also refuses to analyze the *London Journal* as an independent text that helped Boswell accomplish very specific tasks between 1762 and 1763. Critics who grant the *London Journal* this independence, however, have attempted to come to terms with Boswell's place in "the long eighteenth century" by forcing the text to conform to generic, and therefore teachable, conventions. Thus, critics claim that the *London Journal* reads like a novel, looks like a confession, or acts like an autobiography.[4] The most popular generic metaphor that critics use to normalize the *London Journal,* however, has been drama. In response to Boswell's use of the words "scenes" and "character" and his adaptation of dramatic conventions such as dialogue and stage directions to suit a text that is not explicitly a drama, critics such as Patricia Meyer Spacks, Michael Friedman, and Donald Kay have made strong cases for understanding the *London Journal* as Boswell's theatrical performance of identity.[5]

All of these critical approaches use metaphors and similes to tie the *London Journal* to a standard baseline or progressive formal narrative of eighteenth-century literature. The *London Journal* is either "like" the *Life* or it is "like" some other more definable genre. The last word on Boswell is always in relation to something else. This critical approach works insofar as it allows us to witness Boswell's flexibility and investment in complex cultural issues, but there is the danger that, by using metaphor to describe Boswell's specific textual function, we can make Boswell resemble anything we want him to. And we have. Networker, sex addict, genius, director, codependent sham, and celebrity stalker might all be offered to describe Boswell's representation of himself in the *London Journal*. We should note, however, that all of these titles are impositions on a mid-eighteenth-century writer; they are anachronistic titles that attempt to pinpoint Boswell's otherness. Facing a critical stalemate that is in part caused by our own perspective, how are we to read Boswell during the twenty-first century?

To suggest an answer to this question, this chapter interprets James Boswell's *London Journal: 1762–1763* and the canon of criticism surrounding it as a lesson in the limitations and use of eighteenth-century metaphor. In particular, I argue that to comprehend the function that Boswell assigned to his *London Journal*, we must simultaneously juggle two analytical objects: the textual traditions of Boswell's *London Journal* and the eighteenth-century metaphors that writers used to acquire self-knowledge in London. A major point of this chapter is that until we recognize how our metaphors distort Boswell's eighteenth-century metaphors, we will continue to see Boswell through a chain of anachronistic signifiers that subtly rejects the eighteenth century's alterity. Due in part to its 1930 rediscovery and subsequent 1950 publication, the *London Journal* carries a great deal of ideological baggage related to the twentieth century rather than the century in which Boswell wrote it. Thus, when we say that the *London Journal* is "dramatic" and that it "performs selfhood," we use these dramatic metaphors in twentieth-century contexts. One effect of our attempt to interpret historically specific metaphors has been the desire to psychoanalyze Boswell and assign interior motives to his exterior actions. As a result, critics have combed the *London Journal* for moments of Boswell's melancholy, depression, and "unwriteability."[6] These studies offer interesting suppositions about Boswell's psyche, but they frequently exclude discussions related to Boswell's style and form in order to privilege content.

This chapter examines what Boswell's use of dramatic metaphor allowed him to do in 1762. I concentrate here on drama for three reasons. The first reason is biographical. As suggested by his Edinburgh writings that precede his 1762 voyage to London, Boswell was terribly interested in theatrical practice and the performance of written text in particular. Second, Boswell's text blatantly adopts the language and conventions of eighteenth-century theatre. In eighteenth-century London, the overwhelming majority of theatres were located in the Town; in fact, most spaces for formal theatrical performance had vanished from the City of London. Again, London's changed geography contributes to Boswell's literary strategies for comprehending the Town; in particular, Boswell's infamous activities of drinking, socializing, visiting prostitutes, and meeting Samuel Johnson take place in and around Covent Garden, Soho, and the Strand. As I will show, performance literally and metaphorically characterizes this urban space, and the metaphoric self-discipline that we witness Boswell develop as he rereads and rewrites his *London Journal* is the textual habit that shapes—and is shaped by—the Town's marginal administrative environment. In particular, if Addison, Steele, Gay, Fielding, and Pope had never tied their reimagined social functions to London's changed urban environment, then Boswell's version of internalized self-government, so explicitly yoked to the ideas of community and consensus that London represents in his *London Journal,* would not be possible. Third, and not unrelated to the previous reason, drama is the metaphor most accessible to critics for finding and explicating organic unity in the *London Journal.* For many critics, it seems that the only way to interpret Boswell's use of dramatic language and conventions has been to understand them as metaphors. To get a handle on what these conventions do for Boswell, critics see Boswell "as" an actor or "as" a playwright who uses text "as" a stage.

The *London Journal,* however, refers to neither a stage nor a play. Boswell, of course, uses text "like" it is his own stage, but the *London Journal* is not a promptbook that is immediately capable of reproduction on the Drury Lane stage with prologue, epilogue, and cast. We might be able to adapt the text for stage performance, but the fact that the *London Journal* requires adaptation or alteration proves that it is something else.[7] Boswell, the writer, is also not a professional actor. I am not arguing that we should jettison metaphor from critical discourse because it is a defunct or hermeneutically repetitive practice; doing so would bring literary criticism to a violent halt. I am claiming that when we identify what Boswell "looks like" or seems to be doing, we need to historicize the metaphors we use.[8] In particular, criticism has adopted Boswell's dramatic metaphor rather than analyzing it. Boswell's use of dramatic metaphor, however, taps into a complex archive of generic associations and writerly functions that do not refer solely to theatre, actors, and stage properties. During the 1760s, Boswell's dramatic metaphor squarely situated him in a continuing textual tradition of literary and social criticism. That is, an exploration of what "dramatic" meant in 1762 allows us to see that Boswell was a new type of critic and not just "like" one.

"I WAS A MAN MUCH DEVOTED TO FORM"

To understand what "dramatic" meant for Boswell, we need to summarize what type of textual practices surrounded playwriting and theatrical production leading up to 1762. Any discussion of the history of eighteenth-century theatre inevitably begins at the reopening of the theatres by the Stuarts in 1660. Although this occurred a century before Boswell wrote the *London Journal,* Restoration drama is important because following the Interregnum it proposed new baselines for dramatic practice (the proscenium stage, plays written entirely in prose, and performance criticism). No figure was more influential in establishing these new styles for the English theatre than John Dryden. In his *Essay of Dramatic Poesy* (1668) as well as other marginalia to his own plays, Dryden began to consider each play's publication to be an opportunity, or event, for producing a critical essay, preface, prologue, or epilogue. In part a contributor to the proliferation of print, Dryden's career shows us how a new industry of English criticism was developing alongside Restoration drama. One genre (drama) was giving rise to a new and uniquely British genre (literary criticism).

I am arguing that the origins of eighteenth-century criticism exist in the marginalia and essays written to address some of our most canonical Restoration plays.[9] We only need to look at the publishing histories of early dramatic criticism to witness how playwrights doubled as their own critics. For example, William Congreve's "Concerning Humour in Comedy" (1695) first appeared in an anthology that his business partners had conveniently edited: *Letters on Several Occasions: Written By* and Between Mr. Dryden, Mr. Wycherley, Mr. ——, Mr. Congreve, and Mr. Dennis.[10] Jeremy Collier's famous "Short View of the Immorality and Profaneness of the English Stage" (1698) sold so well that Collier, although not a playwright, fed upon drama to generate his own critical publishing house; he later produced *A Defense of the Short View* (1698), *A Second Defense of the Short View* (1700), and *A Farther Vindication of the Short View* (1707).[11]

We need to remember that this supposedly "dramatic" criticism did not merely analyze printed text. Most of this criticism targeted the conduct of characters, audiences, or the anticipated moral ramifications of theatrical performance on English society. It is not surprising, then, to see *The Tatler* and *Spectator* helping to proliferate a brand of social criticism that originated in and around theatrical performance. Beneath the heading that he devotes to "Poetry" ("Will's Coffee-house"), Richard Steele used his first *Tatler* to critique Thomas Betterton's benefit performance of Congreve's *Love for Love:*

> All the Parts were acted to Perfection; the Actors were careful of their Carriage, and no one was guilty of the Affectation to insert Witticism of his own, but a due Respect was had to Audience, for encouraging this accomplished Player. . . . This Place [Will's] is very much altered since Mr. *Dryden* frequented it; where you used to see *Songs, Epigrams,* and *Satyrs,* in the Hands of every Man you met, you have now only a Pack of Cards; and instead of the Cavils about the turn of the Expression, the Elegance of the Style, and the like, the Learned now dispute only about the Truth of the Game.[12]

Steele's concentration upon the audience's conduct and his nostalgia for Dryden's supposedly well-read age are not digressions; they are simply the material of which early eighteenth-century criticism was made. Writing his first periodical paper about (or even in) Dryden's former coffeehouse speaks volumes; Steele mentions Dryden in this passage as though to advertise his willingness to receive the relay baton of critical authority that will allow him instruct a new generation and nation. Drama therefore forms a cornerstone of Addison and Steele's periodical project.[13] Drama is the occasion for producing social criticism and establishing the proper conduct of an urban population. Keeping in mind this unique pairing of drama with the rise and social function of British criticism, we should reapproach Boswell's *London Journal.*

In his memorandum for the entry dated Friday, December 31, Boswell writes, "Be like Sir Richard Steele" (113, n. 5). This command from Boswell to himself instructs him to adopt another person's conduct. Boswell, of course, wishes to be different characters throughout the *London Journal,* and critics have viewed this role-playing maneuver as Boswell's most powerful dramatic metaphor.[14] But in these cocktail-napkin notes that Boswell used as raw data for writing the *London Journal,* we should note that the distinction between dramatic metaphor ("be like" a character) and the function that Boswell associates with Steele's career (refine one's conduct) collapses. Boswell inherited Steele's habit of yoking drama to social criticism. Boswell foregrounds this parallel by peppering the *London Journal* with no less than fourteen separate references to Addison and Steele. Boswell first introduces Addison and Steele into the *London Journal* in a way that allows us to understand how they relate to the goal that Boswell sets for his journal. The authors of the *Tatler* and *Spectator* first appear in the context of a retrofitted flashback narrative:

> When my father forced me down to Scotland, I was at first very low-spirited, although to appearance very high . . . . I was, in short, a character very different from what GOD intended me and I myself chose. I remember my friend Johnston told me one day after my return from London that I had turned out different from what he imagined, as he thought I would resemble Mr. Addison. I laughed and threw out some loud sally of humour, but the observation struck deep. Indeed, I must do myself the justice to say that I always resolved to be such a man whenever my affairs were made easy and I got upon my own footing. . . . Now when my father at last put me into an independent situation, I felt my mind regain its native dignity. I felt strong dispositions to be a Mr. Addison. Indeed, I had accustomed myself so much to laugh at every thing that it required time to render my imagination solid and give me just notions of real life and of religion. But I hoped by degrees to attain to some degree of propriety. Mr. Addison's character in sentiment, mixed with a little of the gaiety of Sir Richard Steele and the manners of Mr. Digges, were the ideas which I aimed to realize. (62)

John Johnston, the same person to whom Boswell posted the *London Journal* in weekly installments,[15] offers Addison's name as a standard by which Boswell may judge his own social conduct. The name "Mr. Addison" triggers a reevaluative narrative episode in which Boswell discusses refining his own conduct. This reevaluation leads to a handy formula that proposes to combine selected traits of Addison, Steele, and (West) Digges (an Edinburgh actor and Boswell's acquaintance). But this passage is important because it assigns value to two keywords, or faculties, that Boswell associates with self-improvement and that Boswell explicitly relates to Addison and Steele's critical project: reflection and imagination. By analyzing Boswell's use of these two words in 1762, we may begin to understand the *London Journal* in terms of an eighteenth-century project. The task of Boswell's particular project is "to render my imagination solid" by means of textual reflection. In order to outline what Boswell means by "imagination" (or "the ideas which I aimed to realize"), we first need to understand the archive of meanings attached to eighteenth-century "reflection."

It is not a trivial detail that the names of Addison and Steele first appear in a passage in which Boswell recounts his upbringing. The passage cited above is an episode of recollection and reflection; it exemplifies the technique for governing or improving oneself that Addison and Steele promoted and exercised in their *Tatler* and *Spectator* papers. I will return to this point in a moment, but for now suffice it to say that in terms of the *London Journal*'s narrative, this episode shows Boswell reflecting not only on his expositional childhood but also on the more immediate moment when he realized that Johnston's observation was correct. I use "reflection" here as Boswell uses it; the word is closer in meaning to "mediation" than the twentieth-century sense of seeing oneself in a mirror. I make this distinction because "reflection" is itself embedded within the history of eighteenth-century dramatic metaphor. In particular, the word relates to Steele's own plays and theories of drama.

Steele's 1722 play, *The Conscious Lovers,* occupies a crucial episode in critical narratives about eighteenth-century theatre. Extremely popular during its first performances, Steele's play launched a "new look" for theater that involved criticizing the social values promoted by an older generation of playwrights.[16] Steele wrote three comedies between 1701 and 1705, but *The Conscious Lovers* was the only comedy to follow his contributions to the *Tatler* and *Spectator.* The play, therefore, is heavily influenced by the techniques Steele had developed to administer proper conduct to an audience. At the close of act 2 of *The Conscious Lovers,* the character John Bevil Jr. is secretly supporting Indiana, a character who knows neither her history nor her identity. Bevil Junior knows Indiana's history, but he does not reveal this history until the play's end. In act 2,

Indiana cannot understand what would motivate an anonymous man to support her existence. Bevil Jr.'s response outlines the conduct of Steele's civilized Briton: "Your hero, madam, is no more than what every gentleman ought to be and I believe very many are. He is only one who takes more delight in reflections than in sensations. He is more pleased with thinking than eating; that's the utmost you can say of him."[17] We should compare this passage with one of the most frequently cited passages from the *London Journal,* a sentence that Boswell uses to introduce the function of the entire text: "Very often we have more pleasure in reflecting on agreeable scenes that we have been in than we had from the scenes themselves" (40). The similarity is not a coincidence.

In 1760, *A View of the Edinburgh Theatre during the Summer Season, 1759* was published in London. The text criticizes 25 plays performed during Edinburgh's 1759 season, one of which is *The Conscious Lovers*. Frederick Pottle has argued that the *View,* although published anonymously, is Boswell's creation, and the text is now commonly attributed to Boswell.[18] What is interesting about the *View* is that it criticizes the conduct of the actors rather than the plays. It claims that its "observations are the result of the strictest attention, guided by a cool equanimity, and mellowed by calm, and unbiased reflection."[19] Even if Boswell did not write the *View,* there is a high probability that because he was living in Scotland during the 1759 season, Boswell attended every play that the *View* discussed. In any case, *The Conscious Lovers* was a staple of Edinburgh's 1759 theatre season and was a play that, in Edinburgh, called attention to critical "reflection" in both the text of the play and the strategies by which it was criticized.

The *London Journal* inherits Steele's dramatic-critical use of reflection, but extends it in a very specific and imaginative way. Boswell represents reflection as textual labor, as evidence of his accomplishing critical work. Consider, for example, the way Boswell's diction relates writing to working: "In recollecting Mr. Johnson's conversation, I labour under much difficulty" (291). My point in tracing the acts of recollection and reflection from Steele to Boswell is to stress that Steele's dramatic-critical project also privileged the act of looking back and recollecting experience as proper and "heroic" meditative work. Using Steele to interpret Boswell's diction, we can see that this work is "heroic" (that is, it possess moral value) because it is a critical activity. What constituted criticism in Steele's *Spectator* papers and his drama were techniques of imaginative government which Steele dictated and exemplified through text. As shown in the introduction, Steele's writing addressed the rise of liberal governmentality. Offering an alternative to a defunct absolutism, his papers proposed to "offer something, whereby such worthy and well-affected Members of the Commonwealth may be instructed, after their reading, *what to think*: Which shall be the End and Purpose of this my Paper . . . ."[20] Reflection looms large in Steele, we should note, because only "after" reading Steele's papers will the reader realize the knowledge that these papers impart. Thus, given the connection that exists between Boswell and Steele in their common use of a critical-dramatic metaphor, we can also see Boswell's agenda in terms of these new forms of governmentality.

Boswell, however, does not simply reproduce the techniques that we have seen Steele develop in the introduction; he extends them. The *London Journal*'s novelty stems from the way Boswell turns Steele's textual strategies for regulating conduct onto himself. In more general terms, Boswell tailors techniques for self-government, judges his own experience, and finally represents this self-governing activity as a new, disciplined type of imagination that eighteenth-century philosophers would have considered morally productive rather than destructive. Boswell's *London Journal* is therefore a critical narrative project, and this label is apt for three reasons.

First, the *London Journal* is criticism in the eighteenth-century sense of the word; it aims to correct and establish proper social values by proposing proper conduct. In the case of the *London Journal,* Boswell's text attempts to conduct and to follow this criticism simultaneously. Second, Boswell maps this type of critical activity onto a narrative. I use "narrative" here in its narratological sense as a "recounting" of events.[21] Reflection and recollection are crucial to the way Boswell tried to order and govern his conduct and imagination. Boswell organized the *London Journal*'s content under dated headings, so his use of narrative to frame some sort of growth or maturity preceding his grand tour is not surprising. What is surprising is that Boswell repeatedly questions whether the *London Journal*'s narrative order is working. Boswell continually tests strategies for "recounting" experience in the *London Journal.* Boswell searches for a textual form that will allow him to criticize and manage both how he thinks and how he acts. Reminiscent of *Tom Jones,* the *London Journal* aligns its content with a narrative structure or habit and then answers, in a very self-conscious tone, questions related to what this structure allows the writer to accomplish. Boswell's self-conscious inquiry into textual form is also completely expected from an eighteenth-century critic. But the *London Journal*'s narrative does not end the way we would expect a novel to end. The day before Boswell leaves London, he recollects and deliberately calls attention to transgressive moral conduct:

> WEDNESDAY 3 AUGUST. I should have mentioned that on Monday night, coming up the Strand, I was tapped on the shoulder by a fine fresh lass. I went home with her. She was an officer's daughter, and born at Gibraltar. I could not resist indulging myself with the enjoyment of her. Surely, in such a situation, when the woman is already abandoned, the crime must be alleviated, though in strict morality, illicit love is always wrong. (332–33)

This is hardly evidence of a reformed Boswell, and its inclusion at the end of the *London Journal* as well as its seemingly hypocritical wavering ("the crime must be alleviated, though in strict morality, illicit love is always wrong") complicate the view that the *London Journal* is a self-contained narrative. We should note that this transgression takes place on Monday evening, yet Boswell delays its recollection until the night before the *London Journal* ends. This deliberate deferral, phrased in retrofitted corrective terms ("I should have mentioned"), is a narrative strategy by which Boswell amplifies what we may consider to be "a bad ending." On a level of content, this interpretation might be true; however, I suggest that Boswell is more concerned in the *London Journal* with perfecting and regulating form rather than content, and this leads me to the third reason why the *London Journal* is a critical narrative project.

If Boswell had censored this final transgression, the *London Journal* would resemble a novel. Boswell deliberately complicates our attempts at substantiating this resemblance because his type of narrative calls attention to the act of correcting rather than to the corrected product itself. The *London Journal* uses narrative episodes, but its inability to end recasts it as a project whose goal is to recruit the imagination as a tool for self-government. Boswell is interested in establishing a narrative process that will manage "the whims that may seize me and the sallies of my luxuriant imagination" (39); he is not interested in narrating a perfect product that would force narration to cease. The *London Journal* does not end in Boswell's perfection; instead, it gestures toward future trials and experiences that test the writing style he was developing. This is what I mean when I write that Boswell is interested not in content but in form; it is as though Boswell looks to London to teach him how to write and think. If my label "critical narrative project" sounds like Fielding's "Heroic, Historical, Prosaic Poem," that is my point. The *London Journal* is Boswell's attempt to strike out in a new direction, to essay upon or critique a new form while writing it.

The remainder of this chapter juggles how the words criticism, narrative, and project can help us see the way the *London Journal*'s formal maneuvers nurture reflection and imagination as tools for effective self-government. In particular, Boswell imagines that textual habit constitutes self-government. This is why Boswell imagines himself as the writer of his own periodical: "The Spectator mentions his being seen at Child's [coffeehouse], which makes me have an affection for it. I think myself like him, and am serenely happy there. There is something to me very agreeable in having my time laid out in some method, such as every Saturday going to Child's" (76). In his attempt to record a dialogue at Child's every Saturday, Boswell organizes his writing and lifestyle into "some method" patterned after the paradigmatic critic, Mr. Spectator. At other moments, Boswell reflects upon his textual conduct: "My present life is most curious, and very fortunately is become agreeable. My affairs are conducted with the greatest regularity and exactness. I move like very clock-work" (183). Boswell's use of passive voice ("my affairs are conducted") suggests that text is organizing and conducting his habitual existence better than he, without writing, could ever do. And there are moments when Boswell is blatant about his governing ability: "I must be called an excellent manager" (184). Writing, for Boswell, is literally habit forming:

> Before I left Scotland, I had a long conversation with Sir David Dalrymple on my future schemes of life. Sir David is a man of great ingenuity, a fine scholar, an accurate critic, and a worthy member of society. From my early years I used to regard him with admiration and awe, and look upon him as a representative of Mr. Addison. . . . I therefore wrote to him, telling him how my affairs went on, and that I wanted to be rationally happy, yet easy and gay, and hoped he would take a charge of me; would let me know what books to read, and what company to keep, and how to conduct myself. . . . I proposed to him that I would write to him on a Saturday, once a fortnight, as I was a man much devoted to form. (188)

"Devoted to form" is a loaded phrase. It follows Boswell's questioning "how to conduct" himself; thus, form seems to be a tool that is synonymous with the words habit, scheme, plan, and method. But this phrase also operates on a metaphorical level.[22] Textual form creates the effect of quotidian devotion and structure. For Boswell, writing evinces self-control or "devotion" as he recollects coffeehouse dialogues every Saturday and mirrors the *Spectator*'s publishing schedule.

Rather than ending the *London Journal* with complete reformation, Boswell concludes with a final commandment: "Let me be manly." "Manly" here expresses Boswell's wish to have mastered a writing style that allows him not only to shape and mold his thoughts but also to correct and refine them. A "manly" style for Boswell is one that disciplines, or conducts, without respite. It, like the grand tour he was about to take, allows a "gentleman" to come into being by means of instructive conduct. The *London Journal*'s critical narrative project was underway.

Boswell's Imagination

If Boswell did not differentiate between writing and governing, then he must have developed some strategy for viewing the relationship between writing and governing as more than just a metaphorical pairing. The faculty that allows Boswell to dissolve the distance between writing and governing and to render it a habit-forming activity is the imagination. As clarified in the introduction, however, *imagination* was a loaded word for eighteenth-century readers because it alluded to epistemological problems that were tied to moral philosophy, poetics, and historical writing. By 1762, imagination was a central topic in critical and philosophical discussions about "human nature" and the capacity to acquire knowledge. Imagination therefore relates to the *London Journal* in two specific ways. First, from a philosophical standpoint, the *London Journal* shows that Boswell was questioning the moral role that imagination should play in his critical narrative project. In particular, should it be "luxuriant" and build "castle[s] in the air" (312) or should it be "solid" (62) and refine images preserved in the memory? Boswell's relationship with David Hume is inevitably bound to this question. Second, from a critical standpoint, Boswell inherited a view of the imagination as the critic's tool for governing people in the place of monarchial absolutism. A series of *Spectator* papers, which are now loosely referred to as "The Pleasures of the Imagination," had already tried to resolve the imagination's social function with liberal governmentality. Inheriting these two strands of debate about the imagination's purpose, Boswell approaches the imagination as a philosophical-critical tool that he can sharpen.

One of the reasons why discussions of the *London Journal* are overburdened with metaphor is because Boswell's ostensible subject is imagination. Taken in its most basic—that is, post-romantic—sense, imagination is a creative mental faculty; its purpose is to invent and envision. This definition raises two corollary assumptions that appear to be self-evident following 1798.[23] First, imagination invokes an alternate reality; it is separate from external facts. One can see what a fertile petri dish this corollary presents for studies of literary metaphor. If imagination is separate from reality, then we can only come to know this alterity by using terms "like" real ones. Metaphor allows critics to dissolve difference and to exercise their own imaginative functions. It is not surprising that the only way literary critics can interpret Boswell's writing is by adding secondary metaphors to those Boswell uses in the primary text. The result is a house of mirrors that exacerbates the inaccessibility of the text's imaginative function rather than clarifying it.

Second, a generative imagination envisions the future. In terms of a plot, it knows or creates what comes next. In the *London Journal,* however, Boswell "never anticipates"; he creates what Pottle has characterized as "a forward-straining tension."[24] Rather than sketching a future, Boswell's imagination reflects on the experience of writing. Pottle also identifies the careful balance Boswell strikes between novelty and textual tradition:

> His kind of confession is almost unique. He is writing, as he himself frequently said, a *history* of his own mind. Not an apologia but a history: the difference is enormous. . . . Boswell approaches the secret places of his own heart and mind with the detachment, the candour, and the responsibility of a historian. Not a mere chronicler, but a historian of the older school, a historian who considers history a branch of literature. That is to say, though he remains scrupulously within the bounds of historical circumstance, he seizes all his material imaginatively, he *creates* it.
>
> . . .
>
> In criticism generally, imagination has meant invention: no invention, no imagination. Actually, the two faculties have no necessary connection. Boswell in his journal is creating, but as he creates he remembers; that is, he is able to refer every stage of his construction to a whole active mass of organized past reactions or experience. His picture must not merely be lifelike and dramatic; it must also be "true." It must keep within the bounds of historical circumstance.[25]

In this passage, Pottle yokes imagination to historical writing and therefore represents Boswell's imagination as a traditional tool for rendering his writing "true." While Pottle's critique is indispensable because it justifies and makes room for discussing a particularly Boswellian imagination, I would like to push Pottle's observation further by revisiting Boswell's relationship between imagination and recollection. That is, Boswell produces "truth" in the *London Journal* not only by mapping imagination onto historical writing, but also by creating and validating the metaphorical fiction or myth that writing constitutes refinement and self-government. Furthermore, given the eighteenth-century philosophical debate over whether Britons should trust or value their imaginations, we should be careful when linking veracity to eighteenth-century versions of imagination. Boswell first had to devise textual strategies for disciplining the imagination before he could link writing to self-government.

In part caused by some of the same metaphorical slippage that we are wrestling with today, David Hume was also skeptical about the imagination's veracity.[26] Hume's attempt in *A Treatise of Human Nature* (1739–40) to separate the imagination into impressions and ideas helped to feed this skepticism. Defining impressions as the "sensations, passions, and emotions, as they make their first appearance in the soul" and ideas as "the faint images of these in thinking and reasoning," Hume set up a hierarchy in which ideas were weaker, or less valuable, than sensory impressions.[27] If Hume considered ideas to be weak reflections of sensory impressions,[28] then ideas were in need of discipline. Boswell cites his letters to Hume throughout the *London Journal;* he even reads Hume's *History of Great Britain* during the long episode in which Boswell battles venereal disease, as though Hume's book confers absolution.[29] Hume relates to Boswell's textual conduct because we can see the *London Journal* partly as an attempt to render Humean ideas reliable and valuable. Consider, for instance, how Boswell anchors the paragraph describing his initial reaction to London's chaotic street level in a concluding, philosophical clause: "I had recourse to philosophy, and so rendered myself calm" (44). We have already seen how Boswell wishes "to render my imagination solid" (62). "Rendering," for Boswell, is synonymous with "disciplining," and Boswell associates this disciplinary activity with imagination and philosophy. In particular, Hume taught Boswell that imagination was in need of discipline. Boswell, however, took imagination to another level when he considered imagination to be a critical tool for disciplining his own conduct. Imagination, therefore, is both the target and the tool for making Boswell's critical narrative project appear useful.

Boswell does not unequivocally vilify or condemn the imagination because he inherits from the *Spectator* the imagination's ability to promote universal "Taste." Addison's "Pleasures of the Imagination" papers (numbers 409, 411–21) introduce literary imagination as a way to "cultivate" taste:

> But notwithstanding this Faculty [Taste] must in some measure be born with us, there are several Methods for Cultivating and Improving it, and without which it will be very uncertain, and of little use to the Person that possesses it. The most natural Method for this Purpose is to be conversant among the Writings of the most Polite Authors. A Man who has any Relish for fine Writing, either discovers new Beauties, or receives stronger Impressions from the Masterly Strokes of a great Author every time he peruses him: Besides that he naturally wears himself into the same manner of Speaking and Thinking.
>
> . . .
>
> Every Man, besides those general Observations which are to be made upon an Author, forms several Reflections that are peculiar to his own manner of Thinking; so that Conversation will naturally furnish us with Hints which we did not attend to, and make us enjoy other Mens Parts and Reflections as well as our own.[30]

"Natural Method," "Impressions," "manner of Thinking," and "Reflections" all gesture towards an Addisonian theory of the imagination, which Addison introduces in terms of a literary project: "I shall next *Saturday* enter upon an Essay *on the Pleasures of the Imagination,* which . . . will perhaps suggest to the Reader what it is that gives a Beauty to many Passages of the finest Writers both in Prose and Verse. As an Undertaking of this Nature is entirely new, I question not but it will be received with Candour."[31] In addition to drawing attention to its own imaginative and critical novelty ("an Undertaking of this Nature is entirely new"), Addison's paper yokes imaginative pleasure to literary criticism. When Addison finally writes this treatise on imagination, its "Speculations" resemble a philosophical essay:

> We cannot indeed have a single Image in the Fancy that did not make its first Entrance through the Sight; but we have the Power of retaining, altering, and compounding those Images, which we have once received, into all the Varieties of Picture and Vision that are most agreeable to the

Imagination . . . .
There are few Words in the *English* Language which are employed in a more loose and uncircumscribed Sense than those of the *Fancy* and the *Imagination.* I therefore thought it necessary to fix and determine the Notion of these two Words, as I intend to make use of them in the Thread of my following Speculations, that the Reader may conceive rightly what is the Subject which I proceed upon.[32]

Addison's goal is to discipline—"to fix and determine"—the proper imagination so that he can stabilize a national "Taste."

All of these excerpts are notable for three reasons. First, Addison never clarifies what "Taste" is beyond labeling it a "Metaphor." While trying to prove "the Propriety of the Metaphor,"[33] he suggests that select individuals are capable of "Cultivating and Improving" taste via the imagination. Second, Addison assumes that readers will respond to this criticism by activating their own imaginations; thus, Addison tries to produce a captive audience that will internalize his strategies for self-conduct. Addison elicits this audience involvement by using phrases such as "the Reader may conceive rightly," and "will perhaps suggest to the Reader." Third, Addison develops value for his own critical writing. If "Conversation with Men of a Polite Genius" (such as the imaginative conversation between writer and reader) "will naturally furnish us with Hints we did not attend to, and make us enjoy other Mens Parts and Reflections as well as our own," then reading *Spectator* 409, for example, will induce the same reflective refinement. Addison makes this logic explicit as he proposes a reading list for his audience: "It is likewise necessary for a Man who would form to himself a finished Taste of good Writing, to be well versed in the Works of the best *Criticks* both Ancient and Modern."[34] When Addison does get close to a practical, that is nonphilosophical, definition of imagination, he distinguishes imagination from its "vulgar" counterpart: "A man of a Polite Imagination is let into a great many Pleasures that the Vulgar are not capable of receiving. He can converse with a Picture, and find agreeable companion in a Statue."[35] Boswell, five days before leaving London for his grand tour, offers a perfect example of this polite conversation: "After service [at St. Paul's], I stood in the center and took leave of the church, bowing to every corner" (331). It is interesting to note how Boswell takes "leave of the church," personifies London's most valuable "Statue," and then proceeds to conclude his *London Journal.*[36]

My point in briefly reviewing the philosophical status of imagination before 1762 is to highlight the fact that Boswell had inherited a way of talking about the imagination that constituted criticizing or disciplining it. In the *London Journal,* we witness Boswell imagining himself to be Addison's elect reader, the "man of Polite Imagination" who:

> meets with a secret Refreshment in a Description, and often feels a greater Satisfaction in the Prospect of Fields and Meadows, than another does in the Possession. It gives him, indeed, a kind of Property in every thing he sees, and makes the most rude uncultivated Parts of Nature administer to his Pleasures: So that he looks upon the World, as it were, in another Light, and discovers in it a Multitude of Charms, that conceal themselves from the generality of Mankind.[37]

The idea that the self-governed man takes "greater Satisfaction in the Prospect" than "the Possession" echoes the reflective man in Steele's *The Conscious Lovers* who "takes more delight in reflections than in sensations . . . more pleased with thinking than eating." The figure who allows "Nature [to] administer to his Pleasures" is the ideal model for liberal governmentality. But the type of imagination that allows Boswell to be a social critic also needs critiquing, as Boswell learned from Hume. Thus, we may view the *London Journal* as a workbook with at least two goals: first, to employ the imagination in order to make writing indistinguishable from governing; and, second, to discipline imagination whenever it focuses on topics unrelated to self-government. For Boswell, these two goals are underwritten by two distinct types or modes of imagination: the analogical and the reflective. To achieve the first goal (to activate the writing-governing metaphor), Boswell frequently heaps together metaphors and analogies to imagine two disparate objects to be similar. To reach the second goal (to discipline what he believes constitutes thought), Boswell reflects upon not only his experiences but also the way he represents these experiences in writing. We should note that both of these goals and their accompanying imaginative modes are made possible by Boswell's generative—that is, creative—imagination.

While recognizing these two goals in the *London Journal,* we must always keep in mind that Boswell differs from Addison, Steele, and Hume because Boswell critiques, manages, and governs *his own conduct* rather than a reader's conduct. The *London Journal* is, after all, a journal. We should also understand that Boswell's reliance upon dramatic-critical metaphor does not make this journal a private confessional but something much more complex and relevant to the social function of text that Boswell had inherited from critics who proceeded him. The *London Journal,* in many ways, answered the hypothetical question of what would happen if Addison, Steele, and Hume critiqued their own writing. In this context, Boswell's running meta-commentary, frequently mistaken for an overanxious self-consciousness, may be Boswell's most insightful contribution to the practice we have come to know as eighteenth-century literary criticism.

"We have no glasses for the mind"

If Boswell inherited from Addison and Steele a model of the imagination as a tool for self-conduct and normalizing "Taste," then Hume's questioning the imagination's truthfulness presented Boswell with a dilemma in 1762. In particular, questions of subjectivity posed by mid-century moral philosophers inevitably undermined Addison and Steele's project to outline a universal blueprint for the proper imagination. Boswell's solution to this philosophical problem was to work the problem out on himself; he internalized the strategies of authorization that Addison and Steele had formerly aimed at a reading public. Viewing the *London Journal*'s dramatic metaphors from their critical foundations therefore allows us to see that rather than wandering through some analogical stage play of his own making, Boswell instead used his journal to imagine himself as both critic and audience. Questions of subjectivity are negligible when Boswell becomes both subject and object. Imagination, as a result, is once again, in the context of Boswell's journal, a tool for urban propriety and unquestioned liberal governmentality.

The most complex aspect about discussing the Boswellian imagination is that Boswell uses the word *imagination* to mean an infinite number of things. The fact that Boswell did not use one definition of *imagination* in the *London Journal* suggests that he was in the process of disciplining this multiplicity. Boswell's indeterminacy was also linked in part to the way the imagination was suspect during the late eighteenth-century. This suspicion is best exemplified in an episode in the *London Journal* when Boswell applauds Thomas Sheridan's observation that society lacks corrective lenses for "show[ing] people their mistakes. We have no glasses for the mind" (182). Faced with this lack, Boswell substitutes text for Sheridan's "glasses for the mind." Writing that recollects past experience, in the self-contained logic that advances the *London Journal,* is as good as, or as close as one should get to, a model of interiority. If the Addisonian imagination was a critical tool for governing society's "Taste," then Boswell sharpens this tool by tailoring it to regulate his own conduct.

By tracing some of the contexts in which Boswell uses the word *imagination*, we can see the analogical and reflective modes of imagination at work. When Boswell employs his analogical mode, he imagines text as a field upon which to shuttle meaning between two disparate objects. Consider, for example, how often Boswell imagines himself some other person. When Boswell leaves for Oxford, he proclaims, "I imagined myself the Spectator taking one of his rural walks" (244). Boswell incessantly attempts to "be like" a figure whose conduct, frequently literary, suits the experience he records ("I think myself like [the Spectator]," "I move like clockwork," "Be like Sir Richard Steele"). There are episodes, however, where Boswell's analogical identities threaten to exceed their proper limits. We can determine what these proper limits are because Boswell always qualifies or judges episodes when he feels that his imagination has reached an improper extremity. One of these extremities occurs during his "voluptuous night" with Louisa: "Louisa had an exquisite mixture of delicacy and wantonness that made me enjoy her with more relish. Indeed I could not help roving in fancy to the embraces of some other ladies which my lively imagination strongly pictured. I don't know if this was fair. However, Louisa had all the advantage" (139–40). The sentence "I don't know if this was fair" is Boswell's version of a moral qualifier. The sentence purposefully destabilizes this episode that Boswell has worked so hard to represent as a victory. Its destabilization also conveniently foreshadows the venereal disease he eventually contracts. Boswell's analogies do not allow him to assume any role without his critiquing the morality of the analogy that allows him to imagine himself "like" another person. Boswell's analogical mode critiques as it imagines.

Boswell not only uses an analogical mode to try to tailor his actions and thoughts to approach London properly, but he also uses the analogical mode to lend credibility to his use of imagination in the first place. Analogies are Boswell's tools for validating an imagination that envisions future goals:

> It is very difficult to be keen about a thing which in reality you do not regard, and consider as imaginary. But I fancy it may do, as a man is afraid of ghosts in the dark, although he is sure there are none; or pleased

> with beautiful exhibitions on the stage, although he knows they are not real. Although the Judgment may know that all is vanity, yet Passion may ardently pursue. Judgment and Passion are very different.
>
> With these notions I am pushing to get into the Guards, where to distinguish myself as a good officer and to get promotion will be my favourite objects. If that does not succeed, I am at least living happily, I am seeing the world, studying men and manners, and fitting myself for a pleasing, quiet life in old age, by laying up agreeable ideas to feast upon in recollection. (79)

This passage is notable for three reasons. First, it mobilizes a string of similes to legitimize Boswell's blatant evocation of "fancy." By switching from "imaginary" in the first sentence to "fancy" in the second, Boswell suggests that his type of imagination is morally distinguished from the mere "imaginary."[38] This change of diction shows that Boswell cannot talk about the imagination without activating some type of imaginative activity. Boswell essentially admits that it is "difficult" to rely upon an imagined future; however, by using his "fancy" to introduce two similes ("as a man is afraid of ghosts in the dark" and "[as] he is pleased with beautiful exhibitions on the stage"), Boswell suggests, or at least proves to himself in his own logic, that imagination is not entirely scandalous. Second, this passage shows how Boswell disciplines the imagination and then immediately embraces this refined imagination by applying it to his own circumstances. Boswell relates the analogical logic from the first paragraph to his own life in the second paragraph. Realizing that "Judgment and Passion are very different," Boswell then judges his own circumstances. This analogical logic ultimately allows Boswell to utilize Humean ideas to imagine or project his future without being in danger of ignoring reality. Boswell's analogical imagination does not threaten to overturn reality because its "castles in the air" are always tethered to the ground by a thread of metaphor. Third, this passage illustrates the relationship between Boswell's analogical mode, which frequently imagines a present or future state, and the reflective mode, which anchors imaginative activity in a more legitimate past or history. Boswell imagines that the *London Journal*'s "studying men and manners" will render him a proper adult "by laying up agreeable ideas to feast upon in recollection." Boswell imagines his future as a time filled with recollection. Again, Boswell ties any projection or anticipation of the future to the safety that a history provides.

Throughout the *London Journal,* Boswell frequently evokes a reflective mode of imagination after employing the analogical mode. After using analogies to make writing look like governing, Boswell then writes about, and therefore governs or judges, past experiences. Boswell's reflective mode accomplishes at least two tasks. First, episodes of reflection act as a distancing technique in which Boswell, in a manner similar to satire, may assume the role of an early eighteenth-century disinterested critic, surveying a prospect of chaos and trying to make sense of it all. Attending the premiere of Mrs. Sheridan's new play, *The Discovery,* Boswell imagines himself as this historical figure: "I wrought myself up to the imagination that it was the age of Sir Richard Steele, and that I was like him sitting in judgment on a new comedy" (177). Here Boswell's simile between Steele and himself not only refers to the judgmental function of dramatic-critical metaphor, but also suggests that the present is less important to Boswell than the way Boswell is able to reimagine that present in writing.

Second, Boswell structures episodes of reflection to question his past conduct and offer answers to this question. This question-and-answer scheme does not prove that Boswell is unsure of what he is doing; instead, it constitutes a strategy of textual self-government in which Boswell judges via reflection whether his past conduct can inform his present problems. Consider, for instance, the question-and-answer session he conducts after sending a letter of rebuke to Louisa reminding her to return the money she borrowed from him: "Am not I too vindictive? It appears so; but upon better consideration I am only sacrificing at the shrine of Justice; and sure I have chosen a victim that deserves it" (175). Boswell's answer to his question shows signs of reflection ("but upon better consideration"), and this reflective meditation results in a supposedly firm judgment. Another example of this knowledge-producing self-reflection occurs during the *London Journal*'s final entry: "Let me recollect my life since this journal began. Has it not passed like a dream? Yes, but I have been attaining a knowledge of the world" (333). Boswell advertises that he has gained self-knowledge while couching this advertisement in a reflective form (the question-and-answer scheme). The reflective imagination does not threaten to overturn reality because it, like the early eighteenth-century novel, imports the value attached to historical writing to validate its claims. Finally, as the above examples of both the reflective and analogical modes show, we should recognize that Boswell develops and disciplines his imaginative activity by alluding to Addison or Steele's critical project.

With these particularly Boswellian modes of imagination in mind, we may now fully understand the context in which Boswell reveals the *London Journal*'s function in its introduction: "INTRODUCTION. The ancient philosopher certainly gave a wise counsel when he said, 'Know thyself.' For surely this knowledge is of all the most important. I might enlarge upon this. But grave and serious declamation is not what I intend at present" (39). It is odd that a journal has an introduction; therefore, we need to pay attention to what this oddity does for Boswell's text. Psychoanalytic critics point to this opening to show that the *London Journal* somehow constructs Boswell's interior; however, we must acknowledge that Boswell qualifies this opening sentiment. He "might enlarge upon this," but does not do so. His task is not to "declaim" an explicit and extensive philosophy about his interior but to question, experiment with, and correct the conduct he, fortunately or unfortunately, presently exhibits. Boswell therefore purposefully complicates this opening disclaimer to advertise how this journal will be different from other diaries.

The rest of this introductory paragraph clarifies that what counts as "knowledge" for Boswell is judgment, refinement, and criticism:

> A man cannot know himself better than by attending to the feelings of his heart and to his external actions, from which he may with tolerable certainty judge "what manner of person he is." I have therefore determined to keep a daily journal in which I shall set down my various sentiments and my various conduct, which will be not only useful but very agreeable. It will give me a habit of application and improve me in expression; and knowing that I am to record my transaction will make me more careful to do well. Or if I should go wrong, it will assist me in resolutions of doing better. I shall here put down my thoughts on different subjects at different times, the whims that may seize me and the sallies of my luxuriant imagination. I shall mark the anecdotes and the stories that I hear, the instructive or amusing conversations that I am present at, and the various adventures that I may have. (39)

Text for Boswell produces a very specific kind of knowledge that is implicit in his choice of action ("know," "judge," "improve") and object ("manner," "conduct," "habit"). This knowledge is also "useful" and "agreeable"; it exemplifies the eighteenth century's requirements for literature to be both instructive and entertaining. The journal therefore exists because it enables Boswell to judge himself in proper critical terms.

Discovery is a critical act; but we must remember that Boswell is writing a critical narrative project that employs narrative episodes but is ultimately unending. "Discovery" is not the ostensible goal of the *London Journal;* Boswell's goal is to develop effective imaginative modes of self-government.

It should not surprise us that Boswell anchors this introductory paragraph's moral posturing to the wrong and uneconomical type of imagination: "luxuriant imagination." This luxuriance is in need of control, discipline, and management; it is the *London Journal*'s critical target. By the end of the *London Journal,* Boswell identifies a "fine imagination" (234)—a newly sharpened and selective faculty. This "fine imagination" not only "preserves many things that would otherwise be lost in oblivion" (40), but also questions how reflective and analogical imaginations might assist Boswell in improving his conduct. The analogical and reflective modes that Boswell develops in the *London Journal* therefore make up the "critical" part of his critical narrative project. Once we recognize that metaphors of taste, drama, and governmentality were trademarks of eighteenth-century critical projects, the task Boswell assigns to the *London Journal* reveals itself to be a critical one. That is, the function of Boswell's "blest imagination" (181) is to criticize rather than to envision or detail a parallel universe. This is an important distinction between the eighteenth-century understanding of the imagination and the romantic version. Imagination constitutes work (in Boswell's perspective) that is anchored to the past and the present rather than in daydreams of an alternate reality. Given this loaded history that is firmly attached to Boswell's use of dramatic metaphor, the remainder of this chapter catalogues how Boswell reimagined dramatic metaphor to launch his own critical narrative project.

"My mind filled with London images"

Although the *London Journal* might be memorable as a record of Boswell's sexual encounters and temptations with London's morally ambiguous diversions and entertainments, these varied experiences do not, for Boswell, adequately constitute all of the threatening aspects of late-century London's heterogeneity. In addition to these fragmented experiences, Boswell considers London to threaten his attempts at self-definition because he inherits too many conflicting textual representations that claim to adequately instruct him. One of the reasons why Boswell assumes that he can relate to London is because his "mind fill[s] with London images" (177); that is, Boswell recognizes London as he recollects "images" that the *Spectator* has taught him to recognize. Addison and Steele's writing contributed to the proliferation of print as an urban phenomenon; its rhetoric succeeds only because it addresses factors that are only present in London: a readership groping for a new mode of government in the wake of 1688 and coffeehouses that serve as both the content and the sites of distribution and reception. Boswell obviously read Addison and Steele before making his first pilgrimage to London in 1760. Thus, Addison and Steele's particular critical imagination or writing style constitutes the lens through which Boswell is able to make sense of London. The "ideas," conduct, and textual styles with which Addison and Steele govern their readers become Boswell's urban guidebook, and Boswell adopts these ideas, conducts, and textual styles with a "when in Rome" approach. This is why the *London Journal* rarely provides a description of the physical city. The *London Journal* instead details Boswell's conduct in, or as he makes his way through, London.

If Boswell values London because he believes that its heterogeneous environment motivates him to better himself, then Boswell is an urbanite in a very different sense than we have come to know him. Most studies that analyze Boswell's relationship to London have focused on the content of Boswell's *London Journal*. From this perspective, Boswell is an urban creature because he is a classical libertine. By concentrating on the way Boswell writes, however, I suggest that Boswell is the ultimate urbanite not because he appears to be over-anxious, obsequious, and hedonistic but because he readily accepts the terms required by both Addison and Steele's urban audience (receptive passivity) and the urban critic (subtle rhetorical didacticism).

The figure of the disinterested critic can help us understand why Boswell relishes passivity. Boswell's beloved Mr. Spectator exhibited a valuable social-critical function because Addison and Steele painted this figure as an aloof, objective observer.[39] Boswell explicitly describes his political relationship to London in these terms:

> I consider mankind in general, and therefore cannot take a part in their quarrels when divided into particular states and nations. . . . This being the case, I am rather passive than active in life. It is difficult to make my feeling clearly understood. I may say, I act passively. That is, not with my

whole heart, and thinking this or that of real consequence, but because so and so things are established and I must submit. (77)

"I must submit" is hardly the war cry of the libertine. Boswell continues to shore up his subtle allegiance to a critical lineage as he considers "a person of imagination . . . such as the Spectator" to be the happiest urban individual:

> In reality, a person of small fortune who has only the common views of life and would just be as well as anybody else, cannot like London. But a person of imagination and feeling, such as the Spectator finely describes, can have the most lively enjoyment from the sight of external objects without regard to property at all. London is undoubtedly a place where men and manners may be seen to the greatest advantage. The liberty and the whim that reigns there occasions a variety of perfect and curious characters. Then the immense crowd and the hurry and bustle of business and diversion, the great number of public places of entertainment, the noble churches and the superb buildings of different kinds, agitate, amuse, and elevate the mind. Besides, the satisfaction of pursuing whatever plan is most agreeable, without being known or looked at, is very great. Here a young man of curiosity and observation may have a sufficient fund of present entertainment, and may lay up ideas to employ his mind in age. (68–69)

Couched in the middle of this passage, which defends the propertyless critic, is Boswell's paean to London's ability to "agitate, amuse, and elevate the mind." The phrase is important because it sketches the narrative formula that Boswell tried to follow in the *London Journal*. Agitation provokes Boswell to write both entertainingly (to "amuse") and instructively (to "elevate"). He immediately qualifies this admission by stressing how "agreeable" it is to be not "known or looked at." Boswell tries to enjoy being the observer rather than the observed.

To concretize his role as his own critic, Boswell even alludes to arguably the most famous *Spectator* paper, commonly known as "Twenty-four Hours in London": "We walked to Hyde Park Corner, from whence we set out at ten. Our spirits were high with the notion of the adventure, and the variety that we met with as we went along is amazing. As the Spectator observes, one end of London is like a different country from the other in look and manners" (153). Boswell references *Spectator* 454 in which the agitated critic, "being restless, not out of Dissatisfaction, but a certain busie Inclination one sometimes has," traverses Court and City to discover that "the Hours of the Day and Night are taken up in the Cities of *London* and *Westminster* by Peoples as different from each other as those who are Born in different Centuries."[40] In this same *Spectator* paper, Steele's narrator visits the City's Exchange and literally ascends into the balcony overlooking the Exchange's courtyard to "Survey" the international trade taking place below. From this privileged, critical perspective, our critic distills his function:

> [D]ear creatures [women shopkeepers working in the Exchange] called to me to ask what I wanted, when I could not answer, only *To look at you*. I went to one of the Windows which opened to the Area below, where all the several Voices lost their Distinction, and rose up in a confused Humming, which created in me a Reflection that could not come into the Mind of any but of one a little too studious; for I said to my self, with a kind of Punn in Thought, *What Nonsense is all the Hurry of this World to those who are above it?*[41]

During "a Reflection," our critic again alludes to the model figure of *The Conscious Lovers* who takes more pleasure in "thinking than eating," in being "above it." Boswell is this type of disinterested critic because he writes himself into, or advertises, this position while using strategies to govern his own conduct. Boswell also defines "the Londoner" in terms similar to those that describe Steele's man of reflection:

> In reality, a person of small fortune who has only the common views of life and would just be as well as anybody else, cannot like London. But a person of imagination and feeling, such as the Spectator finely describes, can have the most lively enjoyment from the sight of external objects without regard to property at all. London is undoubtedly a place where men and manner may be seen to the greatest advantage. (68)

"Men and manner," or self-government and conduct, are at stake in the *London Journal*. As "a person of imagination," Boswell values London because he imagines that the disinterested critic tames its heterogeneity.

"BOSWELL (TO HIMSELF)"

When I claim that the *London Journal* is a critical narrative project, I use "narrative" to allude to the way both form and content change over the

CHAPTER 5: BOSWELL'S *LONDON JOURNAL* 173

course of the *London Journal*. In terms of content, several critics have made strong arguments for the *London Journal*'s self-conscious structure by tracing how certain themes or episodes change over the course of the work. Examples of these episodes include Boswell's attempt to enroll in the Guards, his recovery from venereal disease, his meeting Samuel Johnson, and, of course, his affair with Louisa. The final part of this chapter, however, claims that a formal narrative underwrites this changing content. Boswell designs a plot for not only content but also form. By the end of the *London Journal,* the way Boswell uses textual traditions and rhetorical devices has changed along with Boswell's opinion of himself. In particular, Boswell calls attention to the way different textual strategies gather value for text to such an extent that by the end of the *London Journal,* writing constitutes governing. The formal strategies that undergo this change and assist the analogical and metaphorical imaginations in making writing appear to be a tool for government include genre, tense, and a self-conscious narrative voice. Boswell's imaginative modes, therefore, enable him to do new things to textual traditions. This chapter concludes by detailing the effect of Boswell's imaginative modes on form.

Boswell imports two generic conventions directly into the *London Journal:* dramatic dialogue and the epistolary. In the context of a journal, however, these conventions do not act the same way as they would in a play, essay, novel, or other canonical context. For example, Boswell frames his dialogues in two manners. He either prefaces characters' lines with their name (to resemble a promptbook), or he does not signify the speaker's identity and couches the entire dialogue in a single paragraph (to resemble a Platonic, philosophical conversation). When Boswell uses the promptbook style, he advertises his own participation and function as critic. Consider, for instance, one of Boswell's many dialogues at Child's in which he attempts to make the "PHYSICIAN" character reinterpret his opinion about the recent peace:

> 1 CITIZEN. Pray now, what do you really think of this Peace?
> 2 CITIZEN. That it is a damned bad one, to be sure!
> PHYSICIAN. Damned bad one? Pray what would you be at? Have not you had all that you wanted? Did you not begin the war to settle your boundaries in North America? And have not you got that done, as Mr. Pitt the great champion of the Opposition acknowledged in the House, better than could have been expected? Have not you got a large tract of country ceded to you? Is not the line of division plain and straight?

> BOSWELL. Suppose, Sir, I went out a-hunting with intention to bring home a hare to dinner, and catch three hares. Don't you think that I may also bring home the other two? (75)

Boswell sees his presence managing these characters; he is there to cast their conversations in the correct light. His metaphors guide them to reinterpret their opinions: "I don't think this at all bad. My simile of the hares (my metaphor, rather) is pretty well" (76). Boswell's dialogues are not important for what is said but for how Boswell represents these dialogues in writing.

Boswell's presence also complicates the simple "two people on the stage" model of dialogue. Michael Prince has examined how moral philosophers such as Shaftesbury, Mandeville, Berkeley, and Hume reconceive the dialogue form during the eighteenth century, many of them using dialogues "to make allowance for the increasing autonomy of individual subjects and increasing diversity within social order while still portraying an inevitable consolidation of viewpoints, characters, and interests under a providential scheme."[42] Boswell's dialogues frequently replace this "providential scheme" with "himself." For example, during one of Boswell's promptbook dialogues with Louisa, Boswell assigns lines to "BOSWELL (to himself)"(160). These stage directions do not, however, preface a soliloquy. Boswell is the writer of a journal, recollecting not what he said to Louisa but what he remembers thinking while writing the journal. In the context of a journal, Boswell recollects speaking "to himself" by using a convention of onstage soliloquy—a convention that usually does not include the playwright's own recollections. This is a complex move that is not simply "dramatic"; it is a gesture towards some other, more critical form of writing. This is why we all might be reading Boswell's infamous declaration, "There's conduct for you" (71) rather solipcistically; the "you" might actually refer to Boswell's imagined critical faculty, rather than the reader. Regardless of this complexity, Boswell introduces his appearance in these dialogues as an improvement upon an old scheme: "As I hope to have the honour of a forenoon's conversation with her Ladyship [Northumberland], I shall enrich my journal with it in the form of the original dialogue" (131). Boswell not only rewrites this dialogue but also assigns value to it; he states that this dialogue "enrich[es]" text. Boswell, in a similar manner to Fielding in *Tom Jones,* both dictates what constitutes proper writing and exemplifies it.

When Boswell uses the Platonic style of dialogue, he supplies paren-

CHAPTER 5: BOSWELL'S *LONDON JOURNAL* 175

thetical comments to judge the appropriateness of this mode of representation: "(I think such conversations are best written in the dialogue way)" (89). The conversion that Boswell judges here is with Louisa, and Boswell interestingly frames it as a Platonic dialogue. That is, he uses the form that classical philosophers used to convey knowledge to readers.[43] The idea of framing his conversation with, or "seduction" of, Louisa in terms of a philosophical dialogue with back-and-forth questions and answers represents Boswell's attempt to fill old textual templates with new material. As we witnessed with Fielding, the resulting tone is both satiric and serious.

Consider, also, the way Boswell cites lines from the letters he writes. After citing his entire letter to Lord Eglinton, for example, Boswell moves to a reflective mode and critiques this letter: "I was certain this epistle would please him much. I was pleased with writing it. I felt myself quite serene and happy, my mind unclouded and serenely gay. I never remember to have passed more agreeable moments. All looked fine in my blest imagination." (181). Boswell's letters operate within a journal—a journal that critiques everything that comes before it. Boswell selectively imports these epistolary excerpts into the *London Journal* to remind himself that he writes well. It is therefore not surprising that Boswell reveals the value he assigns to writing as he recollects his opening to a letter to Lord Eglinton: "To the Earl of Eglinton, one of the Lords of his Majesty's Bedchamber, Boswell the Poet, sole Lord of his own, sends such compliments as men of the world generally send to each other" (147). In this satiric opening, Boswell advertises his independence; he, unlike Eglinton, does not work for "his Majesty." Boswell, because he is "the Poet," manages himself and uses writing, including this letter embedded within a journal, both to govern himself and to advertise this governing.

Boswell considers formal enplotment to be an additional strategy for assigning value to writing. In particular, the self-conscious references to his own writing increase as the *London Journal* progresses. He also begins to change tenses more often. These formal maneuvers are neither trivial nor unrelated to Boswell's critical narrative project. In order to imagine that writing constituted critical work because it disciplined, refined, and corrected conduct, Boswell had to make his journal appear as though its self-contained logic was self-evident and natural. Therefore, by the end of the *London Journal,* writing is as much Boswell's topic as his "Self."

To this end, Boswell's imaginative modes begin to produce proof that writing constitutes governing: "What greater proof need be given of dissipation than my forgetting to mark in my journal of yesterday that the hours between one and three were passed in the Little Theatre in the Haymarket under the auspices of Mr. Foote?" (255). Forgetting to write, an action that devalues the critical activity of recollecting, therefore resembles literal proof of moral "dissipation." When Boswell reads historical texts, he seems to adopt a disciplined lifestyle:

> I employed the day in reading Hume's *History,* which enlarged my views, filled me with great ideas, and rendered me happy. It is surprising how I have formerly neglected the study of history, which of all studies is surely the most amusing and the most instructive. As I am now begun to it in earnest, I hope to make good progress. I write my father regularly my observations on each volume, which is of great service to me and gives much satisfaction to him. (197)

Reading and writing, which Boswell interestingly yokes to Hume, history, and his father, are disciplinary tools. They are literally habit-forming practices. Over the course of the journal, Boswell gestures so often to the redemptive quality of his own writing that he even develops the ability to defend his imaginative modes against critique:

> He [William Temple] advised me to force myself to be reserved and grave in a greater degree, otherwise I would just be Jamie Boswell, without any respect. And he said he imagined that my journal did me harm, as it made me hunt about for adventures to adorn it with, whereas I should endeavour to be calm and studious and regular in my conduct, in order to attain by habit a proper consistency of conduct. No doubt consistency of conduct is of the utmost importance. But I cannot find fault with this my journal, which is far from wishing for extravagant adventures, and is as willing to receive my silent and serious meditations as my loud and boisterous rhodomontades. Indeed, I do think that keeping of a journal a very excellent scheme if judiciously executed. (269)

Boswell conducts his journal in the proper manner; he knows when to include "serious meditations" and when to import his "loud and boisterous rhodomontades." The jarring distinction between "meditations" and "rhodomontades" shows that Boswell even tailors his diction to enforce these rules of proper textual conduct. Boswell sees no discrepancy between "endeavour[ing] to be calm and studious and regular in my conduct" and his "judiciously executed" *London Journal.* Indeed, Boswell views the

London Journal not as an unhinged confessional but as a workbook for effective self-government.

We can map Boswell's derivation of this textual value onto the plot of the *London Journal* and trace its first appearance back to his convalescence. At the outbreak of "Signor Gonorrhoea" (155)[44] and prefacing the months of treatment he will undergo, Boswell punctuates his meticulously edited journal with a rare, interruptive dash:

> —What will now become of my journal for some time? It must be a barren desert, a mere blank. To relate gravely that I rose, made water, took drugs, sat quiet, read a book, saw a friend or two day after day, must be exceedingly poor and tedious. Yet I may have some incidents to insert. (166)

Boswell, of course, does not record such minutiae during his convalescence but uses his imagination to establish a conversion narrative. Boswell is not worried that these minutiae may be "exceedingly poor and tedious" to a future reader of the *London Journal;* he is worried that the actual act of writing and reflecting upon these minutiae will offer no opportunities (no "agitation") for governing his conduct. We should note that Boswell values the deterioration of his textual and imaginative habits more than the rotting of his body. The metaphorical trumps the physical here, and this victory moves to the climax of his mini-conversion narrative:

> Upon my word my journal goes charmingly on at present. I was very apprehensive that there would be a dreary vacancy in it for some weeks, but by various happy circumstances I have been agreeably disappointed. I think, too, that I am making a good use of the hint which Captain Erskine gave me, and am taking more pains upon it, and consequently writing it in a more correct style. Style is to sentiment what dress is to the person. The effects of both are very great, and both are acquired and improved by habit. When once we are used to it, it is as easy to dress neatly as like a sloven; in the same way, custom makes us write in a correct style as easily as in a careless, inaccurate one. (186–87)

"As" is the operative word in this climax. Boswell is able to view his writing style as a symptom of his moral fortitude by using an analogy ("Style is to sentiment what dress is to the person"). The analogical imagination is again at work. This climax quickly moves to a reflective mode as Boswell applauds not his dialogue, past conduct, or wit; now, after his conversion takes place, he applauds his own writing style:

> How easily and cleverly do I write just now! I am really pleased with myself; words come skipping to me like lambs upon Moffat Hill; and I turn my periods smoothly and imperceptibly like a skilful wheelwright turning tops in a turning-loom. There's fancy! There's simile! In short, I am at present a genius: in that does my opulence consist, and not in base metal. (187)

This self-reflexive disclaimer hinges on a simile ("like a skilful wheelwright"), and this simile allows Boswell to recognize the foundational tools for his proper vocation: "There's fancy! There's simile! In short, I am at present a genius." A conversion of writing style echoes a conversion of self. The imagination's duty to close the gap between writing and governing is complete.

Beside his episodes of textual self-consciousness, Boswell's most recognizable formal change over the course of the *London Journal* involves his seemingly random shifts in tense. Yet Boswell's shifts in tense accomplish at least three specific things. First, switching to the present tense allows Boswell to decrease the distance between his reflection and his present conduct. It produces a timeline that lends Boswell the impression of moral endurance and immediate enlightenment. Second, switching to the present also allows Boswell to distance himself from an undisciplined past and to stress his present reformation. Although Boswell's shifts in tense are complex, we can interpret them as corollary tools for interrogating Boswell's reflective imagination. Consider, for instance, his entry immediately following his evening with Louisa:

> I dined nowhere, but drank tea at Love's, and at night went to Covent Garden gallery and saw *The Jovial Crew.* My frame still thrilled with pleasure, and my want of so much rest last night gave me an agreeable languor. The songs revived in my mind many gay ideas, and recalled in the most lively colours to my imagination the time when I was first in London, when all was new to me, when I felt the warm glow of youthful feeling and was full of curiosity and wonder. I then had at times a degree of ecstasy of feeling that the experience which I have since had has in some measure cooled and abated. But then my ignorance at that time is infinitely excelled by the knowledge and moderation and government of myself which I have now acquired. (141)

This complex knot of tense changes ("when I was," "I then had," "the experience which I have since had has," "But then my ignorance at that time is infinitely excelled," "which I have now acquired") suggests that Boswell wants to write about his sexual experience (that is, not edit it out) yet frame it in a critical context that permits instantaneous reflection as well as completely reconciles it with the approaching conversion narrative. His writing about the experience therefore allows Boswell, later in the critical narrative project, to judge it incessantly by means of his reflective imagination. Most importantly, Boswell concludes this excerpt by acknowledging "the knowledge and moderation and government of myself which I have now acquired." In many ways, all of these tense changes are aimed at proving Boswell's "government of myself."

Third, Boswell's changes in tense enable him to retrofit past events. Using the same technique that Fielding employed in *Tom Jones* to advertise his "genius" in making seemingly chaotic early events in his plot merge into a single ending,[45] Boswell calls attention to episodes that have already happened in the past but which he failed to include in their proper place: "I have observed in some preceding period of this my journal that making money is one of the greatest pleasures in life, as it is very lasting and is continually increasing. But it must be observed that a great share of anxiety is the constant concomitant of this passion . . ." (185). Boswell's retrofit corrects and refines an earlier conduct. By the end of the *London Journal*, Boswell's retrofitted episodes almost consume the present as he begins his paragraphs with "I should have mentioned Last Sunday . . ." (323), and "I should have mentioned that . . ." (324). We have already seen the narrative importance of Boswell's most important retrofit: "I should have mentioned that on Monday night, coming up the Strand, I was tapped on the shoulder by a fine fresh lass. I went home with her" (332). Boswell's subtle, plotted alterations to genre, self-conscious references to his own writing, and shifts in tense establish a recognizable formal narrative that I have attempted to outline. But this formal narrative ultimately results in the same, open-ended conclusion that accompanies questions about Boswell's reformation. The *London Journal* helps Boswell discover textual techniques that enable him to imagine that writing can govern his conduct, but it remains to be seen, in the other volumes of the critical narrative project that the *London Journal* initiated, whether text can ever represent a finished, polished Boswell. In the end, the only elements driving Boswell's plot forward are turns in and out of reflective episodes. This seems counterintuitive to our traditional ideas about eighteenth-century narrative, yet it constitutes a very specific eighteenth-century textual project.

"O MY JOURNAL! ART THOU NOT HIGHLY DIGNIFIED?"

Writing was sacred to Boswell; he privileged it above all else. He provoked conversations in order to write them down; he bowed to buildings in order to understand or reflect upon why he bowed to them in the first place. Writing, for Boswell, was a moral anchor. He was able to have this relationship with text because he translated an eighteenth-century tradition of social criticism into a personal journal. This translation is Boswell's individual trademark—a trademark completely unrelated to Samuel Johnson. In fact, Boswell suggests that he was enjoying the self-governing benefits of journal writing well in advance of Johnson's suggestion "to keep a journal":

> He [Johnson] advised me to keep a journal of my life, fair and undisguised. He said it would be a very good exercise, and would yield me infinite satisfaction when the ideas were faded from my remembrance. I told him that I had done so ever since I left Scotland. He said he was very happy that I pursued so good a plan. And now, O my journal! art thou not highly dignified? Shalt thou not flourish tenfold? No former solicitations or censures could tempt me to lay thee aside; and now is there any argument which can outweigh the sanction of Mr. Samuel Johnson? He said indeed that I should keep it private, and that I might surely have a friend who would burn it in case of my death. For my own part, I have at present such an affection for this my journal that it shocks me to think of burning it. I rather encourage the idea of having it carefully laid up among the archives of Auchinleck. However, I cannot judge fairly of it now. Some years hence I may. (305)

Boswell obviously never listened to Johnson's suggestion to arrange for burning the work. Johnson simply ratifies something Boswell had valued since he wrote the first page of the journal: textual conduct. This final paean to writing, complete with its archaic personifications ("art thou not," "shalt thou not"), is completely consistent with the *London Journal*'s critical narrative project. It also unabashedly advertises "Boswell the Poet, sole Lord of his own" (147), a figure Boswell was previously able to imagine by writing a letter and then criticizing it within a journal. Boswell's writing governs as it imagines.

Beyond the pages of the *London Journal* and in some "real" life that we will never be able to recover, Boswell might very well have resembled a Dorimant at one moment and a celibate moral philosopher the next. My point is that Boswell includes all of these different conducts in the *London Journal* to exemplify his ability to control when they should appear and when (through editing or censoring) they should not make the final cut. The *London Journal* shows Boswell narrating and justifying his own stylebook. It is both his critique and his validation of his writing.

In the more general terms of eighteenth-century criticism, Boswell used the *London Journal* to envision himself participating in an extended, and definably British, social project. This is really a project of urban conduct in two ways. First, it continues a critical project that began with Dryden, continued with Addison and Steele, and reached a logical conclusion when Boswell internalized all of the tenets of disciplinary self-management attached to eighteenth-century social criticism. Second, Boswell uses dramatic metaphor to respond to an explicitly urban problem: the dangerous heterogeneity that he associated with a print-saturated London. At his arrival in London during the autumn of 1762, Boswell brought with him an archive of literary strategies developed by Addison, Steele, Gay, Fielding, and Pope that were explicitly tied to the Town's administrative novelty and its possibilities for alternative forms of urban government. Boswell also originally came to London to convert to Catholicism, but his own writing style activated the moral reform for which he was searching. Boswell's text is, if nothing else, an example of how valuable metaphor was for imagining alternate modes of self-government during the late eighteenth century. Boswell's analogical and reflective imaginations enabled this metaphor to work in a variety of ways. And the incessant variety of the *London Journal*'s twentieth-century critical assessments may be a testament to Boswell's imagination working in minds other than his own.

What does this interrogation of Boswell's dramatic-critical metaphor suggest for our critical approach to eighteenth-century metaphor? Boswell's *London Journal* shows how much value form had acquired by the 1760s. Boswell's assumption that the style and form in which writers wrote determined their moral character was nothing new. Boswell's particular novelty, however, was to suggest how textual form could define, refine, and improve wayward tendencies by replacing idleness with habits, plans, and schemes. Textual habit, or form, possessed so much concrete value to Boswell that he explicitly states that he was "devoted to form." He writes with this moral in tow. Dramatic metaphor was one of these extremely valuable forms; however, as this chapter has tried to show, it was valuable because it alluded to an archive of critical activity that firmly anchored Boswell in an eighteenth-century critical project of refining and managing imagination. As a result of historicizing this metaphor, we may begin to see Boswell not as an over-anxious, psychologically tormented twenty-two year old who writes incoherently, but as a writer with more control over his craft than we have previously attributed to him. While Boswell's self-policing project was tailored for journal writing, many writers questioned whether other late eighteenth-century genres could sketch out strategies for self-government and self-knowledge. The next chapter explores how women writers such as Frances Burney recognized the novel's potential for governing readers' interiors and contributing to a self-governing populace in London.

6

Frances Burney's "Inward Monitor" and the Self-Governing Woman

If Boswell's experience in a print-saturated London threatened his conception of an authentic self and motivated him to develop strategies of self-government, then Frances Burney's ideas about urban selfhood were even more complex due to gendered notions of urban conduct. In her second novel, *Cecilia* (1782), Burney presents readers with a moment that highlights how London's proliferating print technology presented a new cultural problem to women who tried to navigate the urban landscape on their own. Unlike Boswell's moral anguish over his inability to interpret the innumerable ways a man could relate to London's environment, Burney's problem instead focuses on how these proliferating signs and textual representations did not offer women endless possibilities for self-definition. As Burney experienced them, these proliferating signs and textual representations placed an infinite number of boundaries upon women's urban experiences and cast women as passive objects. Burney recognizes that London's blurred readability was actually limiting a woman's experience of the city.

For example, *Cecilia* records a heroine's experience amid the mobs that inhabited London's street level—the same environment that Boswell had conceived to be dizzying and in need of discipline. Outside "the * * coffeehouse," Cecilia "jump[s] out of the carriage, with the intention to run down the street" in search of her male suitor, Delvile:

> Mean while the frantic Cecilia escaped both pursuit and insult by the velocity of her own motion. She called aloud upon Delvile as she flew to the end of the street. No Delvile was there!—she turned the corner;

> yet saw nothing of him; she still went on, though unknowing whither, the distraction of her mind every instant growing greater, from the inflammation of fatigue, heat, and disappointment. She was spoken to repeatedly, she was even caught once or twice by her riding habit; but she forced herself along by her own vehement rapidity, not hearing what was said, not heeding what was thought. . . . She scarce touched the ground; she scarce felt her own motion; she seemed as if endued with supernatural speed, gliding from place to place, from street to street; with no consciousness of any plan, and following no other direction than that of darting forward where-ever there was most room, and turning back when she met with any obstruction; till quite spent and exhausted, she abruptly ran into a yet open shop, where, breathless and panting, she sunk upon the floor, and, with a look disconsolate and helpless, sat for some time without speaking.[1]

The abstract details of this passage (she visits "the * * coffeehouse" [*C*, 894] and collapses "in — street") combine with its "breathless" litany of emotional experience, punctuated by commas and semi-colons, to represent late eighteenth-century London as an abstract interior experience rather a Dickensian description anchored to clearly detailed external referents. What is unique to a lone woman's experience of London's streets, however, is the feeling of passivity that accompanies this experience. Passive voice saturates this crucial episode ("she was spoken to"; "she was even caught") as though Burney wishes readers to experience the conflicting feelings of independence and passivity that accompany a woman who must interpret London without a male conductor. During this moment, Cecilia lacks self-conscious interpretation or reflection—a dangerous interior condition which Cecilia's external silence tries to represent.

Cecilia's street-level flight exposes the inadequate interpretive skills for navigating London that conduct books and male guardians have bequeathed to her. Burney stresses this failure by trapping the exhausted Cecilia in a nightmare of ambiguous economic signification; that is, the "open shop" to which Cecilia flees is a pawnbroker's shop: "'She's quite crazy,' said the man of the house, who was a Pawn-Broker; 'we had better get rid of her before she grows mischievous'" (*C*, 897). This interpretive house of mirrors continues when the owners mistake her for a prostitute by "concluding at first she was a woman of the town" (*C*, 897). Imprisoned in a pawnbroker's bedroom in an indefinable area of London, Cecilia becomes what both Boswell and Burney had feared they might become while living and writing in a textually saturated London: a misinterpreted, ambiguous textual sign. As a result of Cecilia's lone flight though London's streets, the woman of the pawnbroker shop transforms the "lost" Cecilia into a newspaper advertisement so that other Londoners might be able to read, interpret, and reclaim Cecilia:

> The woman [of the house], growing uneasy from her uncertainty of pay for her trouble, asked the advice of some of her friends what was proper for her to do; and they counselled her to put an advertisement into the papers herself the next morning.
>
> The following, therefore, was drawn up and sent to the printer of the *Daily Advertiser.*
>
> MADNESS
>
> Whereas a crazy young lady, tall, fair complexioned, with blue eyes and light hair, ran into the Three Blue Balls, in — street, on Thursday night, the 2d instant, and has been kept there since out of charity. She was dressed in a riding habit. Whoever she belongs to is desired to send after her immediately. She has been treated with the utmost care and tenderness. She talks much of some person by the name of Delvile.
>
> *N.B.* She had no money about her.

May, 1780 (*C,* 901)

This advertisement interprets Cecilia's exterior features; not only does it describe her as "tall, fair complexioned, with blue eyes and light hair," but also "crazy." With this newspaper excerpt, Burney suggests that London's printed text not only misinterprets a woman's authentic interior but also reproduces these misinterpretations throughout the city, *ad infinitum.* Our reading about Cecilia's madness in a newspaper excerpt *within a novel* is notable because it allows Burney to suggest that London's proliferating print technologies do not refine and specialize knowledge about female Londoners. Instead, printed text helps to misinterpret and to categorize Cecilia as a completely passive creature. Yet *Cecilia* is not the first time that Burney focuses on the debilitating effects of London's proliferating print culture upon women.

Although Burney's first novel *Evelina* (1778) never forces its heroine onto London's streets alone, *Evelina* does examine how the conflicting and ambiguous signs of London inflict confusion and passivity onto women.[2] Consider, for instance, the disjointed, staccato exclamations that characterize Evelina's first London-letter to her male guardian, the Rev. Mr. Arthur Villars:

> This moment arrived. Just going to Drury-Lane theatre. The celebrated Mr. Garrick performs Ranger. I am quite in extacy. So is Miss Mirvan. How fortunate that he should happen to play! We would not let Mrs. Mirvan rest till she consented to go, her chief objection was to our dress, for we have had not time to *Londonize* ourselves. . . .
>   I can write no more now. I have hardly time to breathe—only just this, the houses and streets are not quite so superb as I expected. However, I have seen nothing yet, so I ought not to judge.[3]

Evelina's first letter in London is important for at least three reasons. First, the verb "*Londonize*" introduces the type of female agency that is available to Evelina in London; that is, Evelina fills her London letters with passive constructions rather than active verbs. These passive constructions introduce the city into Evelina's letters:

> The shops are really very entertaining, especially the mercers; there seem to be six or seven men belonging to each shop, and every one took care, by bowing and smirking, to be noticed; we were conducted from one to another, and carried from room to room, with so much ceremony, that at first I was almost afraid to go on. (*E*, 21)

The phrase "we were conducted" summarizes the extent to which Evelina controls her actions in London. Evelina uses passive constructions to describe an infinite number of experiences that she does not know how to interpret or narrate. Second, the image of London that Evelina brings to the city shapes her actual experiences there: "the houses and streets are not quite so superb as I expected." Burney suggests that the printed technologies that shaped Evelina's notion of London (conduct books, parental advice, and perhaps even the writings of Gay, Fielding, and Pope) fail her. Finally, Evelina punctuates her letters to convey a sense of how London's crushing pace and incessant demands for interpretation make it impossible to write. She continually exposes how the demand that she, as a young woman in London, write detailed letters to her male guardian is at odds with the letter's ability to adequately contain and represent all of her actions and thoughts while in London. Thus she proclaims, "I can write no more now. I have hardly time to breathe," yet she continues to write because she has been taught to do so: "I could not forbear writing a few words instantly on my arrival" (*E,* 20). Evelina even apologizes for her formal inadequacy, believing that London, with more time, will make her a better writer: "Pray excuse the wretched stuff I write perhaps I may improve by being in this town, and them letters will be less unworthy your reading" (*E,* 22). Evelina finally confronts the impossibility of interpreting everything that happens to her in London: "I have a vast deal to say, and shall give all this morning to my pen. As to my plan of writing every evening the adventures of the day, I find it impracticable; for the diversions here are so very late, that if I begin my letters after them, I could not go to bed at all" (*E,* 22). Evelina concedes that she is exhausted by the irresolvable difference between London's advertised image and her ability to authentically record her experience. In turn, Evelina yokes her inability to conduct herself properly to her "London letters": "And here I conclude my London letters,—and without any regret; for I am too inexperienced and ignorant to conduct myself with propriety in this town, where everything is new to me, and many things are unaccountable and perplexing" (*E,* 40). In Evelina's attempt to provide her male guardian with her initial reaction to London, Evelina submits to London's "perplexing" environment and the apparent agency it has over her knowledge and actions.

With these examples, Burney suggests that a thoroughly print-drenched London requires women to imagine new interpretive strategies to avoid their being written into a state of passivity. When Evelina writes about the demand "to *Londonize* ourselves," she advertises a passivity inflicted upon women citizens not only by a personified "London," but also by a specific style of writing that characterized London epistles. For Burney, "Londonization" is a process that renders both Evelina and Cecilia passive. For instance, neither heroine fully comprehends Londonization. London is a place where neither heroine wishes to be. Evelina and Cecilia are repeatedly delayed in London (it is almost impossible for Burney to express this detail without using passive voice), and they repeatedly wish to return to the country. These captive writers offer a unique twist on letter writing; they literally navigate or conduct themselves through an environment that previous texts designed to be unmaneuverable to the unmarried woman. In particular, writing becomes a survival skill that exercises imagination and explores agency in both a setting and textual tradition that imposed supposedly natural limitations on what women could say and write. Burney uses Evelina's personal letters to advertise these limitations: "And yet, I must confess, that I am not half so happy here at present as I was ere I went to town: but the change is in the place, not in me" (*E,* 98). This confession, with its qualifying disclaimer, "the change is in the place, not in me," shows Evelina granting a large amount of agency to an entity that she distinguishes from herself: her environment.[4] This separation and the confession which encourages it appear both dangerous and artificial. This personification of place is, Burney suggests by writing *Evelina* and *Cecilia,* a side effect of textual representation. The difference between Evelina's reliance upon writing and the role that letters in *Cecilia* play can therefore suggest how Burney reimagined a woman's relationship to a London that was now saturated with a type of printed text that attempted to control and conduct her.

It is, of course, arguable whether Cecilia's self-navigating flight through London is "realistic"; however, my point is that Burney's novels represent how women experienced late eighteenth-century London—how women *felt* while interpreting not only London's spaces but also any writing that originated in the city. Burney's own experiences, recorded in her journals and letters, further support this claim. For instance, as early as 1768, Burney's journal records the suspicion and ambiguity that accompanies letters from London:

> Oh my dear, I have received the *finest* letter that ever was wrote—sure!—while we were at Dinner, a packet came from London—papa opened it—& among other Epistles, was the following to me—
>
> To Miss Frances Burney
> When first I saw thee, Fanny, move
> Ah me! what meant my throbbing heart?
> Tell me—oh tell me—is it Love
> That is Lodged here within my Breast?
> Incognitus[5]

Although Burney's mother eventually attributes its authorship to a family member,[6] this letter nonetheless exhibits how Burney had been acclimated to London's ambiguous signs and letters early in her life. While "Incognitus" is on a first-name basis with Burney, she is left to interpret the Londoner's textual puzzle. In a 1777 letter to her sister Susanna, Burney details the volumes of urban literature that she and her family's friends consume as they anticipate a return to London:

> *We Read:* Mr. Crisp pores over Critical Reviews to Sir John Hawkins; Mrs. Hamilton, the Tradesmen's Bills; Miss Cook, her own pocket Book, or *Ladies Memorandum,* and I,—am studying, against I return to Town, *Le Diable Boiteux,* which contains no few moral sentences, proper for those who dwell in a great *Methropolis* [sic]."[7]

Amid these frenzied descriptions of her circle's varied reading lists, Burney emphasizes her "studying" Le Sage's novel for its "moral sentences" and its instructive conduct. Under the heading of *"We Read,"* Burney reveals to her sister the textual and interpretive preparation that conditioned her return to London. Thus, Burney's experience with interpreting London-based texts involves not only being attracted to endless diversions and agitation (like Boswell's experience) but also—and this is the new cultural problem that a woman's experience brings to the foreground—being pulled (in passive voice) from one attraction to another by writerly authorities, many of them unknown men.[8] Burney thoroughly recognized the textual techniques that Gay, Fielding, and Pope had established to control others, especially as she represented her experiences in London.

Given the boundaries which Burney felt London's printed text was placing on women, late eighteenth-century London clearly presented Burney with a new cultural problem: how to acquire an authentic sense of selfhood amid an infinite number of competing, confusing, and frequently ambiguous textual signs and conventions in London that were designed to limit and control a woman's urban experience. In writing *Evelina* and *Cecilia,* Burney faced an important question: if a previous generation of authors (such as Gay, Fielding, and Pope) governed the female experience of London by imagining passivity to be part of that experience, then how might women salvage printed text to reimagine their urban agency? Burney answers this question on a formal level by rejecting the epistolary novel as a vehicle for self-knowledge. Refusing to be governed by unrelated, disparate texts that saturated the marketplace as they attempted to control London's populace, Burney writes *Cecilia* as an experiment in imaginative self-government. Burney does not write *Evelina* and *Cecilia* to govern readers; rather, she offers readers (particularly women readers) new interpretive strategies for governing themselves within a London that is not of their own making—a London they did not originally imagine. For this reason, *Cecilia* trains the interpretive skills of its readers so that rather than relying upon the imagined governance of Gay, Fielding, and Pope, these readers might govern themselves.

This chapter therefore views Burney's first two novels beyond a critical narrative that privileges confession as the eighteenth-century novel's only mode of interiority.[9] At the same time, the goal is not to present Burney's first two novels as anomalies in a narrative about the eighteenth-century novel but to view Burney's modes of interiority as viable alternatives to confession. In particular, I argue that *Evelina* and *Cecilia* constituted a project in which Burney rejected confessional and interior revelation as signs of feminine health or proper conduct. Writing about women and their relationship to a city previously defined by male writers such as Gay, Addison, and Steele, Burney suggests that highly self-conscious interpretative activity should replace epistolary confession. For Burney, this substitution results in a woman's proper definition of urban independence and generates a type of self-government that could counter London's proliferation of ambiguous and confusing printed advice. This at first seems counterintuitive to twenty-first-century interpretations of eighteenth-century interiority. Burney's rejection, however, does not mean that she reinscribed herself within a masculine paradigm; instead, it allowed Burney to suggest how urban geography and textual traditions could recommend new ways for women writers to compete with male writers for imagined sites of authority in London.

I focus on *Evelina* (1778) and *Cecilia* (1782) instead of addressing Burney's final two novels, *Camilla* (1796) and *The Wanderer* (1814), for two reasons. First, London is a virtual character in *Evelina* and *Cecilia*. Each novel attempts to illustrate London's dizzying influence on a woman's "entrance into the world"; the heroine of each novel learns things about herself when she learns things about London. Burney therefore mapped her specific brand of interiority onto London to make her version legible to an urban audience.[10] Lacking a Freudian vocabulary or an elaborate tradition of free indirect discourse, Burney anchored her idea of interiority to a literal cityscape. This literal cityscape, however, was simply an imaginative starting point for Burney.[11] Burney assumed that her readers would be familiar with either London's geography or classical textual traditions. Thus, the metaphor of conduct is an important tool for Burney since this metaphor could at some times refer directly to the way conduct books produced urban knowledge, and at other times, this metaphor could help readers imagine new geographic relationships (a critical self-awareness that replaced male guardians in the literal cityscape) or forms (new modes, voices, or narratives that replaced epistolarity). By evoking the metaphor of conduct while describing London, Burney outlined a version of interiority that did not require the pain and humiliation that Jane Austen would continue to yoke to self-knowledge.

Burney's urban project not only tested the inherent, moral nature of a heroine, but it also judged the effects of the city on its inhabitants' values as the city became a dominant model for governing British people. By referring to "the city" as an "it" with "its" own archive of moral qualities, I mean to highlight a unique personification that Burney questions throughout these novels. If there is a common task shared by *Evelina* and *Cecilia,* it is to link interiority to abstract representations of London. Burney helped to build the idea that London—as a character with its own disposition—exhibited an agency that Burney's characters must either blindly accept or carefully question.

Another reason why I view *Evelina* and *Cecilia* as components of a novelistic project involves they way Burney used *Cecilia* to rewrite *Evelina.* Both novels launch a young orphaned woman into London. Both novels carefully detail moments of crisis that are unique to women who lack proper conductors, guardians, or parents. Both novels substitute London for proper parents.[12] Both novels self-consciously exploit epistolarity. I argue that the formal and thematic similarities between *Evelina* and *Cecilia* allow us to view the two novels as a single project that attempted to outline, clarify, and validate feminine authority in London. *Evelina* and *Cecilia* constituted a single project because, as I will show, Burney imagined that her writing in and beyond an epistolary mode could change or at least guide the way women conceptualized their relationship to authority in London. It is difficult to see this project in either *Evelina* or *Cecilia* alone; however, by comparing the two novels' treatments of textual traditions and geographical boundaries, we may begin to identify how Burney imagined that she was, first, redesigning women's interior selves, and second, representing these interiors as proper and natural elements of the self-governed Londoner.

When I call the *Evelina-Cecilia* pair a "project," I refer to Burney's use of the word. There is a crucial episode in *Cecilia* when our heroine, during her first days in London, proposes "to become mistress of her own time" (*C,* 55). In a chapter Burney titles, "A Project," Cecilia uses her imagination to understand why Londoners' exteriors do not reveal their interior qualities:

> . . . she determined no longer to be the only one insensible to the blessings within her reach, but by projecting and adopting some plan of conduct,

better suited to her taste and feelings than the frivolous insipidity of her present life, to make at once a more spirited and more worthy use of the affluence, freedom and power which she possessed.

A scheme of happiness at once rational and refined soon presented itself to her imagination. She purposed, for the basis of her plan, to become mistress of her own time, and with this view, to drop all idle and uninteresting acquaintance, who while they contribute neither to use nor pleasure, make so large a part of the community, that they may properly be called the underminers of existence: she could then shew some taste and discernment in her choice of friends, and she resolved to select such only as by their piety could elevate her mind, by their knowledge improve her understanding, or by their accomplishments and manners delight her affections. (*C*, 54–55)

During this episode of "projecting," Cecilia imagines a "plan of conduct" that will help her relate to London and that does not involve confession or interior revelation. Cecilia imagines that she can transform desire into social action because Cecilia interprets her own desires rather than requiring others to do so for her. Burney also expresses Cecilia's imagination in a style that rejects Evelina's beloved epistles. Cecilia organizes her plan in her mind—not in a letter. As I will show, Burney's conceptualization of self-government and urban independence required her to reinterpret the epistolary novel's formal constraints. *Evelina* and *Cecilia* critique the ways in which epistolarity promotes written confession as an exercise in, or physical proof of, virtue and identity. The way the confessor-interpreter relationship produces truth parallels the way in which the epistolary novel's writer-reader relationship produced truth. While confession's artifice attained a certain transparency during the twentieth century, I am suggesting that *Evelina* and *Cecilia* attempted to expose this transparency to an eighteenth-century audience.

By calling the *Evelina-Cecilia* pair a project, I am also arguing that *Evelina* harbors several unanswered and open-ended questions. Most notably, although London is incessantly recalled throughout the novel's final volume in both content and the style in which Evelina writes, the city suddenly drops out of the novel after the second volume. I do not attempt to close off this open-endedness but to interpret Burney's next novel, *Cecilia,* as a sequel to *Evelina.* As a sequel, *Cecilia* reinterpreted what London and the textual traditions women used to record their urban experiences could and could not do for "women of letters." Because they are Burney's strategies of self-authorization in both novels, the textual traditions and urban geography Burney used between 1778 and 1782 require critical contextualization.

Urban Epistolarity (or, Confessing in Print)

A mimetic approach to epistolarity is partly to blame for the claim that Burney solely values confessional interiority in *Evelina*. Letters, so the argument goes, are vehicles for self-revelation; letters more adequately reveal truths about an abstract and timeless human condition than more "fictional" vehicles such as poetry or novels do. However, we must remember that eighteenth-century letters did not simply magnify an individual self that hived itself off from a social self or community. For example, we need to recall that the eighteenth-century letter was "an art . . . naturally looked upon as a continuation of the art of conversation . . . an art which at its best should be the triumph of wit and humor and imagination."[13] Conversation, which Addison and Steele considered to be the basis of imagination, was a social activity; thus, epistolary conversation was not only a private transaction but also a social art.[14] In his study of Samuel Richardson's epistolary techniques, Tom Keymer considers this artistry to focus upon "the experience of *writing*—on the efforts of engaged parties to describe, make sense of, and often advance particular purposes in, their world."[15] In this way, the eighteenth-century familiar letter, the foundational unit of the epistolary novel, harbored a social function that exercised both the reader's and writer's imaginations as the letter produced, performed, and replicated a writer's versions of self-knowledge and truth. The eighteenth-century letter was a highly crafted form of writing. Indeed, some of the most famous examples from the growing industry of conduct books were not books but collections of letters: Hester Chapone's *Letters on the Improvement of the Mind, Addressed to a Young Lady* and Wetenhall Wilkes's *A Letter of Genteel and Moral Advice to a Young Lady* are two of the most famous examples.[16] The letter not only brought with it a normalized writing style, but also delivered rules of social conduct to readers. This perspective suggests that eighteenth-century letter writing was not always an activity that privileged an interior self over considerations about its readers.

Epistolarity is only initially part of Burney's novelistic project; she experiments with the form in *Evelina*, but, in *Cecilia*, rejects certain limitations that writing an epistolary novel had allowed her to recognize. This is not to say that Burney, as an eighteenth-century woman novelist, was able to discard the myth that writing epistles was a feminine skill;[17] however, by making *Cecilia* inherit only faint traces of epistolarity, Burney was able not only to expose the inherent limitations that the epistolary form assigned to women writers, but also to exploit the myth that only epistolary talent could produce a marketable woman novelist.

Another way to interpret the relationship between *Evelina* and *Cecilia* is to place the *Evelina-Cecilia* project in the context of the proliferation of eighteenth-century writing about London. By 1777, Londoners had access to a variety of works written by men that professed to help readers understand their relationship to an urban community: John Gay's *Trivia,* John Rocque's 1746 map, Addison and Steele's periodicals, Samuel Johnson's "London," to name but a few. Therefore, from an urban context, there are at least two ways to explain why Burney began her *Evelina-Cecilia* project with an epistolary novel. First, the epistle remained a textual tradition associated with producing and performing feminine virtue.[18] Second, the function of the epistle had increasingly been associated with instructing women. By casting *Evelina* as an epistolary novel and then writing *Cecilia* as a retrospective critique of the epistolary novel's influence on the way women related to London, she initiated a project that explored how genres became gendered and meaningful. Thus, *Evelina* began a project that attempted to respond to Evelina's awareness of a gaping void in the literary marketplace: "But, really, I think there ought to be a book, of the laws and customs *à-la-mode,* presented to all young people upon their first introduction into public company" (*E,* 70). The specificity of Evelina's request ("of the laws and customs *à-la-mode*") suggests that conventional conduct books were not adequately doing their job, especially for young women introduced to the public. Like the strategies of self-government in Boswell's *London Journal,* Burney's novels are made possible by London's changed urban environment since she and her fictional characters are dealing with their inheritance of Fielding's, Gay's, and Pope's contributions to imaginative governance and strategies for shared consensus. Unlike Boswell, however, Burney's London is complicated by gendered forms of writing and the gendered spaces that these forms construct.

The History of a Young Lady's Entrance into the World (or *Evelina*)

Despite *Evelina*'s epistolary template, Evelina is not comfortable writing letters. Consider, for example, Evelina's unease as she forces herself into her first epistle: "Lady Howard insists upon my writing!—yet I hardly know how to go on"; "I am half ashamed of myself for beginning this letter"; "I almost repent already that I have made this confession" (*E*, 18–19). Confession generates Evelina's anxiety; it is the source of her "shame." Evelina's untamed style—her dashes, her exclamations, her spontaneous modal auxiliaries—exposes the assumptions that women letter-writers unknowingly perpetuated: "I made a resolution when I began, that I would not be urgent; but my pen—or rather my thoughts, will not suffer me to keep it—for I acknowledge, I must acknowledge, I cannot help wishing for your permission" (*E*, 18–19).[19] Evelina anxiously corrects her diction to accept the dutiful position of a letter writer: "I acknowledge, I must acknowledge." This self-editing—her injection of the modal "must" between subject and verb—distances Evelina from agency. Evelina also corrects her elision between "thoughts" and "pen" because the private letter, as the eighteenth-century myth claims, is supposed to be an unhinged, natural confessional that conceals nothing. By having Evelina correct her writing, Burney foregrounds this myth and therefore immediately destabilizes the logic that underwrites the epistolary novel that follows.

Although *Evelina* is an epistolary novel, Evelina's style and the content of her letters make it clear that the epistle is not an adequate form to record a "history of a young lady's entrance" into London. For example, Evelina is aware that her letters must satisfy Villars and his desire to read—or judge—the most quotidian details of her maturation in London. If Evelina is uncertain of her success in mastering the urban epistle, Villars's first response, which resembles a reader's report, assures her that her uncertainty and suffering are proof of maturity: "I am sure I need not say, how much more I was pleased with the mistakes of your inexperience at the private ball, than with the attempted adoption of more fashionable manners at the ridotto. But your confusion and mortifications were such as to entirely silence all reproofs on my part" (*E*, 46). Burney crafts this response carefully; it judges Evelina's conduct and then interprets her "confusion and mortifications" as evidence of her proper maturation. If, as Evelina wrote earlier, she feels "compelled to confess my absurdity" (*E*, 32), Villars's letter naturalizes this compulsive feeling; his letter naturalizes confession as proper conduct. The letter promotes Evelina's shame, her blushing ("yet I blush to write it to you!" [*E*, 33]), as an external marker of internal propriety and natural virtue. According to Villars, feelings of humility and shame adequately stand in for his presence in London as her guardian.

Villars writes his response letter (letter XV, volume I) on April 16; however, according to the order in which Burney presents the letters, Evelina does not receive Villars's report card until the very end of letter XXII (volume I), which Evelina writes on April 18. That is, the delay between Villars's writing and Evelina's reading (we read four lengthy letters written by Evelina before we witness her receiving Villars's letter) renders Villars's reaction obsolete, his power negligible. In fact, Burney interrupts the novel with an extended dash and a row of asterisks to suggest that the letter is impractical as a vehicle for uninterrupted guidance and surveillance:

> To-night we go to the Pantheon, which is the last diversion we shall partake of in London, for to-morrow—
> . . .
> This moment, my dearest Sir, I have received your kind letter.
> If you thought us too dissipated the first week, I almost fear to know what you will think of us this second . . . . (*E,* 87)

To make the epistolary work, Evelina needs to write to someone whom she imagines possesses the authority to critique her conduct. In the form through which Evelina must express her thoughts, Villars represents a particularly masculine position of authority because he acts as the distanced, Addisonian observer-critic who interprets what he sees or reads.

Throughout *Evelina,* Villars's letters validate Evelina's writing as social conduct. Villars is Evelina's reader and her literal conductor or guardian; we readers are merely voyeurs, reading over his shoulder.[20] When Villars judges Evelina's experiences, he uses a vocabulary of conduct:

> . . . I am led to apprehend that his [Mr. Macartney] unhappy situation is less the effect of misfortune, than of misconduct . . . .
> . . .
> . . . the right line of conduct is the same for both sexes, though the manner in which it is pursued, may somewhat vary, and be accommodated to the strength or weakness of the different travellers.
> . . .
> As to Sir Clement Willoughby, I know not how to express my indignation at his conduct. (*E,* 180–81)

Evelina's final letter to Villars, which she writes after marrying Orville, need only be three sentences long because the entire dynamic upon which her epistle rested (the need for a male guardian or interpreter) is now rendered obsolete by her marriage:

> All is over, my dearest Sir, and the fate of your Evelina is decided! This morning, with fearful joy, and trembling gratitude, she united herself for ever with the object of her dearest, her eternal affection.
>
> I have time for no more; the chaise now waits which is to conduct me to Berry Hill, and to the arms of the best of men. (*E,* 336–37)

Burney ingeniously spotlights Evelina's resignation of agency in this passage. For the first time in the novel, Evelina represents herself in the third-person voice; "she" is being conducted "to the arms of the best of men." Evelina's letters, in both form and content, end in a telescopic diminution of agency. *Cecilia,* however, strives to reclaim this third-person voice.

Although *Evelina* ends in confession and reconciliation, I have focused on several episodes to suggest that all is not well in Burney's canonical epistolary novel. Part of *Evelina*'s target is the dysfunction of epistolarity and the confessional tactics it uses to construct feminine interiority. These tactics include passive constructions, shameful revelation, and the myth (strengthened by her reader, Mr. Villars) that letters (the feminine "pen") expose women's natural "thoughts" for all to see. And although volume three of *Evelina* resembles a canonical eighteenth-century novel in its content, Burney taints our reception of this content because we can no longer unequivocally state that the form that delivers this content to us is an adequate representational vehicle.[21] In the end, *Evelina* the novel and Evelina the character are urban products. If *Evelina* details "The History of a Young Woman's Entrance into the World," then Evelina's history irretrievably shapes her to be an urban creature. One of the more dangerous side effects of employing a confessional mode of interiority in London is that it tends to personify and therefore empower "place" as a separate, indomitable entity. How strange for Burney to draw attention to the dysfunction of confessional interiority without designing anything to replace it; how stranger yet for us to consider *Evelina* to be Burney's last word on women's agency in London.

MEMOIRS OF AN HEIRESS (OR *CECILIA*)

If we can call *Evelina* Burney's performance of the side effects and limitations of confessional interiority, then *Cecilia* represents her attempt to move beyond these limitations. Whereas *Evelina* shows that Burney was conscious of the ways an epistolary novel inherently supported confessional tactics, *Cecilia* shows Burney imagining ways not only to explode the self-evident assumptions promoted by epistolarity, but also to suggest that interpretative skill should replace confession. *Cecilia* accomplishes these tasks in both its form and its content.

Burney narrates *Cecilia* in the third person. By rejecting the strictures of the epistolary novel that *Evelina* had briefly outlined, *Cecilia* renders everything that occurred between *Evelina*'s letters, those previously ineffable gaps, narratable. A sustained, self-conscious critique of form therefore becomes part of the narrator's agenda in *Cecilia*. Formal concerns, however, are no longer disruptions as they were in *Evelina*. Throughout *Cecilia*, Burney draws attention to the ways Cecilia's interior depends upon Cecilia's acquiring agency over her textual (epistolary) and social (male) conductors in London. One way to claim this authority, Burney suggests, is for women to reimagine their relationship to those who read their letters. For example, by imagining that she is guided not by a male reader but by an "inward monitor" (*C*, 585) of her own creation, Cecilia is able to act in ways that would normally be socially unacceptable for women in London. In particular, Cecilia rectifies a situation that even Burney's male characters cannot handle properly: a suicide that occurs at Vauxhall, which was one of the most public arenas in eighteenth-century Britain. Burney's genius involves her ability to rally sympathy for Cecilia's socially unacceptable response to her guardian's suicide, and thereby to depict the unacceptable as completely proper. Cecilia, reacting to the suicide of her legal guardian, begins to imagine how she may become her own guardian via descriptive, analytic, and interpretative strategies. By depicting this chaotic scene at Vauxhall as well as peppering Cecilia's relatives throughout London, Burney's novel shapes and is shaped by marginally administered areas of London and therefore contributes to the city's traditions of imaginative governance by writers.

Recognizing the imaginary authority that Villars possessed in *Evelina* as that of Evelina's reader-conductor, Burney develops ways for Cecilia to internalize this imaginary role. Consider, for example, the extremely performative beginning of *Cecilia*. In contrast to her heroine's delayed entrance in *Evelina*, Burney begins *Cecilia* by citing the heroine's "secret prayer":

> "PEACE to the spirits of my honoured parents, respected be their

remains, and immortalized their virtues! may time, while it moulders their frail relicks to dust, commit to tradition the record of their goodness; and Oh may their orphan-descendant be influenced through life by the remembrance of their purity, and be solaced in death, that by her it was unsullied!"

Such was the secret prayer with which the only survivor of the Beverley family quitted the abode of her youth, and residence of her forefathers; while tears of recollecting sorrow filled her eyes, and obstructed the last view of her native town which had excited them.

Cecilia, this fair traveller, had lately entered into the one-and-twentieth year of her age. (*C,* 5)

Cecilia does not address this prayer to a male guardian via a letter; in fact, Burney advertises that it is "secret." *Cecilia* therefore begins by rejecting confession and valuing internalized secrecy. By describing Cecilia as a "traveller," Burney introduces us to a woman who conducts herself to London and through this novel. Cecilia's inner monologue speaks to none but herself.

Burney relocates *Evelina*'s reader-conductor within Cecilia. Consider how Cecilia responds to the barrage of advice she receives before leaving for London from a coterie of landed male gentry (Mr. Monckton, Mr. Belfield, Captain Aresby, and Mr. Morrice). Bombarded by aphoristic quotations from Pope and Shakespeare and warnings about the imagination, Cecilia finds herself in the middle of "an argument" (the chapter's title) about individual, or female, agency in an urban environment:

> "All this," answered Mr. Monckton, "is but the doctrine of a lively imagination, that looks upon impossibilities simply as difficulties, and upon difficulties as mere invitations to victory. But experience teaches another lesson; experience shews that the opposition of an individual to a community is always dangerous in the operation, and seldom successful in the event;—never, indeed, without a concurrence strange as desirable, of fortunate circumstances with great abilities."
>
> "And why is this," returned Belfield, "but because the attempt is so seldom made? The pitiful prevalence of general conformity extirpates genius, and murders originality; man is brought up, not as if he were 'the noblest work of God,' but as a mere ductile machine of human formation . . . ." (*C,* 15)

Monckton and Belfield loosely personify the two positions in the continuing argument between sovereignty and self-government. Both men attempt to become Cecilia's conductor in London. Burney, however, exposes their debate over imagination and conduct as a pseudo-philosophical struggle for artificial authority over Cecilia. This struggle extends to another trivial argument over who, in Monckton's house, has the proper right "to conduct" Cecilia into the chaise that will conduct her to London:

> The usual ceremonies of leave-taking now followed, and the Captain, with most obsequious reverence, advanced to conduct Cecilia to the carriage; but in the midst of the dumb eloquence of his bows and smiles, Mr. Morrice, affecting not to perceive his design, skipped gaily between them, and without any previous formality, seized the hand of Cecilia himself; . . . .
>
> The Captain shrugged and retired. But Mr. Monckton, enraged at his assurance, and determined it should nothing avail him, exclaimed "Why how now, Morrice, do you take away the privilege of my house?"
>
> "True, true," answered Morrice, "you members of parliament have an undoubted right to be tenacious of your privileges." (*C*, 19)

Monckton wins the right by following the proper rules of conduct; it is his house. Throughout this chapter, Monckton assumes a Polonius-like role (immediately following Belfield's quoting *Hamlet*) and assigns Cecilia the task of going to London to mature yet remain unchanged:

> "Be upon your guard," he [Monckton] cried, "with all new acquaintance; judge nobody from appearances; form no friendship rashly; take time to look about you, and remember you can make no alteration in your way of life, without greater probability of faring worse, than chance of faring better. Keep therefore as you are, and the more you see of others, the more you will rejoice that you neither resemble nor are connected with them."
>
> . . .
>
> Mr. Monckton, in leading her to the chaise, again begged permission to wait upon her in town . . . and Cecilia, gratefully thanking him for his solicitude in her welfare, added "And I hope, sir, you will honour me with your counsel and admonitions with respect to my future conduct, whenever you have the goodness to let me see you."
>
> This was precisely his wish. (*C*, 18, 19)

Although she appears to choose Monckton as her conductor in London, Cecilia grows disgusted with the inadequacy of all those in whom she is supposed to confide or to whom she is to confess her feelings.

Cecilia reaches this conclusion after an instructive and satirical cram-session on London's populace provided by Mr. Gosport. Gosport is valuable to Cecilia because he, like the Restoration's rake, utilizes a specialized vocabulary for talking about the urban scene:

> The TON misses, as they are called, who now infest the town, are in two divisions, the SUPERCILIOUS, and the VOLUBLE. The SUPERCILIOUS, like Miss Leeson, are silent, scornful, languid, and affected, and disdain all converse but with those of their own set: the VOLUBLE, like Miss Larolles, are flirting, communicative, restless, and familiar, and attack without the smallest ceremony, every one they think worthy their notice. (*C,* 40)

Cecilia immediately mobilizes this vocabulary, and she uses it to interpret her own appearance: "'Probably, then,' said Cecilia, 'I have passed to night, for one of the VOLUBLES; however, all the advantage has been with the SUPERCILIOUS, for I have suffered a total repulse'" (*C,* 40). It is important to note that, given a lexicon for understanding her place in London, Cecilia interprets this language rather than uncritically draping it over herself. This is why Cecilia relates to Gosport throughout the novel; they both understand how language generates urban authority and reputation. They also both understand that language requires active interpretation rather than passive acceptance.

When Cecilia proposes "to make a visit herself to each of [her guardians], to observe their manners and way of life" (*C,* 56), she commits to a comprehensive tour of London. In particular, Burney maps Cecilia's three guardians onto three areas of London: the Delviles live on St. James's Square (Delviles equate with the Court), Mr. Briggs lives on an unnamed street in "the city" (Briggs equate with the City of London), and the Harrels live on Portman Square (Harrels equate with the *nouveau riche* suburbs bordering upon the space between Court and City). Burney's even distribution of Cecilia's legal guardians throughout these different areas of London weakens *Evelina*'s suggestion that London was a single, authoritative entity with an indomitable agency over its populace. The Court, City, and middle ground are not abstract administrative objects, but are represented by families who characterize the spaces they inhabit. Burney may therefore play on the idea that London stands in for Cecilia's parents; she may reinterpret *Evelina*'s Londonization by using a familial analogy.

When Burney maps Cecilia's surrogate parentage onto London's geography, she assumes a certain amount of familiarity on the part of her readers. Burney suggests that in order to sympathize with Cecilia, readers must acquire a familiarity with this geography. In *Cecilia,* an antiquated love of surname and bloodline characterizes the Court; a hyperobsessive economic awareness and self-inflicted poverty characterize the City; and an inordinate desire for both bloodline and money by those who have neither characterizes the middle ground. But Burney also introduces the idea of "an inward monitor" (*C,* 585) and presents it as a way to know both the city and, by analogy, the inner self. Cecilia defines this inward monitor in response to the absence of proper escort; that is, Burney has Cecilia develop it as a contrast to Monckton's empty (that is, economically self-interested) role as Cecilia's male conductor. Cecilia's project for acquiring agency hinges upon interpreting London as an extension of her inner self. London, again, is an essential part of Burney's novelistic project for proposing alternatives to confessional interiority.

On two specific occasions, however, Cecilia's agency exceeds the bounds of metaphor. At Vauxhall Cecilia stumbles into a situation where she must test the extent to which imaginative agency, or metaphor, can produce legitimate authority. Suicide was, by itself, an extremely complex act for eighteenth-century Britons to interpret; however, a suicide on the public pathways at Vauxhall heaped more ideological baggage onto an already uninterpretable act. Narrating the ride to Vauxhall, Burney prepares readers for an episode that will require hypersensitive interpretative skills: "During the rest of the ride not another word was said; Mrs. Harrel wept, her husband guarded a gloomy silence, and Cecilia most unpleasantly passed her time between anxious suspicions of some new scheme, and a terrified wonder in what all these transactions would terminate" (*C,* 397–98). The words "scheme" and "transactions" advertise that readers need to mobilize their interpretive skills to "transact" Harrel's approaching suicide. This is Burney's technique for conducting her readers.

Burney frames Harrel's suicide at Vauxhall in indecipherability because people from all three regions of London converge in Vauxhall's environment. Mr. Simkins cannot understand the Captain's French idioms ("you said something of a blank?" [*C,* 408]); the Captain gives Cecilia "an unmeaning smile" (*C,* 408); and Sir Robert responds to Mr. Hobson's city-inflected ideas by crying, "What do you mean by that, fellow?" (*C,*

411). During this scene where no one can interpret anyone else, Harrel runs off and shoots himself. Upon hearing the pistol, the rest of the men flee Cecilia's Vauxhall box, leaving Cecilia and Mrs. Harrel without male escorts and alone in London's infamous public space. Burney casts this episode in slow-motion:

> Mrs. Harrel and Cecilia were now left to themselves, and their horror was too great for speech or motion: they stood close to each other, listening to every sound and receiving every possible addition to their alarm, by the general confusion which they observed in the gardens, in which, though both gentlemen and waiters were running to and fro, not a creature was walking, and all amusement seemed forgotten.
>
> From this dreadful state they were at length removed, though not relieved, by the sight of a waiter, who, as he was passing shewed himself almost covered with blood! (*C*, 414)

Burney's passive phrases "were now left to themselves" and "were at length removed" produce a claustrophobic terror (the women see nothing beyond the confines of their "box") and pin Cecilia into a corner from which any attempt to leave (to wander about Vauxhall alone or to attend to her guardian's corpse) would be improper. When Cecilia learns that Harrel's wound may not be fatal and that a surgeon might be able to save him, she again tries to literalize her metaphor of imaginary agency and conduct:

> "A surgeon!" exclaimed Cecilia, recovering from one surprize by the effect of another, "is it then possible he may be saved?"
>
> And without waiting to have her question answered, she ran out of the box herself, flying wildly about the garden, and calling for help as she flew, till she found the house by the entrance; and then, going up to the bar, "Is a surgeon sent for?" . . . . Nor would she quit the bar, till two or three waiters were called, and received her orders. And then, eager to see them executed herself, she ran, fearless of being alone, and without thought of being lost, towards the fatal spot whither the crowd guided her. (*C*, 415)

Cecilia reacts to Harrel's suicide because no one else does; more importantly, she wishes to act properly in this occasion by receiving Harrel's deathbed confession and granting last rites: "Cecilia, though greatly disappointed, still determined to make way to [Harrel], that she might herself enquire if, in his last moments, there was any thing he wished to communicate, or desired to have done: but, as she struggled to proceed, she was next met and stopt by Sir Robert Floyer, who, forcing her back, acquainted her that all was over!" (*C,* 416). Cecilia's agency in this passage involves damage control; she wants to end this episode as quickly yet as properly as possible. Cecilia also wants to interpret Harrel's "insane" act properly. Sir Robert Floyer's "forcing her back," however, wakes Cecilia from the imaginary relationship she has constructed with Harrel. Previously "fearless of being alone, and without thought of being lost," Cecilia now faces the terrifying task of conducting a widow—and herself—back to Portman Square without Mr. Harrel, their proper male conductor.

Burney forces Cecilia to deal with some terrifyingly quotidian details related to Harrel's suicide. Cecilia must deliver Mrs. Harrel to a coach without seeing her husband's body, choose an appropriate escort for the corpse, secure a coffin, and find a place to inter the body until the funeral. All of the men, however, are more interested in who has the proper right to conduct Cecilia, not Harrel's lifeless body, back to Portman Square. As in the "Argument" chapter, Cecilia encounters men vying to be her conductor:[22]

> "*My* coach, Sir," said Mr. Marriot, "will be ordered when the ladies are ready, and I hope to have the honour myself of conducting them to town."
>
> "No, Sir," cried the Baronet, "that can never be; my long acquaintance with Mrs. Harrel gives me a prior right to attend her, and I can by no means suffer any other person to rob me of it." (*C,* 419)

Anticipating the potential for another duel for which she would be responsible, Cecilia must reconcile her proper choice of a male conductor with a feminine code of urban conduct which stipulates that women do not travel alone from Vauxhall to town:

> ... the impossibility that two ladies could go to town alone, in a hackney coach, and without even a servant, at near four o'clock in the morning, they mutually urged, vehemently entreating that she would run no such hazard.
>
> Cecilia was far other than insensible to these representations: the danger, indeed, appeared to her so formidable, that her inclination the

> whole time opposed her refusal; yet her repugnance to giving way to the overbearing Baronet, and her fear of his resentment if she listened to Mr. Marriot, forced her to be steady, since she saw that her preference would prove the signal of a quarrel. (*C,* 420–21)

Cecilia stands paralyzed between two manifestations of Burney's metaphor of conduct: urban travel and masculine honor. For Cecilia alone, this situation is irresolvable. Burney dissolves the stalemate by having Cecilia meet young Delvile by "surprise" (*C,* 421). Burney curtails the suicide's disruption of *Cecilia*'s narrative with a *deus ex machina* that guides Cecilia to her future husband, Mortimer Delvile. The narrator's switching to Sir Robert and Marriot's perspective at the close of the chapter also shores up an end to this disruption: "Sir Robert and Mr. Marriot, confounded though enraged, saw [Cecilia and Delvile's] departure in passive silence: the right of attendance they had so tenaciously denied to each other, here admitted not of dispute: Delvile upon this occasion, appeared as the representative of his father, and his authority seemed the authority of a guardian" (*C,* 423). We witness a literal changing of the guard in this passage. Young Delvile "appears" or "seems" to replace the dead Harrel as Cecilia's "guardian." The males who are denied this privileged position leave Vauxhall and end this chapter "in passive silence."

Although Harrel's suicide normalizes Cecilia's relationship to a male conductor, Cecilia's agency in this scene (her ability to interpret how to react properly to Harrel's act) stems from her desire to follow her "project" to "become mistress of her own time." Thus, Burney suggests how interpretative activity can produce action and, in turn, serve as signposts of interior virtue. Consider, for example, Mrs. Delvile's response to Cecilia's actions at Vauxhall:

> Charming Miss Beverley! how shall I ever tell you half the admiration with which I have heard of your conduct! The exertion of so much fortitude at a juncture when a weaker mind would have been overpowered by terror, and a heart less under the dominion of well-regulated principles, would have sought only its own relief by flying from distress and confusion, shews such *propriety of mind* as can only result from the union of good sense with virtue. You are indeed a noble creature! (*C,* 425, emphasis Burney's)

Mrs. Delvile reaches her conclusion about Cecilia's "*propriety of mind*" by evaluating not our heroine's letter-writing skills, as Villars does in *Evelina,* but our heroine's "conduct."[23] Mrs. Delvile's comments privilege interpretation rather than confession. Delvile lauds Cecilia for her ability to render herself "well-regulated" rather than being "overpowered by terror." Burney shores up this paradigmatic change in feminine interiority by having Cecilia read Harrel's suicide letter. It is no accident that Harrel's deranged suicide letter takes the form of a confession ("To bring myself to this final resolution, hard, I confess, have been my conflicts" [*C,* 431]). This letter also ends with the only textual break or gap in *Cecilia* (*C,* 432). As in *Evelina,* the epistle's validity as a representational vehicle is suspect. Cecilia interprets Harrel's suicide note as an "incoherent letter" (*C,* 432).

Because Cecilia is aware of confession's manipulative qualities, she reinterprets letter writing as a self-conscious, interpretative craft rather than an unaware, revelatory vehicle for confession. Consider, for example, Cecilia's important letter to young Delvile in which she revokes her consent to marry him. Cecilia writes this letter to reject Delvile as her male conductor; thus, Cecilia approaches letter writing as a tool for acquiring agency:

> Cecilia . . . determined to act consistently with her professions and her character, and, by one great and final effort, to conclude all her doubts, and try to silence even her regret, by completing the triumph of fortitude over inclination.
>
> She called, therefore, for pen and ink, and without venturing herself from the room, wrote the following letter. (*C,* 584)

Burney casts Cecilia's letter writing as an active choice ("she called . . . for pen and ink") rather than a passive compulsion. Cecilia's careful diction maintains this agency: "I blush at this tardy recantation, and I grieve at the disappointment it may occasion you: but I have yielded to the exhortations of an inward monitor, who is never to be neglected with impunity. Consult him yourself; and I shall need no other advocate" (*C,* 585). Cecilia does not "blush" in response to confessing; her "blushing" in the above excerpt is rhetorical. For Cecilia, it is a stylistic device of proper letter writing now divorced from the supposedly "natural" confessional drive nurtured by epistolarity. This letter also names the alternative mode of interiority that Burney has been developing: "an inward monitor." Highly self-conscious interpretative skills constitute Cecilia's inward monitor; they also take the place of an "exterior monitor" previously held by her male conductors.

Although Cecilia advertises that this inward monitor renders her independent ("I shall need no other advocate"), she also genders her interior monitor as male ("Consult him yourself"). We may wish to interpret this as a failure on Burney's part to escape the epistolary control of a male reader. While I have not argued that *Cecilia* is a revolutionary treatise, I suggest that we contextualize Burney's gendering this inward monitor in terms of the situation in 1782. Addison and Steele's concept of the disinterested observer play directly into Burney's concept of "monitoring." Thus, by gendering her metaphor, Burney was able to empower women writers while not fully rejecting letter writing as an unproductive tradition. Cecilia's inward monitor takes the place of an external male reader.

Eighteenth-century conduct books did valorize feminine "passivity."[24] I see the *Evelina-Cecilia* project as Burney's successful attempt to write herself out of these epistolary limitations. Burney understands that her project for replacing confession with interpretation belongs to a slow process that has painful side effects, and it is from this perspective that we may interpret Cecilia's eventual madness. In fact, Cecilia's insanity follows another of her attempts to literalize her imagined authority. Prefacing Cecilia's impromptu flight through London's streets, Burney details how Cecilia's project for acquiring agency has become problematic, especially because it stands in direct contrast to marriage:

> It seemed once more in her power to be mistress of her destiny; but the very liberty of choice she had so much coveted, now attained appeared the most heavy of calamities; since, uncertain even what she ought to do, she rather wished to be drawn rather than to lead, rather desired to be guided than to guide. She was to be responsible not only to the world but to herself for the whole of this momentous transaction, and the terror of leaving either dissatisfaction, made independence burthensome, and unlimited power a grievance. (*C,* 621–22)

Equivocation dominates this passage; Cecilia's imagined agency battles an imagined satisfaction in "be[ing] drawn" and "be[ing] guided." Burney represents this equivocation as both painful and the "work of mental reformation" (*C,* 790). Cecilia considers her interpretative activity to be laborious; thus, Burney's novel writing, as interpretative activity, appears to effect "work." In the case of Cecilia's street flight, Burney's task is to question the boundaries of feminine agency.

While hastily trying to interpret one of Delvile's letters, Cecilia concludes that he has mistakenly assumed her having an affair with Belfield. We should note that a series of misinterpretations (by both Devile and Cecilia) cause Cecilia to take to the streets:

> These thoughts, which confusedly, yet forcibly, rushed upon her mind, brought with them at once an excuse for his conduct, and an alarm for his danger; "He must think," she cried, "I came to town only to meet Mr. Belfield!" then, opening the chaise-door herself, she jumpt out, and ran back into Portland-street, too impatient to argue with the postilion to return with her.... (*C,* 889)

Cecilia runs to unnamed coffeehouses and confronts a coachman who, while insisting upon his payment, physically restrains Cecilia from pursuing her imagined agency:

> "Let me go! let me pass!" cried she, with encreasing eagerness and emotion; "detain me at your peril!—release me this moment!—only let me run to the end of the street,—good God! good Heaven! detain me not for mercy!"
>
> ... a mob was collecting: Cecilia, breathless with vehemence and terror, was encircled, yet struggled in vain to break away; and the stranger gentleman, protesting, with sundry compliments, he would himself take care of her, very freely seized her hand.
>
> This moment, for the unhappy Cecilia, teemed with calamity; she was wholly overpowered; terror for Delvile, horror for herself, hurry, confusion, heat and fatigue, all assailing her at once, while all means of repelling them were denied her, the attack was too strong for her fears, feelings, and faculties, and her reason suddenly, yet totally failing her, she madly called out, "He [Delvile] will be gone! he will be gone! and I must follow him to Nice!" (*C,* 895–96)

We should note that this excerpt clarifies that Cecilia "goes mad" before her street pursuit. Burney's altered style (the barrage of commas and short paragraphs of exclamation) as well as Burney's describing the way Cecilia "madly call[s] out" to nobody expresses Cecilia's insanity. Cecilia's failure to interpret her situation ends in a confessional outburst on the streets of London, and this outburst attracts a mob, the ultimate urban marker of ill conduct. Burney continues to punish her heroine's uncritical "horror for herself" as she describes Cecilia "gliding from place to place, from street to street; with no consciousness of any plan . . ." (*C,* 897). Cecilia lacks "any plan" and therefore lacks "consciousness." Without interpretation, Cecilia lacks a proper "inward monitor" and, using a metaphor of conduct, she lacks a proper conductor. Thus, when Cecilia enters a pawnbroker's shop, the owners at first misinterpret her to be a prostitute. As I reviewed at the beginning of this chapter, it is at this point where the pawnbrokers easily translate Cecilia into a piece of printed text in *The Daily Advertiser.* Due in part to this textual imprisonment, Cecilia experiences a condition that epitomized for eighteenth-century Britons a complete lack of self-government: madness.

Although Cecilia's pursuit through London's streets is highly complex because of its eighteenth-century novelty, we need to remind ourselves that neither a disembodied "London" nor its abstract streets drive Cecilia mad. Cecilia's cessation of interpretative activity is the source of her breakdown; it leads her imagination to create groundless fictions about Delvile. In the absence of a Freudian lexicon for describing interior struggle, Burney casts Cecilia onto the streets alone, and, by having Cecilia exhibit improper conduct, is able to represent Cecilia's mental breakdown. Because Burney's metaphor of conduct refers both to literal geography and figurative mental activity, the impropriety of Cecilia's flight through the unknown streets echoes the mental crisis she experiences. This scene also helps Burney examine the way in which language and literature were distancing London from human agency. Cecilia questions *Evelina*'s claim that "the change is in the place, not in me" and offers to rephrase it as "the change is in me, not in the place."

Cecilia's flight through the streets of London may appear to represent the failure of Burney's experiment with imaginative agency. What heals Cecilia, however, is not confession but meticulous editing and concealment. In particular, the physician who attends to Cecilia's recovery, Dr. Lyster, is versed in more than just physic and medicine; he resembles a narratologist: "He [Lyster] went, however, to Cecilia, and gave her this narration, suppressing whatever he feared would most affect her, and judiciously enlivening the whole by his strictures" (*C,* 925). An edited narrative brings Cecilia back to life not only in Lyster's narrative, but also in the narrative Burney's writes; that is, Burney must ignore certain parts of Cecilia's struggle for agency in order to reach the *telos* of marriage. In an urban environment that values language and narrative, there is a ruthless need for incessant interpretation. Pausing from this interpretative activity can almost prove fatal. Burney calls attention to Lyster's narrative function when she temporarily imbues him with the power of an omniscient narrator who seems to proclaim the novel's moral from a position outside the novel's confines:

> "The whole of this unfortunate business," said Dr. Lyster, "has been the result of PRIDE and PREJUDICE, Your uncle, the Dean, began it, by his arbitrary will, as if an ordinance of his own could arrest the course of nature! and as if *he* had power to keep alive, by the loan of a name, a family in the male branch already extinct. . . . Yet this, however, remember; if to PRIDE and PREJUDICE you owe your miseries, so wonderfully is good and evil balanced, that to PRIDE and PREJUDICE you will also owe their termination . . . ." (*C*, 930)

Lyster's concluding moral, of course, leaves certain things out in order to make its summary possible. In particular, Lyster edits the disruptions to create a sanitized product. That Austen supposedly fed upon these lines to launch her own career suggests that Lyster's words tie off an unfinished project in which Austen sensed more work was needed.

By using London's geography as a metaphor for Cecilia's interior breakdown, Burney is able to detail Cecilia's participation in an unprecedented and supposedly immoral experience on London's streets. Evelina would have never been able to represent, express, or confess such an experience in a letter because a letter is the mythic repository for proper feminine conduct. *Cecilia,* however, uses London's geography and the gendered archives of conduct associated with that geography to convey an eighteenth-century woman's experience with madness. If Cecilia cauterizes her imagined agency and exposes her metaphor for what it really is (that is, imagined) by relying upon a male conductor (that is, Delvile), we should not automatically assume that *Cecilia,* as a novelistic project, fails to reach Burney's goals. The novel offers no immediate solution to the problem of how to express this new model of interiority, but, then again, solutions are not the immediate goals of "a project." Burney points to interpretive activity as a way for Cecilia to become aware of the imprisoning effects of confessional interiority in London. Burney does not point to interpretative activity as a way to enjoy a dangerous urban independence that jettisons standards of proper social conduct altogether.

Although one might be tempted to say that Cecilia's imagined agency and independence ultimately end in marriage, Burney's imagined authority is a different story. Burney reimagines form and, in turn, reimagines what constitutes interiority. Burney's exposure of the limitations of confession and epistolarity suggests that she valued the imagination's ability to critique existing social and textual conducts. From this perspective, *Cecilia* is Burney's most valuable contribution to helping her readers interpret their relationship to eighteenth-century London and literature about London in general.

Burney's "inward monitor" constitutes an innovative strategy for female self-government that originated in a gendered experience of London's ambiguous signs and textual artifacts. The frenzied confusion that Cecilia experiences as she flees London's streets and arrives at the London pawnbroker's shop parallels Burney's experience as a woman writer living in London's print-saturated environment of the late eighteenth century. This environment caused Burney to ask the same questions that Cecilia inevitably asked herself: How did we get here? In an environment that is shaped by others (the imaginative vestiges of early eighteenth-century writers), how am I to realize my authentic self? Burney's strategies for self-government attend to the need for new interpretive skills that carefully reconsider the types of London-based authorities to whom women should defer. Burney's answer is simple: a woman needs to defer to her authentic self. However, due to the calcified layers of printed text and cultural conducts that attached themselves during the early eighteenth century to this authenticity, Burney acknowledges that this is an extremely difficult task. Burney writes *Cecilia* to wade through these layers of print-saturation, retire the epistolary novel, and reclaim a highly interpretive third-person narration.

We may therefore register a major paradigm shift between *Evelina* and *Cecilia* by understanding the different functions that Burney assigns to the disruptive episodes in each novel. In *Evelina,* for example, forged letters destabilize the epistolary logic that underwrites Burney's epistolary novel. In *Cecilia,* by contrast, the disruptive scenes (Cecilia's confrontation with the mob, Harrel's suicide at Vauxhall, and Cecilia's street flight) normalize Cecilia's interpretative activity by forcing it to confront its practical limitations. What this reveals is that what was experimental in *Evelina* was normalized in *Cecilia;* the gaps in *Evelina* become interpretable parts of narrative in *Cecilia.* Thus, we may recognize *Cecilia* as Burney's attempt to understand the ways form and urban geography in *Evelina* forced her to write in a specific way. Burney's textual project, like Cecilia's imagined project, is an interpretative one.

Considering self-conscious interpretation as a way to understand feminine agency, Burney was able to view London as an unfinished project. Women could participate in this urban project only if they seized the sites of agency (geography and textual traditions) that these novels performed. This is why Burney's activity as a writer, like Gay's activity, becomes part of the text's project. Burney performed her own rhetoric to make her readers recognize the writer as a proper interpretative authority. But Burney did more than just raise awareness of these strategies of authorization; she made her readers realize that these strategies could fashion and authorize ideas of gender. Just as Burney, the novelist, doubles as our letter writer and conductor in *Evelina* and *Cecilia,* we, the readers, double as the interpreters of Evelina and Cecilia. Burney stresses the slipperiness between these double roles in order to show her readers how these imaginary yet authoritative roles made gender meaningful. London, Burney seems to say, did not have to be this way for women. Epistolary confession, Burney suggests, did not have to be the only means for knowing oneself. When Cecilia launches herself onto the streets, gender's constructed boundaries become as opaque as epistolarity's truth claims. If we recognize the visibility that Burney's novels lent to epistolarity and confession between 1778 and 1782, Burney may suggest to us that our own model of confessional interiority, psychoanalysis, never had to be our only means for knowing ourselves.

Conclusion

Throughout this book I have argued that by closely reading the metaphors that eighteenth-century writers developed in London—as well as contextualizing these metaphors in terms of London's government following the Glorious Revolution and the proliferation of printed text in London during the late eighteenth century—we may understand how eighteenth-century literature tried to reimagine London. In their attempts to reimagine London, these writers design projects that speculate upon (or "conjecturally anticipate") not only an alternative urban present, but also a more socially engaged role for the urban writer. This role casts writers as indispensable managers of a reader's imagination. Since this role was imagined, we may claim that these projects were destined to fail, especially if we wish to define "failure" as the inability to produce political change. As the speculative goal of late-century writers changes from governing others to governing the self, we witness their desperate attempts to reverse this failure and to make writing valuable to the individual. Yet their inability to cause substantive political change does not render them culturally ineffectual; instead, these eighteenth-century projects are important in London's cultural history since they represent imaginative alternatives to the type of politics that now organize London as we know it. These eighteenth-century projects imagine alternative futures, and these imaginative acts are crucial to defining London's *imagined* sense of community. From this perspective, urban imagination indeed serves a social function.

Analyzing these imaginative and speculative techniques has allowed me to outline three conclusions as well as define several fields where more research is necessary to grasp the full extent to which printed text projected and speculated upon futures for eighteenth-century London that are distinctly different from the one twenty-first-century Londoners (and other urbanities) are living. The first conclusion involves the fluctuating status of eighteenth-century genre and how this fluctuation represents eighteenth-century writers' acknowledgment that both topography and textual traditions have the potential to become convenient tools for categorization and organization. For example, John Gay recognizes that London's geography was a physical manifestation of social change, and Gay seizes this fact to explore the ways that changes in literary form could attend to changes in urban form. All of these altered textual traditions, such as Gay's mock-georgic long poem, Fielding's civil prose, Pope's verse epistle essay, Boswell's journal, and Burney's nonepistolary novel, provide the terms in which writers and readers attempted to negotiate these geographical changes. In the end, genre and geography constitute familiar templates that writers are able to fill with new meaning. In particular, these writers use genre and geography to train readers to understand the metaphor of conduct as a natural and inherent structure of the mind.

The second conclusion suggested by my study clarifies the governing role that eighteenth-century writers in London shaped for themselves. This role may be likened to a conductor—a figure who, in the wake of 1688, led readers to recognize the boundaries of London's geography as well as the boundaries of literary genre. The writers that I examine in this book cater to these urban needs by creating texts that sketch experimental modes of interiority (Burney and Boswell), yoke abstract notions of morality to a literal cityscape (Gay), recast the relationships between textual traditions and civic projects (Pope), and advertise writers as credentialized artisans of London's administration (Fielding). In this way, the metaphor of conduct sometimes offers to instruct public behavior, and at other times it refers to the imaginative guidance which only a writer could provide. For Pope, conduct referred to the practical execution of an abstract theory, and for Boswell and Burney, it referred to and outlined what we now call the conscience. Most importantly, conduct refers to emerging theories of genre—as well as how to read these genres—because it could accomplish imaginative tasks in excess of its literal meaning. In particular, eighteenth-century writers transformed conduct to resemble a commodified object that printed texts could transmit to readers as well as guide them to functional models of urban self-government. London's literal, physical geography helped to legitimize the figurative work of the metaphor of conduct.

A final conclusion is that the tradition of imaginative writing about eighteenth-century London is much larger than previously assumed. In each chapter, I have attempted to recover the subtle nuances of what it mean to "imagine" in eighteenth-century printed text about London; however, literary criticism is far from comprehending the eighteenth century's alternate conception of the imagination (if there is one) that preceded the romantic imagination. This is where more work in eighteenth-century studies may be concentrated. With this work, we may discover that London's urban setting performed the same function for eighteenth-century writers that nature performed for Wordsworth; that is, the local conditions of the urban environment encouraged writers to imagine their role in new ways.

I have also stressed throughout this book that much of London's eighteenth-century literature offers an archive of alternatives to our notions of not only genre but also urban phenomena. For example, Gay's *Trivia* promotes not only "an Art of Walking the Streets" but also an art of reading street-level behavior as the main strategies for knowing London. Gay imagines a future city in which citizens inhabit and indulge in street-level experience not as a means to an end, but as a communal experience in its own right. In fact Gay's street level is where the urban community organizes itself and where it interacts. In this way, Gay's street-level, interpretative techniques stand as distinct alternatives to knowing a city by gaining a bird's-eye view of its geography—a perspective so common with modern maps. From Gay's perspective, one need not disengage oneself atop a skyscraper's observatory or a Millennium Wheel, surveying ant-like citizens in order to know the city. Instead, Gay considers the way street-level interpretation and social engagement enact the proper form of urban knowledge. Another notable alternative is presented by Boswell's *London Journal*. In particular, Boswell internalizes Gay's interpretive skills and applies them to his textually represented self. For Boswell, disciplined writing and rereading offered the possibility of successful self-government, especially in their attempt to become viable substitutes for the police forces outside one's head.

I have not highlighted these urban alternatives to suggest that we try to recover these eighteenth-century alternatives or (impossibly) reinhabit their conditions of possibility; instead, I have written this book to provoke questions about the ways we have been trained to read eighteenth-century literature about London. The self-evident truth that all of the different alternatives presented in this book ask us to question is, quite simply, the inevitability of our urban present. For example, how have we come to privilege maps rather than street-level experience? How have we come to rely upon police rather than experimental forms of self-discipline? And most importantly, how have histories of writing in nineteenth-century London as well as histories of reading literature during the twentieth and twenty-first centuries been able to virtually erase these eighteenth-century experiments in imaginative social engagement? These are questions whose answers are likely to be found in the distance between Frances Burney's and Ian McEwan's London. They are also questions whose answers will help us approach an understanding as to why eighteenth-century London appears historically foreign yet architecturally familiar at the same time.

Exploring the intersection of these issues in eighteenth-century London's imaginative writing may also assist us in finally tracing imagination's alternate history—a history that suggests how our ideas about how to create, manage, and police centralized populations in urban settings do *not* have to be viewed as the culmination of an inevitable process. Indeed, when the 9/11 Commission Report proclaims a "failure of imagination" to be the reason for a twenty-first-century city's vulnerability, it uses imagination in a very practical way. This usage suggests that the post-romantic concept of a unified imagination has apparently retained its eighteenth-century usage. And from this perspective, writing about eighteenth-century London may present twenty-first-century readers with not only histories of their present government, but also solutions for realizing a different future.

Glossary

Critical works that contribute to the following definitions are abbreviated as follows: *LC* = Ed Glinert, *The London Compendium: Exploring the Hidden Metropolis* (London: Allen Lane, 2003); and *BG* = Ylva French, *London: the Blue Guide,* 7th ed. (New York: W.W. Norton & Co., 1998).

absolutism Literally "all-powerful," the term refers to the sixteenth- and seventeenth-century trends of monarchial rule throughout Europe in which the monarch establishes a society where individuals are defined by the degree to which they are "subjects" to the King.

Bow Street Not only a literal street in the City of Westminster but also a conceptualized English space that is synonymous with enforcing civil law in London. Its name originates in its supposed shape (a bow) and was first yoked to legislative matters when Thomas de Veil "opened London's first magistrates court here in 1740, a time when there was little official protection for members of the public" (*LC* 108–9). The novelist Henry Fielding presided over the Bow Street court beginning in 1747; he therefore acquired the name "the Bow Street Magistrate." Bow Street's liminal geographic position between Court and City allowed Fielding to pursue new types of authority for urban writers. For example, Bow Street stands directly across from the Royal Opera House in Covent Garden; this geographic intersection of opera and law represents a visible reminder of how eighteenth-century writers (such as novelists) may have viewed urban, legislative authority as an additional "art" of civilization to which they were uniquely entitled.

City of London, the An explicitly defined, conceptualized English space that is synonymous with "the City"—an administrative space characterized by the ancient "square mile" of London consisting of guilds, vestries, and aldermen. Britons frequently associate the phrase "the City" with mercantile activity and thereby distinguish this phrase from the governing activities of "the Court."

Conduct A metaphor valued by writers for its connotative flexibility. For the writers in this study, conduct may refer to: instructive public behavior, imaginative guidance which only a writer could provide, the practical execution of a theory, the mental activities we now associate with the conscience, or the set of specific rules that a reader followed to make sense of, and engage with, printed text. In this sense, conduct refers to the stylistic and generic maneuvers in printed text.

Court, the A conceptualized space that informally refers to England's governing apparatus and royally determined governing bodies. It is frequently a synonym for "the City of Westminster" in opposition to "the City of London." Generically, the term refers to the English monarchy.

Covent Garden To eighteenth-century Londoners, a public square patterned after the piazzas of Italy, bordered on its west side by Inigo Jones's St. Paul's Church and on the east side by the Royal Opera House. The area is "built on what was the Saxons' Thames port of Lundenwic and is probably the same as Bede's 'Metropolis . . . a mart of many peoples coming by land and sea,' which was abandoned *c.* 900. After Westminster Abbey bought the lands at the beginning of the thirteenth century it established a *convent* garden, later Covent Garden, which grew into London's major flower and vegetable market, giving its name to the area in a corrupted form . . ." (*LC* 98). When Londoners refer to "the Town," Covent Garden stands at the center of this reference and therefore occupies a crucial space between Court and City for writers such as Fielding (Bow Street) and Boswell (who first met Samuel Johnson at Davies's Bookshop just east of the square).

Fleet Street Thoroughfare connecting the City of London to the Town. Fleet Street turns into the Strand on its westernmost end. *See* the Strand, Whitehall

Genre A textual tradition that carries with it specific conventions of writing, reading, and interpreting. These conventions may be defined by the writer or, more importantly, brought to the text by the reader. For eighteenth-century literature, genre is rarely a stable, theorized entity; instead, it is a concept in continual change and historical flux.

Glorious Revolution of 1688, the James the Second, heir to Charles the Second's throne, leaves England due to the public perception that James is too overtly Catholic to rule a Protestant country still reeling from the Puritan Revolution. The Protestant-friendly William and Mary are therefore given rule of England, and this monarchial realignment is deemed "glorious" since no blood was shed. For late Restoration and early eighteenth-century Londoners, however, the Glorious Revolution signifies the destabilization of absolute monarchy and the contested disruption of a seamless Stuart lineage.

liberal governmentality A twentieth-century term theorized mainly by Michel Foucault to describe a mode of government that appears after the Glorious Revolution destabilizes absolutism. The term refers to the resulting "arts of government" that develop as alternatives to absolutism. These arts involve the work of politicians, clergy, writers, alderman, and institutions that clamored to fill the absolutist void of 1688. Foucault theorizes the term in his 1978 lecture, "Governmentality."

London Due to its history, the term "London" has inherited two distinct meanings: one local and one global. In locally specific terms, "London" refers to the "the City of London." In global terms, "London" has become an umbrella-term for not only the ancient City of London but also the City of Westminster, the boroughs, counties, and suburbs surrounding the more formally defined Cities of London and Westminster. *See also* City of London, the City of Westminster, the Court, and the Town.

self-government In contrast to sovereign monarchy and absolutist states, the term refers to a form of authority in which the individual is stressed over an all-powerful monarch or police force. Self-governed people are therefore individuals rather than subjects whose status in English society was determined by their being "subject" to the ruling monarch.

Soho A traditionally bohemian area of the Town between Court and City characterized during the eighteenth century by coffeehouses, theaters, and housing for artists. The marginal qualities of this area are evinced in the origin of its name; when hunters wished to call attention to their sighting a pheasant in the fields that bordered between Court and City, they yelled, "so-ho!" to alert their gunmen while pointing towards the animal. This rural hunting call now refers to this decidedly urban area and emphasizes the rapid transition many marginal areas experienced as they were transformed from field, to suburb, and finally, to city.

Strand, the Named after the shore (or "beach") against which the Thames ran during the late seventeenth century, the Strand is the thoroughfare that connects Court to City. In particular, the Strand is located in the Town, originating in Whitehall on its west end and Fleet Street on its east end. Due to its position between Court and City, the Strand represents the "middling" environment of the Town—a street of publishers, shops, and housing for writers and other artists.

Thames, the Titled by Caesar as "the River Tamesis" (*BG* 347), London's tidal river supported the creation of "Londinium," the town newly founded by the Romans. For eighteenth-century writers, the Thames became a convenient, organic metaphor for a type of natural, urban harmony since the river unapologetically connected the administratively foreign areas of Court, Town, and City.

Town, the A generic term for the marginally policed parishes located between Parliament and the City of London. Although technically under the jurisdiction of the City of Westminster, "the Town" refers to the unregulated "liberties of the Strand." During the eighteenth century, the Town was characterized by bohemian artistry, rampant crime and poverty, and most importantly, London's theatres. Due to its administrative liminality, the Town presents a number of opportunities and problems to writers in London, including the opportunity to yoke morality to geography (John Gay); the problem of Westminster Bridge (Alexander Pope); the opportunity for performative self-government (James Boswell); and the chance to navigate explicitly gendered spaces (Frances Burney).

Westminster Bridge Completed in 1749, Westminster Bridge spans the Thames and connects the City of Westminster with southern England. When Pope crafted his *Epistle to Burlington,* Westminster Bridge represented a highly contested symbol between the city's self-government and Westminster's traditional governing bodies. Today's Westminster Bridge was designed by Thomas Page and built in 1862 (*BG* 349).

Westminster, the City of The formal title for the area of London containing the governing bodies of England, including the Houses of Parliament, the royalty of St. James's Palace, and aristocratic estate homes. The City of Westminster is markedly separate from the City of London in terms of rulers and legislation.

Whitehall The street upon which the Houses of Parliament anchor themselves. Britons use the term to refer to "the Court" or a body of royal government.

Notes

Notes to Preface

1. Ian McEwan, *Saturday* (New York: Doubleday, 2005), 3.
2. Critics who study eighteenth-century London for its "early modern" traits usually do so to explain why modern London looks the way it does. In many ways, the phrase "early modern London" presupposes that a "modern London" is the triumphant goal which any city of the past aimed to realize. For examples of what I call these "narratives of London's historical inevitability," see the essays included in J. F. Merritt's anthology *Imagining Early Modern London: Perceptions and Portrayals of the City from Stow to Strype, 1598–1720*, edited by J. F. Merritt (Cambridge: Cambridge University Press, 2001); Lawrence Manley, *Literature and Culture in Early Modern London* (Cambridge: Cambridge University Press, 1995); and Elizabeth McKellar's *The Birth of Modern London: The Development and Design of the City, 1660–1720* (Manchester: Manchester University Press, 1999). In all of these titles, a recognizable entity called "early modern London" figures prominently.

   While these narratives of London's early modern history are valiant enterprises since they attempt to understand our urban inheritance of the past, especially McKellar's detailed study of London's post-Fire design and architecture, I am more interested in tracing the *alternatives* to our modern notions of "the urban" that eighteenth-century Londoners devised. I am interested in London's "otherness" for two reasons. First, as shown by the work I have just cited, connections between eighteenth-century London and the modern city have been almost thoroughly explored elsewhere, and I refer readers to these studies to understand these connections. Second, the alternatives that eighteenth-century writers imagined for London's future strike me as crucial elements for understanding not only the function of eighteenth-century literature about London but also the problems that modern cities presently face. These urban social problems—poverty, policing, suburban sprawl, to name a few—do not always have their origins solely in a decision of the past, and literature from the past may frequently offer solutions (aka alternatives) to these supposedly inevitable problems of urban civilization.
3. Stuart Sim and David Walker provide a succinct review of the Glorious Revolution's importance in *The Discourse of Sovereignty, Hobbes to Fielding: the State of Nature and the Nature of the State* (Burlington: Ashgate Press, 2003):

"[T]he sovereignty issue continued to bedevil English political life throughout the reign of Charles II, to break out into open revolution once again in the events of 1688–89, when his brother James II was driven from the throne in favour of a Protestant succession. At least part of the problem with the later Stuart monarchy was the attraction that absolute monarchy held for them, and that proved a critical element in the emergence of party politics in this period, with the Tories, broadly speaking, supporting the absolutist ideal and the Whigs opposing it" (4).

4. Robert B. Shoemaker shows how the reformation of manners campaigns of the 1690s also contributed to the dissemination of extralegal power following the Glorious Revolution of 1688, and that "the reformation of manners campaign was as much about social reform as it was about religious reform," especially given the fact "that reformers were far more active in cities than in the countryside" ("Reforming the City: the Reformation of Manners Campaign in London" in Stilling the Grumbling Hive: the Response to Social and Economic Problems in England, 1689–1750 edited by Lee Davison, Tim Hitchcock, Tim Keirn, and Robert B. Shoemaker [New York: St. Martin's Press, 1992], 100).

5. Carol Kay, *Political Constructions: Defoe, Richardson, and Sterne in Relation to Hobbes, Hume, and Burke* (Ithaca: Cornell University Press, 1988), viii. Kay expands this notion of sovereignty on 38–44.

6. Kay, *Political Constructions*, viii.

7. See John Brewer and Roy Porter, Introduction to *Consumption and the World of Goods*, edited by John Brewer and Roy Porter (London: Routledge, 1993): "But it would be a mistake to assume that the new world of goods was primarily or overwhelmingly domestic, merely to do with the building of 'home.' As Tim Breen argues, personal accoutrements, perhaps clothes above all, created styles which established public identities, by processes of assimilation and distinction" (5); see also 3–5.

8. See Lawrence E. Klein, *Shaftesbury and the Culture of Politeness: Moral Discourse and Cultural Politics in Early Eighteenth-Century England* (Cambridge: Cambridge University Press, 1994), especially 27–47 and 123–53; and Kay, *Political Constructions*, 19–44 and 131–40.

9. Linda Colley, *Britons: Forging the Nation, 1707–1837.* (New Haven: Yale University Press, 1992), see especially 67–68: "The Protestant ruling order established by the Revolution of 1688, and ensured by the Hanoverian succession of 1714, supplied traders with positive advantages. One of its foremost innovations, after all, was annual sessions of Parliament, and this was of considerable value to men and women hungry for parliamentary intervention and sympathetic legislation." Colley sees Protestantatism and war as factors that were more important than trade in contributing to Britain's communal identity: "For it was the British government's huge investment in the navy, together with the imperial reach that this increasingly made possible, that allowed overseas trade to grow in the way that it did, and with the speed that it did. In this sense, it was actually trade that was parasitic on the resources of the nation state" (68). See also 64 for Colley's description of London's unique position as "the hub of British commerce" as well as "the meeting place of Parliament."

10. See Michael McKeon, *The Origins of the English Novel, 1660–1740.* (Baltimore: the Johns Hopkins University Press, 1987): "Genre theory cannot be divorced from the history of genres, from the understanding of genres in history" (1).

11. Erin Mackie, *Market à la Mode: Fashion, Commodity, and Gender in The Tatler and The Spectator* (Baltimore: the Johns Hopkins University Press, 1997), 4. Mackie's focus on "the *discourse* of fashion" as her "central category of analysis" has injected the verb "fashion" into critical discussions of how writing tried to shape public consensus after 1688. Mackie's Marxist interpretation of *The Tatler* and *The Spectator* attempts to exhibit "some of the structures of distinction, prescription, and exclusion that underlie the very formulation of these promises [of liberation and inclusion], which, after all, can only be fulfilled through an internalized adoption of quite particular, class-based ideological regulations. These regulations follow the modern paradoxes of a bourgeois, hegemonic social order whose most formidable strengths lie not in outright censorship but in widespread consensus garnered through the free assent of each individual; not in coercive and repressive prohibition but in the deep subjective identification of each person with sociocultural norms that become integral to his or her very psyche; not in the performance of power and authority as imperious display but in the fashioning of each strand of the fabric of everyday life through the management of taste, style, and manners" (262). In particular, Mackie's dialectic between individual free will and hegemonic consensus extends the dialectic that McKeon outlines in *The Origins of the English Novel.*

While adopting these historically situated lenses to read eighteenth-century literature, I differ from McKeon's and Mackie's methods of analysis since I claim that writers such as Boswell and Burney do understand this dialectic tension between "free assent" and "widespread consensus" as they reimagine London— that they are not deluded individuals whose writings are solely economically determined. My discussion on eighteenth-century imagination in the chapter on Boswell (chapter five) will clarify this distinction.

12. Michel Foucault's lectures on governmentality are responsible for sketching the methodologies to historically reassess an eighteenth century "art of government" (See especially Foucault, "Governmentality," in *The Foucault Effect: Studies in Governmentality, with Two Lectures and an Interview with Michel Foucault,* ed. Graham Burchell, Colin Gordon, and Peter Miller [Chicago: University of Chicago Press, 1991], 87–104). Critics who extend Foucault's arguments to address the English political sphere in particular most notably include John Bender (*Imagining the Penitentiary: Fiction and the Architecture of the Mind in Eighteenth-Century England* [Chicago: the University of Chicago Press, 1987]) and Mackie (*Market à la Mode*). I expand upon and qualify the ways this work bears upon London in the introduction.

13. See T. F. Reddaway, *The Rebuilding of London after the Great Fire* (London: Jonathan Cape, Ltd., 1940); and McKellar, *The Birth of Modern London,* especially 12–92.

14. Kay, *Political Constructions,* viii.

15. John Bender, *Imagining the Penitentiary: Fiction and the Architecture of the Mind in Eighteenth-Century England* (Chicago: the University of Chicago Press, 1987), 228. In particular, Bender's seventh chapter entitled "The Aesthetic of Isolation as Social System" argues for the imaginative foundation of urban self-discipline: "The penitentiary suspends the offender within a tightly specified topography of spectatorship which reproduces, as physical practice, an invisible masterplot that structures mental life in metropolitan society. This plot is capable of full enactment only through sympathetic construction, in the imagination, of those material particulars that govern the sensibility and behavior of others. Thus the penitentiary does not need to be accessible to visitors, or even physically present to view (in fact, by contrast with the old prisons, they came increasingly to be located outside of cities) because its rules are one and the same as those that govern consciousness itself. Citizens at large function, in imagination, as the beholders of penitentiary punishment, picturing themselves at once as the objects of supervision and as impartial spectators enforcing reformation of character on the isolated other.... The impartial spectator is a personification, not a personality: its character exists, like the grammatical procedures of free indirect discourse, only as a general code. Although Bentham and other architects were able to specify every detail of structures in which the principle of inspection could be played out bodily—and in the mature Panopticon scheme every guard and turnkey, not just offenders, would have been subject to the gaze of others—inspection is not so much a physical condition as a way of living in a transparent world" (228).

16. Whereas Bender relies upon the work of eighteenth-century philosophers (Adam Smith and Thomas Hobbes), painters (William Hogarth and Joseph Wright of Derby), and "the role of novelistic representation in institutional formation" (*Imagining the Penitentiary,* 2) as cultural evidence for his argument, I am interested primarily in the role that printed text and literary style plays for writers who are trying to attend to the specific topographical demands of eighteenth-century London.

17. Bender's *Imagining the Penitentiary* also examines the eighteenth-century psychological motivations for this categorization, following Foucauldian theorizations of "disciplining" knowledge via genres, education, and degrees.

18. In my attempt to show how writers used literary form to "render London a knowable object," I contribute to the work mainly done by Cynthia Wall and Elizabeth McKellar, which examines the relationship between literary genre and urban planning.

19. See especially J. Paul Hunter, *Before Novels: the Cultural Contexts of Eighteenth-Century English Fiction* (New York: W.W. Norton & Co., 1990), 4–5 and 223–24. Wall's *The Literary and Cultural Spaces of Restoration London* also stresses how easily it may be to misinterpret the stability of what writers considered to be eighteenth-century generic categories; see especially xii.

20. For Johnson on genre and readers, see especially *The Rambler* Nos. 8, 36, 37, and especially 125.

21. G. Gabrielle Starr, *Lyric Generations: Poetry and the Novel in the Long Eighteenth Century* (Baltimore: the Johns Hopkins University Press, 2004), 201.

22. Hunter, *Before Novels*, x.

23. Hunter also highlights the reader's role in generic innovation as he explores Providence and Wonder Books and their connection to the English novel: "Readers often were surprised around the borders of popular kinds they knew and depended on, for writers learned to use the ambiguities of generic overlap and exploit the claims that title pages made. And readers (consciously or not) are complicitous by their participation in the generic pretense, which they explicitly join at the moment they pass the title page and begin to discover where it was—and where it was not—honest in promising what lay beyond" (*Before Novels*, 223).

24. My characterization of eighteenth-century writers in London as "conductors" is meant to specify both the literal and figurative work that I see writers trying to accomplish in the city. Therefore, I use "conductor" here to allude to a very specific type of guidance espoused by the more generalized tradition of eighteenth-century Guide-literature, a textual tradition outlined by Hunter: "By far the most popular of the identifiable 'kinds' in all the didactic para-literature of the time—and the closest in spirit to the novel—is the Guide. . . . Many Guides offer practical instruction in manual arts, the procedures of a particular craft, or the demands of a certain discipline. The social history of eighteenth-century London, is, in fact, well preserved in the treatises on cookery, conversation, ciphering, writing letters, dancing, playing games, keeping a household, and performing the duties of a trade, for the most of them plainly state social expectation while implying which aberrations are the most popular. . . . Print culture took over functions that the oral culture could no longer handle, becoming a vehicle for social change as well as a measure of it" (*Before Novels*, 252–53).

25. McKellar, *Birth of Modern London*, 219.

26. Bender also stresses the need to understand eighteenth-century literature, particularly novels, as "the vehicles, not the reflections, of social change" in *Imagining the Penitentiary* (1), and he elaborates as to why a mimetic mode misleads readers: "But we can see more in works of art than mere reflections. They clarify structures of feeling characteristic of a given moment and thereby predicate those available in the future. This is the specific sense in which they may serve as a medium of cultural emergence through which new images of society, new cultural systems, move into focus and become tangible. I use the term 'structure of feeling' to identify qualities that are contained within a culture at any given moment and that emerge *in process* as conventions play out their relationships within literary and visual forms. . . . Such forms have constructive force as the bearers of a culture's organizing principles and master narratives" (7, emphasis Bender's).

In this way, Bender's theorization of "structures of feeling" as templates for emergent social change are crucial to my ability to argue that eighteenth-century literature about London contains alternatives to our notions of "the urban." Some of these alternatives we have embraced; others we have rejected. The task of the twenty-first-century literary critic, as I see it, is to understand the contexts and research the terms in which these choices were made.

27. For more on the different connotations attached to imagining and reading during the eighteenth-century (as opposed to during the romantic and post-

romantic eras), see the idea of the "lyric-turn" theorized by Clifford Siskin in *The Historicity of Romantic Discourse* (Oxford: Oxford University Press, 1988), 3–66.

28. See especially Mikhail Bakhtin, *The Dialogic Imagination: Four Essays*, translated by Caryl Emerson and Michael Holquist (Austin: University of Texas Press, 1981).

29. See Reddaway, *The Rebuilding of London*, 42–90 and especially 67. After a careful review of the political negotiations leading to the proclamations for rebuilding London in late September 1666, Reddaway argues that "the extent of the improvement possible was clearly defined by the funds available to pay for it" (67). See also Raymond Williams, *The Country and the City* (New York: Oxford University Press, 1973), especially 302–6.

30. Wall, *Literary and Cultural Spaces*, 52 and 39, respectively.

31. Wall, *Literary and Cultural Spaces*, 60 and 53.

32. Wall, *Literary and Cultural Spaces*, 63; see especially 63–70.

NOTES TO INTRODUCTION

1. Abraham Cowley, "On the Queen's Repairing Somerset House," in *Selected Poems of Abraham Cowley, Edmund Waller, and John Oldham*, ed. Julia Griffin (London: Penguin Group, 1998), p. 30, lns. 33–38 and 43–46.

2. Cowley, "Somerset House," lns. 47–54.

3. Cowley, "Somerset House," ln. 80.

4. In particular, Pearl questions whether the City of London was authentically "Puritan" in its sympathies leading to the revolutionary crises. Her thesis is that "the subsequent political standpoint of the leading groups in the chartered trading companies [of the City of London] strengthens the thesis of this work (although it cannot, of course, be said to confirm it) that their sympathies in the crisis of 1641 and 1642 lay primarily with the crown and that the eventual alignment of London with Parliament was the result of *force majeure*, that is to say, of the seizing of power in the City by the parliamentary puritans" (*London and the Outbreak of the Puritan Revolution: City Government and National Politics, 1625–43* [Oxford: Oxford University Press, 1961], 184). See also 1–37 and 237–84.

5. For a detailed account of this building boom, see John Summerson, *Georgian London* (Harmondsworth: Penguin Books Ltd., 1962). For an account of Restoration London's growth from a perspective of "town-planning," see Steen Eiler Rasmussen, *London: The Unique City* (Cambridge, MA: The MIT Press, 1991), especially 99–122. See also McKellar, *Birth of Modern London*, especially 15–21. McKellar calls the Strand "a major commercial nexus linking the City and the Court" (24) and stresses the way Defoe and Addison advertised the Court-City binary (22). I push McKellar's brief discussion of literature's relationship to the Court-City binary further by suggesting that literature was as important to shaping London as were the surveyors, carpenters, and the writers of technical handbooks

that she analyzes. McKellar includes excerpts from Defoe and Addison but does not move beyond a claim that these excerpts prove that "Addison as a propagandist for a new form of polite urban culture naturally emphasized the gap between Court and City, whereas Defoe, with a sharper eye for the economic pulse of the town, discerned the umbilical cord which linked the two worlds, namely money" (22). The goal of my work is not to speculate upon the politics of urban writers but to outline the textual strategies that writers used to make themselves appear valuable to urban society.

6. Alexander Pope, "Windsor Forest," *The Poems of Alexander Pope*, ed. John Butt (New Haven: Yale University Press, 1963), p. 208–9, lns. 377–81.

7. Richard Steele, *Spectator* 454, 11 August 1712, in *Selections from The Tatler and The Spectator*, ed. Angus Ross (London: Penguin Books, 1988), 306–7.

8. Steele, *Spectator* 454, 11 August 1712, 306.

9. Daniel Defoe, *A Tour through the Whole Island of Great Britain*, ed. Pat Rogers (London: Penguin Group, 1986), 306.

10. Roy Porter, *London: A Social History* (Cambridge, MA: Harvard University Press, 1995), 389.

11. John Strype, *A Survey of the Cities of London and Westminster: Containing the Original, Antiquity, Increase, Modern Estate, and Government of those CITIES*, ch. 7, vol. 4, (London, 1720), 104.

12. Francis Sheppard, *London: A History* (Oxford: Oxford University Press, 1998), 195. See also 188–89.

13. John Entick, *A New and Accurate History and Survey of London, Westminster, Southwark and Places Adjacent* (London, 1766), vol. 4, 400, in *An Enquiry into the Late Increase of Robbers and Related Writings*, ed. Malvin R. Zirker (Middletown: Wesleyan University Press, 1988), 2, n. 2. A "Liberty" was also a "district, extending beyond the bounds of the city . . . subject to the control of the municipal authority" (*Oxford English Dictionary*, 2nd ed., s.v. "liberty").

14. For a study of the earlier cycles of stability in medieval London and the first appearance of "a string of elastic, stretched and twisted between a hand at Westminster and a hand in the City of London" (365), see Christopher N. L. Brooke and Gillian Keir, *London, 800–1216: The Shaping of a City* (London: Secker & Warburg Ltd., 1975).

15. Lawrence Manley, *Literature and Culture in Early Modern London* (Cambridge: Cambridge University Press, 1995), 566.

16. Manley, *Literature and Culture*, 565.

17. Manley's *Literature and Culture* shows how the seventeenth-century city's experience with reformation and revolution actually reinscribed Londoners into resurrected forms of social control; in other words, they read literature about London and became complicit in what Manley calls the New Historicist "dialectic of subversion and containment" (13). For example, as Manley argues, sixteenth- and seventeenth-century writers described—or reinvented—London to encourage a type of absolutist "neofedualism" in which new ideas of "radical justice" revalidated medieval notions of "radical power" (20). For example, during the sixteenth

century, London's expanding commercialism overlapped with print technologies "to establish new priorities of communal life, to refashion the corporate identity of what was coming to be called the 'common weal' or 'commonwealth,'" and much of the resulting literature equated the health of the city with that of the absolutist state (63). Although writers such as Sir Thomas More and William Bullein represented Tudor London to be a center of reformation, they simultaneously contained this sense of unbounded reform by centralizing it within London; or in Manley's terms, "the more radical the reform projected, the more radical the concentration of power in London" (see 110 and 113–22). This results in "fictions of settlement" (210) in which London is linguistically invented rather than reflected, and Manley suggests that the decrease in civic community and corresponding increase in bourgeois privacy in seventeenth-century London exposes these fictions to be such.

Like Manley, I do not view "New Historicist dialectic of subversion and containment" as the point of my study (13). Unlike Manley, I consider the way writers believed they were genuinely guiding the imaginations of Londoners to enact new urban projects, some of which never posed "containment" as their goal.

18. Ian Archer also identifies different manifestations of seventeenth-century absolutism before and after the Puritan Revolution: "[I]t is striking how the different elements of popular political discourse . . . contributed to the antagonism between Londoners and the priorities of James's and Charles's government in the 1620s: Protestantism, xenophobia, civic chivalry and the defence of the integrity of the civic community all intersected in growing disillusionment. Londoners remained loyal to the Crown, but they had constructed their grounds for loyalty on a very different basis from that insisted upon by Charles I" ("Popular Politics in the Sixteenth and Early Seventeenth Centuries," in *Londinopolis: Essays in the Cultural and Social History of Early Modern London,* Paul Griffiths and Mark S.R. Jenner, eds, [Manchester: Manchester University Press, 2000], 41).

19. J. A. Downie acknowledges as well as accounts for the degree of authority that writers such as Swift and Defoe seemed to accrue after the Glorious Revolution: "Daniel Defoe and Jonathan Swift were the mainstays of the Oxford ministry's propaganda machine. [Robert] Harley [earl of Oxford] had succeeded in winning over the two most potent pamphleteers of his day, and the curious thing is that at the beginning of the year [1710] they were both actively involved with the whigs. . . . The simple fact that Harley should *bother* to accommodate men who had no real political power, and who might just as easily have been silenced, is a signal indication of his awareness of the importance of propaganda and the need to appeal to public opinion" (*Robert Harley and the Press: Propaganda and Public Opinion in the age of Swift and Defoe* [Cambridge: Cambridge University Press, 1979], 129, emphasis Downie's). Downie's phrase "no real political power" refers to writers' extralegal strategies of authority which they developed after 1688. I argue that after 1688, although writers' power is not traditionally "real" in the absolutist sense, it nonetheless affects how "real" political power is now structured, debated, and mobilized. Downie admits this as well by stressing Harley's concentration upon Defoe and Swift as important players on the political stage. See also Downie, 195.

20. For histories that focus upon "aristocratic versus bourgeois," see Peter Lake, "From Troynouvant to Heliogabulus's Rome and Back: 'Order' and Its Others in the London of John Stow," in *Imagining Early Modern London*, 217–249; M.J. Power, "The Social Topography of Restoration London," in *London, 1500–1700: the Making of a Metropolis*, eds. A.L. Beier and Roger Finlay (London: Longman, 1986), 199–223; and M.J. Kitch, "Capital and Kingdom: Migration to Later Stuart London," in *London, 1500–1700*, 223–251.

For histories focusing on Protestant versus noncomformist, see J. F. Merritt, "The Reshaping of Stow's *Survey*: Munday, Strype, and the Protestant City" in *Imagining Early Modern London*, 52–88; for apocalyptic Hell versus City of God, see Nigel Smith, "'Making Fire': Conflagration and Religious Controversy in Seventeenth-Century London" in *Imagining Early Modern London*, 273–293; for Court versus City, see Paul Griffiths, "Politics Made Visible: Order, Residence, and Uniformity in Cheapside, 1600–45" in *Londinopolis*, 176–196.

21. Archer, "Popular Politics," in *Londinopolis*, 27. Archer's point is that seventeenth-century Londoners did not always defer to the elite; instead, Archer examines the impact of civic concerns on the City's decision-making apparatus. These concerns, (as revealed in the previous footnote), include "Protestantism, xenophobia, civic chivalry and the defence of the integrity of the civic community" (41).

22. J. F. Merritt, "Perceptions and Portrayals of London, 1598–1720" in *Imagining Early Modern London*, 23.

23. Mark S. R. Jenner and Paul Griffiths, "Introduction," in *Londinopolis*, 8, emphasis Jenner and Griffiths's.

24. Hunter reviews eighteenth-century Guide-literature in a similar way, making the point that Guide-literature is symptomatic of larger cultural change: "The context that led to the extensive production of Guides involves lost personal contact and radically changed institutions and situations" (*Before Novels*, 273). The "radically changed institutions" upon which I focus in this study include sovereignty and urban administration.

25. Hunter, *Before Novels*, 261.

26. John Gay, *Trivia, or the Art of Walking the Streets of London* in *Poetry and Prose*, ed. Vinton A. Dearing with the assistance of Charles E. Beckwith (Oxford: Clarendon Press, 1974), p. 172, Book III, lns. 415–16.

27. It is in my concentration on conduct's metaphoric connotations that my study differs from Hunter's work on "the metaphor of guidance" (*Before Novels*, 261) since Hunter uses the label "Guide-literature" to refer to an enormous body of didactic texts providing technical and spiritual guidance (exclusive of the novel, poetry, and drama) whereas conduct-literature refers to a very specific body of writing (including the novel, poetry, and drama). Hunter sees "guidance" and "conduct" to be separate categories as well: "didacticists enforced the metaphor of guidance and direction as something the written word could provide. The verbal guidance of books began to replace the sense that exemplary personal guidance—of parents, pastors, or patriarchs—was necessary to proper conduct" (*Before Novels*, 261). For Hunter, "guidance" (written direction for the individual)

transforms into "conduct" (interpretive behavior for the communal body *and* mind) during the act of reading, and it is this imaginative transformation that I aim to detail.

28. Dieter A. Berger, "Maxims of Conduct into Literature: Jonathan Swift and *Polite Conversation*," in *The Crisis of Courtesy: Studies in the Conduct-Book in Britain, 1600–1900,* ed. Jacques Carré (Leiden: E.J. Brill, 1994), 81.

29. Nancy Armstrong, *Desire and Domestic Fiction: A Political History of the Novel* (New York: Oxford University Press, 1987), 63.

30. Armstrong, *Desire,* 69.

31. Nancy Armstrong and Leonard Tennenhouse, "The Literature of Conduct, the Conduct of Literature, and the Politics of Desire: An Introduction," in *The Ideology of Conduct: Essays on Literature and the History of Sexuality,* ed. Nancy Armstrong and Leonard Tennenhouse (New York: Methuen & Co., 1987), 1.

32. See Berger, "Swift and *Polite Conversation*," in *The Crisis of Courtesy,* especially 81–88, for the way Jonathan Swift's "non-ironic tracts are marked by an endeavor to heighten the matter of conversational conduct—by referring it to Enlightenment ideals, uniting it with a general criticism of culture, bringing in aspects of gender, and admonishing the reform of aristocratic refinements—and to enliven the stylistic presentation with personal impressions and amusing anecdotes. In spite of this their overall didactic intent is not to be overlooked. In *Polite Conversation,* however, one of the last books he saw through the press before his mind became distorted, the approach to the subject of courtesy is one of literary alienation. Although an equal weight is put on instruction, the entertaining factor is of even greater importance. Now the concept of conversation as an art is also presented in the form of a literary work of art" (87–88).

Berger argues for the stylistic artistry of Swift's *Polite Conversation* since "apart from its utility to Swift's contemporaries, it still appeals to us by the brilliant transformation of courtesy material into art by the playful fusion of parody and irony with satire. Even a reader abhorring conduct literature must be delighted with it" (91). Although appealing to post-romantic conceptions of literary "art," Berger's argument is important to my study since it explores how conduct literature's stylistic maneuvers allow us to interpret the tradition as socially engaged literature.

Lawrence A. Klein's *Shaftesbury and the Culture of Politeness* examines how Anthony Ashley Cooper, the third earl of Shaftesbury, writes his *Characteristics of Men, Manners, Opinions, and Times* (1711) as a treatise on politeness with political underpinnings that coped with the changed environment of the Glorious Revolution: "[Shaftesbury's] moralism, his deism, and his aesthetic interests were all harnessed to a political project. Moreover, far from being an exercise in Whig radicalism, that project was nothing less than the legitimation of the post-1688 Whig regime. As, in his view, the Revolution had definitely established the dominance of gentlemen over English society and politics, so it ushered in an era of gentlemanly culture, the norms and content of which he was attempting to envision" (1). Like Klein, I examine conduct literature for its stylistic strategies "to envision" (or, in my terms "speculate" or "imagine") an alternate future. I differ from Klein's argument in that many of the writers in my study are, unlike Shaftesbury, not strictly interested in the political ramifications of their imaginative acts.

33. See Neils Haastrup, "The Courtesy-Book and the Phrase-Book in Modern Europe," in *The Crisis of Courtesy* for a summary of the "unfortunate borderlines" that the disciplines of literature, linguistics, and history encounter when faced with the task of historicizing politeness and courtesy (76).

34. For more detailed discussions of these different seventeenth-century traditions, see Carré, *The Crisis of Courtesy*, especially 11–64. Gilles Duval explores the changes that chapbook literature experienced during the eighteenth century in "Standardization Vs. Genre: Conduct-Books and English Chap-Literature" in *The Crisis of Courtesy*, 41–49.

By the eighteenth-century, "good manners" refer to "a universal of human nature, and therefore attainable for everybody relying on reason" whereas "good breeding" refers to "the particular rules of courteous behavior, also known as ceremony or etiquette, . . . acquired only by personal effort, either by the observation of social practice or by the study of books" (Berger, "Swift and *Polite Conversation,*" *The Crisis of Courtesy*, 83).

35. Carré, *The Crisis of Courtesy*, 2. For discussions on the nature of these generic alterations, see Carré's introduction to his anthology, *The Crisis of Courtesy:* "the demise of courtly values did not mean a loss of interest in the substance of courtesy, but essentially a dissemination of its treatment in the whole spectrum of literature" (8). Tim McLoughlin's essay "Fielding's *Essay on Conversation:* A Courtesy Guide to *Joseph Andrews?*" in *The Crisis of Courtesy*, revives Catherine Sobra Green's use of the term "conduct/courtesy novel" to describe the novelistic variations of seventeenth-century conduct literature (93). Georges Lamoine attempts to make connections between Chesterfield's *Letters to his Son Philip Stanhope* and other eighteenth-century conduct literature (Swift, Johnson, Burney, and Austen) in "Lord Chesterfield's *Letters* as Conduct-Books," in *The Crisis of Courtesy*, 105–17.

36. The "crisis" to which the title of Jacques Carré's anthology, *The Crisis of Courtesy*, refers involves Carré's perception that the "spiritual significance of courtesy" declined during the eighteenth century: "The fatal decline of the British courtesy-book, a genre so brilliantly illustrated in the sixteenth century, should not in fact be traced to the Victorian and Edwardian age and its obsession with social solecisms. . . . The crisis of courtesy and its attendant decline into mere conduct . . . was in fact older, and may be described as a lengthy and gradual process extending through the seventeenth and eighteenth centuries. What is more, it did not simply lead to the narrowing down of a genre into repetitive, uninspired, although (for modern readers) occasionally hilarious manuals of etiquette; but rather it involved the dissemination of its subject-matter into a broad range of literary genres, such as, preeminently, the novel. The decline of the courtesy-book in fact meant the rebirth of the literature of conduct in other, often much more sophisticated, forms. . . ." (2).

I agree with Carré's claim that "the great age of the metamorphosis of conduct-literature in England . . . was clearly the Augustan Age"; however, I do not interpret eighteenth-century writers' use of "conduct" to strictly equate with litanies of rules and/or etiquette. Instead, as I show in the close of the introduction, writers recognized that the metaphoric connotations of conduct in poems and novels and their influence upon readers' experiences of traversing and comprehending London constituted part of this "dissemination" of the traditional functions of seventeenth-century conduct literature.

37. Carré, introduction, *Crisis of Courtesy,* 2–4.

38. These writers use conduct as a metaphor in the purest sense of the term, with a tenor, vehicle, and ground. A metaphor produces knowledge by comparing a previously unknown entity (the tenor) to a familiar entity (the vehicle), and is only successful at a point when the two entities are similar (the ground).

39. For example, Pope uses conduct to mean "execution" in his 1711 *An Essay on Criticism* (in *Poems of Alexander Pope,* p. 152):

> In ev'ry Work regard the Writer's End,
> Since none can compass more than they Intend;
> And if the Means be just, the Conduct true,
> Applause, in spite of trivial Faults, is due. (lns. 255–58)

40. See Jürgen Habermas, *The Structural Transformation of the Public Sphere: An Inquiry into a Category of Bourgeois Society,* trans. Thomas Burger with the assistance of Frederick Lawrence (Cambridge, MA: The MIT Press, 1991) and Foucault, "Governmentality," *Foucault Effect,* 87–104.

41. See Colin Gordon, "Governmental Rationality: An Introduction," *Foucault Effect,* 1–52; Graham Burchell, "Peculiar Interests: Civil Society and Governing 'The System of Natural Liberty,'" *Foucault Effect,* 119–50; and Mary Poovey, *A History of the Modern Fact* (Chicago: University of Chicago Press, 1998), especially xix–xx and 144–13.

42. Foucault, "Governmentality," *Foucault Effect,* 92.

43. Poovey, *Modern Fact,* xx.

44. Judith Butler, *Precarious Lives: the Powers of Mourning and Violence* (London: Verso, 2004), 55–56.

45. Butler, *Precarious Lives,* 52.

46. For J. A. Pocock's suspicion of liberal "interpretations of history," see *Virtue, Commerce, and History* (Cambridge: Cambridge University Press, 1985), 71.

47. Pocock, *Virtue, Commerce, and History,* 49. In the way Pocock describes it, manners reconciled any ethical problems with London's materialism and "at last, a right to things became a way to the practice of virtue, so long as virtue could be defined as the practice and refinement of manners" (50).

48. Colley offers "recurrent Protestant wars, commercial success, and imperial quest" as three additional modes of national and governmental consensus—a consensus that depended not upon "an integration and homogenisation of disparate cultures" but rather "an array of internal differences in response to contact

with the Other, and above all in response to conflict with the Other" (*Britons*, 375 and 6, respectively).

49. See Habermas, *The Structural Transformation of the Public Sphere*. Habermas's conceptualization of the public sphere "as a sphere between civil society and the state" (Thomas McCarthy, introduction to Habermas, *Structural Transformation*, xi), which seems to have originally meant to clarify ideas of power in eighteenth-century London, has itself become a twenty-first-century abstraction. Habermas's theory informs my arguments in so much as it describes the historical conditions (such as coffeehouse culture) in which urban modes of liberal governmentality appeared.

50. Miles Ogborn in *Spaces of Modernity: London's Geographies, 1680–1780* (New York: The Guilford Press, 1998) implies that if we can interpret social treatises published on the Strand, we can gain access to a modern process (see especially 1–38 and 201–230). Although Ogborn defines modernity in an eighteenth-century context, the assumption still seems to be that this modernity relates to us today: "As a 'project' modernity is less a realised set of relationships, institutions and experiences than a series of claims and attempts to make and remake the future. . . . Read in this way the 'spaces of modernity' considered here might be seen as anachronisms: spaces that were self-consciously novel, spaces that didn't fit, spaces that sought to constitute a different future. Just as modernity involves a transformation of space, these were its spaces of transformation, spaces where change was possible and desirable" (28). Although I use the word "project," I do not refer to the forward-looking sense in which Ogborn uses the word. In the chapters on Fielding and Gay, I salvage Ogborn's ideas of "spaces that were self-consciously novel" and "spaces where change was possible and desirable"; however, in doing so, I want to strip from them any tinge of the "modern" and show that writers such as Gay and Fielding were rarely thinking about "constitut[ing] a different future." Instead, they were focusing on the immediate present. These writers were not imagining a future that someone, somewhere would bring into being; they were instead reimagining their own present. Modernity has in many ways become a meaningless abstraction; thus, I avoid suggesting that the act of imagining alternative futures characterizes modernity.

51. Daniel Defoe, *An Essay upon Projects*, (New York: AMS Press, Inc., 1999), 13.

Notes to Chapter 1

1. Wall, *Literary and Cultural Spaces*, 78. According to Wall, "the first surviving printed map of London, the 'Copperplate,' dates from about 1559" (227, n. 5).
2. Wall, *Literary and Cultural Spaces*, 80 and 84, respectively.
3. Wall, *Literary and Cultural Spaces*, 96.
4. Wall, *Literary and Cultural Spaces*, 76, emphasis Wall's.
5. Wall, *Literary and Cultural Spaces*, 83 and 90–111.

6. The degree of the "modernism" exemplified in John Stow's *Survey of London* is still avidly contested. Whereas Patrick Collinson and J. F. Merritt argue that Stow's *Survey of London* enmeshed early modern London in Reformation rhetoric (see Patrick Collinson, "John Stow and Nostalgic Antiquarianism," in *Imagining Early Modern London*, 27–51 and J. F. Merritt, "The Reshaping of Stow's *Survey*," in *Imagining Early Modern London*, 52–88), Cynthia Wall argues that Stow's "narrativized antiquities . . . disappeared under a welter of alphabetized and cross-referenced *lists* of street names" (*Literary and Cultural Spaces*, 76).

7. Collinson, "Nostalgic Antiquarianism," in *Imagining Early Modern London*, 34.

8. Merritt, "The Reshaping of Stow's *Survey*," in *Imagining Early Modern London*, 88. Merritt specifies the nature of the *Survey*'s reassuring fiction of continuity: "Perhaps it is not too fanciful to suggest that the preservation of medieval London in the pages of the *Survey*, where it blended almost effortlessly (indeed confusingly) with the present, may have provided a much-needed sense of stability and identity" (88).

9. Wall, *Literary and Cultural Spaces*, 100. Wall's examples of these grammatical constructions stem from a specific moment of Stow's *Survey*: "after that is Grubstreets, more then halfe thereof to the strightning of the streete, next is Whitecrosse streete, up to the end of Bech lane, and then Redcrosse street wholy, with a Parte of Goldingland, even to the Posts there placed, as a bounder . . . and so haue you all the boundes of Criplegate warde without the walles" (Stow qtd. in Wall, 100).

10. Wall, *Literary and Cultural Spaces*, 103 and 111.

11. Wall, *Literary and Cultural Spaces*, 133. Wall also argues that "unlike Swift's and Pope's, Gay's poem read confidently, optimistically, the need for negotiation or containment not urgently ideological but practical, sensible" (133). As I will argue, I instead interpret *Trivia*'s "practical, sensible" tone to be the effect of a very urgent and ideological literary project to inject writers into the developing discourses of governmentality.

12. Paula McDowell, *The Women of Grub Street: Press, Politics, and Gender in the London Literary Marketplace, 1678–1730* (Oxford: Clarendon Press, 1998), 10.

13. See McDowell, especially 33–179.

14. See McDowell, especially 82–90 and 128–79.

15. Adrian Johns, *The Nature of the Book* (Chicago: The University of Chicago Press, 1998), 36.

16. See David Nokes, *John Gay: A Profession of Friendship* (Oxford: Oxford University Press, 1996), 206.

17. See Tom Woodman, "'Vulgar Circumstance' and 'Due Civilities': Gay's Art of Polite Living in Town," in Lewis and Wood, *Gay and the Scriblerians*, 83–93. See also Nokes, *Profession*, especially 197–230.

18. Woodman, "'Vulgar Circumstance,'" 88. Woodman presents the most detailed (and overdue) comparison of *Trivia* to Virgil's *Georgics*, cataloguing what grants *Trivia* the right to align itself with anything "classically georgic."

19. See Nokes, *Profession,* 206–7.

20. Pat Rogers, *Grub Street: Studies in a Subculture* (London: Methuen & Co. Ltd., 1972), 162.

21. Wall, *Literary and Cultural Spaces,* xv.

22. For accounts that suggest views of Court and City "space" in this manner, see especially Roy Porter, *London: A Social History* (Cambridge: Harvard University Press, 1994) and M. Dorothy George, *London Life in the Eighteenth Century* (London: Penguin Books Ltd., 1985).

23. The best summary of the variety of contemporary critical reactions to *Trivia* can be found in Stephen Copley and Ian Haywood's "Luxury, Refuse and Poetry: John Gay's *Trivia,*" in *John Gay and the Scriblerians,* ed. Peter Lewis and Nigel Wood (New York: St. Martin's Press, 1988), 62–82.

24. Vinton A. Dearing's annotations to *Trivia* in *John Gay: Poetry and Prose,* vol. 2 (Oxford: Clarendon, 1974) support my view of *Trivia*'s specificity. Dearing's annotations are entirely necessary because they suggest—rather than recover—eighteenth-century traditions of London. In turn, the notes show how many jokes and satiric jabs are lost on the modern reader. I push this issue further in this chapter to claim that we do not "get" *Trivia*'s references because we neither recognize nor "read for" the type of knowledge which this long poem ostensibly offers to us.

25. I do not write "what we would now recognize as" urban planning for a very specific reason; I wish to preserve an "otherness" of the work Gay's poem accomplishes. The practice of urban planning, as we know it, is a system of credentialized study in which "a long poem" is not a likely vehicle for building a city. The eighteenth-century long poem is a genre of the eighteenth century which we have now lost; therefore, *Trivia*'s textual vehicle is foreign to us. For these reasons, Gay is not an "urban planner"; he is, during a lack of any credentialized practice of urban planning, an eighteenth-century version of our urban planner. In this chapter, difference and otherness underwrite my approach to *Trivia.*

26. Gay's *The Beggar's Opera* (1728) has also suffered this fate due to what is too often seen to be an anarchic stance towards "genre" and the text's "re-birth" into the historical context surrounding *The ThreePenny Opera.*

27. Jeremy Collier, "A Short View of the Immorality and Profaneness of the English Stage, Together with the Sense of Antiquity Upon this Argument," in *British Dramatists from Dryden to Sheridan,* ed. George H. Nettleton and Arthur E. Case (Carbondale and Edwardsville: Southern Illinois University Press, 1969), 391. I use Collier's quotation here because Collier's use of "stand" has particular ramifications for Gay's use of "walking"; the glosses, "like rocks," literally exist beyond the metrical rhythm of pace of this poem designing "the Art of Walking."

28. Indexes for eighteenth-century long poems seem to count as a twentieth-century version of critical work. I refer to the constant demand for indexes and variorum editions to eighteenth-century long poems. Gay's index to *Trivia* obviously satirizes the motives and values behind this editorial—or even "literary"—work.

29. The prostitute also appears in an entry of the first type I have just described: "*Whores, the Streets where they ply.*"

30. One example of Gay's "satiric ordering" is pertinent here: the entry "*Cheese not lov'd by the Author*" immediately follows "Cheapside" (an entry referring the reader to the episode in the poem where the walker-poet enters streets surrounding this area of east London).

31. Hunter, *Before Novels,* 273.

32. Hunter, *Before Novels,* 273 and 248–72.

33. John Gay, *Trivia: or, the Art of Walking the Streets of London, John Gay: Poetry and Prose,* ed. Vinton A. Dearing with the assistance of Charles E. Beckwith, vol. 1 (Oxford: Clarendon Press, 1974), 134–181, lns. 19–20. I internally cite all subsequent references to *Trivia* by book and line number.

34. In this peripatetic context, "to tread" also implies "to shape" or to cut a new path.

35. Elkanah Settle, as Dearing notes, was "the last" poet to occupy this position of "city-poet"—"an office not actually aspired to by a poet of Gay's caliber" (in *John Gay: Poetry and Prose,* vol. 2, 550).

36. For the remainder of this chapter, I use "London" to refer to a composite of City, Town, and Court. Part of *Trivia*'s goal is to make "London" an identifiable referent.

37. To fit the iambic pentameter of line six, "conduct" must be a verb with the stress on the second syllable. However, Gay does use conduct as a noun elsewhere in the poem (see 3.310), and it is from Gay's alternate usage that I derive my reading of conduct in its double meaning.

38. For standard summaries about the ways abstract space has been theorized since the eighteenth century, see Henri Lefebvre, *The Production of Space,* trans. Donald Nicholson-Smith (Oxford: Blackwell, 1991); Mary Poovey, *Making a Social Body: British Cultural Formation, 1830–1864* (Chicago: University of Chicago Press, 1995), especially chapter 2, "The Production of Abstract Space"; and James Epstein, "Spatial Practices/Democratic Vistas," *Social History,* October 1999, 24.3, especially footnote 5.

39. Miles Ogborn, *Spaces of Modernity: London's Geographies 1680–1780* (New York: The Guilford Press, 1998), 113.

40. Dearing offers this etymological root of the figure of Trivia in his annotations, *John Gay: Poetry and Prose,* vol. 2 (Oxford: Clarendon Press, 1974), 548–49.

41. I refer to our poet's persona as our "walker-poet" to distance the poet of *Trivia* from the walker—the figure whom the walker-poet addresses and simultaneously designs as a "reader." To claim that our poet is simply a "walker" ignores the distinct sense of distance (common in the eighteenth-century prospect poem) between poet and reader which Gay does preserve by using only the first-person when the poet retreats from his object during a moment of extreme danger or when the poet envisions public praise for his text while writing. Furthermore, the walker-poet might be Gay himself, and I use "walker-poet" and "Gay" interchangeably throughout this section because *Trivia*'s poetic persona blatantly

incorporates the act of writing into the poem itself (a claim that I specify in the next section). However, Gay's association with *Trivia*'s poetic persona—as a poet radically opposed to a shoulder-to-shoulder walk with the reader—still maintains a distinction between poet and the walking audience.

42. "The Play," is, of course, an activity that characterized the areas surrounding the Strand; however, given the general inconclusiveness over the type of audience (courtly or otherwise) of early eighteenth-century plays, it is possible that Gay here refers to a theatre-scene attended primarily by patrons of the Court.

43. Woodman stresses that *Trivia* considers walking to be an "art of reading codes of dress and speech," but he concludes that these codes only function "to respond appropriately to strangers in the confusing new conditions" (Woodman, "'Vulgar Circumstance,'" 88). I am suggesting here that Gay creates what is "appropriate" instead of merely offering ways of "respond[ing] appropriately" to others. Furthermore, what I call "protocols of reading" apply not only to "dress and speech" but to the immediate physical surroundings such as buildings and signage. I also differ from Woodman here in calling Gay's idea of reading a "skill" rather than "an art"—a distinction I clarify later.

44. Wall, *Literary and Cultural Spaces,* 121. See also 131–33.

45. The accompanying glosses to these sections also nurture this sensitivity: "Signs of cold Weather," "Signs of fair Weather, and "Signs of rainy Weather."

46. A "Glazier" performs the rather specialized job of placing plates of glass in window "sashes." The joke here is that the glazier aims the ball towards the Penthouse windows and, as a result, produces more work for his guild. The "gingling Sashes" allude to the anxiety surrounding the "falling tiles" of the rooftops of Juvenal's Rome (see *Satire III,* in *The Sixteen Satires,* trans. by Peter Green [London: Penguin Books, 1974], lns. 269–70). Gay almost directly quotes this line, as Dearing notes, on 2.270.

47. As I will explore in the next section, Gay shores up his connection of walking to virtue in the final lines to book two: "O rather give me Sweet Content on Foot, / Wrapt in my Vertue, and a good *Surtout!*" (2.589–90).

48. The face-tracing that this particular couplet establishes seems to influence Blake's first quatrain of his pedestrian poem, "London" (here quoted from *Blake: Complete Writings with Variant Readings,* ed. Geoffrey Keynes [Oxford: Oxford University Press, 1992], p. 216, lns. 1–4):

> I wander thro' each charter'd street,
> Near where the charter'd Thames does flow,
> And mark in every face I meet
> Marks of weakness, marks of woe.

49. Woodman focuses on Gay's reference on 2.45 to "Due Civilities" in his essay "'Vulgar Circumstance'"; however, my approach differs in that I consider the function of these "Civilities" to fashion space whereas Woodman sees these "Civilities" strengthening "the traditional hierarchical analogy between reason and nature" in London (Woodman, 88–89 and 92).

50. I also use "moral" here to highlight its present-day ambiguity—an ambiguity which *Trivia* dissolves by making "morality" visible in the way people conduct themselves through different areas of London. That is, *Trivia* makes morality an *observable* quality capable of being registered and evaluated by others.

51. Alexander Pope's Cloacina episode for the Fleet-diving scene of *The Dunciad* resembles Gay's episode. It is important to note that no glosses appear during this origin-myth; that is, this origin-myth is beyond the type of knowledge nurtured by the glosses.

52. See especially Peter Stallybrass and Allon White's *The Politics and Poetics of Transgression* (Ithaca: Cornell University Press, 1986) for the relationship of eighteenth-century carnivalesque to satire and the "infraction of binary structures" (18) that results from high-low comparisons.

53. Dearing, *John Gay: Poetry and Prose,* vol. 2, 557–58.

54. Both Gay and Pope write verse "Epistles" to Lord Burlington: Gay's *To the Right Honourable the Earl of Burlington* (1715) and Pope's *To Richard Boyle, Earl of Burlington* (1731).

55. See Dearing, *John Gay: Poetry and Prose,* vol. 2, 563.

56. Dearing, *John Gay: Poetry and Prose,* vol. 2, 550.

Notes to Chapter 2

1. Tim Wales, "Thief-Takers and Their Clients in Later Stuart London," in *Londinopolis,* 68 and 72, respectively.

2. For an account of the historical tension between the governing bodies of Westminster and the City of London, see Roy Porter, *London: A Social History* (Cambridge, MA: Harvard University Press, 1994). Part of Porter's thesis is that "London was above all the uncontrolled city. . . . London has no unifying municipal government" (8), and this argument informs my conception of eighteenth-century London as a collection of dispersed sites of administrative authority

3. Francis Sheppard, *London: A Social History* (Oxford: Oxford University Press, 1998), 195. See also 188–89.

4. John Entick, *A New and Accurate History and Survey of London, Westminster, Southwark and Places Adjacent,* vol. 4 (London, 1766), 400, cited in *An Enquiry into the Late Increase of Robbers and Related Writings,* edited by Malvin R. Zirker (Middletown: Wesleyan University Press, 1988), 2, n. 2. Local conditions separate from the Court and the City, no matter how informal, seemed to have ruled these districts, of which the Strand was part. The full title of the *Charge* also details Fielding's realm of authority over "the City and Liberty of Westminster, & c." (Henry Fielding, *A Charge Delivered to the Grand Jury at the Sessions of the Peace held for the City and Liberty of Westminster, & c. on Thursday the 29th of June, 1749* in *Related Writings,* 1).

5. Entick cited in Zirker, *Related Writings*, 2–3, n. 2.

6. John Strype, *A Survey of the Cities of London and Westminster: Containing the Original, Antiquity, Increase, Modern Estate and Government of those CITIES*, ch. 7, vol. 4 (London, 1720), 104.

7. Tim McLoughlin's essay, "Fielding's *Essay on Conversation: A Courtesy Guide to Joseph Andrews?*" in *Crisis of Courtesy*, concludes with the argument that "[t]he *Essay on Conversation* can be read as a guide to the general principles of good breeding which inform *Joseph Andrews*, but more tantalising is the possibility that Fielding, realising the restrictions inherent in the mode of the *Essay*, turned to the novel as a more open kind of discourse in which to express his perceptions of what kind of person a man of good conduct might be" (102). My study of Fielding's civil prose and its connection to *Tom Jones* agrees that Fielding indeed turned to the novel to devise new conceptions of urban conduct; however, as I seek to show in the following chapter, the "man of good conduct" that results from *Tom Jones* is the Author himself.

8. I use "discourse" throughout this chapter in its Foucauldian sense of a set of statements that, through habitual practice and systematic usage, take on the appearance of truth. See Michel Foucault, *The Archaeology of Knowledge and the Discourse on Language*, trans. A. M. Sheridan Smith (New York: Pantheon Books, 1972) and *The Order of Things: An Archaeology of the Human Sciences* (New York: Random House, 1994).

9. Establishing a specific "conduct" or certain way knowledge is produced is intimately tied to Foucault's concept of discourse itself. Fielding's discussions of conduct are a primitive version of the disciplinary specificity needed to establish discourse and, eventually, to validate practices that become "professional" because they possess their own, specific way of acting, performing, and generating ways of knowing. In this way, Fielding's emphasis on conduct participates in the larger project of distinguishing types and practices of knowledge from one another.

10. For evidence of this overlap, see especially Martin C. Battestin with Ruthe R. Battestin, *Henry Fielding: A Life* (London: Routledge, 1989), 439–53. Battestin also suggests that the dedication to *Tom Jones* is an epistle of gratitude to two men, George Lyttleton and John Russell, the Duke of Bedford, who helped elect Fielding as Magistrate (459).

11. J. Paul Hunter, *Occasional Form: Henry Fielding and the Chains of Circumstance* (Baltimore: Johns Hopkins University Press, 1975), 202–3.

12. Henry Fielding, *The History of Tom Jones, a Foundling*, ed. Martin C. Battestin and Fredson Bowers (Hanover: Wesleyan University Press, 1975), 6.1.268. Hereafter cited internally, marked by *T* and relevant book, chapter, and page number(s).

13. Leo Damrosch, *God's Plot and Man's Stories: Studies in the Fictional Imagination from Milton to Fielding* (Chicago: the University of Chicago Press, 1985), 302 and 300, respectively. For more on *Tom Jones* and providential readings, see Patrick Reilly, *Tom Jones: Adventure and Providence* (Boston: Twayne Publishers, 1991), especially the conclusion, (135–37) for the supposed reasons to explain modern readers' adversity to classical, comic endings.

14. The reader will recall that Jones gives the money that he makes from selling the horse and the Bible to Black George so that George's family may purchase food. Fielding dissolves two of the mock-trials included in this list in the same way he dissolves Jenny Jones's mock-trial: with versions of the word, "dismissed." (*T*, 3.4.131 and 3.8.143).

15. Fielding, *An Enquiry into the Late Increase of Robbers* in Zirker, *Related Writings*, 73.

16. See Malvin R. Zirker, introduction to *Related Writings*, xxv: "Relatively few of the many thousands of charges delivered to grand juries in the eighteenth century have survived (the Webbs cite only ten charges published in the eighteenth century before Fielding's), but we may safely assume that, when not totally perfunctory, the chairman's charge focused on those social disorders he considered particularly in need of redress."

17. Sir John Gonson's *Five Charges to Several Grand Juries* (London, 1740) collects four examples of charges delivered to the "Grand Jury of the City and Liberty of Westminster" and one City charge delivered to "the Grand Jury of the Royalty of the Tower of London, and Liberties and Precincts thereof." In the British Library's fourth-edition copy of Gonson's collection, Fielding's *Charge* of 1749 is an unlisted yet appended as part of the anthology and stands as a sixth example.

18. "The presiding justice's charge to the grand jury was one of the signal public events in the legal process of assizes and quarter sessions. The ceremonies attached to assizes were generally grander, for they involved the semi-annual visitation of the king's justices to the counties . . . ." Zirker, introduction to *Related Writings*, xxiv.

19. See Zirker, introduction to *Related Writings*, xxviii–xxxi.

20. Henry Fielding, *A Charge Delivered to the Grand Jury* in Zirker, *Related Writings*, 4. All subsequent references to this text will be cited internally.

21. *Oxford English Dictionary*, 2nd ed., s.v. "Charge."

22. *Oxford English Dictionary*, 2nd ed., s.v. "Charge."

23. Zirker, introduction to *Related Writings*, xxv and xxx.

24. Clifford Siskin reads William Wordsworth's *The Prelude* in the same manner. See Siskin, *The Work of Writing: Literature and Social Change in Britain, 1700–1830* (Baltimore: The Johns Hopkins University Press, 1998), 1–26.

25. See Zirker for the most detailed account of Penlez's initial claims against Owen's bawdy-house, introduction to *Related Writings*, xxiv.

26. See also Zirker, introduction to *Related Writings*, xl–xli.

27. Fielding, *A True State of the Case of Bosavern Penlez* in Zirker, *Related Writings*, 58. All subsequent references to this text will be cited internally.

28. The factor that distinguishes the public from the private is the number of rioters involved (see *Case*, 35–40).

29. Zirker, introduction to *Related Writings*, liii.

30. *Oxford English Dictionary*, 2nd ed., s.v. "inquiry."

31. Fielding, *An Enquiry into the Late Increase of Robbers* in Zirker, *Related Writings*, 73. All subsequent quotations of this text will be cited internally.

32. Fielding devotes Section VI entirely to questions on how to deal with "Vagabonds" who commit crimes *specifically* in the Town: "Now, however, useful this excellent Law [to prevent crimes committed by wanders] may be in the Country, it will by no means serve the Purpose in this Town" (*Enquiry*, 142).

Notes to Chapter 3

1. See the title page to Nicholas Hawksmoor's *A Short Historical Account of London-Bridge; with a Proposition for a New-Stone Bridge at Westminster* (London, 1736).

2. Michel Baridon's "The Gentleman as Gardner: Pope, Shenstone, Mason," in *The Crisis of Courtesy* argues that "It is no exaggeration to say that in his *Moral Epistles* Pope took his cue from the *Spectator*. His intention was the same, to provide moral standards for the post-1688 age, but his tone was different, even when he spoke of gardens, a theme which Addison had developed in several numbers of the *Spectator*" (130). Baridon considers this "different" tone to stem from Pope's yoking morality to property, his visual aesthetics, his poetic psychology, and his "giving a literary expression to the phantasmal forms" of scientists. This leads Baridon to conclude that "in spite of their attraction to solitude, the gentlemen-gardeners of the eighteenth century contributed actively to the movement of ideas. As such, albeit implicitly, they can be considered active promoters of new patterns of behavior" (141).

The art of gardening takes on a very communal function when looking at Pope's career, and critics such as Maynard Mack and Baridon stress how "cultivating the garden" becomes an operative metaphor for guiding the philosophical, scientific, and aesthetic imaginations of the community, city, and nation. Therefore, I agree with Baridon's claim that the cultivation of "solitude" is not Pope's immediate goal.

3. See Maynard Mack, *The Garden and the City: Retirement and Politics in the Later Poetry of Pope, 1731–1743* (Toronto: University of Toronto Press, 1969). Mack's epilogue substantiates this metaphoric connection: "For Pope—so my argument runs—the garden and the grotto supplied [literally and figuratively, a place to stand, an angle of vision]. They supplied a rallying point for his personal values and a focus for his conception of himself—as master of a poet's 'kingdom,' a counter-order to a court and ministry that set no store by poets. . . . Through them his retreat at Twickenham became, not only in his own eyes but in those of a number of his contemporaries, a true country of the mind" (232–33); "[In Pope's satires of the '30s], all play their part in an extended fiction (which is by no means all fiction) of the virtuous recluse who ventures in and out of London to remind his contemporaries of the City a little further up-river. Though the throne is empty, there remains an alternative center, and a power of a different kind: the poet-king-philosopher in his grotto, midway between the garden and the river" (236).

4. Pope, *An Essay on Criticism* in *Poems*, p. 153, lns. 322–23.

5. Pope establishes this "Poet-Critic" as early as lines 17–18 of the *Essay:*

"Authors are partial to their Wit, 'tis true, / But are not Criticks to their Judgment too?"

6. Cynthia Wall, introduction to *The Rape of the Lock*, edited by Cynthia Wall (Boston: Bedford Books, 1998), 4 and 5, respectively.

7. According to Joyce D. Kennedy, Michael Seidel, and Maximillian E. Novak's headnote to Defoe's *An Essay upon Projects*, "Projector evokes stereotypes—the cockeyed virtuosi; economic alchemists; the figure the *OED* describes as invidious, 'a schemer; one who lives by his wits; a promoter of bubble companies; a speculator, a cheat'" (xxi).

Yet Kennedy, Seidel, and Novak stress that "it is almost as if the reign of William after the [Glorious] Revolution provided the opportunity to rid the nation of that proliferative breed of schemers and virtuosos left over from Stuart times" (xxiv). These critics' emphasis upon the change in projecting after 1688 may be attributed to the burgeoning "art of government" in which writers increasingly participate.

8. Kennedy, Seidel, and Novak, headnote to Defoe's *An Essay upon Projects*, xxiv and xxv, respectively. The authors' characterization of Defoe's work also echoes Fielding's work, which I have detailed in the preceding chapter: "By proposing, as he will, that there are two ways to look at the projector's art, Defoe lays the groundwork for his own legitimacy" (xxv).

9. For detailed histories of the building of Westminster Bridge, see Morris R. Brownell, *Alexander Pope and the Arts of Georgian England* (Oxford: Clarendon Press, 1978), 301–4; and R. J. B. Walker, *Old Westminster Bridge: The Bridge of Fools* (Newton Abbot: David and Charles Publishers, 1979), especially 77–104.

10. *Daily Journal* (26 January 1721/2) quoted in Walker, *Old Westminster Bridge*, 48.

11. See G. Gabrielle Starr, *Lyric Generations*. In particular, Starr sees lyric episodes in eighteenth-century novels creating an intermediary realm between "truth and lie" as "chiastic sites": "These figures help create the novelistic ideal of the 'fictional' as a category distinct from truth or lie, a category closely tied to the emergence of the novel as a cultural force" (108). Starr's conception of a lyric imagination is important, especially in its relation to "projection": "The spaces of memory, projection, and personification are the imaginative and hence sympathetic spaces of the mid-century lyric" (109–110).

12. For a recent study that has served to analyze this Augustan-romantic divide by focusing upon the birth of the romantic imagination, see James Engell, *The Creative Imagination: Enlightenment to Romanticism* (Cambridge, MA: Harvard University Press, 1981).

13. For examples of the foundational type of work that has created this interpretative space for questions about eighteenth-century views of the imagination, see David Fairer, *Pope's Imagination* (Manchester: Manchester University Press, 1984) and Leopold Damrosch, Jr., *The Imaginative World of Alexander Pope* (Berkeley: University of California Press, 1987).

14. I am therefore arguing that although eighteenth-century notions of the imagination may have appeared socially complex, Pope's *To Burlington* offers a way to discipline this complexity during a specific historical episode. Dennis

Todd also argues that Pope had tried to represent the function of imagination in his poetry; however, Todd examines the final stage of Pope's career to argue that an anxious link exists in *The Dunciad* between "Dulness" and imagination (see Dennis Todd, *Imagining Monsters: Miscreations of the Self in Eighteenth-Century England* [Chicago: the University of Chicago Press, 1995], 179–216). In contrast to Todd's argument, I see Pope disciplining the imagination to accomplish a social duty much earlier. I also see Pope designing the imagination to be a socially relevant tool rather than what Todd sees Pope approaching as an alienating faculty or even "monstrous" (216) entity (see especially Todd, 183–92).

15. See Brownell, *Georgian England,* 291; especially 276–325 for a detailed discussion of the characteristic traits of, and Pope's relationship to, Palladianism.

16. See Julian Ferraro, "Taste and Use: Pope's *Epistle to Burlington,*" *The British Journal of Eighteenth-Century Studies,* 19, no. 2 (Autumn 1996), 141–59.

17. See Maynard Mack, *Last and Greatest Art, Some Unpublished Poetical Manuscripts of Alexander Pope* (Newark, 1984), 156–63; and Ferraro, "Taste and Use."

18. See Ferraro, 156, n. 9: "The revisions discussed in this paper are principally those from the first edition, the various editions of the 1735 *Works,* together with that of 1739 and the *Four Ethic Epistles* of 1744."

19. Ferraro's thesis is that "[the different versions of *To Burlington*] are poems the various versions of which have a different resonance, scope, and meaning at different points in their history, rather than being supplanted by subsequent revisions in a straightforwardly teleological development" ("Taste and Use," 155). Because I am interested in the various generic reincarnations of this poem, this chapter uses the Twickenham's version of *To Burlington,* included under the title Pope gave to the epistles in 1744, *Moral Essays.* My choice does not mean that I am privileging this version above all other earlier versions. The Twickenham version has simply become a "standard" edition of the poem; thus, I use this convention as a means of arguing my claims about this poem to a wider audience.

20. Although we have come to recognize *To Burlington* as *Epistle IV* of the *Moral Essays,* Pope wrote *To Burlington* between 1730–31 and published it in 1731, well before his other three epistles ("Epistle to Bathurst" [1733], "Epistle to Cobham" [1734], and "Epistle to a Lady" [1735]). Thus, *To Burlington* initiated an epistle sequence; it started a larger project. Combined with its multiple revisions and various published versions, these details suggest a reason why *To Burlington* has received the most attention of the four *Moral Essays.*

21. Quoted in John Butt, preface to *Poems,* ix.

22. See George S. Fraser, *Alexander Pope* (London: Routledge and Kegan Paul, 1978), 76.

23. Poovey argues in *A History of the Modern Fact* that the English essay was an attempt "to replicate experience instead of demonstrating propositions" and that this constituted an alternate form of knowledge production (212; see especially 210–13). I will return to Poovey's argument to detail how it can suggest new approaches to Pope's poetry.

24. For discussions about the otherness of the eighteenth-century imagination in relation to Pope, see again Damrosch, *The Imaginative World of Alexander Pope* and David Farber, *Pope's Imagination,* especially 1–7.

25. T. G. Nelson, "Pope, Burlington, Architecture, and Politics: A Speculative Revisionist Review," *Eighteenth-Century Life* 21 (February 1997), 46. If written by Pope himself, *The Master Key* supports the argument that Pope recognized how crucial it was to instruct readers on how to read the content of *To Burlington* properly; the *Key* provides satiric instructions to solve this inane (and in Pope's opinion, interpretative) problem in 1732, a period before his revising the title of the four epistles.

26. *The Master Key to Popery,* quoted in Brownell, 313.

27. Alexander Pope, *Epistle IV. To Richard Boyle, Earl of Burlington,* in *Poems,* lns. 19–22. Hereafter cited internally by line number(s).

28. Frank Stack, *Pope and Horace: Studies in Imitation* (Cambridge: Cambridge University Press, 1985), 29–30.

29. See Pope's *The First Epistle of the First Book of Horace Imitated* (1738); *The Sixth Epistle of the First Book of Horace Imitated* (1738); *The First Epistle of the Second Book of Horace Imitated* (1737); *The Second Epistle of the Second Book of Horace Imitated* (1737); and *The Seventh Epistle of the First Book of Horace Imitated in the Manner of Dr. Swift* (1739).

30. Stack, 116.

31. R. A. Brower, "The *Moral Essays,*" in *Critics on Pope: Readings in Literary Criticism* (Coral Gables: University of Miami Press, 1972), 97.

32. Brower, 99.

33. My concept of *To Burlington*'s narrative is similar to Brower's summary of the poem, cited above. But I do not believe that the poem ends with "a single bad case and its nobler opposite" (Brower, 97). Pope extends beyond this Horatian ending. In fact, Pope's ending, as I will soon show, is where he deviates from Horace and outlines his imaginative project.

34. Brower, 101.

35. See especially Ferraro, 146.

36. Richard Steiger, "Pope's *Epistle to Burlington,* 11, 47–50," *Explicator* 48 (Fall 1989), 14.

37. Steiger, 14.

38. See Stack and his discussion of Shaftesbury's detailing "the self-consciousness of the Horatian manner" (15, 116–49), and especially the section entitled "The Poet's Public Self" (128–31).

39. Horace, "Satire I.x.11–14," in *Horace: Satires, Epistles, and Ars Poetica,* trans. H. Rushton Fairclough (Cambridge, MA: Harvard University Press, 1999), 117.

40. Pope also co-titled his *Epistle to Bathurst,* the second poem in this project, "Of the Use of Riches." This detail supports my claim that *To Burlington* initiates an imaginative project centering upon wealth's relationship to a new imperial powerhouse.

41. The social value that the essay acquired during the 1750s is foreign to the twentieth century. See Poovey, p. 213: ". . . the proliferation of some new genres

of imaginative writing in the eighteenth century (the novel) and the persistence of others (poetry) demonstrates that Britons still cultivated modes of knowledge production that departed from the systematic idea of philosophy. Indeed, during the eighteenth century, then increasingly at century's end, these imaginative modes briefly came to seem at least as appropriate as moral philosophy to the crucial task of exploring the human motivation that underwrote liberal governmentality. The reign of the modes of writing that we call literature over the domain of subjectivity was relatively short-lived, however . . . ."

42. Poovey, 204, 198.

43. Ferraro's argument also centers upon the visibility of Pope's transition from "Taste" to "Use"; however, while Ferraro succeeds in detailing this transition through Pope's manuscripts and revisions, he does not interpret its significance beyond an argument about Burlington himself (see especially 155).

44. For this reason, perhaps an even more fitting title for *To Burlington* would have been "Of Use."

45. William A. Gibson, "Three Principles of Renaissance Architectural Theory in Pope's 'Epistle to Burlington'" in *Studies in English Literature* 11 (1971), 490.

46. Quoted in Ferraro, 152.

47. I refer the reader to the infamous etching, "Taste, or Burlington Gate" (1732), a print previously attributed to William Hogarth that depicts Pope tottering above a scaffold, whitewashing the word "TASTE" carved over the entrance to Burlington's main gate. I would add that this etching has also been a contributing factor to interpretations that view *To Burlington* solely in terms of Pope's relationship to an architect.

48. Mack qtd. in Ferraro, 154.

49. See Gibson, preface, "The Art of Architecture: A Poem" (Los Angeles: University of California, 1970), viii.

50. *Oxford English Dictionary,* s.v. "use."

51. I would argue that Pope's multiple revisions to this poem also support the claim that Pope wrote *To Burlington* to address very specific conditions of the early 1730s.

52. Pope, n. to lines 195–204, "To Burlington," *Poems,* 595.

53. See the title page to Nicholas Hawksmoor's *A Short Historical Account of London-Bridge; with a Proposition for a New-Stone Bridge at Westminster* (London, 1736).

54. Hawksmoor's *Proposition* was just one of many plans submitted to the Commissioners for the Westminster Bridge (a committee headed by William Pulteney and of which Burlington himself was a member beginning in 1737). Thomas Ripley and Colen Campbell also had submitted plans. Construction of Westminster Bridge began in 1738 and was completed in 1749. (Again, see Brownell, *Georgian England,* 301–4; and Walker, *Old Westminster Bridge,* especially 77–104).

55. For more on Labelye's design, see Walker, *Old Westminster Bridge,* especially 77–87.

56. Hawksmoor, *Proposition*, 11 and 16.
57. Hawksmoor, *Proposition*, 11.
58. Hawksmoor, *Proposition*, 3.
59. Lord Burlington transitively relates to Hawksmoor via Pope, but Burlington served as an informal advisor to the Bridge Committee headed by William Pulteney. Although Burlington strongly recommended an architect of his Palladian agenda, Colin Campbell, to Pulteney's committee in addition to hiring "two eminent mathematicians, Edmund Halley and Dr. Arbuthnot, to check Campbell's design" (Walker, *Old Westminster Bridge*, 47), portfolios from a variety of different architectural camps poured into the committee in hopes of securing a public works project that was a cultural lynchpin for London.

NOTES TO CHAPTER 4

1. See James Raven, *Judging New Wealth: Popular Publishing and Responses to Commerce in England, 1750–1800* (Oxford: Clarendon Press, 1992); William B. Warner, *Licensing Entertainment: The Elevation of Novel Reading in Britain, 1684–1750* (Berkeley, University of California Press, 1998); and Jon P. Klancher, *The Making of English Reading Audiences, 1790–1832* (Madison: University of Wisconsin Press, 1987).

2. For numerical data outlining these proliferating phenomenon, see especially Raven, "The Publication of Fiction in Britain and Ireland, 1750–70," *Publishing History* 24 (1998); Jan Fergus, "Provincial Servants' Reading in the Late Eighteenth Century," *The Practice and Representation of Reading in England*, edited by Raven, Helen Small, and Naomi Tadmor (Cambridge: Cambridge University Press, 1996), 202–225; James Raven and Antonia Forster, *The English Novel 1770–1829: A Bibliographical Survey of Prose Fiction Published in the British Isles,* vol. 1: 1770–1799 (Oxford: Oxford University Press, 2000), especially 15–121; Raven, "From Promotion to Proscription: Arrangements for Reading and Eighteenth-Century Libraries," in *Practice and Representation*, 175–201; Raven, *British Fiction, 1750–1770: A Chronological Check-List of Prose Fiction Printed in Britain and Ireland* (Newark: University of Delaware Press, 1987); and Raven, *Judging New Wealth,* 19–82.

3. Raven, *Judging New Wealth,* 66. Raven anchors this proliferation to an urban sphere: "The presses of London, Dublin, and Edinburgh responded eagerly, proclaiming the instructional value of their publications" (66).

4. Raven, *Judging New Wealth,* 68–69.

5. See John Entick, *A New and Accurate History and Survey of London, Westminster, Southwark, and Places Adjacent,* 3rd ed., (London, 1766), vol. 3, 266. In William Henry Irving's study of Gay's London, Irving also refers to such a law, but dates it to 1762 ("The overhanging signs grew so numerous and so elaborate that finally, in 1762, the law had to interfere and they were removed"); see Irving, *John Gay's London,* (Cambridge, MA: Harvard University

Press, 1928),168. Because Irving does not reference the actual law, I am relying upon Entick's citation. I also thank Alison O'Byrne (University of York) and the Eighteenth-Century Listserv for helping me to locate references to this act.

6. "The humble representation of the commissioners of the sewers and pavements within the said city and liberties" quoted in Entick, *A New and Accurate History,* vol. 3, 266.

7. Raven, *Judging New Wealth,* 163.

8. John Trusler, *The London Adviser and Guide* (London, 1786), 121–124 and 126, respectively.

9. R. Campbell, *The London Tradesman* (London, 1757), 129, emphasis Campbell's.

10. R. Campbell, *The London Tradesman,* 130.

11. Warner, *Licensing Entertainment,* xi.

12. Warner, *Licensing Entertainment,* 279, emphasis mine.

13. Warner, *Licensing Entertainment,* 39.

14. See especially Warner's "Conclusion: The Freedom of Readers," *Licensing Entertainment,* 277–94.

15. See especially chapter 2 of Warner, *Licensing Entertainment,* 45–87.

16. Klancher, *The Making of English Reading Audiences,* 20.

17. Klancher, *The Making of English Reading Audiences,* 23. Klancher considers the 1790s to be a turning point when "new periodical writing . . . foregrounds the discontinuity of publics" (44). If this is true, then Boswell and Burney represent a prehistory that leads to this late-century "foregrounding"; in other words, Boswell and Burney try to reappropriate their predecessors' textual strategies to react to the proliferation of print and develop new modes of self-government in which "the London individual" may be realized.

18. See Mackie, *Market à la Mode,* 4.

Notes to Chapter 5

1. James Boswell, *Boswell's London Journal: 1762–1763,* ed. Frederick A. Pottle (New Haven: Yale University Press, 1950), 44. Hereafter cited internally with relevant page number(s).

2. See Pottle, introduction, *London Journal,* 5–7.

3. David Harvey theorizes the imaginative power of these "'God-like' vision[s]" as he introduces his study of "the city in imagination" in his introduction to *The Urban Experience* (Baltimore: The Johns Hopkins University Press, 1989), 1.

4. For an analysis of the *London Journal*'s novelistic similarities, see Robert H. Bell, "Boswell's Notes Toward a Supreme Fiction from *London Journal* to *Life of Johnson,*" *Modern Language Quarterly* 38, no. 2 (June 1977): 132–48. For discussions of the *London Journal*'s autobiographical and confessional qualities, see Frederick A. Pottle, introduction to *Boswell's London Journal,* ed. Frederick A. Pottle (New Haven: Yale University Press, 1950), 10–16.

5. See Patricia Meyer Spacks, *Imagining a Self: Autobiography and Novel in Eighteenth-Century England* (Cambridge, MA: Harvard University Press, 1976), especially chs. 8 and 9; Michael D. Friedman, "'He Was Just a Macheath': Boswell and *The Beggar's Opera*," *The Age of Johnson: A Scholarly Annual* 4 (1991): 97–114; and Donald Kay, "Boswell in the Green Room: Dramatic Method in the *London Journal*," *Philological Quarterly* 57, no. 2 (Spring 1978): 195–212. Kay describes the *London Journal* as a "dramatic autobiographical journal" ("Green Room," 195), but his article mainly addresses these different genres under what he sees as Boswell's "dramatic method" ("Green Room," 195).

6. For studies that interpret Boswell's melancholy, see Ronald Primeau, "Boswell's 'Romantic Imagination' in the *London Journal*," *Papers on Language and Literature* 9, no. 1 (Winter 1973): 13–27; and Susan Manning, "'The Philosophical Melancholy': Style and Self in Boswell and Hume," in *New Light on Boswell: Critical and Historical Essays on the Occasion of the Bicentenary of* The Life of Johnson, ed. Greg Clingham (Cambridge: Cambridge University Press, 1991), 126–40. Manning posits the idea of melancholy's "unwriteability" ("Melancholy," 139) in the *London Journal*.

7. This dramatic adaptation has, in fact, occurred in the form of a 1984 BBC television production, *Boswell in London*. See Irma S. Lustig, "On the Making of *Boswell's London Journal* and *Boswell for the Defence*," and Kay Sloan, "Boswell for the Defence/*Boswell's* London Journal," *Eighteenth-Century Life* 16, no. 2 (May 1992): 136–39 and 142–44, respectively.

8. I owe the methodology I am using here to two essays that have reappropriated the discourses of metaphor and genre in history. First, Erin O'Connor tackles the rhetoric of Victorian medical metaphors in her essay "Breast Reductions," in *Raw Material: Producing Pathology in Victorian Culture* (Durham: Duke University Press, 2000), 60–101. O'Connor's thesis is that we need to "consider catachresis as a historical, textual, and analytical entity. . . . Thinking catachresis in turn forces us to think more carefully about what constitutes 'context' and about what we mean when we say that signifying practices are 'political'" (100–1). Second, Mary Poovey's essay "The Model System of Contemporary Literary Criticism," emphasizes the need to understand genre as an "organizing metaphor" that itself has a history in the professionalization of literary criticism (*Critical Inquiry* 23, no. 3, 408-38). Both of these studies highlight the need for us to understand the history of the metaphors we use to explicate text.

9. Aphra Behn, in addition to many other playwrights, followed Dryden's lead. Critics stress Behn's postscript to *The Rover,* "I hang out the sign of Angellica," (see *Oroonoko, The Rover, and Other Works,* ed. Janet Todd [London: Penguin Books, 1992], 248), because it offers a meta-commentary, interpretation, and social critique of her own play.

10. See *Restoration and Eighteenth-Century Comedy,* ed. Scott McMillin (New York: W.W. Norton & Company, 1997), footnote †, 474.

11. See *Restoration and Eighteenth-Century Comedy,* ed. Scott McMillin (New York: W.W. Norton & Company, 1997), footnote †, 474.

12. Richard Steele, *Tatler* 1, Tuesday, 12 April 1709, in *Selections from* The

Tatler *and* The Spectator, ed. Angus Ross (New York: Penguin Books, 1982), 67.

13. One of the most famous *Spectator* papers is Steele's *Spectator* 65, Tuesday, 15 May 1711. It is famous because it addresses George Etherege's *The Man of Mode* (1676). Critics and professors of eighteenth-century drama frequently use it to understand the contemporary reaction to the play, particularly the rake Dorimant. Not surprisingly, Steele reflects in this paper upon the "unnatural" conduct of the characters (see Ross, *Selections,* 407).

14. There are extended evaluations about how Boswell wishes to be Macheath (see especially Friedman), but few studies have interpreted Boswell's obsession with Addison and Steele with the same vigor.

15. See Pottle, introduction, 40, n. 4. Boswell elaborates on his weekly plan to send these installments to the Scottish Johnston within the *London Journal:* "In the evening I went to Douglas's, where I found a letter from my friend Johnston which gave me much satisfaction, brought many comfortable ideas into my mind, and put me on a regular plan of sending him my journal" (68). Johnston's vetting this journal suggests another reason why we should trace Boswell's strategies for refining and managing his own conduct.

16. See George H. Nettleton and Arthur E. Case's critical preface to *The Conscious Lovers* in *British Dramatists from Dryden to Sheridan,* ed. Nettleton and Case (Carbondale and Edwardsville: Southern Illinois University Press, 1969), 435–36.

17. Richard Steele, *The Conscious Lovers,* II.ii.314–19, in Nettleton and Case, *Comedy,* p. 452.

18. Boswell's authorship of the *View* was in a way sealed in 1976 when the Augustan Reprint Society published the text in facsimile with Boswell's name on the cover. In his introduction to this edition, David W. Tarbet, states that "circumstantial evidence favors the claim for Boswell. The dedication to Boswell's current idol, West Digges, and the extravagant praise of Mrs. Cowper, Boswell's current passion, suggest his enthusiasms. The evidence of his letters shows a strong and early interest in the theatre, and an indirect reference in a 26 September 1759 letter to John Johnston appears to make an amused claim of the authorship for part of the *View* which had earlier appeared in the June and July numbers of the *Edinburgh Chronicle.*" (David W. Tarbet, introduction to *A View of the Edinburgh Theatre during the Summer Season, 1759,* by [James Boswell] [Los Angeles: University of California, 1976], i).

19. [James Boswell], *A View of the Edinburgh Theatre during the Summer Season, 1759* (Los Angeles: University of California, 1976), iii.

20. Richard Steele, *Tatler* 1, 12 April 1709, in *Selections,* 65 (emphasis Steele's).

21. See Gerald Prince, *A Dictionary of Narratology* (Lincoln: University of Nebraska Press, 1987), s.v. "narrative."

22. I argue that Boswell is conscious of his own use of metaphor. For an example of this self-consciousness, see when Boswell calls attention to, or reflects upon, his own artful handling of metaphors following his participation in a Saturday-dialogue at Child's coffeehouse: "I don't think this at all bad. My simile

of the hares (my metaphor, rather) is pretty well" (76).

23. I choose 1798 because it is the year Samuel Taylor Coleridge and William Wordsworth began to circulate this "romantic" view of a creative imagination in the *Lyrical Ballads*.

24. Pottle, introduction to *London Journal,* 12. For a discussion of the relevance of Pottle's description to a discussion of narrative and plot, see Arnold W. Cushner, "Plot and Episode in James Boswell's *Grand Tour Journal*," *English Language Notes* 32, no. 1 (September 1994): 53–62, especially 57.

25. Pottle, introduction to *London Journal,* 13–14.

26. See Alan R. White, *The Language of Imagination* (Oxford: Basil Blackwell Ltd., 1990), 5: "It was an emphasis on this active strand in imagination which, despite its still unsevered tie to the sensory image, opened the way to a view of imagination as the instigator of novelty, inventiveness, and originality, and as the source of the power, displays, flights, and feats of imagination. It is this strand, often under the Aristotelian name of 'fancy,' which Hobbes and later aesthetic theory praised for its wit, beauty, and art, and Descartes, Locke, and Hume disparaged for its unreality, extravagance, and lack of discipline."

27. David Hume, *A Treatise of Human Nature,* ed. David Fate Norton and Mary J. Norton (Oxford: Oxford University Press, 2000), 7. For further analysis of this hierarchy, see White's summary of Hume's theories about imagination, 35–43.

28. See White, *Language,* 35.

29. In fact, a new volume of Hume's *History* appeared during Boswell's residence in London (1762).

30. Addison, *Spectator* 409, Thursday, 19 June 1712, 366.

31. Addison, *Spectator* 409, Thursday, 19 June 1712, 367.

32. Addison, *Spectator* 411, Saturday, 21 June 1712, 368–9. As Angus Ross points out in his notes to the Penguin edition, Addison fails to make this distinction between "fancy" and "imagination" (549, n. 2). The distinction may primarily be a post-eighteenth-century phenomenon.

33. Addison, *Spectator* 409, Thursday, 19 June 1712, 365.

34. Addison, *Spectator* 409, Thursday, 19 June 1712, 367. The most famous example of Boswell's continued obsession with Addisonian self-government takes place on 18 October 1763, during the second month of his studies at Utrecht, as he composes his "Inviolable Plan: To be read over frequently." This "Plan," written entirely in a commanding, second-person voice, offers an explicit example from Boswell's journals of how he considers the delayed interpretation of his writing to constitute the source of self-knowledge and "certain fact." Consider how Boswell uses the Plan's preamble to reinterpret everything that came before this day in Holland:

> Let those years be thought of no more. You are now determined to form yourself into a man. . . . You studied with diligence. You grew quite well. This is a certain fact. You must never forget it. Nor attempt to plead a real incurable distemper; for you cured it, when it was

at its very worst, merely by following a proper plan with diligence and activity. This is a great era in your life; for from this time you fairly set out upon solid principles to be a man. (Boswell, *Boswell in Holland, 1763–1764,* ed. Pottle [New York: McGraw-Hill Book Co., Inc., 1952], 387)

Boswell uses this preamble to reflect upon the past and establish two "certain fact[s]": first, Boswell can bring a previously agentless illness ("a real incurable distemper") into his own control; and second, he can obtain his own "cure" and become his own agent by "following a proper plan with diligence and activity." I claim that the source of Boswell's "proper plan" is the disciplined writing and reading of his journals because he concludes his "Inviolable Plan" with the same Delphic mantra that marks the threshold of his *London Journal:* "Know Thyself" (*Holland* 390). Thus, the plan of the *London Journal* and his "Inviolable Plan" share objectives; that is, Boswell's idea of "the individual"—of "an excellent character"—stems from incessant, textual self-monitoring.

35. Addison, *Spectator* 411, Saturday, 21 June 1712, 369.
36. Boswell also details another "bowing" episode as he leaves Edinburgh:

> I made the chaise stop at the foot of the Canongate; asked pardon of Mr. Stewart for a minute; walked to the abbey of Holyroodhouse, went round the Piazzas, bowed thrice: once to the Palace itself, once to the crown of Scotland above the gate in front, and once to the venerable old Chapel. I next stood in the court before the Palace, and bowed thrice to Arthur Seat, that lofty romantic mountain on which I have so often strayed in my days of youth, indulged mediation, and felt the raptures of a soul filled with ideas of the magnificence of GOD and his creation. (41–42)

Amid these bouts of bowing, it is interesting to see how Boswell transfers the value of bowing from Edinburgh to London over the course of the *London Journal*'s narrative. Boswell also attaches an unregulated language of imagination ("mediation," "raptures," "magnificence") to the Edinburgh episodes. This diction is striking in comparison to the way Boswell bows to St. Paul's in London.

37. Addison, *Spectator* 411, Saturday, 21 June 1712, 369.
38. It is important to remember that "fancy" and "imagination" were still used interchangeably by many eighteenth-century authors including Addison, Steele, and Pope. (In Pope's case, see especially David Fairer, *Pope's Imagination* [Manchester: Manchester University Press, 1984], 2–3). Boswell here is trying to develop his own rules for distinguishing the two words from each other.
39. For other examples of this critical distancing strategy, see Addison, *Spectator* 69, 19 May 1711 where the narrator visits the Royal Exchange and imagines perspectives from the King's courtyard that surveys, and therefore manages, the activity below.
40. Steele, *Spectator* 454, Monday, 11 August 1712, 306.

41. Steele, *Spectator* 454, Monday, 11 August 1712, 309–10.

42. Michael Prince, *Philosophical Dialogue in the British Enlightenment: Theology, Aesthetics, and the Novel* (Cambridge: Cambridge University Press, 1996), 15.

43. Dryden's *Essay of Dramatic Poesy* also used dialogue to convey critical knowledge to his readership.

44. In order to understand, contextualize, and know what his condition is, Boswell again uses similes: "I this day began to feel an unaccountable alarm of unexpected evil: a little heat in the members of my body sacred to Cupid, very like a symptom of that distemper with which Venus, when cross, takes it into her head to plague her votaries" (149).

45. Boswell's tense shifts seem to parallel Fielding's strategies of authorization, and it is tempting to say that the *London Journal* is novelistic. However, the *London Journal* is an urban project that is both similar to and distinct from the novel in the same way it is similar to and distinct from every other canonical genre of the time: history, drama, epistolary, diary.

Notes to Chapter 6

1. Frances Burney, *Cecilia, or Memoirs of an Heiress,* ed. Peter Sabor and Margaret Anne Doody (Oxford: Oxford University Press, 1999), 897. All subsequent references to this text will be cited internally, marked by "*C*" and the relevant page number(s).

2. Catherine Gallagher's *Nobody's Story: The Vanishing Acts of Women Writers in the Marketplace, 1670–1820* (Berkeley: University of California Press, 1994) explores Burney's wrestling with the effects of female authorship in chapter 5 of her book, "Nobody's Debt: Frances Burney's Universal Obligation." In this chapter, Gallagher offers a comprehensive analysis of Burney's interactions with Samuel Johnson and other literary celebrities as they shape her publishing career. Unlike Gallagher, however, I am interested in how Burney used her first two novels to represent the experience of passivity on London's streets and in London's spaces in order to suggest alternate interpretive strategies that might cauterize this passivity.

3. Frances Burney, *Evelina, or, The History of a Young Lady's Entrance into the World,* ed. Stuart J. Cooke (New York: W.W. Norton and Company, 1998), 70. All subsequent references to this work will be cited internally and marked with an "*E*" and relevant page number(s).

4. The immediate cause of Evelina's unhappiness is the return of Captain Mirvan and Madame Duval to Howard Grove. Evelina continues, "But do not suppose *London* to be the source of these evils; for, had our excursion been anywhere else, so disagreeable an addition to our household, must have caused the same change at our return" (*E,* 98). Regardless of this qualifier, "place" acquires value in this passage as something separate from Evelina's self ("me").

5. Burney, "Saturday," Journal 1768, in *The Early Journals and Letters of Fanny Burney,* ed. Lars E. Triode (Montreal: McGill-Queen's University Press, 1988), vol. 1, 8.

NOTES TO CHAPTER 6   253

6. "[A]s soon as Mama saw it she immediately knew the Hand—it was Stephen's—I am sure *I* should never have suspected it was by the same Hand came to Hetty— . . . ." (Burney, "Saturday" Journal 1768, in *The Early Journals,* vol. 1, 9).

7. Burney, Letter to Susanna Burney, 15 March 1777, in *The Early Journals,* vol. 2, 221–22.

8. When Burney writes about traversing London's streets in her journal, an abstract threat infiltrates her language:

> We stayed very late, to avoid the Crowd, but the [King's Opera] House emptied very slowly, the Pit & Boxes being quite full. When we went down, we got with difficulty to our Coach; but, after the usual perils & dangers, we were drove out of Haymarket, & into Suffolk Street. Here we concluded we were safe,—but, as we afterwards found, there had been left a load of Gravel in the street, which the shade (of a moonlight) hid from the Coach man. We found ourselves suddenly mounting on one side—Mama, who is soon alarmed, cried out, "We are going! we are going!" I sat quite quiet, thinking it a false alarm: but presently the Coach was entirely overturned. . . .
>
> . . .
>
> . . . some people immediately gathered about the Cariage [sic], &, I believe, opened the Door, which was now at the Top of the Coach. . . . I made shift to stand up—& a Gentleman lifted me out. He had no Hat on, being come out of a Neighbouring House. He beg'd me to go with him, & promised to take care of me:—but I was now terified [sic] for Mama & Susan. . . . I quite wrung my Hands with horror—This Gentleman took hold of me, & almost used violence to make me go away—I remember I called out to him, as I broke from him, that he would drive me distracted! . . . However he would not leave me, for which I believe I am very much obliged to him, as I was surrounded by a mob . . . (Burney, Journal, 13 February 1773, in *The Early Journals,* vol. 1, 239–40)

9. In literary histories, Frances Burney's career is almost exclusively represented by *Evelina*. One of the reasons for *Evelina*'s overstated singularity involves the novel's supposed participation in the epistolary tradition of confessional interiority. I argue that our approaching *Evelina* in this manner, however, discounts the alternate modes of interiority that Burney was outlining.

10. Patricia Meyer Spacks has argued that "locating polarized qualities in opposed social spheres, [*Clarissa* and *Evelina*] use London and its class structure as way of rendering internal division. Impulse toward indulged passion and desire for restraint, these contrasted sides of female nature find correlatives in the fictional city" ("Women and the City," in *Johnson and His Age,* ed. James Engell [Cambridge, MA: Harvard University Press, 1984], 505). While I agree that Burney uses London "as a way of rendering internal division," I disagree

with Meyer Spacks that "the city implies an alternative to traditional patriarchal arrangements, but Burney finally evades that alternative" (507). I do not see *Evelina* by itself detailing an elaborate "alternative"; rather, the novel destabilizes the form though which Burney conveys these "traditional patriarchal arrangements" to the reader.

11. William Galperin's essay "The Radical Work of Frances Burney's London" (*Eighteenth-Century Life* 20 [November 1996]) claims that "while Burney's London remains, in many respects, a site of radical hope and possibility, her novel [*Evelina*]—as it asks to be read—assuredly does not" (47). Similar to Galperin, Meyer Spacks reads London as holding out "ingenious possibilities for female self-assertion" that *Evelina* ultimately refuses (Spacks, "Women," 492). Part of my argument in this chapter is that we should not draw conclusions about "Burney's London" until we understand *Cecilia*'s formal relationship to *Evelina*.

12. For more about London's "synechdoch[al]" qualities, see Spacks, "Women," 485–507, especially 488.

13. Herbert Davis, "The Correspondence of the Augustans," in *The Familiar Letter in the Eighteenth Century*, ed. Howard Anderson, Philip B. Daghlian, and Irvin Ehrenpreis (Lawrence: University of Kansas Press, 1966), 13. Bruce Redford's argument in *The Converse of the Pen: Acts of Intimacy in the Eighteenth-Century Familiar Letter* (Chicago: The University of Chicago Press, 1986) also emphasizes the way "intimate" letter-writing adopts the textual strategies of conversation: "the eighteenth-century familiar letter, like the eighteenth-century conversation, is a performance" (2).

14. Irene Tucker points out that we need to distinguish "the particular representational paradoxes of the letter form and the ways in which these paradoxes are complicated by being placed within the frame of a novel" (Irene Tucker, "Writing Home: *Evelina*, the Epistolary Novel, and the Paradox of Property," *English Literary History* 60 [1993]: 422). While I agree that Tucker's distinction is important (and will catalogue what I find to be "paradoxes" specific to *Evelina* and *Cecilia* later in this chapter), it is nonetheless necessary to historicize eighteenth-century familiar letter writing to see the public-private tension that was built into the epistolary novel's development.

15. Tom Keymer, *Richardson's Clarissa and the Eighteenth-Century Reader* (Cambridge: Cambridge University Press, 1992), xvi. Keymer interprets letters as social performances by detailing the two approaches to "epistolary discourse" taken by Pope and Johnson: "Where Pope stresses representational fidelity, Johnson dismisses the notion of the epistolary window as a prelapsarian dream, and finds in letter-writing instead an inevitable gravitation towards disguise. Taken together, their rival explanations mark the two extremes between which all epistolary discourse may be supposed to lie—on one hand, the pure, *un*dressed, expressive ideal; on the other, its impure, *ad*dressed, manipulative antithesis" (15).

16. See Amanda Gilroy and W.M. Verhoeven, introduction to *Epistolary Histories: Letters, Fiction, Culture,* ed. Amanda Gilroy and W. M. Verhoeven (Charlottesville: University Press of Virginia, 2000), 3.

17. "[U]ntil quite recently, critical discourse has on the whole accepted female epistolary skill as a truth universally acknowledged, and has subscribed to the fiction of the feminine, private letter," (Gilroy and Verhoeven, introduction, 3).

18. For studies that have examined the relationship between epistolarity and women writers, see especially Nancy Armstrong, *Desire and Domestic Fiction: A Political History of the Novel* (New York: Oxford University Press, 1987) and Janet Gurkin Altman, *Epistolarity: Approaches to a Form* (Columbus: Ohio State University Press, 1982), and Gilroy and Verhoeven, introduction, especially 1–14.

19. Janine Barchas's *Graphic Design, Print Culture, and the Eighteenth-Century Novel* (Cambridge: Cambridge University Press, 2003) analyzes the epistolary's graphics (in particular, the dashes, asterisks, *fleurons,* and *hederas* of Samuel Richardson's *Clarissa*) as interpretable elements of "the novel's temporal authenticity" and representative of "the space of time": "Richardson revives the non-ornamental qualities of the printer's ornament. He activates, as it were, the ancient function of the *hedera* as a mark of punctuation. When Richardson awakens this ability of the ornaments to punctuate, organize, and mark emphasis, he gains greater control over the fiction's temporal dimensions. He then exploits this control to give the readers an indication of the psychology of his characters" (133 and 152, respectively).

I agree that Burney's *Evelina* adopts Richardson's dashes and their function of "temporal authenticity"; however, Burney's novel also draws attention to moments where letters fail to represent Evelina's actual experiences, disruptions, meals, etc.

20. Gina Campbell's essay "How To Read Like a Gentleman: Burney's Instructions to Her Critics in *Evelina*" (*English Literary History* 57 [1990]: 557–84) also interprets Villars as someone trained in "textualizing Evelina" (581). Whereas Campbell argues "that Burney includes a model of reading within *Evelina* that resembles conduct literature in its emphasis on propriety and that is meant to serve Burney's literary ambitions by teaching her critics how they *ought to read* her work" (557), I do not see Burney detailing an elaborate mechanism for correcting her male audience's reading practices. Rather, Burney signals and performs the problems associated not with "a bad reader" (as Campbell deems Villars [565]) but with a flawed and gendered representational form (the epistolary) in general. Thus, I agree with Campbell that "Villars's interpretive method thus brings to the personal, private sphere the rules of conduct that apply to young women in the world, namely that anything secret or clandestine is incriminating" (566); however, I see this interpretive method in terms of its religious origin in confession. I differ from Campbell's argument when I claim that Burney suggests a reformation not in her male readers but in the work that women imagine their letters accomplishing. When viewed from the perspective of *Cecilia, Evelina* signals Burney's attempt to reject or write beyond the epistolary's limitations. These limitations included the authoritative position it assigned to its male readers in order for the form to be able to regulate feminine conduct.

21. Analyzing Richardson's epistolary techniques in *Clarissa* and *Pamela,*

Terry Castle details additional limitations that are inherent in epistolary novels—limitations that may have influenced Burney's attempt to acquire social authority: "The absence of authorial rhetoric and the shifting of authority to the reader makes the classic epistolary novel marvelously unfit, obviously, for didacticism of any kind. The epistolary novelist can never express moral or social "messages" with the relative precision and clarity available to a novelist using other narrative forms" (*Clarissa's Ciphers: Meaning & Disruption in Richardson's Clarissa* [Ithaca: Cornell University Press, 1982], 168). But Castle distinguishes *Evelina* not as a "classic epistolary novel" (in which there are "multiple-correspondent[s] ... in which each letter writer is given approximately the same amount of space in the text") but rather as an epistolary novel in which "the letters of a single character (usually the heroine) tend to dominate the sequence" (*Clarissa's Ciphers*, 168). Castle admits that this nonclassical epistolary novel involves a loss of narrative authority: "The choice of the letter form inevitable entails a weakening of authorial *power*" [emphasis Castle]; [t]he very proliferation of fictional voices—the diffuse, babbling effect of correspondence—allows the reader a kind of participation and freedom not granted in other forms of narration" (*Clarissa's Ciphers*, 167). If this is true, then the third-person voice of Burney's *Cecilia* suggests that Burney desired a strengthening of "authorial power" so that she could distribute her ideas of internalized self-government to a reader's unadulterated attention.

22. The male contest to conduct Cecilia is an omnipresent pattern in *Cecilia*. (See especially "The Masquerade" [chapter three, book two] and "An Affray" [chapter four, book two]). Cecilia incessantly attempts to divert or delay these contests.

23. According to Doody and Sabor, Burney probably italicized "*propriety of mind*" to "suggest a general conduct-book phrase, or a more specific allusion" (see endnote referring to p. 425, *C*, 985). This detail therefore shows Mrs. Delvile accepting Burney's new model of conduct that nurtures interiority by rejecting confession and privileging interpretation.

24. See Hester Chapone, *Letters on the Improvement of the Mind, Addressed to a Young Lady* (1778; Wellington, 1809), 50, letter 4 in *Evelina*, ed. Cooke, 341.

Works Cited

Allen, Emily. "Staging Identity: Frances Burney's Allegory of Genre." *Eighteenth-Century Studies* 31, no. 4 (1998): 433–51.

Altman, Janet Gurkin. *Epistolarity: Approaches to a Form.* Columbus: The Ohio State University Press, 1982.

Archer, Ian. "Popular Politics in the Sixteenth and Early Seventeenth Centuries." In *Londinopolis: Essays in the Cultural and Social History of Early Modern London,* edited by Paul Griffiths and Mark S. R. Jenner, 26–46. Manchester: Manchester University Press, 2000.

Armstrong, Nancy. *Desire and Domestic Fiction: A Political History of the Novel.* New York: Oxford University Press, 1987.

Armstrong, Nancy, and Leonard Tennenhouse. "The Literature of Conduct, the Conduct of Literature, and the Politics of Desire: An Introduction." In *The Ideology of Conduct: Essays on Literature and the History of Sexuality,* edited by Nancy Armstrong and Leonard Tennenhouse, 1–24. New York: Methuen & Co., 1987.

Bakhtin, Mikhail. *The Dialogic Imagination: Four Essays.* Translated by Caryl Emerson and Michael Holquist. Austin: University of Texas Press, 1981.

Barchas, Janine. *Graphic Design, Print Culture, and the Eighteenth-Century Novel.* Cambridge: Cambridge University Press, 2003.

Baridon, Michel. "The Gentleman as Gardener: Pope, Shenstone, Mason." In *The Crisis of Courtesy: Studies in the Conduct-Book in Britain, 1600–1900,* edited by Jacques Carré, 129–44. Leiden: E.J. Brill, 1994.

Bateson, F.W., ed. Preface and Introduction to *Epistles to Several Persons (Moral Essays),* by Alexander Pope. London: Methuen & Co., 1951.

Battestin, Martin C., and Ruthe R. Battestin. *Henry Fielding: A Life.* London: Routledge, 1989.

Behn, Aphra. *The Rover.* In *Oroonoko, The Rover, and Other Works.* Edited by Janet Todd. London: Penguin Books, 1992.

Bell, Robert H. "Boswell's Notes toward a Supreme Fiction from *London Journal* to *Life of Johnson.*" *Modern Language Quarterly* 38, no. 2 (June 1977): 132–48.

Bender, John. *Imagining the Penitentiary: Fiction and the Architecture of the Mind in Eighteenth-Century England.* Chicago: the University of Chicago Press, 1987.

Berger, Dieter A. "Maxims of Conduct into Literature: Jonathan Swift and Polite Conversation." In *The Crisis of Courtesy: Studies in the Conduct-*

Book in Britain, 1600–1900, edited by Jacques Carré, 81–92. Leiden: E.J. Brill, 1994.
Blake, William. *Blake: Complete Writings with Variant Readings.* Edited by Geoffrey Keynes. Oxford: Oxford University Press, 1992.
Boswell, James. *Boswell's London Journal, 1762–1763.* Edited by Frederick A. Pottle. 1950. Reprint, New Haven: Yale University Press, 1992.
———. *Boswell in Holland, 1763–1764.* Edited by Frederick A. Pottle. New York: McGraw-Hill Book Co., 1952.
[Boswell, James]. *A View of the Edinburgh Theatre during the Summer Season, 1759.* Edited by David W. Tarbet. Los Angeles: University of California, 1976.
Brewer, John and Roy Porter, eds. *Consumption and the World of Goods.* London: Routledge, 1993.
Brooke, Christopher N.L. and Gillian Keir. *London, 800–1216: the Shaping of a City.* London: Secker & Warburg, 1975.
Brower, R.A. "The *Moral Essays*." In *Critics on Pope: Readings in Literary Criticism,* edited by Judith O'Neill, 96–103. Coral Gables: University of Miami Press, 1972.
Brownell, Morris R. *Alexander Pope and the Arts of Georgian England.* Oxford: Clarendon Press, 1978.
Burchell, Graham, "Peculiar Interests: Civil Society and Governing 'The System of Natural Liberty.'" In *The Foucault Effect: Studies in Governmentality, with Two Lectures and an Interview with Michel Foucault,* edited by Graham Burchell, Colin Gordon, and Peter Miller, 119–50. Chicago: University of Chicago Press, 1991.
Burney, Frances. *Cecilia, or Memoirs of an Heiress.* Edited by Peter Sabor and Margaret Anne Doody. Oxford: Oxford University Press, 1999.
———. *The Early Journals and Letters of Fanny Burney.* Volumes 1 and 2. Edited by Lars E. Triode. Montreal: McGill-Queen's University Press, 1988.
———. *Evelina, or, The History of a Young Lady's Entrance into the World.* Edited by Stuart J. Cooke. New York: W.W. Norton and Company, 1998.
Butler, Judith. *Precarious Lives: the Powers of Mourning and Violence.* London: Verso, 2004.
Campbell, Gina. "How To Read Like a Gentleman: Burney's Instructions to Her Critics in *Evelina.*" *English Literary History* 57 (1990): 557–83.
Campbell, R. *The London Tradesman. Being an Historical Account of All Professions, Arts . . . Now Practised in . . . London and Westminster.* Third Edition. (London, 1757).
Carré, Jacques. Introduction to *The Crisis of Courtesy: Studies in the Conduct-Book in Britain, 1600–1900,* edited by Jacques Carré, 1–10. Leiden: E.J. Brill, 1994.
Castle, Terry. *Clarissa's Ciphers: Meaning & Disruption in Richardson's Clarissa.* Ithaca: Cornell University Press, 1982.
Chapone, Hester. *Letters on the Improvement of the Mind, Addressed to a Young Lady.* 1778; Wellington, 1809. 50, letter 4. In *Evelina, or, The History of a*

Young Lady's Entrance into the World, edited by Stuart J. Cooke, 341 and 343. New York: W.W. Norton and Company, 1998.

Colley, Linda. *Britons: Forging the Nation, 1707–1837.* New Haven: Yale University Press, 1992.

Collier, Jeremy. "A Short View of the Immorality and Profaneness of the English Stage, Together with the Sense of Antiquity Upon this Argument." In *British Dramatists from Dryden to Sheridan,* edited by George H. Nettleton and Arthur E. Case, 389–91. Carbondale and Edwardsville: Southern Illinois University Press, 1969.

Collinson, Patrick. "John Stow and Nostalgic Antiquarianism." In *Imagining Early Modern London: Perceptions and Portrayals of the City from Stow to Strype, 1598–1720,* edited by J. F. Merritt, 27–51. Cambridge: Cambridge University Press, 2001.

Copley, Stephen, and Ian Haywood. "Luxury, Refuse and Poetry: John Gay's *Trivia.*" In *John Gay and the Scriberlians,* edited by Peter Lewis and Nigel Wood, 62–82. New York: St. Martin's Press, 1988.

Cowley, Abraham. *Selected Poems of Abraham Cowley, Edmund Waller, and John Oldham.* Edited by Julia Griffin. London: Penguin Group, 1998.

Cushner, Arnold W. "Plot and Episode in James Boswell's *Grand Tour Journal.*" *English Language Notes* 32, no. 1 (September 1994): 53–62.

Damrosch, Leopold, Jr. *God's Plot & Man's Stories: Studies in the Fictional Imagination from Milton to Fielding.* Chicago: the University of Chicago Press, 1985.

———. *The Imaginative World of Alexander Pope.* Berkeley: University of California Press, 1987.

Darlington, Ida and James Howgego. *Printed Maps of London Circa 1553–1850.* Foreword by R. A. Skelton. London: George Philip & Son Ltd., 1964.

Davis, Herbert. "The Correspondence of the Augustans." In *The Familiar Letter in the Eighteenth Century,* edited by Howard Anderson, Philip B. Daghlian, and Irvin Ehrenpreis, 1–13. Lawrence: University of Kansas Press, 1966.

Defoe, Daniel. *An Essay on Projects.* Edited by Joyce D. Kennedy, Michael Seidel and Maximillian Novak. New York: AMS Press, Inc., 1999.

———. *A Tour through the Whole Island of Great Britain.* Edited by Pat Rogers. London: Penguin Group, 1986.

Doornick, Marcus Willemsz. *Platte Grondt der Verbrande Stadt London.* Amsterdam. 1666.

Downie, J. A. *Robert Harley and the Press: Propaganda and Public Opinion in the Age of Swift and Defoe.* Cambridge: Cambridge University Press, 1979.

Duval, Gilles. "Standardization vs. Genre: Conduct-Books and Chap-Literature." In *The Crisis of Courtesy: Studies in the Conduct-Book in Britain, 1600–1900,* edited by Jacques Carré, 41–50. Leiden: E.J. Brill, 1994.

Engell, James. *The Creative Imagination: Enlightenment to Romanticism.* Cambridge, MA: Harvard University Press, 1981.

Entick, John. *A New and Accurate History and Survey of London, Westminster, Southwark, and Places Adjacent.* Volumes 3 and 4 (London, 1766).

Epstein, James. "Spatial Practices/Democratic Vistas." *Social History* 24, no. 3 (October 1999): 294–310.

Faden, William. *A New Pocket Plan of the Cities of London & Westminster With the Borough of Southwark, Comprehending the New Buildings and Other Alternations to the Year 1790.* 1790.

Fairer, David. *Pope's Imagination.* Manchester: Manchester University Press, 1984.

Fergus, Jan. "Provincial Servants' Reading in the Late Eighteenth Century." In *The Practice and Representation of Reading in England,* edited by James Raven, Helen Small, and Naomi Tadmor, 202–25. Cambridge: Cambridge University Press, 1996.

Ferraro, Julian. "Taste and Use: Pope's *Epistle to Burlington.*" In *The British Journal of Eighteenth-Century Studies,* 19 no. 2 (Autumn 1996), 141–59.

Fielding, Henry. *An Enquiry into the Late Increase of Robbers and Related Writings.* Edited by Malvin Zirker. Middletown: Wesleyan University Press, 1988.

———. *The History of Tom Jones, A Foundling.* Edited by Fredson Bowers. Hanover: Wesleyan University Press, 1975.

Foucault, Michel. *The Archaeology of Knowledge and the Discourse on Language.* New York: Pantheon Books, 1972.

———. "Governmentality." In *The Foucault Effect: Studies in Governmentality, with Two Lectures and an Interview with Michel Foucault,* edited by Graham Burchell, Colin Gordon, and Peter Miller, 87–104. Chicago: University of Chicago Press, 1991.

———. *The Order of Things: An Archaeology of the Human Sciences.* New York: Random House, 1994.

Fraser, George S. *Alexander Pope.* London: Routledge and Kegan Paul, 1978.

French, Ylva. *London: The Blue Guide.* Seventh Edition. New York: W.W. Norton & Co., 1998.

Friedman, Michael D. "'He Was Just a Macheath': Boswell and *The Beggar's Opera.*" *The Age of Johnson: A Scholarly Annual* 4 (1991): 97–114.

Gallagher, Catherine. *Nobody's Story: The Vanishing Acts of Women Writers in the Marketplace, 1670–1820.* Berkeley: University of California Press, 1994.

Galperin, William. "The Radical Work of Frances Burney's London." *Eighteenth-Century Life* 20 (November 1996): 37–48.

Gay, John. *Trivia, or the Art of Walking the Streets of London.* In *Poetry and Prose.* 2 vols. Edited by Vinton A. Dearing with the assistance of Charles E. Beckwith. Oxford: Clarendon Press, 1974.

George, M. Dorothy. *London Life in the Eighteenth Century.* London: Penguin Books Ltd., 1985.

Gibson, William A. Preface to "The Art of Architecture: A Poem," by Anonymous. Los Angeles: University of California, 1970.

———. "Three Principles of Renaissance Architectural Theory in Pope's *Epistle to Burlington.*" *Studies in English Literature* 11 (1971): 487–501.

Gilroy, Amanda, and W. M. Verhoeven. Introduction to *Epistolary Histories:*

Letters, Fiction, Culture, edited by Amanda Gilroy and W.M. Verhoeven, 260–61. Charlottesville: University Press of Virginia, 2000.

Glinert, Ed. *The London Compendium: Exploring the Hidden Metropolis.* London: Allen Lane, 2003.

Gonson, John. *Five Charges to Several Grand Juries.* London, 1740.

Gordon, Colin, "Governmental Rationality: An Introduction." In *The Foucault Effect: Studies in Governmentality, with Two Lectures and an Interview with Michel Foucault,* edited by Graham Burchell, Colin Gordon, and Peter Miller, 1–52. Chicago: University of Chicago Press, 1991.

Griffiths, Paul. "Politics Made Visible: Order, Residence and Uniformity in Cheapside, 1600– 45." In *Londinopolis: Essays in the Cultural and Social History of Early Modern London,* edited by Paul Griffiths and Mark S. R. Jenner, 176–96. Manchester: Manchester University Press, 2000.

Griffiths, Paul and Mark S. R. Jenner. Introduction to *Londinopolis: Essays in the Cultural and Social History of Early Modern London,* edited by Paul Griffiths and Mark S. R. Jenner, 1–23. Manchester: Manchester University Press, 2000.

Haastrup, Niels. "The Courtesy-Book and the Phrase-Book in Modern Europe." In *The Crisis of Courtesy: Studies in the Conduct-Book in Britain, 1600–1900,* ed. Jacques Carré, 65–80. Leiden: E.J. Brill, 1994.

Habermas, Jürgen. *The Structural Transformation of the Public Sphere: An Inquiry into a Category of Bourgeois Society.* Translated by Thomas Burger with the assistance of Frederick Lawrence. Cambridge, MA: The MIT Press, 1991.

Harvey, David. *The Urban Experience.* Baltimore: The Johns Hopkins University Press, 1989.

Hawksmoor, Nicholas. *A Short Historical Account of London-Bridge; with a Proposition for a New-Stone Bridge at Westminster.* London, 1736.

Henry, Avril, and Peter Dixon. "Pope and the Architects: A Note on the *Epistle to Burlington.*" *English Studies: A Journal of English Language and Literature* 51 (1971): 437–41.

Hibbard, G. R. "The Country House Poem of the Seventeenth Century." In *Essential Articles for the Study of Alexander Pope,* ed. Maynard Mack, 439–75. Hamden: Archon Books, 1968.

Horace. "Satire I.x.11–14." In *Horace: Satires, Epistles, and Ars Poetica,* trans. by H. Rushton Fairclough. Cambridge, MA: Harvard University Press, 1999.

Hume, David. *A Treatise of Human Nature.* Edited by David Fate Norton and Mary J. Norton. Oxford: Oxford University Press, 2000.

Hunter, J. Paul. *Before Novels: the Cultural Contexts of Eighteenth-Century English Fiction.* New York: W.W. Norton & Co., 1990.

———. *Occasional Form: Henry Fielding and the Chains of Circumstance.* Baltimore: the Johns Hopkins University Press, 1975.

Irving, William Henry. *John Gay's London.* Cambridge, MA: Harvard University Press, 1928.

Johns, Adrian. *The Nature of the Book.* Chicago: The University of Chicago Press, 1998.

Juvenal. *The Sixteen Satires*. Translated by Peter Green. London: Penguin Books, 1974.

Kay, Carol. *Political Constructions: Defoe, Richardson, and Sterne in Relation to Hobbes, Hume, and Burke*. Ithaca: Cornell University Press, 1988.

Kay, Donald. "Boswell in the Green Room: Dramatic Method in the *London Journal*." *Philological Quarterly* 57, no. 2 (Spring 1978): 195–212.

Kennedy, Joyce D., Maximillian Novak, and Michael Seidel. Headnote to *An Essay on Projects by Daniel Defoe*, edited by Joyce D. Kennedy, Maximillian Novak, and Michael Seidel, xix–lii. New York: AMS Press, Inc., 1999.

Keymer, Tom. *Richardson's Clarissa and the Eighteenth-Century Reader*. Cambridge: Cambridge University Press, 1992.

Kitch, M. J. "Capital and Kingdom: Migration to Later Stuart London." In *London, 1500–1700: The Making of a Metropolis*, edited by A.L. Beier and Roger Finlay, 224–51. New York: Longman, 1986.

Klancher, Jon P. *The Making of English Reading Audiences, 1790–1832*. Madison: University of Wisconsin Press, 1987.

Klein, Lawrence E. *Shaftesbury and the Culture of Politeness: Moral Discourse and Cultural Politics in Early Eighteenth-Century England*. Cambridge: Cambridge University Press, 1994.

Lake, Peter. "From Troynouvant to Heliogabulus's Rome and Back: 'Order" and its Others in the London of John Stow." In *Imagining Early Modern London: Perceptions and Portrayals of the City from Stow to Strype, 1598–1720*, edited by J.F. Merritt, 217–49. Cambridge: Cambridge University Press, 2001.

Lamoine, Georges. "Lord Chesterfield's *Letters* as Conduct-Books." In *The Crisis of Courtesy: Studies in the Conduct-Book in Britain, 1600–1900*, edited by Jacques Carré, 105–18. Leiden: E.J. Brill, 1994.

Lefebvre, Henri. *The Production of Space*. Translated by Donald Nicholson-Smith. Oxford: Blackwell, 1998.

Lustig, Irma S. "On the Making of *Boswell's London Journal* and *Boswell for the Defence*." *Eighteenth-Century Life* 16, no. 2 (May 1992): 136–39.

McCarthy, Thomas. Introduction to *The Structural Transformation of the Public Sphere: An Inquiry into a Category of Bourgeois Society*, by Jürgen Habermas. Cambridge, MA: The MIT Press, 1991.

McDowell, Paula. *The Women of Grub Street: Press, Politics, and Gender in the London Literary Marketplace, 1678–1730*. Oxford: Clarendon Press, 1998.

McEwan, Ian. *Saturday: a Novel*. New York: Doubleday, 2005.

McKellar, Elizabeth. *The Birth of Modern London: The Development and Design of the City, 1660–1720*. Manchester: Manchester University Press, 1999.

McKeon, Michael. *The Origins of the English Novel, 1600–1740*. Baltimore: Johns Hopkins University Press, 1987.

McLoughlin, Tim. "Fielding's *Essay on Conversation*: a Courtesy Guide to *Joseph Andrews?*" In *The Crisis of Courtesy: Studies in the Conduct-Book in Britain, 1600–1900*, edited by Jacques Carré, 93–104. Leiden: E.J. Brill, 1994.

McMillin, Scott, ed. *Restoration and Eighteenth-Century Comedy*. New York: W.W. Norton & Company, 1997.

Mack, Maynard, ed. *The Last and Greatest Art: Some Unpublished Poetical Manuscripts of Alexander Pope*. Newark: University of Delaware Press, 1984.

———. *The Garden and The City: Retirement and Politics in the Poetry of Pope, 1731–1743*. Toronto: University of Toronto Press, 1969.

Mackie, Erin. *Market à la Mode: Fashion, Commodity, and Gender in The Tatler and The Spectator*. Baltimore: the Johns Hopkins University Press, 1997.

Manley, Lawrence. *Literature and Culture in Early Modern London*. Cambridge: Cambridge University Press, 1995.

Manning, Susan. "'The Philosophical Melancholy': Style and Self in Boswell and Hume." In *New Light on Boswell: Critical and Historical Essays on the Occasion of the Bicentenary of The Life of Johnson*, edited by Greg Clingham, 126–40. Cambridge: Cambridge University Press, 1991.

Merritt, J. F. Introduction to *Imagining Early Modern London: Perceptions and Portrayals of the City from Stow to Strype, 1598–1720*, edited by J. F. Merritt, 1–24. Cambridge: Cambridge University Press, 2001.

———. "The Reshaping of Stow's *Survey:* Munday, Strype, and the Protestant City." In *Imagining Early Modern London: Perceptions and Portrayals of the City from Stow to Strype, 1598–1720*, edited by J. F. Merritt, 52–88. Cambridge: Cambridge University Press, 2001.

Nelson, T.G. "Pope, Burlington, Architecture, and Politics: A Speculative Revisionist Review." *Eighteenth-Century Life* 21 (February 1997): 45–61.

Nettleton, George H., and Arthur E. Case, eds. Preface to *The Conscious Lovers*, by Richard Steele, 435–36. In *British Dramatists from Dryden to Sheridan*. Carbondale and Edwardsville: Southern Illinois University Press, 1969.

Nokes, David. *John Gay: A Profession of Friendship*. Oxford: Oxford University Press, 1996.

O'Connor, Erin. "Breast Reductions." In *Raw Material: Producing Pathology in Victorian Culture*. Durham: Duke University Press, 2000.

Ogborn, Miles. *Spaces of Modernity: London's Geographies, 1680–1780*. New York: The Guilford Press, 1998.

Pearl, Valerie. *London and the Outbreak of the Puritan Revolution: City, Government, and National Politics, 1625–43*. Oxford: Oxford University Press, 1961.

Pocock, J. G. A. *Virtue, Commerce, and History: Essays on Political Thought and History, Chiefly in the Eighteenth Century*. Cambridge: Cambridge University Press, 1985.

Poovey, Mary. *A History of the Modern Fact*. Chicago: University of Chicago Press, 1998.

———. *Making a Social Body: British Cultural Formation, 1830–1864*. Chicago: University of Chicago Press, 1995.

———. "The Model System of Contemporary Literary Criticism." *Critical Inquiry* 27, no. 3 (Spring 2001): 408–38.

Pope, Alexander. *The Poems of Alexander Pope*. Edited by John Butt. New Haven: Yale University Press, 1963.

Porter, Roy. *London: A Social History.* Cambridge, MA: Harvard University Press, 1995.
Pottle, Frederick A. Introduction to *Boswell's London Journal, 1762–1763.* 1950. Reprint, New Haven: Yale University Press, 1992.
Power, M. J. "The Social Topography of Restoration London." In *London, 1500–1700: The Making of a Metropolis,* edited by A. L. Beier and Roger Finlay, 199–223. London: Longman, 1986.
Primeau, Ronald. "Boswell's 'Romantic Imagination' in the *London Journal.*" *Papers on Language and Literature* 9, no. 1 (Winter 1973): 13–27.
Prince, Gerald. *A Dictionary of Narratology.* Lincoln: University of Nebraska Press, 1987.
Prince, Michael. *Philosophical Dialogue in the British Enlightenment: Theology, Aesthetics, and the Novel.* Cambridge: Cambridge University Press, 1996.
Rasmussen, Steen Eiler. *London: The Unique City.* Cambridge, MA: The MIT Press, 1991.
Raven, James. *British Fiction, 1750–1770: A Chronological Check-List of Prose Fiction Printed in Britain and Ireland.* Newark: University of Delaware Press, 1987.
———. *Judging New Wealth.* Oxford: Clarendon Press, 1992.
———. "From Promotion to Proscription: Arrangements for Reading and Eighteenth-Century Libraries." In *The Practice and Representation of Reading in England,* edited by James Raven, Helen Small, and Naomi Tadmor, 175–201. Cambridge: Cambridge University Press, 1996.
———. "The Publication of Fiction in Britain and Ireland, 1750–70." *Publishing History* 24 (1998): 31–47.
Raven, James and Antonia Forster. *The English Novel 1770–1829: a Bibliographical Survey of Prose Fiction Published in the British Isles.* Volume I: 1770–1779. Oxford: Oxford University Press, 2000.
Reddaway, T. F. *The Rebuilding of London after the Great Fire.* London: Jonathan Cape Ltd., 1940.
Redford, Bruce. *The Converse of the Pen: Acts of Intimacy in the Eighteenth-Century Familiar Letter.* Chicago: The University of Chicago Press, 1986.
Reilly, Patrick. *Tom Jones: Adventure and Providence.* Boston: Twayne Publishers, 1991.
Rogers, Pat. *Grub Street: Studies in a Subculture.* London: Metheun & Co. Ltd., 1972.
Sheppard, Francis. *London: A History.* Oxford: Oxford University Press, 1998.
Shoemaker, Robert B. "Reforming the City: the Reformation of Manners Campaign in London." In *Stilling the Grumbling Hive: the Response to Social and Economic Problems in England, 1689–1750,* edited by Lee Davison, Tim Hitchcock, Tim Keirn, and Robert B. Shoemaker, 99–120. New York: St. Martin's Press, 1992.
Sim, Stuart and David Walker. *The Discourse of Sovereignty, Hobbes to Fielding: The State of Nature and the Nature of the State.* Burlington: Ashgate Publishing Co., 2003.

Siskin, Clifford. *The Historicity of Romantic Discourse*. Oxford: Oxford University Press, 1988.
———. *The Work of Writing: Literature and Social Change in Britain, 1700–1830*. Baltimore: the Johns Hopkins University Press, 1998.
Sloan, Kay. "*Boswell for the Defence*/Boswell's *London Journal.*" *Eighteenth-Century Life* 16, no. 2 (May 1992): 142–44.
Smith, Nigel. "'Making Fire': Conflagration and Religious Controversy in Seventeenth-Century London." In *Imagining Early Modern London: Perceptions and Portrayals of the City from Stow to Strype, 1598–1720*, edited by J.F. Merritt, 273–93. Cambridge: Cambridge University Press, 2001.
Spacks, Patricia Meyer. *Imagining a Self: Autobiography and Novel in Eighteenth-Century England*. Cambridge, MA: Harvard University Press, 1976.
———. "Women and the City." In *Johnson and His Age*, edited by James Engell, 485–507. Cambridge, MA: Harvard University Press, 1984.
Stack, Frank. *Pope and Horace: Studies in Imitation*. Cambridge: Cambridge University Press, 1985.
Stallybrass, Peter, and Allon White. *The Politics and Poetics of Transgression*. Ithaca: Cornell University Press, 1986.
Starr, G. Gabrielle. *Lyric Generations: Poetry and the Novel in the Long Eighteenth Century*. Baltimore: Johns Hopkins University Press, 2004.
Steele, Richard. *The Conscious Lovers*. In *British Dramatists from Dryden to Sheridan*, edited by George H. Nettleton and Arthur E. Case, 436–469. Carbondale and Edwardsville: Southern Illinois University Press, 1969.
Steele, Richard and Joseph Addison. *Selections from The Tatler and The Spectator*. Edited by Angus Ross. London: Penguin Books, 1992.
Steiger, Richard. "Pope's *Epistle to Burlington*, 11. 47–50." *Explicator* 48 (Fall 1989): 12–14.
Strype, John. *A Survey of the Cities of London and Westminster: Containing the Original, Antiquity, Increase, Modern Estate, and Government of those CITIES*. 6 vols. London, 1720.
Summerson, John. *Georgian London*. Harmondsworth: Penguin Books Ltd., 1962.
Tarbet, David W. Introduction to *A View of the Edinburgh Theatre during the Summer Season, 1759*, by [James Boswell], i–x. Los Angeles: University of California, 1976.
Todd, Dennis. *Imagining Monsters: Miscreations of the Self in Eighteenth-Century England*. Chicago: University of Chicago Press, 1995.
Trusler, John. *The London Adviser and Guide: Containing Every Instruction and Information Useful and Necessary to Persons Living in London and Coming to Reside There . . . .* (London, 1786).
Tucker, Irene. "Writing Home: *Evelina*, the Epistolary Novel, and the Paradox of Property." *English Literary History* 60 (1993): 419–39.
Wales, Tim. "Thief-Takers and their Clients in Later Stuart London." In *Londinopolis: Essays in the Cultural and Social History of Early Modern London*, edited by Paul Griffiths and Mark S.R. Jenner, 67–84. Manchester: Manchester University Press, 2000.

Walker, R. J. B. *Old Westminster Bridge: The Bridge of Fools.* Newton Abbot: David and Charles Publishers, 1979.

Wall, Cynthia. *The Literary and Cultural Spaces of Restoration London.* Cambridge: Cambridge University Press, 1998.

———. Introduction to *The Rape of the Lock.* Edited by Cynthia Wall, 3–38. Boston: Bedford Books, 1998.

Warner, William. *Licensing Entertainment: The Elevation of Novel Reading in Britain, 1684–1750.* Berkeley: University of California Press, 1998.

White, Alan R. *The Language of Imagination.* Oxford: Basil Blackwell Ltd., 1990.

Williams, Raymond. *The Country and the City.* New York: Oxford University Press, 1973.

Woodman, Tom. "'Vulgar Circumstance' and 'Due Civilities': Gay's Art of Polite Living in Town." In *John Gay and the Scriberlians,* edited by Peter Lewis and Nigel Wood, 83–93. New York: St. Martin's Press, 1988.

Zirker, Malvin R., ed. Introduction to *An Enquiry into the Late Increase of Robbers and Related Writings.* Middletown: Wesleyan University Press, 1988.

Index

absolutism: destabilization of, x–xiii, 10, 12, 69; governmentality and, 19, 24. *See also* Glorious Revolution (1688); sovereignty
Act of Union (1707), xii
Addison, Joseph: Boswell and, 136, 140–41, 151–53, 157–64; Burney and, 196, 207; the City vs. Westminster and, 226–27n5; community and, 21, 26; conversation and, 193; imagination and, 161–64, 167; objectivity and, 251n39; Pope and, 241n2; proliferation of print and, 170–72, 194
administrative geography, 3–8. *See also* London: the Town
aldermen, 13
alternative models of urban governance: Boswell and, 140, 215; Burney and, 197–212; Fielding and, 77, 90, 94–95; Gay and, 34–35, 67, 215, 235n25; historical alterity and, xviii, 11, 28, 214–16; Pope and, 121, 125–26
Archer, Ian, 11, 228n18, 229n21
architecture: the Fire and, xxi–xxii; Gay and, 65–67; Pope and, 98–103, 105–6, 108–10. *See also* Palladianism
Armstrong, Nancy, 14–15
Arnold, Matthew, xix
Austen, Jane, 191

Bakhtin, Mikhail, xxi
Barchas, Janine, 255n19
Baridon, Michael, 241n2
Battestin, Martin, 239n10
Battestin, Ruthe R., 239n10
Beggar's Opera, The (Gay), xvi, 235n26
Behn, Aphra, 21, 248n9
Bender, John, xiv, 224n17, 225nn15–17, 225n26
Berger, Dieter A., 14, 230n32, 230n34
Blake, William, 237n48
Bleak House (Dickens), xix
Bloom, Harold, 97
Boswell, James: drama and, 25–26, 147–58; genre and, 12, 212; proliferation of print and, 139, 141; the self-governed Londoner and, xvii, xxii, 1–2, 16, 22, 25, 135–47; self-discipline and, xxii, 142–82, 249n15, 250–51n34; Steele and, 13; the Town and, 7
Bow Street Magistrate. *See* Fielding, Henry: Bow Street and
Bow Street Runners, 90, 95, 129
Boyle, Richard. *See* Burlington, Earl of (Richard Boyle)
Brewer, John, xii, 222n7
Brooke, Christopher N. L., 227n14
Brower, R. A., 106–7, 244nn32–34
Brownell, Morris R., 243n15, 244n26
Burchell, Graham, 19
Burlington, Earl of (Richard

268   INDEX

Boyle), 64–66, 98, 102
Burney, Frances: Boswell and, 189; London's geography and, xv, 211–12, 253n8, 253–54nn10–12; genre and, 12, 212; *Journals* and, 188–89, 253n6, 253n8; male writers and, 190; projects and, 191–93, 212; proliferation of print and, 183–90, 211–12; Queen Charlotte and, 13; self-discipline and, xxii; the self-governed Londoner and, xvii, xxii, 1–2, 16, 22, 25; women's agency and, 26, 184–85, 211–12
Butler, Judith, 19–20

Campbell, Colin, 246n59
Campbell, Gina, 255n20
Campbell, R., 132–33
Carré, Jacques, 15, 230n35, 231n34, 231–32n36
Case, Arthur E., 249n16
Castle, Terry, 255–56n21
Cecilia (Burney): the City in, 201–2; *Evelina* and, 189–94, 206; genre and, 18; geographic metaphor in, 208–10; imagination and, xix; "inward monitor" and, 198–212; letter writing in, 206; madness in, 183–85, 208–9; metaphor of conduct in, 205, 256nn22–23; narratology and, 209–10; passivity and, 184–85, 203–4, 207; projects and, 191–93, 210–12; proliferation of print and, 211–12; rejection of epistolary confession in, 26–27, 191–94, 197–212; street-level experience and, 183–85, 207–9; the Town in, 201–2; Westminster in, 201–2
Cervantes, Miguel de, 27
Chapone, Hester, 256n24

Charge Delivered to the Grand Jury, A (Fielding), 70, 80–84
Charles II, 5
Charlotte, Queen, 13
City (of London). *See* London: the City
City of Westminster. *See* London: Westminster
Civica Corona, 67
civil society: consensus and, 9–10, 19; Fielding and, 79–96; Gay and, 55, 67; Pope and, 111, 115–16, 118. *See also* community; consensual rule; liberal governmentality
Civil War, 4, 9–10
Colley, Linda, xii, 222n9, 232–33n48
Collier, Jeremy, 41, 151, 235n27
Collinson, Patrick, 234nn6–7
community: consensus and, xii; imagination and, xxi, 213–16; the individual and, 21; writing and, xix. *See also* civil society; consensual rule; liberal governmentality
conduct: Boswell and, 174; Burney and, 190, 192, 194; discourse distinguished from, 239n9; Fielding and, 77–79; Gay and, 53–60; guidebooks and, 229–30n27; as a governing abstraction, 1, 28; knowledge production and, 19, 214; manners distinguished from, 20; as metaphor for genre, 18, 214; as metaphor for space, 45, 52; politeness and, 15; urban geography and, 12–19. *See also* government: metaphors of; metaphor: urban knowledge production and conduct literature: governmentality and, 2, 14–19; passivity and, 256n24; Pope and, 99; pro-

INDEX 269

liferation of, 132–33, 231–32n36; the urban marketplace and, xvii. *See also* conduct
Congreve, William, 150
Conscious Lovers, The (Steele), 153–54, 163, 172
consensual rule, xii, 9, 12, 21, 223n11
Corporation of the City of London. *See* London: the City
Court. *See* London: Westminster
Cowley, Abraham, 3–4, 6
criticism: literary critic and, xvi; urban authority and, xvi

Daily Journal, 100
Damrosch, Leo, 74
Darlington, Ida, 32
Davis, Herbert, 254n13
Dearing, Vinton, 56, 62, 235n24, 236n35, 236n40; 238nn55–56
Defoe, Daniel: the City vs. Westminster and, 6, 8, 226–27n5; Pope and, 99, 242nn7–8; political authority and, 228n19; projects and, 28; travel and, 45; urban geography and, xix
Dickens, Charles, xix, 184
didacticism: Fielding and, 70–72; imagination and, xv, xx; Pope and, 98, 104; Town-literature and, 16
Dodington, Bubb, 106
Dombey and Son (Dickens), xix
Doody, Margaret Anne, 256n23
Doornick, Marcus Willemsz, 32
Downie, J. A., 228n19
drama. *See* theater
Dryden, John, 150, 181, 252n43
Dunciad, The (Pope), 120

Enquiry into the Late Increase of Robbers, An (Fielding), 70, 90–95, 240n15, 241n32
Entick, John, 69, 82, 131, 227n13, 238n4, 247n6
epic, 62–63
epistle essay, 99–121
Epistle to Burlington (Pope): essay form and, 104–21; Horatian imitation and, 106–12, 120, 122; publishing history of, 103–4, 243n18–19, 245n51; readers and, 110; as urban artifact, 23; wealth's function and, 112–26; Westminster Bridge and, xv, 24, 97–101, 121–26
epistolary confession: conversation and, 254n15; Burney and, 26, 186–97, 253n9; imagination's function in, 119–21; Richardson and, 255–56n21. *See also* Cecilia: rejection of epistolary confession in
essay form. *See* epistle essay
Essay on Criticism (Pope), 98, 232n39, 241–42n5
Essay of Dramatic Poesy (Dryden), 150, 252n43
Essay on Man (Pope), 104
Essay on Projects (Defoe), 99, 242nn7–8
Evelina (Burney): *Cecilia* and, 189–94, 206, 211–12; epistolary confession in, 186–97; passivity in, 26–27, 185–87, 195–97, 252n4

Faden, William, 33
Ferraro, Julian, 103, 243nn18–19, 244n35, 245n43, 245n46, 245n48
Fielding, Henry: administrative discourse and, 79–80; Bow Street and, xv, 8, 13, 23, 69–71, 79–96; Gay and, 91; genre and, 12, 214; as interpretive guide, xx; law and, 75–77, 79–96; metaphor and, 16; as textual magistrate, xv, xvii, 68,

79–96; the Town and, 68–70, 80–96
Fielding, Sir John, 141
Fire of London (1666): Boswell and, 144; empty space and, xxii, 5; maps and, 31–34; rebuilding London and, xiii, xxi. *See also* architecture: the Fire and
Five Charges to Several Grand Juries (Gonson), 240n17
Fortescue, William, 64–65
France, 7
Fraser, George S., 243n22
Freud, Sigmund, 139, 190, 209
Friedman, Michael, 148
Foucault, Michel, 19

Gallagher, Catherine, 252n2
Galperin, William, 254n11
Gay, John: Fielding and, 9; genre and, 12, 60–64, 214; as interpretive guide, xx; London's topography and, xv, xvii; metaphors of space and, 16, 22–23, 34–53; the Poet's function and, 60–67; as spatial architect, 66
gender: Burney and, 8, 26, 183–212; genre and, 26; proliferation of print and, 136, 183–90; space and, 26; the Town and, 8; *See also* Burney, Frances: women's agency and
genre: Boswell and, 147–48, 181–82; compared to geography, xv–xvi, xxii, 214; definitions of, xv–xvii; as imaginative tool, xv, 213–14; Gay and, 60–64; metaphor and, 248n8; Pope and, 101–21; relation to conduct literature, 2, 18; theories of, xvii. *See also* conduct literature; government: genre and; mock-genres; novel

geography: distinguished from topography, xxii; as metaphor, 17; morality and, 36; physicality and, xxii; relationship to genre, xv–xvii, xxii, 214; textual citations of, xix, 13. *See also* London: changing geography of
George I, 85, 87
Georgics (Virgil), 62
Gibson, William, 114, 245n49
Gilroy, Amanda, 254nn16–17
Glorious Revolution (1688): administrative void left by, x–xiv, xvii, 12; crime and, 68; 221n3; Londoners and, 1; opportunities created by, 19, 213–14; urban geography and 3–4, 8–9
Gonson, Sir John, 240n17
Gordon, Colin, 19
government: as an art, xiv, xvi, xx, 2, 19–22; genre and xv; governing ideas, xiii; metaphors of, xix, 12–19; writers' role and, xvii. *See also* genre; liberal governmentality
governmentality. *See* liberal governmentality; government: as an art
Great Fire of London (1666). *See* Fire of London
Griffiths, Paul, 11
Grub Street, 8
guidebooks: Gay and, 31, 40–43, 60; proliferation of print and, 132–33. *See also* Hunter, Paul: guidebooks and

Haastrup, Neils, 231n33
Habermas, Jürgen, 19, 21
Harvey, David, 247n3
Hawksmoor, Nicholas, 24, 97–101, 121–26
Haywood, Eliza, 21–22

historical alterity: genre and, 18; space and, 45; theorizations of, xviii
Horace, 104, 106–7, 111, 120, 122, 244n29
Howgego, James, 32
Hume, David: Boswell and, 158, 160, 163–64, 176; essays and, 112–13; imagination and, 28, 160; Pope and, 24
Hunter, Paul: genre and, xv, xvii, 225n23; guidebooks and, 13, 42, 225n24, 229n24, 229–30n27; on *Tom Jones,* 71

imagination: alternate futures and, xviii; Boswell and, 164–69; *Cecilia* and, xix; conduct and, 12–19, 28; creative vs. didactic, 16, 28, 98, 104–5, 242n12, 250n23; eighteenth-century definitions of, xix–xxi, 101–2, 121, 161–63, 169, 214–16, 242n13; Fielding's Bow Street and, 96; Pope and, 101, 118–21; *Tom Jones* and, xix; as tool of self-government, xiv, 161–69, 213–16; urban community and, xviii, xxi; urban experience and, xxi. *See also* Addison, Joseph; imagination and; alternative models of urban governance; *Cecilia:* imagination and; community: imagination and; didacticism: imagination and; epistolary confession: imagination's function in; Hume, David: imagination and; *London Journal, The* (Boswell): imagination's function and; Pope: imagination and; *Spectator,* imagination and; *Tom Jones:* imagination and; writerly authority: imagination and

interiority: Boswell and, 140–82; Burney and, 190–212; letters and, 193; movement towards, 129; proliferation of print and, 135–37; the Town and, 8
Irving, William Henry, 40, 246–47n5

James II, 17, 69
Jenner, Mark S. R., 11
Johns, Adrian, 36
Johnson, Samuel, xvii, 149, 180, 194, 254n15
Juvenal, 237n46

Kay, Carol, xi–xii, xiv, 222n6
Kay, Donald, 148, 247–48n5
Keir, Gillian, 227n14
Kennedy, Joyce D., 99, 242nn7–8
Keymer, Tom, 193, 254n15
Klancher, Jon, 130, 133–34
Klein, Lawrence, xii, 15, 230–31n32

Labelye, Charles, 124
Lamoine, Georges, 15
law: consensual rule and, xii; Fielding and, 75–77, 79–96; Gay and, 66; signage and, 131–32; urban writers and xvi
Lefebvre, Henri, 45
letter-writing. *See* epistolary confession
liberal governmentality: absolutism and, xiii, 24, 36; Burney and, 200; conduct and, 28; definition of, 19–22; Gay and, 55–56, 64–67; Pope and, 115–16, 126
liberties. *See* London: Liberty of the Dutchy of Lancaster
Life of Johnson, The (Boswell), 147
Lintott, Bernard, 67
literary criticism. *See* criticism

Locke, John, 17

London:
  changing geography of, 3–11
  the City: Burney and, 201–2; community and, xxii; definition of, 4, 7; Gay and, 54–56; Fielding and, 93; revolution and, 226n4; Westminster vs., xvi, 4–8, 39, 100–2, 125
  difficulty in naming, x–xi, 1–8, 238n2
  oversimplified binaries of, 11
  periodizations of: early modern London, xviii, 8–11, 34, 227–28n17; medieval London, xxi, 9, 227n14; nineteenth-century London, xix; Restoration London, xxiii; speculative rebuilding and, 5; twenty-first century London, ix–x, xiv, xvi
  personal experience and, 11–12
  places in: Arundell Street, 65; Billingsgate, 54; Bond Street, 5; Bow Street, xv, 69–70; Camden, 4; Covent Garden, 50–51, 149; Drury Lane, 54; Fitzroy Square, ix; Fleet Ditch, 61–62; Fleetstreet, 13, 46, 54; Grub Street, 8; Holborn, 8; Hyde Park Corner, 171; the King's Road, 46; Lambeth, 100; Liberty of the Dutchy of Lancaster, 7, 69; Ludgate Hill, 7; the Monument, 143–44; Pall Mall, 46; Portman Square, 204; Red Lion Square, 5; Seven Dials, 40; Soho, xiii; Somerset House, 3–5; Southwark, 4; the Strand, 3, 44, 51, 62, 65–66, 81, 149; St. Paul's, 144; the Thames, 3, 65, 100; Vauxhall, 202–5; Watling Street, 40; Westminster Bridge, 96–101, 121–26; Whitehall, 7, 46
  population changes in, x
  post-Fire rebuilding and, xxi, 1–2, 5
  proliferation of print and heterogeneity in, 2, 25, 129–37
  the Town: Boswell and, 7; Burney and, 201–2; community and, xiii; definition and boundaries of, 5, 7–8; Fielding and, 68–70, 80–96; Gay and, 56–59, 64–67, 237n42; liberties and, 7; marginal novelty of, 7–8, 44–45
  Westminster: Burney and, 201–2; the City vs., xvi, 4–8, 100–2, 125; definition of, 7; Fielding and, 93; Gay and, 39, 46–47, 56–59; Pope and, 121–26;
  women's experience in, 189

London Adviser and Guide, The (Trusler), 132

London Journal, The (Boswell): agitation and discipline in, 140–47; analogy and, 165–66, 169, 177–78; Bow Street in, 141; dialogue and, 173–75; drama and, 7, 25–26, 147–58, 173–74; epistolarity and, 175; genre and, 18, 147–48, 181–82; the Grand Tour journals and, 250–51n34; Hume and, 158, 160; imagination's function and, 153, 158–82; *Life of Johnson* and, 147; narrative and, 172–79, 252n45; as a project, 27; proliferation

of print and, 139–40, 169–72; psychoanalysis and, 168; reflection and, 153, 155, 163–72, 179; self-government and, 138–39; 142–82; Steele and, 151–55; tense and, 178–79, 252n45; *Tom Jones* and, 155, 157, 179; topography and, 251n36; the Town and, 7, 149
London Tradesman (Campbell), 132–33

Mack, Maynard, 98, 103, 116–17, 241nn2–3
Mackie, Erin, xii, 223n11
Macky, John, 34
Mandeville, Bernard, 111, 115, 119
Manley, Lawrence, 9–10, 227–28nn16–17
manners, 20
Manning, Susan, 248n6
maps, xxii, 13, 31–35, 215
Marxism, xxi
Master Key to Popery, A, 105–6
materialism, xxi, 20, 36, 131
McDowell, Paula, 35–36
McEwan, Ian, ix, 216
McKellar, Elizabeth, xviii, 226–27n5
McKeon, Michael, xii, xv, 223n10
McLoughlin, Tim, 15, 231n35, 239n7
Merritt, J. F., 11, 34, 234n6, 234n8
metaphor: dramatic, 25–26, 147–50, 181–82; urban knowledge production and, xix, 12–19, 96, 232n38; genre and, 248n8; taste and, 161–64. *See also* government: metaphors of; metaphor of conduct
metaphor of conduct, 16–19, 68–69; 77–79
mock-genres, xvi, 18, 37. *See also* genre
modernity, xviii–xix, 233n50

Moll Flanders (Defoe), xix
monarchy, xi–xii. *See also* absolutism; Charles II; Charlotte, Queen; George I; James II
Moral Essays (Pope), 104, 111–12, 120, 241n2, 243nn19–20, 243n20. *See also* Epistle to Burlington (Pope)
moral philosophy, 112–14

Nelson, T. G., 244n25
Nettleton, George H., 249n16
New and Accurate Survey of London, A (Entick), 69
New Criticism, xviii, 98
Nokes, David, 234n16, 235n19
Novak, Maximillian, 99, 242nn7–8
novel: epistolary, 193–212, 255–56n21; Fielding and, 68, 70–79, 96; *London Journal* and, 156, 167; proliferation of, 133; urban geography and, xix; women and, 185–212. *See also* genre; mock-genres

O'Connor, Erin, 248n8
Ogborn, Miles, 45, 233n50
On the Conduct of the Understanding (Locke), 17
"On the Queen's Repairing Somerset House" (Cowley), 3–4

Palladianism, 98–103, 108, 121, 124. *See also* architecture
Parliament, xi, 47, 57
Pearl, Valerie, 4, 226n4
Penlez, Bosavern, 84–90
performance, 20, 147–58. *See also* theater
Pocock, J. A., 20, 232nn46–47
police, xvii–xviii, 15, 90, 95
politeness, 15
Poovey, Mary, 19, 113, 243n23, 244–45n41, 248n8
Pope, Alexander: Burlington and,

102; epistolarity and, 254n15; genre and, xvii, 12, 99–121, 212; Hawksmoor and, 121–26; imagination and, 104–5, 118–19; liberal governmentality and, 126; as moral interpreter, 102–3, 110, 116–17; projects and, 99–101; the Town and, 6; trade and, 102; Westminster Bridge and, xv, 97–101, 121–26
Porter, Roy, xii, 222n7, 227n10, 238n2
Pottle, Frederick, 154, 159, 247n2
Prince, Gerald, 249n21
Prince, Michael, 174
professionalization, xx
projects: Boswell and 156, 181; definition of, 27–28; Fielding and, 96; Pope and, 99–101; urban planning and, xix, 8, 213–16
proliferation of print: Boswell and, 139, 141; Burney and, 191–93, 211–12; cultural problem of, xiii, xviii, 1, 22, 24–25, 213–16; Gay and, 35–36; gender and, 136; history of, 129–37; individual identity and, 135–37; street signs and, 131–32; unified London and, 131, 134–35
Proposition for a New Stone-Bridge at Westminster (Hawksmoor), 24, 97–101, 123–26
prospect poetry, 62–63
Protestantism, xi–xii, 11, 222n9
public sphere, xxii
Pulteney, William, 246n59
Puritan Revolution. See Civil War

Rape of the Lock (Pope), 98–99
Raven, James, 130–33, 246n3
Reddaway, T. F., xxi, 223n13, 226n29
Redford, Bruce, 254n13
Reilly, Patrick, 239n13
Richardson, Samuel, 255n19, 255–56n21
Riot Act, 85, 87–88, 94
Rocque, John, 194
Rogers, Pat, 37–38
romanticism, xx, 16, 28, 250n23

Sabor, Peter, 256n23
Satires (Horace), 106, 111
Saturday (McEwan), ix
Seidel, Michael, 99, 242nn7–8
self-government. See liberal governmentality
Settle, Elkanah, 67, 236n35
Sheppard, Francis, 227n12, 238n3
Sheridan, Thomas, 164
Shoemaker, Robert B., 222n4
Sim, Stuart, 221–22n3
Siskin, Clifford, 226–27n27, 140n24
sovereignty: governmentality and, 20, 24; the Restoration and, xi, xxii, 119, 221–22n3; self-government and, 138, 200. See also absolutism; Glorious Revolution (1688); writerly authority: sovereignty and
space. See urban space
Spacks, Patricia Meyer, 148, 253–54nn10–12
Spectator: Boswell and, 151–55, 158; the City, Town, and Westminster in, 6, 171–72; consensus and, xii, 21; Gay and, 41; imagination and, 161–63, 165; objectivity and, 170, 172, 251n39; Pope and, 241n2; proliferation of print and, 170–72
speculation, xxi, 5, 213. See also alternative models of urban governance; imagination: alternate futures and; commu-

nity: imagination and speculative building, 5
Stack, Frank, 106, 244n38
Stallybrass, Peter, 238n52
Starr, G. Gabrielle, xvii, 242n11
Steele, Richard: Boswell and 13, 136, 140, 151–65, 167; the City, Town, and Westminster and, 6; governing readers and, 26; proliferation of print and, 170–72; social projects and, 181; conversation and, 193; Burney and, 207
Steiger, Richard, 110
Stow, John, 7, 34, 69
Strype, John, 7, 34, 69
Survey of the Cities of London and Westminster (Stow), 7, 69
Swift, Jonathan, 72, 228n19, 230n32

Tarbet, David W., 249n18
Tatler, xii, 21, 41, 151, 153
Tennenhouse, Leonard, 14–15
Thames. *See* London, the Thames
theater: Boswell and, 7, 147–58, 173–74; Gay and, 237n42
thief-taking, 68
Todd, Dennis, 242–43n14
Tom Jones (Fielding): administrative discourse and, 79; Bow Street and, xv, 23, 70–72, 79; *A Case* and, 86–87; *A Charge* and, 82; epistolary and, 73; imagination and, xix; proposals and, 72; law and mock-trials in, 75–79; metaphor of conduct and, 77–79; plot and, 74–75; reading instructions and, xx; as urban artifact, 23; as urban project, 27
Tories, 7, 11, 39
Tour through the Whole Island of Great Britain (Defoe), 6, 34
Town. *See* London: the Town

trade, 11–12, 20, 99–100, 102, 111–26
Trivia, or the Art of Walking the Streets of London (Gay): alterity in, 235n25; the City vs. Westminster in, 39, 46–47, 54–57; epic and, 62–63; georgic and, xx, 36–37, 61, 63–64; as a guidebook, 40–43, 60; geographic citation and, 17–18, 22–23, 36; historical specificity and, 23, 39; maps and, 13, 31–35; metaphor of conduct and, 34, 45–60; mock-genre and, xvi, 18, 31, 37, 60–64; morality and, 36, 57, 238n50; novelty and, 43; the Poet's function in, 13, 57, 60–67, 236–37n41; Pope and, 238n51; prospect poetry and, 62–63; reading and, 36–37, 47–50, 57–67, 237n45; space and, 38, 43, 45, 52–53; street-level experience and, 34, 39, 44–53, 50–51; tone in, 37–38; the Town and, 53–58, 62, 64–67
True State of the Case of Bosavern Penlez, A (Fielding), 70, 84–90
Trusler, John, 132–33
Tucker, Irene, 254n14

Universal Register Office, 129
urban planning, xix, 37, 39, 96, 235n25. *See also* projects: urban planning and urban space: the Fire and, xxii; Gay's definition of, 38–39, 45, 52, 59–60; metaphors of, 16
urban writers: as conductors, xvii; governing roles and, xvii; as knowledge producers, xv; problem of administrative geography and, 8; relationship to readers, xvi; as urban

guides, xv
utopia, xx, 101

Vanbrugh, John, 105
Verhoeven, W. M., 254nn16–17
View of the Edinburgh Theatre during the Summer Season, 1759, A, 154
Virgil, 62
Vitruvius, 117, 118, 121

Wales, Tim, 68
Walker, David, 221–22n3
Walker, R. J. B., 124, 242n10, 245n55, 246n59
Wall, Cynthia: Gay and, 31–34, 38, 47–48, 234n11; maps and, 223n3; Pope and, 242n6; rebuilding London and, xxi; space, 234n10; Stow and, 234n6, 234n9
Walwyn, William, 9
Warner, William, 130, 133
West-End. *See* London: Westminster
Westminster. *See* London: Westminster
Westminster Bridge. *See* London: Westminster Bridge
Whigs, 7, 11, 39
White, Alan R., 250n26, 250n28
White, Allon, 238n52
Whitehall. *See* London: Westminster
Wild, Jonathan, 68
Williams, Raymond, xxi
Windsor Forest (Pope), 5
Woodman, Tom, 37, 234nn17–18, 237n43, 237n49
Wordsworth, William, xx, 28, 240n24
writerly authority: agency and, xxi; imagination and, xxi; metaphors and, xix, xx; sovereignty and, 13; urban authority and, xiv, xxi

Zirker, Malvin, 80, 82, 90, 240n16, 240n18, 240nn25–26

Urban Life and Urban Landscape
Zane L. Miller, Series Editor

The series examines the history of urban life and the development of the urban landscape through works that place social, economic, and political issues in the intellectual and cultural context of their times.

Lake Effects: A History of Urban Policy Making in Cleveland, 1825–1929
Ronald R. Weiner

High Stakes: Big Time Sports and Downtown Redevelopment
Timothy Jon Curry, Kent Schwirian, and Rachael A. Woldoff

Suburban Steel: The Magnificent Failure of the Lustron Corporation, 1945–1951
Douglas Knerr

New York City: An Outsider's Inside View
Mario Maffi

Merchant of Illusion: James Rouse, America's Salesman of the Businessman's Utopia
Nicholas Dagen Bloom

The Failure of Planning: Permitting Sprawl in San Diego Suburbs, 1970–1999
Richard Hogan

Faith and Action: A History of the Catholic Archdiocese of Cincinnati, 1821–1996
Roger Fortin

Regionalism and Reform: Art and Class Formation in Antebellum Cincinnati
Wendy Jean Katz

Making Sense of the City: Local Government, Civic Culture, and Community Life in Urban America
Edited by Robert B. Fairbanks and Patricia Mooney-Melvin

Suburban Alchemy: 1960s New Towns and the Transformation of the American Dream
Nicholas Dagen Bloom

Visions of Place: The City, Neighborhoods, Suburbs, and Cincinnati's Clifton, 1850–2000
Zane L. Miller

A Right to Representation: Proportional Election Systems for the Twenty-First Century
Kathleen L. Barber

Boss Cox's Cincinnati: Urban Politics in the Progressive Era
Zane L. Miller

Columbus, Ohio: A Personal Geography
Henry L. Hunker

Domesticating the Street: The Reform of Public Space in Hartford, 1850–1930
Peter C. Baldwin

The Rise of the City, 1878–1898
Arthur Meier Schlesinger

Lancaster, Ohio, 1800–2000: Frontier Town to Edge City
David R. Contosta

Cincinnati in 1840: The Social and Functional Organization of an Urban Community during the Pre-Civil War Period
Walter Stix Glazer

For the City as a Whole: Planning, Politics, and the Public Interest in Dallas, Texas, 1900–1965
Robert B. Fairbanks

History in Urban Places: The Historic Districts of the United States
David Hamer

Main Street Blues: The Decline of Small-Town America
Richard O. Davies

Getting Around Brown: *Desegregation, Development, and the Columbus Public Schools*
Gregory S. Jacobs

Changing Plans for America's Inner Cities: Cincinnati's Over-the-Rhine and Twentieth-Century Urbanism
Zane L. Miller and Bruce Tucker

Visions of Eden: Environmentalism, Urban Planning, and City Building in St. Petersburg, Florida, 1900–1995
R. Bruce Stephenson

Designing Modern America: The Regional Planning Association of America and Its Members
Edward K. Spann

The Poetics of Cities: Designing Neighborhoods That Work
Mike Greenberg

Welcome to Heights High: The Crippling Politics of Restructuring America's Public Schools
Diana Tittle

Planning for the Private Interest: Land Use Controls and Residential Patterns in Columbus, Ohio, 1900–1970
Patricia Burgess

The Mysteries of the Great City: The Politics of Urban Design, 1877–1937
John D. Fairfield

The Lost Dream: Businessmen and City Planning on the Pacific Coast, 1890–1920
Mansel G. Blackford

The New York Approach: Robert Moses, Urban Liberals, and Redevelopment of the Inner City
Joel Schwartz

Hopedale: From Commune to Company Town, 1840–1920
Edward K. Spann

Suburb in the City: Chestnut Hill, Philadelphia, 1850–1990
David R. Contosta

Cincinnati: Queen City of the West
Daniel Aaron

Cincinnati Observed: Architecture and History
John Clubbe

Plague of Strangers: Social Groups and the Origins of City Services in Cincinnati, 1819–1870
Alan I. Marcus

Polish Immigrants and Industrial Chicago: Workers on the South Side, 1880–1922
Dominic A. Pacyga

Washing "The Great Unwashed": Public Baths in Urban America, 1840–1920
Marilyn Thornton Williams

Fragments of Cities: The New American Downtown and Neighborhoods
Larry Bennett

Silent City on a Hill: Landscapes of Memory and Boston's Mount Auburn Cemetery
Blanche Linden-Ward

Building Chicago: Suburban Developers and the Creation of a Divided Metropolis
Ann Durkin Keating

www.ingramcontent.com/pod-product-compliance
Lightning Source LLC
Chambersburg PA
CBHW020943230426
43666CB00005B/138